CHRISTOPHER HAMPTON: COLLECTED SCREENPLAYS

Christopher Hampton was born in the Azores in 1946. He wrote his first play, *When Did You Last See My Mother?*, at the age of eighteen. Since then, his plays have included *The Philanthropist*, *Savages*, *Tales From Hollywood*, *Les Liaisons Dangereuses*, *White Chameleon* and *The Talking Cure*. He has translated plays by Ibsen, Molière, Horváth, Chekhov and Yasmina Reza (including *Art* and *Life Times Three*). His television work includes adaptations of *The History Man* and *Hotel du Lac*. His screenplays include *The Honorary Consul*, *The Good Father*, *Dangerous Liaisons*, *Mary Reilly*, *Total Eclipse*, *Carrington* and *The Secret Agent*, the last two of which he also directed.

by the same author

CHRISTOPHER HAMPTON PLAYS ONE
(*The Philanthropist, Total Eclipse, Savages, Treats*)

ABLE'S WILL: A PLAY FOR TELEVISION
LES LIAISONS DANGEREUSES
WHITE CHAMELEON
TALES FROM HOLLYWOOD

adaptations
George Steiner's
THE PORTAGE TO SAN CRISTOBAL OF A.H.
Lewis Carroll's
ALICE'S ADVENTURES UNDER GROUND

screenplays
DANGEROUS LIAISONS
THE GINGER TREE
CARRINGTON
TOTAL ECLIPSE
THE SECRET AGENT and NOSTROMO

translations
from Molière
DON JUAN
TARTUFFE
from Ödön von Horváth
TALES FROM THE VIENNA WOODS
DON JUAN COMES BACK FROM THE WAR
FAITH, HOPE AND CHARITY
from Ibsen
THE WILD DUCK
HEDDA GABBLER and A DOLL'S HOUSE
AN ENEMY OF THE PEOPLE
from Yasmina Reza
ART
THE UNEXPECTED MAN
CONVERSATIONS AFTER A BURIAL
LIFE X 3

musical
SUNSET BOULEVARD
(with Don Black and Andrew Lloyd Webber)

CHRISTOPHER HAMPTON

Collected Screenplays

Dangerous Liaisons

Carrington

Mary Reilly

A Bright Shining Lie

The Custom Of The Country

Introduced by the Author

faber and faber

First published in 2002
by Faber and Faber Limited
3 Queen Square London WC1N 3AU
Published in the United States by Faber and Faber Inc.
an affiliate of Farrar, Straus and Giroux LLC, New York

Typeset by Country Setting, Kingsdown, Kent CT14 8ES
Printed in England by Mackays of Chatham plc, Chatham, Kent

A CIP record for this book
is available from the British Library

ISBN 0-571-21457-6

2 4 6 8 10 9 7 5 3 1

CONTENTS

INTRODUCTION

DANGEROUS LIAISONS

My Dinner with Miloš

What follows is a brief account of how my play *Les Liaisons Dangereuses*, which opened at The Other Place (now sadly defunct) in Stratford in September 1985 for a scheduled twenty-three performances, eventually (and somewhat miraculously) led on to the Warner Brothers' film *Dangerous Liaisons*, which opened in America in December 1988. It was a far from straightforward journey, with more than its fair share of diversions, blind alleys and reckless driving, during which a little of Laclos's military training might often have come in handy: I shall try to confine myself to the principal landmarks.

I sold the film rights to my first play in 1967; since when the bidding for film rights to my work has hardly been brisk. However, in this case, offers for the rights had begun to arrive even before the Royal Shakespeare Company brought the play in to The Pit in January 1986, and in the course of the year, despite the RSC's absent-minded dropping of the play from its schedule for three months, the bids proliferated. I was busy with other things. Still, there seemed to be plenty of time, and I thought it was simply a matter of weighing up the various options and making a careful choice. As it turned out, this naive way of thinking contained a number of important errors.

Not that the film rights could have been sold before the disposition of the New York rights. A management putting an English play on (or off) Broadway traditionally shares with the London management forty per cent of any film or TV sales; and the cost of mounting a play in New York is now so alarming that the absence of these ancillary rights rules out any possibility of a production. There's a corollary to this: any proposal for a film which seeks to keep costs down by suggesting profit participation rather than a large up-front payment (and there were one or two interesting approaches along these lines) is unlikely to be approved of by the theatre managers or their investors.

In fact, the New York rights had been disposed of, without my knowledge, before the play had even opened. The RSC had an arrangement with an American producer, James Nederlander, whereby, in return for a certain amount of money, he had first option on any new play the RSC presented. As it turned out, Mr Nederlander had a genuine love for the play and proved more than reasonable, allowing for example the director, Howard Davies, and myself to persuade him, against what I suspect was his commercial instinct, to bring over the British company, rather than recasting with American actors: all the same, the arrangement itself is hardly one of which an author could be expected to approve. And one of its consequences was to put any decision about the film on ice until the Broadway opening in April 1987.

The play's first preview at the Music Box Theatre on 45th St was a more than usually ghastly occasion. During the day the temperature rose steeply and in the course of the afternoon it was discovered that the delicate amplification necessary in so large a house had not been balanced against the air-conditioning, which effectively drowned it. A dispute between the rival claims of art and comfort was decided in favour of the former more or less as the audience filed in. Within a few days, the cast had adjusted to the dimensions of the theatre and were giving as good an account of the play as it had ever received: but there simply had not been enough time to prepare, and on this occasion the performance was muted and tentative. Nevertheless, alongside the representatives from the major studios and other perspiring celebrities, the three chief executives from the Lorimar film division, Bernie Brillstein, Peter Chernin and Ileen Maisel, decided they wanted to acquire the film rights.

Peter and Ileen came to see me the following day. Ileen had been told about the play by Norma Heyman, the English producer for whom I had written a film based on *The Honorary Consul*. The film hadn't turned out quite as we'd hoped, for a variety of reasons, but I'd been very impressed with Norma's commitment, tenacity and attention to detail. One of Lorimar's proposals was that I should co-produce the film (with Norma); obviously, in addition to working with someone I knew well, this would give me the advantage of having some say in the choice of director, cast and so on. Just as important, however, was the fact that I immediately liked

Ileen and Peter (and, when I subsequently met him, Bernie) and felt they were to be trusted. I came back to England, deciding to follow my instinct and relieved that the much-deferred disposal of the film rights could finally be made.

Easier said than done. Lorimar, I was assured, was not offering enough money. Furthermore, the company was on the brink of bankruptcy. Various incomprehensible articles to this effect in the trade papers began to arrive weekly in my mail. Most seriously of all, the RSC refused to agree to countersign my contract.

Reading contracts is not one of my skills and I had failed to notice that the RSC had reserved this unlikely right of veto. It was also my understanding that they had handed over ninety per cent of their participation in the film rights to Frank and Woji Gero as part of the West End transfer negotiations. They were therefore entitled to two per cent of the film rights. This meant that for them to achieve an extra thousand pounds the basic offer would need to increase by the best part of a hundred thousand dollars. Nevertheless they were adamant. Complete stalemate ensued.

Adjacent or sideways to this was the matter of Miloš Forman. He had been sighted early on in the run of the play at The Pit, more than once by all accounts. He was pointed out to me at the première in New York. Now, a friend of Mr Nederlander's, Salah Hassanein, at this time head of distribution for United Artists, declared an interest in acquiring the rights for Mr Forman, with whom he had attended a screening of Roger Vadim's 1959 film *Les Liaisons Dangereuses* in New York. Would I go with him to meet Mr Forman in Paris? Unfortunately, I was very busy and couldn't get away. In that case, could we all meet the following weekend in London? Of course.

Mr Hassanein and I arrived at Mr Forman's hotel at the appointed hour on Saturday 30 May. He had not checked in. We waited a while, then moved on to a restaurant, where we enjoyed an excellent meal. We reminisced about a school we had both attended in Alexandria. The atmosphere was convivial. Mr Forman, however, failed to join us. I went home.

The stalemate persisted through the summer. I went on holiday with my family to Crete. There, I was telephoned by my agent, who told me that Miloš Forman had announced his intention to make a film based on *Les Liaisons Dangereuses*. It would be called *Valmont* and it would have nothing to do with my play. The good news was that the RSC had been sufficiently galvanised by this information to countersign the contract with Lorimar. Too late, I said. I was convinced that in these circumstances no one would ever go ahead with our film.

I returned to New York in September in a melancholy frame of mind. The British cast had completed its Equity-permitted twenty weeks on Broadway and the play closed, breaking the theatre's house record in its final week. The air was thick with valediction. However, Lorimar seemed as optimistic as ever. They were still talking to Miloš Forman's agents and lawyers (the man himself being notably hard to come by); indeed they were talking to all kinds of people. I should go back to England and stand by.

A month passed; then, in the manner of films, forced inactivity was suddenly transformed into frantic haste. Mr Forman was sitting with his writer in Connecticut, beavering away. We were now months behind. Unless we caught up with, not to say overtook, the opposition, all was lost. The first draft was written in less than a month and delivered on Thanksgiving weekend, 1987. It was enthusiastically received, but my sense is that the following three weeks or so were the most perilous of the entire saga. Fortunately, I know no details of what went on and all that can be said in retrospect is that Bernie Brillstein managed to overcome whatever doubts and difficulties remained; at last, the questions of director and cast, the subject of endless theoretical discussions, could be addressed in some concrete way.

Lorimar had one instinct in common with all the other companies who had negotiated for the rights: a disinclination to cast anyone connected with the play. They didn't ask for big stars; they didn't even demand American actors; they simply wanted a fresh start. I often wondered whether their decision had anything to do with the circumstances of that first preview in New York; they denied this and insisted, however hard I argued, that what they felt was necessary was a cast who would arrive on the set not carrying any kind of baggage.

An actor whose name began to surface frequently in our discussions was John Malkovich; so, in the week before Christmas, I went back to New York and saw the play in which he was appearing, Lanford Wilson's *Burn This*. The performance was an astonishing tour de force. Afterwards, I went backstage, knocked on his dressing room door, introduced myself and handed him the script. His immediate acceptance of the part of Valmont felt like a great breakthrough: finally, we were up and running.

At the same time I persuaded Lorimar to let me show the script to Stephen Frears. Such reluctance as they had displayed was entirely to do with the fact that he had never before made a large-budget film. It's always seemed to me more logical to be wary of a man who has never made a small-budget film, but there we are. Anyway, back in London, I went round to hand him the script on New Year's Day 1988.

He seemed to like it. And so, a few weeks later, it was back to New York for Stephen to meet Bernie Brillstein. The atmosphere at lunch was initially somewhat strained and Stephen, who to mark the solemnity of the occasion had invested in a new pair of sneakers, was asked how soon he was able to begin work. After an impressive pause for reflection, he said, 'Tuesday.' He then proposed a five-week trial period, during which he and I could work on the script, while he investigated the feasibility of the budget and timetable and began to assemble a team. As to the casting, he was more than happy with John Malkovich and before his stay in New York was over and a delighted Lorimar could realistically contemplate the prospect of beginning shooting in a little over three months, he had agreed to offer the part of the Marquise de Merteuil to Glenn Close.

I had met Glenn the year before with Howard Davies, when we had asked her to head the American company we had expected to take over the play on Broadway when the RSC's permitted time was up. She had accepted and had then, no doubt, been as startled as we were when the management decided not to extend the run. Apart from any other considerations, it therefore seemed only just that the part should eventually come to her.

The next three months sped by in a blur. Exhaustive script discussions took place (mostly in aeroplanes) and I wrote two more drafts; the enormous apparatus of pre-production trundled forward; location hunts established, to general relief, that it was scarcely more expensive to shoot in France than in Eastern Europe or elsewhere; rehearsals took place at Glenn's house in the country (she was about to have a baby). A good deal of time was devoted to the casting of Madame de Tourvel, and Stephen and I met some impressive candidates both in New York and Los Angeles. We decided to offer the part to Michelle Pfeiffer. A mysterious silence ensued. Subsequently it turned out that she had simultaneously been offered the part of Madame de Merteuil in Miloš Forman's film. For a week, as everyone at our end hyperventilated, she had been driving to work (she was shooting *Tequila Sunrise*) with both scripts on the seat beside her. Eventually, to our great good fortune, she made her choice.

At last, we were standing, soon after dawn, inadequately protected from the drizzle, outside Château Maisons-Lafitte, a grandiose pile playing the part of Madame de Rosemonde's country house. There were still a good many surprises in store, not the least of which was that in that first week of shooting, the film was bought lock, stock and barrel by Warner Brothers, in a deal separate from their interminable negotiations to buy Lorimar. We were to suffer none of the interference often associated with big studios and they proved exemplary custodians of the film: which now began, as John Malkovich paused at the top of a flight of stone steps, silhouetted against a leaden sky, and slapped his boot with his glove. It was 30 May: a year to the day since I'd failed to have dinner with Miloš Forman.

Published screenplays often consist of the writer's final draft or shooting script. The inevitable differences between such a text and the finished film can be fascinating, but seem sometimes to imply a kind of reproach or criticism. In this case, since the film was a genuinely collaborative venture, I wanted the screenplay to resemble the final cut as closely as possible. It follows that I owe thanks to all those who contributed to the final shape of the film, principally, of course, Stephen Frears, but also the actors, the editing room, the camera team, designers, continuity, the sound department, fellow producers, executives, preview audiences in Pasadena and just about anybody who put a head round the door and lobbed in a suggestion. I'm extremely grateful.

CARRINGTON

The White Elephant

The gestation period of *Carrington* (more or less eighteen years) was so grossly excessive and its halting progress so convoluted and strewn with landmines, it seemed worth attempting an account, especially in view of the fact that its entirely unexpected conclusion has brought about a radical alteration in my life.

As far as I recall, it was Barry Krost, then a London-based agent, who in the mid-seventies gave me Michael Holroyd's monumental and ground-breaking biography of Lytton Strachey. He was convinced there was some sort of film to be derived from it and had already suggested this to his friend and future client John Osborne, who had sensibly declined, although he was sufficiently impressed by the strange story of Lytton and Carrington to use elements of it in his underrated play of that year *Watch It Come Down.* I was less prudent: I was so shaken and haunted by Holroyd's devastating book that I told Barry if he could find some credible source of finance for what was obviously an unconventional subject, I'd be more than happy to take it on, even though I had no clear idea how I might extrapolate from this mass of material some manageable narrative.

A year or so later, I was working with Stephen Frears, rehearsing my first original play for television, when Barry called to say that an executive from Warner Brothers was in London and was expressing some interest in commissioning a script which might in some way encompass the nebulous but then fashionable subject of Bloomsbury. Could I lunch with him? I should add that the mid-seventies sprouted one of the very occasional oases in the featureless desert which is the British film industry of the last thirty years. These brief periods of relief always baffled and angered the government of the day, which would eventually devise some countermeasure, the closure, say, of some harmless tax loophole or the threatened penalisation of potential foreign investors or even some entirely illogical and unhelpful strengthening of the currency. Anything, in short, to put a stop to the embarrassing prospect of producing in any given year more than the usual dribble of Poverty

Row features. In 1976, then, someone at the Department of Trade and Industry had nodded; the dollar was strong, and things British became fleetingly attractive to the Hollywood studios.

A car came to collect me from the Acton Hilton (the BBC rehearsal rooms) and whisked me into the West End. According to the piece of paper someone had handed me, I was to lunch with a Mr Elephant, which seemed, like most things I associated with Hollywood, unlikely but not impossible. Mr Elephant greeted me warmly, a man more bearish than owlish, and, in traditional fashion, chatted affably of this and that, not uttering the word 'Bloomsbury' until the arrival of coffee, and even then with an apologetic intonation. I admitted that I had little or no interest in Bloomsbury as such, but that I was touched and fascinated by the story of Carrington, which I proceeded to relate to him. He listened in a thoughtful and sympathetic manner and pronounced himself very interested; I explained I had to get back to my rehearsals and thanked him for an excellent lunch, addressing him as 'Mr Elephant', which he gave every appearance of taking on the chin. Only as the car pulled away and I looked back at the restaurant did it seem likely that some clerical error had occurred: we'd been lunching at The White Elephant.

Nevertheless and somewhat to my amazement, a contract very soon arrived and I retired to my house in Oxfordshire, a Georgian rectory within walking distance of the spot where Carrington began her campaign to seduce Gerald Brenan in 1921, and settled down for what was very probably the most enjoyable year of my writing life. It was the first time I'd worked for one of the big studios and I found them endlessly accommodating. No sooner did you make an enquiry about the entire Lytton–Carrington correspondence stored on microfiche in the British Museum than a truck would arrive with cartons and cartons of photocopies. After the tropical rigours of 1976, the summer of '77 was the full buzzing and humming genuine British article (very similar, in fact, to the summer of 1994, when the film was eventually shot), and I strung a hammock between the trees at the top of the garden (there was a new baby in the house) and immersed myself in another world. Six months of planning gave way to three months' writing through the height of the summer and a first draft completed by the middle of September. I knew it was about twice as long as it should be, but I was pleased with the script and confident that a good director would know where to apply the machete.

I imagine the delivery of the *Carrington* script must have caused some consternation at Warner Brothers. Certainly Mr Elephant (whose real name turned out to be Marty Elfand, so not too much of a clerical error) had long since been released and whoever inherited the project must have been more than a little bewildered. Nevertheless, they buckled down to it, and within four or five months I was asked if I could go over to Los Angeles and spend a couple of weeks working with the designated director, Herbert Ross. By all means, I said, provided they were able to cope with the fact that I couldn't drive.

It turned out that the only hotel within walking distance of Herb Ross's house was one of the most expensive in Beverly Hills. Indeed, the suite they installed me in was so extensive I couldn't at first find the bed and it was only when I was settling down on the sofa that I finally spotted the discreet staircase which led up to the three bedrooms above. Mr Ross had a play in preview and a film in pre-production, both by his usual collaborator, Neil Simon, so he was a little distracted, but I was happy to get back to the hotel in time for the daily distribution of free caviar at six p.m. in the Roof Bar, and our script discussions were extremely straightforward and constructive. Finally, on the last day, Barry Krost hosted a lunch in a private room at Mr Chow's. I was sitting between Herb Ross and his wife, the late Nora Kaye, a formidable and celebrated ex-ballet dancer and principal of the American Ballet Theater. The two of them were soon engaged in a ferocious argument about China: during a frosty silence I turned to Nora and, thinking a change of subject might be helpful, asked her if she had read the script. 'I read some of it,' she said.

Her tone was unambiguous, but for some reason I persisted and asked her what she thought of it. She told me she didn't like it. How much of it had she read? I asked. Nine pages, she admitted. Perhaps, I suggested, it wasn't fair to judge it quite so definitively on so short an extract and she should give it another chance. She looked straight at me. 'I don't want to read about a lot of pissy English people,' she remarked.

I looked at Barry Krost: he had gone white. At this point, the door burst open and a girl in hot pants erupted into the room. She was carrying a cake which said *Carrington* in pink icing. The next day I flew back to London and never heard another word.

1980 was Lytton Strachey's centenary and the *South Bank Show* asked Michael Holroyd to write a programme about him. In the course of our mutual vicissitudes, Michael and I had become friends and he suggested that extracts from my script might be used to illustrate the programme. Warner Brothers kindly consented to a maximum of eight minutes from the script being used, and so it was that Joanna David, Edward Petherbridge and the late Geoffrey Burridge were the first to incarnate scenes from the script. The programme was well received, won a prize in America and was seen by my friend Peter Gill, who, three or four years later, asked if he could use the script for actors' exercises in the National Theatre Studio, which he ran at that time.

Sometime in 1984, Peter rang me to say that he had decided to give a staged reading of *Carrington* as one of his studio nights at the Cottesloe. It was done with a couple of dozen actors (some reading the stage directions) sitting on plain chairs on the Cottesloe stage. The theatre was full and the occasion was, for me, a full seven years after completing the script, extremely moving. And the following day I had two enquiries from television companies. One of these was from Linda Agran at Thames TV who, with enormous determination, eventually persuaded the company to buy back the rights from Warner Bros. at a mere seven times my original salary (perhaps the caviar had not, after all, been free). No sooner had this transaction been completed than Linda, following some pattern I had begun to recognise as inevitable, lost her job. Her successor, however, an ebullient New Zealander called Andrew Brown, liked the script very much, as did his colleague John Hambley, the head of Thames TV's film division, Euston. There seemed no reason on earth why the film should not now smoothly proceed to production.

On the plus side we also had the enthusiastic support of Jeremy Isaacs and David Rose at Channel 4; Andrew Brown brought in Mike Newell, for whom I had already written a screenplay from

Peter Prince's novel *The Good Father*, and we had made contact with two French companies which were extremely interested in the project: Pyramide, run by Francis Boespflug and Fabienne Vonier and Noréa, which was Phillipe Carcassonne's shingle. But every positive was to be undone by some over-achieving negative. The powers-that-were at Thames had some deep objection to the script (its cost perhaps), which caused them to declare that, while they had no fundamental objection to the film being made, they were certainly not going to put any money into it themselves; hardly a confidence-inspiring posture in the eyes of potential investors. Then David Rose's successor at Channel 4, David Aukin, finally admitted his blanket aversion to so-called 'period drama'; Andrew Brown convinced himself, when the money was finally all in place, that Mike, who was editing *The Enchanted April*, would not have sufficient time for pre-production, and unilaterally appointed another director, which caused the French investors to withdraw at once and finally, to put the old tin lid on it, Thames lost its franchise.

I have an office in Notting Hill Gate where friends occasionally come and stay: one such is Ronnie Shedlo, who had bought the film rights of my first play in the mid-sixties and has been a friend ever since. Rooting around during a bout of insomnia, he found a script of *Carrington*, with which he proceeded to fall in love. He and his English partner, John McGrath, also an old friend, took up the cause and began painstakingly to try to reglue what had so comprehensively fallen part. Needless to say, they initially encountered the established pattern of setbacks and rejections, but within a mere eighteen months came a couple of decisive strokes of luck: Emma Thompson, who had given a memorably good screen test back in the days when she was only just known, agreed at once, when reapproached, to play Carrington; and Polygram, who had taken a share in Phillipe Carcassonne's company, suddenly agreed to put up all the necessary finance to make the film.

It seemed scarcely believable: only sixteen years after the delivery of the script, and here it was, set to go forward. Mike cast Jonathan Pryce and a date was agreed for the summer of 1994 when both actors were available. At which point, I received a phone call from Mike. He was dispirited about the prospects of the film he was then editing. 'It's just a little English film,' he said. 'It won't do anything. I can't go straight into another little English film. I have to go to Hollywood and make a proper movie.' He was unpersuadable, adamantine. The film he was working on was called *Four Weddings and a Funeral.*

All kinds of directors were frantically canvassed. They were all unavailable, uninterested or unfinanceable. And eventually, late one evening, Phillipe Carcassonne called to say that in France it was not unprecedented for the writer to direct his script. 'Oh, no,' I said. 'I've never wanted to do that.' And I hadn't. But on the other hand, if I let the opportunity slip, who was to say it wouldn't be another decade or two before the actors, the dates and the money were there? So that when Emma rang a couple of days later and made the same suggestion, I was already weakening. And then, the strangest thing: like a virgin in a pornographic novel, having resisted so staunchly for so long, I found I couldn't get enough of it. And Carrington, who specialised in changing men's lives, had now changed mine.

Carrington has passed, over the years, through a minimum of eight or nine drafts, reducing, in the process, to not much more than half its original length. The final cuts were made, painfully, after the completion of the film. It seemed right, however, to print here a text as close to the finished film as might be; and this is what will be found in the following pages.

MARY REILLY

More Blood

After the rigours of *A Bright Shining Lie*, *Mary Reilly*, adapted from Valerie Martin's poignant and haunting novel, came as a great relief; so much so that I was able to write a first draft in no more than a week. It was received at TriStar (and this perhaps is where the first warning bells should have sounded for me) with tremendous enthusiasm; indeed, I can't remember anything I've ever written being more fervently welcomed. A modest feeding frenzy began immediately among actresses; and the director was already attached: the distinctive and imaginative Tim Burton. Tim was shooting *Batman Returns*, so early meetings tended to take place on a vast refrigerated set in Burbank, surrounded by electronic penguins and a pervasive smell of fish. Working with Tim was a fascinating process; but early on he fell into a dispute with Sony, who wanted him to make *Ed Wood* (if he insisted on making it at all) in colour, rather than the burnished black-and-white he eventually achieved: and they dumped him.

I learned of this in a call from Stephen Frears, whom the studio had approached to take over. The prospect of working with him again (and Norma Heyman, whom Stephen had proposed as our producer) was, of course, extremely exciting; and we began the business of re-examining the script and casting the film. Stephen, no doubt thinking to protect himself against the possible interference of the studio, decided to add a powerful American producer to the mix: Ned Tanen, who had run Paramount during its glory days, and who brought with him, as a third producer, his wife, Nancy Graham Tanen. And so, in October 1993, a mere two years after the completion of the first draft, Stephen and I found ourselves flying to Chicago to meet Julia Roberts, who struck me as being as intelligent as she was beautiful, an opinion I've since found no reason to revise. In short: so far, so good.

However, I'm not sure that Stephen had considered the possibility that, as an ex-studio boss, Ned might be *plus royaliste que le roi*. In any event, anxieties about the script were beginning to present themselves ever more insistently: it was too hermetic ('Couldn't we have some, like, dinner parties?'), too enigmatic ('Shouldn't there be a voice-over, so we know where she's coming from?') and, above all, too restrained ('I think it just needs more blood'). This was difficult, since what I had ringing in my mind was Nabokov's injunction: 'Please completely forget, disremember, obliterate, unlearn, consign to oblivion any notion you may have had that *Jekyll and Hyde* is some kind of a mystery story, a detective story or movie.'

I resisted as best I could, clinging to my quietist, atmospheric psychological drama. I found myself wanting to quote Mallarmé ('the ideal is to *suggest*') in script meetings, never a good idea. But slowly, inexorably, the blood began to flow. First, Sir Danvers Carew, MP, was elaborately murdered on camera, rather than described over the kitchen sink; then Mary was sent on an errand with Hyde, charged with securing organs from both an abattoir (streets foaming with blood) and a hospital operating-room; thirdly, Mrs Faraday, the brothel-keeper, met a gruesome end; next the obligatory transformation scene (which I had mischievously transferred to the end of the story, defying convention by showing Hyde turn into Jekyll instead of vice-versa) became an affair of deliquescing muscles and splitting flesh; finally (and here I drew the line, though the scene was, nevertheless, most ingeniously shot) Mary's appalling father had his throat cut by Hyde in a graveyard. Mr. Hyde, I kept protesting, is not a social worker; he murders for pleasure, not like some conscientious neighbourhood vigilante. But it was a losing battle. Finally, a suite was taken for me at the Lanesborough Hotel; I tried to point out that I actually lived in London, but to no avail: Ned and Nancy wanted me continually on hand so that I might be available at any moment to commit some new atrocity or kill off yet another hapless character in our story. I used to slip off home at the end of the day and return at dawn, and to my knowledge nobody ever noticed; but those days in that chintzy suite were the low-point of pre-production.

Unusually among directors, Stephen Frears likes and, if possible, insists upon the presence of the writer on the set; but by some malign destiny, having waited six years for a film to start after *Dangerous Liaisons*, I found that *Mary Reilly* was to begin shooting the same week as *Carrington*. Stephen was so put out by this, he kindly offered, if we postponed, to direct *Carrington* himself; but plans were too far advanced to make this a practical solution. So I was only able to visit Pinewood on Saturdays (whenever he had a six-day week and I didn't) and at the very end of shooting; and my contributions were more or less confined to a few rewrites faxed in the evenings from whichever location I found myself, as I trundled round the country.

Nobody (including myself) had ever been very happy with the script's ending; and when filming came to a rather abrupt end in August 1994 (because of the stars' schedules), it was on the understanding that we would all reconvene to deal with the problem. Unfortunately, it was six months before this could happen, which gave time for me to be cajoled into providing no fewer than two dozen alternative endings, of which, I believe, three were eventually shot. The basic concept, namely that Hyde (like Valmont in *Dangerous Liaisons*) is destroyed by his one uncharacteristically decent impulse (in Valmont's case, falling in love; in Hyde's, refraining from his usual orgy of rape and murder), remained consistent, but it was given so many different variants I imagine we were all fairly bewildered by the time it came to choose one of them.

Eventually, one horrible spring day in 1995, I flew from Paris to London, met Stephen, flew on to Los Angeles and then, in the Sony jet, to some pink mall in San Diego, where large numbers of people in shorts failed to take very much interest in the travails of poor Mary. The scores, in short, were no better than average.

Over the next year, the struggle intensified. A second cut, two weeks later, seemed to be less good than the first (I told Stephen I thought this, resulting in our one moment of *froideur*) and indeed scored less well at the preview. The score continued to slide, as further cuts were shown. The studio begged Stephen to fire me and find a new writer (a plea I was by then enthusiastically seconding) but he remained adamant. Finally, a new editor was brought in over Stephen's head, a young and evidently lively presence, who re-syncopated Victorian Edinburgh (another minor source of confusion, since the script had been set in London) to the more restless and familiar rhythms of a music video. Sadly, this version scored the lowest of all, whereupon the studio threw its hands up and asked Stephen to return: which he agreed to do, on the condition that his next version would be regarded, previews or no previews, as the final cut. Something of the studio's annoyance at all this inevitably seeped out; and when the film finally received its perfunctory release in, I think, May 1996, it was patronised and dismissed by the American critics, a response parrotted in the customary way by their British counterparts.

I happened to be in Tahiti when the film was released, and went to see it, dubbed euphoniously into French, at the Papeete Odeon, where the Saturday night crowd was hushed and appreciative. And I remain extremely fond of *Mary Reilly*; and pleased that discerning judges like David Thomson and *Cahiers du Cinéma* have begun to speak up in its favour. It does perhaps seem unwise, in retrospect, to spend forty-two million dollars on a story about two people in a house; and not necessarily an advantage to be able to fly the director and the writer on a day return on the Concorde to discuss three lines of dialogue. But the text printed here, although it does retain some features of that bloodless early draft, is sufficiently close to Stephen's final version (and its eventually selected ending) to act, I hope, as an endorsement of the finished film: which, at the very least, must be the only studio picture of recent years to contain a significant number of hidden quotations from Baudelaire.

A BRIGHT SHINING LIE

Blaming the Vietnamese

At the very end of the eighties, Allyn Stewart, who was at that time working at Warner Bros., sent me a vast doorstop of a book by Neil Sheehan, the former *New York Times* correspondent and unveiler of the Pentagon Papers. Despite its Pulitzer Prize and National Book Award, I may have opened *A Bright Shining Lie* a shade reluctantly; but I was almost immediately immersed in what was nothing less ambitious than an attempt (successful, I believe) to embody the complex catastrophe of the Vietnam War within the biography of a single untypical, indeed remarkable American, Lt. Col. John Paul Vann. For sixteen years, ever since attending Vann's dramatically polarised funeral, Mr Sheehan had been grappling with a mountain of confusing and often contradictory material, in the ill-lit basement of his Washington home: and the result, in many people's opinion, was *the* book of America's disastrous adventure in Vietnam.

Vann arrived in Vietnam early on, as one of President Kennedy's 1962 batch of advisers; he died in a helicopter crash ten years later, by which time he was, effectively, the only civilian general in American military history. Most unusually among Americans, he not only understood the Vietnamese, but actually loved them; which, of course, put him in a perfect position to yield finally to an irresistible temptation: which was to betray them. As I read on with growing excitement, I could see that the subject offered a matchless opportunity to do something which no previous Vietnam film, however admirable, had managed to achieve: namely, to give an account of that brutal and unnecessary conflict, which did not, either directly or by implication, lay the blame for the war squarely on the shoulders of the Vietnamese.

It took about a year of enjoyably absorbing research and quarrying to carve out the unwieldy shape of a bulky first draft. The usual conversations then ensued with various Warner Bros. executives; with the producers, Lois Bonfiglio and Jane Fonda, whose then husband, Ted Turner, memorably attended one of our discussions, on the grounds that he'd never been at a script meeting before; and, most usefully for me, with Neil Sheehan. My greatest anxiety had been writing dialogue for a largely American cast of characters and I had spent inordinate amounts of time studying the turns of phrase of the interviewees on the sackful of tapes Neil Sheehan had kindly handed over to me, which also included a number of lectures delivered to Vietnam rookies in the harsh, clipped tones of Vann himself: time well spent, it seemed, since no one ever said a word about the language, confining themselves instead to unfathomable (at least, to me) subjects, such as whether or not the character of Vann was too unsympathetic to be acceptable to this or that celebrated actor.

Clearly what was needed at this juncture was a director: and I was delighted when the choice adventurously fell on Phil Joanou, still in his twenties, whose new film, *State of Grace*, about a policeman infiltrating a Hell's Kitchen gang, took a familiar subject and made it into something extraordinary and fresh. He turned out to be extremely lucid and easy to work with and we hacked away at the shapeless heap of material, working in Los Angeles, in Atlanta (where Phil was shooting a U2 video) and in New York, until we had the version of the screenplay printed here, with which everybody seemed reasonably pleased.

That August I was in Paris, enjoying the absence of Parisians, when I received a call from Lucy Fisher of Warner Bros. She said she had good news. This turned out to be that Oliver Stone had passed through the office, picked up the script and liked it enough to say he would direct it. 'What are the ethics of this?' I remember stupidly saying, at which Lucy was obliged patiently to explain certain obvious realities. 'At least your film will get made', she ended by saying.

A few months later I was waiting in the Santa Monica offices of Oliver Stone while he finished up a conference call. I couldn't help noticing that one wall was lined with enormous cartoons, labelled, I saw as I drifted irresistibly towards them, 'NVA boots' or 'ARVN helmets'. Obviously I'd come to the right shop. Oliver, when he appeared, though a little *distrait* (he was editing two films simultaneously, *Heaven and Earth* and *Natural Born Killers*), was admirably clear and straightforward: his notes basically consisted of a number of scenes he liked in the book which I'd left out in the screenplay. I said I thought the length of the script was already probably up around three hours: to which he replied I was to let him worry about that. All this seemed fair enough: the only point at which I balked somewhat was when he asked for a voice-over narration; it seemed to me that Vann was nothing if not entirely unself-conscious. Then pick someone else to narrate, he said. I could never work this out and eventually rather impudently suggested he write the narration himself.

The fact of the matter, of course, is that Oliver never made the film. The financial failure of *Heaven and Earth* (a very interesting film about culture shock which, to be fair, certainly didn't blame the Vietnamese) and the added blow that Tom Cruise respectfully declined the role of Vann, discouraged him and caused him to back away; whereupon, after a long silence, Warner Bros. decided to hand the whole project over to HBO, which they had recently acquired, to make a Cable TV movie.

This is a brief account: but I'd now been involved in the material for more than five years and found myself writing to Jane Fonda as follows:

> . . . while I certainly have nothing against made-for-TV films, having perpetrated a good many of them myself in the past, I can't help feeling that the *scale* of our enterprise is not really one which would lend itself very comfortably to a TV format.
>
> I've always thought that the essential line of our story . . . is uniquely equipped to illuminate the whole sorry business (of the war) from both an American and (which is important, because so rarely considered) a Vietnamese perspective; it's the trajectory of *Lawrence of Arabia*, and I see no reason why it

shouldn't be possible to make a film of equal size and importance, with the added advantage that it deals with a series of events embedded in the public consciousness . . .

The year 2000 is the twenty-fifth anniversary of the end of the war: wouldn't that be a good moment to bring out an ambitious film . . . which would deal distinctively with one of the central turning-points in American history? So many treatments of the subject in the past have, whatever their virtues, been narrowly nationalistic; but it seems to me that Vann, with all his flaws and complexities a genuine tragic hero, illustrates both the conduct of the war and the reasons for its inevitable failure . . .

I'm well aware that these decisions are made for hard-headed, pragmatic reasons which are really none of my business: but of all the many and various projects I've worked on, none has ever engaged me as passionately or seemed as worthwhile (and potentially universal). So I hope you'll forgive me for sending out the deathbed appeal.

I can't say I really expected an answer; and none came. Ron Hutchinson, to my pleasant surprise, made an astute and careful compression of the script for HBO; at which point the whole project took the kind of turn these things so often do: an entirely new script was written (by the director) in a matter of weeks. Sometimes contractual subtleties make it impossible to take one's name off a script: but, in this case, in an unusual act of clemency, the Writers' Guild of America did it for me. And the finished film did at least find one intriguing variant from the norm: it blamed the South Vietnamese.

THE CUSTOM OF THE COUNTRY

Girl Behaving Badly

I was sent Edith Wharton's great novel by two New York producers, Joan Kramer and David Heeley; and immediately fell in love with it. Wharton's greatest success, achieving sales which made Henry James blanch with envy, it is one of those rare masterpieces (like *Les Liaisons Dangereuses*) which deals with the run-up to a pivotal moment in history (in this case, the turn of the twentieth century, when America decided to slough off its ill-founded belief in European moral and cultural superiority and forge its own brand of world leadership) by telling a story of attractive people (in this case, a spectacularly beautiful young woman) exploiting the contradictions of an imploding social system by behaving very badly. This is a novel Margaret Mitchell must have studied with some care before sitting down to write *Gone with the Wind*; and, as a supreme social comedy, I felt it was far more readily dramatisable than some of Wharton's more tragic and subtly gradated pieces.

What was needed was obviously the precisely correct actress to play the magnificently named Undine Spragg; and so I suggested that we send the novel to Michelle Pfeiffer. It took her some time to read it, but when she did, she responded with great enthusiasm and joined us as a producer, together with her partner Kate Guinzberg. And in 1992, the year after *Mary Reilly*, the first draft was written.

Timing was against us: while we were searching for a director, Michelle was offered another Wharton project, the very different *Age of Innocence*, directed by Martin Scorsese. In my view, the result was a marvellously textured and beautifully acted film; but it was far from profitable; and the studio (once again, it was Sony) wavered. The success, the following year, of *Sense and Sensibility* briefly renewed their faith in period pictures; but then the relative failure (I speak in purely commercial terms) of Jane Campion's *Portrait of a Lady* brought back all their feelings of insecurity: and at around this time, Michelle, though remaining with us as an executive producer, tactfully withdrew from the role of Undine; and we slid back into what is often described as development hell, but which more closely resembles the lulling waters of the Bermuda Triangle.

I shall leave it there: it is a constitutional requirement in this area of my profession that one remains unreasonably but permanently crazed with optimism; and it is in this spirit that I venture to hope that one day, sooner or later, I shall be able to make this film.

CHRISTOPHER HAMPTON

Dangerous Liaisons

For Stephen Frears

CAST AND CREDITS

Warner Bros. presents a Lorimar Film Entertainment picture of an NFH Limited Production, based on the play by Christopher Hampton, adapted from the novel *Les Liaisons Dangereuses* by Pierre-Ambroise-François Choderlos de Laclos. The cast included:

MARQUISE DE MERTEUIL	Glenn Close
VICOMTE DE VALMONT	John Malkovich
MADAME DE TOURVEL	Michelle Pfeiffer
MADAME DE VOLANGES	Swoosie Kurtz
CHEVALIER DANCENY	Keanu Reeves
MADAME DE ROSEMONDE	Mildred Natwick
CÉCILE DE VOLANGES	Uma Thurman
AZOLAN	Peter Capaldi
GEORGES	Joe Sheridan
JULIE	Valerie Gogan
ÉMILIE	Laura Benson
ADELE	Joanna Pavlis
MAJORDOMO	Nicholas Hawtrey
CASTRATO	Paulo Abel Do Nascimento
CURÉ	François Lalande
BELLEROCHE	François Montagut
ARMAND	Harry Jones
BAILIFF	Christian Erickson
OPERA SINGER	Catherine Cauwet

Director	Stephen Frears
Screenplay	Christopher Hampton
Producers	Norma Heyman, Hank Moonjean
Director of Photography	Philippe Rousselot
Production Designer	Stuart Craig
Film Editor	Mick Audsley
Co-Producer	Christopher Hampton
Music	George Fenton
Costume Designer	James Acheson
Production Supervisor	Suzanne Wiesenfeld
Casting	Juliet Taylor and Howard Feuer

INT. MERTEUIL'S DRESSING ROOM. DAY

The gilt frame around the mirror on the Marquise de Merteuil's dressing table encloses the reflection of her beautiful face. For a moment she examines herself; critically, but not without satisfaction.

Another angle shows the whole large room, the early afternoon light filtering through gauze curtains.

It's midsummer in Paris in 1788.

INT. VICOMTE DE VALMONT'S BEDROOM. DAY

Valmont is an indistinct shape in his vast bed. His valet-de-chambre, Azolan, leads a troupe of male servants into the room. One raises the blind and opens enough of a curtain to admit some afternoon light; another waits with a cup of chocolate steaming on a tray; a third carries a damp flannel in a bowl; another pours water into a bathtub.

Valmont stirs, his face still unseen, and reaches for the flannel.

INT. MERTEUIL'S DRESSING ROOM. DAY

Three or four female servants wait, disposed around the room, as Merteuil's chambermaid leans over Merteuil, polishing her shoulders with crushed mother-of-pearl.

INT. VALMONT'S BEDROOM. DAY

Valmont's face is swathed in hot towels, his head tilted back. A young manicurist, on his knees, attends to Valmont's nails. Several other servants wait gravely to play their part in the elaborate ritual of dressing Valmont. The barber produces a pair of tweezers and delicately plucks a hair from one of Valmont's nostrils.

INT. MERTEUIL'S DRESSING ROOM. DAY

Merteuil's maid straps a pair of bamboo panniers on to Merteuil's waist.

INT. VALMONT'S BEDROOM. DAY

Azolan opens a walk-in closet, which contains innumerable rows of boots and shoes. He and another servant choose a couple of pairs of shoes each and bring them out. Valmont's hand comes into shot, indicating a black pair with red heels. Azolan hands them to a bootboy, who hurries away, breathing on them as he goes.

INT. MERTEUIL'S DRESSING ROOM. DAY

A second dressing table is covered with extravagant numbers of perfume boxes. Merteuil, now in corset, chemise and underskirt, sits, surrounded by her maids. Eventually she makes a choice and indicates a box. A maid opens the box and begins to apply the perfume (in the form of a cream) to Merteuil's neck, lightly massaging it in.

INT. ANTEROOM TO VALMONT'S BEDROOM. DAY

Valmont's perruquier waits attentively as Valmont, seen from behind, stands in front of the three tiers of featureless wooden heads that carry his collection of wigs. Eventually, he points to one.

INT. MERTEUIL'S DRESSING ROOM. DAY

Merteuil's stomacher is now in position and she stands, arms outstretched, as two maids move forward with her dress, guiding her arms into it as if it were an overcoat. This done, Merteuil's seamstress approaches and begins the delicate process of sewing her into her dress. The back of her dress is lifted so that one of her maids can tighten her corset.

INT. VALMONT'S BEDROOM. DAY

A bizarre paper cone with gauze-covered eyeholes conceals Valmont's face as the perruquier blows powder at his wig. As the powder drifts away, Valmont slowly lowers the cone and we see for the first time his intelligent and malicious features. Another angle shows the complete magnificent ensemble; or not quite complete, for Azolan now reaches his arms round Valmont's waist to strap on his sword.

INT. CORRIDOR IN MERTEUIL'S HOUSE. DAY

Merteuil emerges triumphally from her dressing room, her expression serene.

INT. VALMONT'S BEDROOM. DAY

Valmont, surrounded by his servants, frozen in postures of respectful silence, sets off with a spring in his step to begin his day's work.

EXT. COURTYARD OF MERTEUIL'S TOWN HOUSE. DUSK

Valmont's handsome black carriage comes to a halt and he emerges, resplendent. Above, at the window, peering curiously down at Valmont, is a demure fifteen-year-old blonde, Cécile Volanges.

INT. ANTE-ROOM TO GRAND SALON IN MERTEUIL'S HOUSE. DUSK

Cécile turns away from the window, thoughtful.

INT. MERTEUIL'S GRAND SALON. DUSK

A panoramic view of the great room. In one corner Merteuil is playing piquet with her cousin Madame de Volanges: in the centre of the room, the huge chandelier has been lowered to within a foot of the floor and two footmen with tapers are lighting its candles.

Cécile moves across the room. The large playing cards slap down on one another.

VOLANGES Sequence.

Merteuil looks across the long expanse of room at Cécile's profile. Eventually she speaks.

MERTEUIL Well, my dear . . .

Cécile doesn't at first realise it's she who's being addressed: then she starts and half turns.

So how are you adapting to the outside world?

CÉCILE Very well. I think.

VOLANGES I've advised her to watch and learn and be quiet except when spoken to.

Merteuil looks Cécile up and down, frankly appraising her.

MERTEUIL We must see what we can devise for your amusement.

The mirrored double doors open and Merteuil's Majordomo, carrying a silver tray, advances unhurriedly across the room. The chandelier is fully lit now and the footmen begin to raise it. Merteuil glances up at her Majordomo and reaches for the card on his tray. She replaces the card, looks up at him and nods. Gradually, as the chandelier rises, Merteuil's perfect, mask-like face becomes fully lit.

Valmont is here.

Volanges reacts with a trace of alarm.

VOLANGES You receive him, do you?

MERTEUIL Yes. So do you.

Volanges turns to her daughter, whose interest has been caught by this exchange.

VOLANGES Monsieur le Vicomte de Valmont, my child, whom you very probably don't remember, except that he is conspicuously charming, never opens his mouth without first calculating what damage he can do.

CÉCILE Then why do you receive him, Maman?

VOLANGES Everyone receives him.

She breaks off as the Majordomo reappears, escorting Valmont, who crosses to bow formally to Merteuil in a gesture that also takes in the others.

VALMONT Madame.

MERTEUIL Vicomte.

VOLANGES What a pleasant surprise.

VALMONT Madame de Volanges. How delightful to see you.

VOLANGES You remember my daughter, Cécile?

VALMONT Well, indeed, but who could have foretold she would flower so gracefully?

Volanges is not best pleased by this remark; meanwhile Valmont turns his attention back to Merteuil.

I wanted to call on you before leaving the city.

MERTEUIL Oh, I'm not sure we can allow that. Why should you want to leave?

VALMONT Paris in August, you know; and it's time I paid a visit on my old aunt. I've neglected her disgracefully.

VOLANGES Madame de Rosemonde has been good enough to invite us to stay at the château. Will you please give her our warmest regards?

VALMONT I shall make a point of it, madame.

Volanges, made uneasy by Valmont's professional scrutiny of Cécile, speaks to her daughter more sharply than she intends.

VOLANGES I think it's time we took you home.

Cécile responds, still nervously aware of Valmont's unwavering stare.

CÉCILE I'm used to being in bed by nine at the convent.

VALMONT So I should hope.

She breaks away, mysteriously alarmed, and hurries across to Volanges. Merteuil has summoned a footman. Valmont bows and we watch from his point of view as the footman shows out Volanges and Cécile. When they've gone, Merteuil crosses back towards Valmont, speaking in an entirely different tone of voice.

MERTEUIL Your aunt?

VALMONT That's correct.

MERTEUIL I thought she'd already made arrangements to leave you all her money.

He smiles without answering. She arrives beside him.

Do you know why I summoned you here this evening?

VALMONT I'd hoped it might be for the pleasure of my company.

MERTEUIL I need you; to carry out an heroic enterprise. You remember when Bastide left me?

Valmont feigns a sympathetic expression.

VALMONT Yes.

MERTEUIL And went off with that fat mistress of yours whose name escapes me.

VALMONT Yes, yes.

MERTEUIL No one has ever done that to me before. Or to you, I imagine.

VALMONT I was quite relieved to be rid of her, frankly.

MERTEUIL No, you weren't.

Silence. She now has his undivided attention.

For some years now, Bastide has been searching for a wife. He was always unshakeably prejudiced in favour of convent education. And now he's found the ideal candidate.

INT. CONVENT. DAY

Cécile, superintended by a couple of nuns, waits inside an enclosure, her face framed between the bars of a wooden partition.

VALMONT (*voice over*) Cécile Volanges.

MERTEUIL (*voice over*) Very good.

EXT. CONVENT. DAY

Volanges's magnificent carriage, silhouetted against the walls of the convent.

VALMONT (*voice over*) And her sixty thousand a year, that must have played some part in his calculations.

A nun peeps through the grille in the gate of the convent.

MERTEUIL (*voice over*) None whatsoever.

INT. CONVENT. DAY

Volanges, escorted by nuns, moves along a vaulted stone corridor.

MERTEUIL (*voice over*) His priority, you see, is a guaranteed virtue.

VALMONT (*voice over*) I wonder if I'm beginning to guess what it is you're intending to propose.

Volanges hasn't seen Cécile for years. She advances tentatively towards the partition. Still on the other side of it, Cécile curtsies respectfully.

MERTEUIL (*voice over*) Bastide is with his regiment in Corsica for the rest of the year. That should give you plenty of time.

INT. MERTEUIL'S GRAND SALON. DUSK

Valmont rises into frame.

VALMONT You mean to . . .?

Merteuil arrives at his shoulder.

MERTEUIL She's a rosebud.

VALMONT You think so?

MERTEUIL And he'd get back from honeymoon to find himself the laughing-stock of Paris.

VALMONT Well . . .

MERTEUIL Yes. Love and revenge: two of your favourites.

Silence. Valmont considers for a moment. Finally, he shakes his head.

VALMONT No, I can't.

MERTEUIL What?

VALMONT Really, I can't.

MERTEUIL Why not?

VALMONT It's too easy. It is. She's seen nothing, she knows nothing, she's bound to be curious, she'd be on her back before you'd unwrapped the first bunch of flowers. Any one of a dozen men could manage it. I have my reputation to think of.

Merteuil frowns, displeased. Valmont moves over to sit next to her.

I can see I'm going to have to tell you everything.

MERTEUIL Of course you are.

VALMONT Yes. Well. My aunt is not on her own just at the moment. She has a young friend staying with her.

EXT. FORMAL GARDENS OF ROSEMONDE'S CHATEAU. DAY

Madame de Tourvel's strong, beautiful, untroubled face, as she moves through the gardens. She's accompanied by Valmont's eighty-year-old aunt, Madame de Rosemonde, who chooses flowers, which Tourvel then cuts and lays in a basket.

VALMONT (*voice over*) Madame de Tourvel.

INT. MERTEUIL'S GRAND SALON. DUSK

Merteuil turns to him, genuinely surprised.

MERTEUIL You can't mean it.

VALMONT To seduce a woman famous for strict morals, religious fervour and the happiness of her marriage: what could possibly be more prestigious?

MERTEUIL I think there's something degrading about having a husband for a rival. It's humiliating if you fail and commonplace if you succeed.

EXT. ROSEMONDE'S GARDENS. DAY

Tourvel supports Rosemonde as they move back towards the château.

MERTEUIL (*voice over*) Where is Monsieur de Tourvel anyway?

VALMONT (*voice over*) Presiding over some endless case in Burgundy.

MERTEUIL (*voice over*) I don't think you can hope for any actual pleasure.

VALMONT (*voice over*) Oh, yes.

INT. MERTEUIL'S GRAND SALON. DUSK

Valmont leans in, his tone more intimate.

VALMONT You see, I have no intention of breaking down her prejudices. I want her to believe in God and virtue and the sanctity of marriage and still not be able to stop herself. I want the excitement of watching her betray everything that's most important to her. Surely you understand that. I thought betrayal was your favourite word.

MERTEUIL No, no, cruelty: I always think that has a nobler ring to it.

He contemplates her for a moment, lost in admiration.

INT. CORRIDOR OF MIRRORS. DUSK

The first-floor landing in Merteuil's house is an immense gallery of mirrors. She and Valmont pass down the corridor, their images shifting and multiplying in the candlelight.

VALMONT How's Belleroche?

MERTEUIL I'm very pleased with him.

VALMONT And is he your only lover?

Merteuil pretends to give this a moment's consideration.

MERTEUIL Yes.

VALMONT I think you should take another. I think it most unhealthy, this exclusivity.

MERTEUIL You're not jealous, are you?

VALMONT Of course I am. Belleroche is completely undeserving.

MERTEUIL I thought he was one of your closest friends.

VALMONT Exactly, so I know what I'm talking about.

INT. LANDING. DUSK

Valmont and Merteuil emerge on to the landing at the top of the broad and imposing staircase which leads down to the entrance of the house.

VALMONT No, I think you should organise an infidelity. With me, for example.

Merteuil stops and looks up at him, smiling.

MERTEUIL You refuse me a simple favour and then you expect to be indulged?

VALMONT It's only because it *is* so simple. It wouldn't feel like a conquest. I have to follow my destiny. I have to be true to my profession.

INT. STAIRCASE. DUSK

Valmont plants a chaste kiss on Merteuil's bosom and sets off down the stairs. Merteuil's voice stops him in his tracks.

MERTEUIL All right, then: come back when you've succeeded with Madame de Tourvel.

VALMONT Yes?

MERTEUIL And I will offer you . . . a reward.

VALMONT My love.

MERTEUIL But I shall require proof.

VALMONT Certainly.

MERTEUIL Written proof.

VALMONT Ah.

MERTEUIL Not negotiable.

Valmont recovers quickly.

VALMONT I don't suppose there's any possibility of an advance?

MERTEUIL Goodnight, Vicomte.

She grants him a dazzling smile and leaves him.

INT. CORRIDOR OF MIRRORS. DUSK

Merteuil stops in front of one of the mirrors. It turns out to be a door, which she opens.

INT. SPIRAL STAIRCASE. DUSK

A candle at the top sheds a dim light; Merteuil begins to ascend her secret staircase.

INT. MERTEUIL'S BEDROOM. DUSK

Belleroche, a beautiful blockhead of about thirty, springs to his feet as Merteuil emerges from what is ostensibly a cupboard door. He hurries over to embrace her.

BELLEROCHE Where have you been? Time has no logic when I'm not with you: an hour is like a century.

MERTEUIL I've told you before: we shall get on a good deal better if you make a concerted effort not to sound like the latest novel.

She closes the door purposefully.

INT. PRIVATE CHAPEL IN ROSEMONDE'S GROUNDS. DAY

The sound of the little silver bell which summons the congregation to take Communion: close on Tourvel as her hands part to reveal her face. Rosemonde kneels next to her and is now being helped to her feet by Valmont.

Valmont escorts Rosemonde up the stairs to the altar rail, Tourvel remaining on the other side of her. The rest of the congregation consists

of Rosemonde's domestic staff, in a segregated portion of the chapel; and they file up towards the altar, respectfully waiting their turn. Tourvel kneels at the altar rail as Valmont helps Rosemonde to kneel beside her. Then Tourvel looks up, slightly surprised, as Valmont moves off to one side, instead of taking his place at the rail. By now, the elderly Curé, intoning the Latin mass, is approaching Tourvel with the large Communion wafer. Valmont watches intently.
Valmont's point of view: the wafer is placed on Tourvel's lower lip and slowly vanishes into her mouth.
Tourvel's point of view: Valmont, his expression respectful, his demeanour humble.

EXT. ROSEMONDE'S PRIVATE CHAPEL. DAY

Beautiful summer's day. The chapel is in the grounds of Rosemonde's château, the turrets of which are visible in the distance. Her open carriage stands waiting, as the congregation emerges into the sunlight. The coachman jumps down, but Rosemonde dismisses him with a gesture.

ROSEMONDE It's such a beautiful day, I believe we'll walk.

A little way off, Tourvel shyly approaches Valmont.

TOURVEL You didn't take the sacrament today.

VALMONT No.

TOURVEL May I ask why?

VALMONT I have this appalling reputation, as you may know . . .

TOURVEL Oh, yes, I have been warned about you.

VALMONT You have? By whom?

TOURVEL A friend.

EXT. GROUNDS OF ROSEMONDE'S CHATEAU. DAY

Valmont and Tourvel stroll back across the sunlit lawns.

VALMONT The fact is I've spent my life surrounded by immoral people; I've allowed myself to be influenced by them and sometimes even taken pride in outshining them.

TOURVEL And now?

VALMONT Now what I feel most often is unworthiness.

TOURVEL But it's precisely at such moments you start to become worthy.

Valmont appears to give this assertion his serious consideration.

He glances back to see Azolan, who is flirting with Tourvel's young chambermaid, Julie.

VALMONT I certainly believe that one should constantly strive to improve oneself.

Long shot: the two of them among the entire household, moving back towards the austere and massively imposing shape of the château, as, on sound, the passionate climax of the aria 'O malheureuse Iphigénie' from Gluck's Iphigénie en Tauride *begins to swell.*

INT. MERTEUIL'S BOX AT THE OPERA. EVENING

The aria continues; the opera is in progress. Volanges and Cécile, in the box, stare down at the stage. Merteuil, however, opera glasses pressed to her face, is scanning the audience.

INT. OPERA HOUSE. EVENING

Merteuil's point of view, as her gaze comes to rest on the face of a handsome young man of not more than twenty, listening intently, tears streaming down his face: the Chevalier Danceny.

INT. MERTEUIL'S BOX. EVENING

A knock at the door and Danceny, charmingly shy and uncertain, bows deeply to Merteuil.

MERTEUIL Chevalier, I don't believe you know my cousin, Madame de Volanges. This is Chevalier Danceny. And madame's daughter, Cécile.

All this has taken place very quickly and now Danceny becomes aware of Cécile for the first time: he looks at her, tongue-tied, obviously smitten, eventually managing to utter a strangled greeting. Merteuil observes him shrewdly.

Tell us what we should think of the opera.

DANCENY Oh, it's sublime. Don't you find?

MERTEUIL Monsieur Danceny is one of those rare eccentrics who come here to listen to the music.

DANCENY I do look forward to our next meeting.

He bows to Cécile, blushing deeply, and leaves the box. Cécile's eyes are shining. Merteuil is watching her closely.

MERTEUIL Charming young man. Penniless, regrettably. He's one of the finest music teachers in the city.

Close on Cécile: the idea occurs to her at the very moment Merteuil expresses it.
Perhaps you should employ him.

EXT. ROSEMONDE'S CHATEAU. DAWN
Julie steps out on to the balcony of Tourvel's room.

EXT. COURTYARD AT ROSEMONDE'S CHATEAU. DAWN
Below, Valmont and Azolan, who carries a long musket over his shoulder, descend a staircase and crunch across the gravel.
Another angle reveals a figure in stealthy pursuit of them: Tourvel's footman, Georges.

INT. TOURVEL'S BEDROOM. DAWN
Julie comes in from the balcony and bends to wake Tourvel and murmur in her ear.

EXT. WOODS. DAWN
Valmont and Azolan stride through the waist-high grass.
VALMONT How are you getting on with Madame de Tourvel's maid?
AZOLAN Julie? Tell you the truth, it's been a bit boring. If I wasn't so anxious to keep your lordship abreast, I think I'd have only bothered the once. Still, you know, what else is there to do in the country?
VALMONT Yes, it wasn't so much the details of your intimacy I was after, it was whether she's agreed to bring me Madame de Tourvel's letters.
AZOLAN She won't steal the letters, sir.
VALMONT She won't?
AZOLAN You know better than me, sir, it's easy enough making them do what they want to do; it's trying to get them to do what you want them to do, that's what gives you a headache.
VALMONT And them, as often as not. I need to know who's writing to her about me.
AZOLAN I shouldn't worry if I was you, sir. She told Julie she didn't believe you went hunting in the mornings. She said she was going to have you followed. So I'd say it was only a matter of time.

They carry on through the woods. Behind them, Georges blunders incompetently from tree to tree.

EXT. BOUNDARY OF ROSEMONDE'S LAND. DAY

Azolan unlocks a gate in the wall enclosing Rosemonde's property to let Valmont through. The latter hesitates, looking back.

VALMONT Terrible noise he's making.

AZOLAN He should get the news back to her twice as quickly.

VALMONT I don't think we should make it too easy for him.

He takes the musket from Azolan and suddenly fires it into the undergrowth.

EXT. UNDERGROWTH. DAY

Georges, panic-stricken, hurls himself to the ground as the echoes of the shot die away.

EXT. VILLAGE SQUARE. DAY

The village consists of half a dozen wattle-and-daub huts disposed around a muddy clearing, where pigs graze and barefoot children wander. The poverty is as stark and absolute as that of a village in India. A small crowd is gathered around one of the huts, Armand's, out of which a couple of men, supervised by the Bailiff, are carrying a plain deal table, which they dump down next to three wooden chairs. A gaunt woman follows them, miserably wringing her hands.

Valmont and Azolan arrive: the former takes in the situation and turns to confront the Bailiff.

VALMONT What exactly do you think you're doing?

BAILIFF I am impounding these effects, sir.

VALMONT Has it not been explained to you? Monsieur Armand is not well.

BAILIFF I don't make the laws, sir, I just do what I'm told. Everybody has to pay his taxes.

VALMONT How much does he owe?

BAILIFF Well . . .

VALMONT How much?

BAILIFF Fifty-six livres.

Valmont takes a large, jingling purse out of his pocket and hands it to Azolan.

VALMONT Pay him.

AZOLAN Yes, my lord.

Valmont ducks into Armand's hut, as Georges arrives on the fringes of the crowd and hurries to Armand's window.

INT. ARMAND'S HUT. DAY

Georges's point of view: Valmont stands looking down at Armand, a man of not more than fifty, who looks ancient, gnarled and battered by work, his hair long, thick and white.

VALMONT Monsieur Armand. You don't know me.

ARMAND Of course I do, Monsieur le Vicomte.

VALMONT Please, don't get up.

Armand is struggling up out of his large pallet bed covered with sacking.

ARMAND I have to, sir. They're taking the bed.

VALMONT Not at all. No one is taking anything.

EXT. VILLAGE SQUARE. DAY

Valmont leaves the hut, pursued by Armand, who falls to his knees to kiss Valmont's hand, as his wife (the gaunt woman) embraces Valmont's other hand.

VALMONT Azolan.

Another angle shows Valmont and Azolan surrounded by villagers and their children. Valmont distributes gold coins to the clamouring crowd.

Just to tide you over. I insist.

EXT. BOUNDARY OF ROSEMONDE'S LAND. DAY

Azolan unlocks a compartment in one of the brick gateposts and takes out a wooden mailbox with a slot in the top. Then he takes a pin from his wig and begins delicately to probe the lock of the mailbox as they talk.

VALMONT Fifty-six livres to save an entire family from ruin, that seems a genuine bargain.

AZOLAN These days, my lord, you can find half a dozen like that, any village in the country.

VALMONT Really? I must say the family was very well chosen. Solidly respectable, gratifyingly tearful, no suspiciously pretty girls. Well done.

AZOLAN I do my best for you, sir.

VALMONT And all that humble gratitude. It was most affecting.

AZOLAN Certainly brought a tear to my eye.

The lock yields to his manipulations, the mailbox opens and after a brief inspection he hands two letters to Valmont, who glances at the postmarks and hands one of them straight back to Azolan.

VALMONT Dijon. That's from her husband.

He holds the other letter, which is in a distinctive, somewhat pretentious envelope, up to the light.

This must be from that officious friend of hers.

He passes it back to Azolan, who returns it to the mailbox and closes it. They move off, back in the direction of the house.

Tell me, where do you and Julie meet?

AZOLAN Oh, in my room, sir.

Azolan unlocks the gate and they pass through it.

VALMONT And is she coming tonight?

AZOLAN Afraid so.

VALMONT Then I think I may have to burst in on you. See if blackmail will succeed better than bribery. About two o'clock suit you? I don't want to embarrass you, will that give you enough time?

AZOLAN Ample, sir.

INT. GRAND SALON IN ROSEMONDE'S CHATEAU. DAY

Valmont looks up from his book, as Rosemonde bustles into the room, followed by Tourvel. He rises to greet them.

ROSEMONDE Is this true about Monsieur Armand?

VALMONT I don't believe I know anyone of that name . . .

TOURVEL You may as well own up, monsieur. My footman happened to be passing when you were in the village this morning.

VALMONT I don't think you ought to pay too much attention to servants' gossip.

ROSEMONDE It is true, isn't it?

VALMONT Well, I . . . Yes, it is.

He looks up, ostensibly deeply embarrassed, to catch Tourvel's admiring gaze. Rosemonde spreads her arms.

ROSEMONDE You dear boy, come and let me give you a hug!

Valmont crosses to her and they embrace. Then Valmont turns and advances towards Tourvel. Before she can escape, he's embraced her and, for a second, she's in his arms. Meanwhile Rosemonde's steward has entered, with the mail laid out on a salver. As Tourvel escapes from Valmont's arms, she finds the steward at her elbow. Ashen, she shakily reaches out her hand for the two letters.

INT. GRAND SALON IN ROSEMONDE'S CHATEAU. NIGHT

Valmont is reading and Tourvel is looking over her letter from Paris, the one with the distinctive envelope. Eventually, she looks up at him and breaks the silence.

TOURVEL I can't understand how someone whose instincts are so generous could lead such a dissolute life.

VALMONT I'm afraid you have an exaggerated idea both of my generosity and of my depravity. If I knew who'd given you such a dire account of me . . .

Tourvel folds up her letter, her expression sheepish.

. . . since I don't, let me make a confession. I'm afraid the key to the paradox lies in a certain weakness of character.

TOURVEL I can't see how so thoughtful an act of charity could be described as weak.

VALMONT Because it was simply a response to a strong new influence in my life: yours.

Tourvel looks away. Valmont sighs.

You see how weak I am? I promised myself I was never going to tell you. It's just, looking at you . . .

TOURVEL Monsieur.

VALMONT You needn't worry, I have no illicit intentions. I wouldn't dream of insulting you. But I do love you. I adore you.

The letter slips from Tourvel's fingers. Valmont is across the room in an instant, on his knees in front of her, handing her the letter and then taking her hand in his.

Please help me.

Tourvel scrambles to her feet, horrified, and begins to move away across the great room, her pace increasing as she realises that Valmont is pursuing her.

INT. MAIN STAIRCASE. NIGHT

Tourvel hurries up the vast, wide staircase. Below, Valmont, in pursuit, emerges into the hallway.

INT. CORRIDOR. NIGHT

Tourvel's back recedes down the corridor. Presently, Valmont comes into frame, catching her up. But Tourvel disappears into her room and there's the sound of a heavy bolt.

Valmont arrives at her door and drops to his knees, pressing his eye to her keyhole.

INT. TOURVEL'S BEDROOM. NIGHT

Keyhole shot: Tourvel, panting, distressed, begins to loosen her bodice.

INT. CORRIDOR. NIGHT

Valmont stands up. There's a look of satisfaction on his face as he begins to tiptoe away.

INT. AZOLAN'S BEDROOM. NIGHT

Azolan is in bed with Julie, they're asleep in each other's arms. Suddenly the door bursts open. Valmont stands in the doorway in his dressing gown, holding a candlestick. In its flickering light, Azolan and Julie wake, Julie genuinely terrified and Azolan (since this has been prearranged) convincingly dismayed.

VALMONT I rang a number of times.

AZOLAN Didn't hear, sir.

VALMONT I require some hot water.

AZOLAN Right away, sir.

He jumps out of bed, uncovering Julie. She reaches for the sheets but Valmont speaks sharply, stopping her in her tracks.

VALMONT Don't move.

As Azolan puts on a dressing gown and hurries to the door, Valmont settles himself on the end of the bed, his eyes burning into Julie.

Azolan.

AZOLAN Sir.

VALMONT Wait for me in my room.

Azolan hurries out. Valmont continues to stare at Julie, who is becoming increasingly uncomfortable.

You know I can't condone this sort of behaviour, Julie.

JULIE I know, sir . . .

VALMONT But you may rely on my discretion –

JULIE Oh, thank you, sir.

VALMONT – providing, of course, that you agree to my price.

There's a silence, during which Julie thinks she understands what he means. Her expression changes as she tries to work out how best to react. But Valmont shakes his head.

No, no, nothing like that. No, all I want is to see every letter Madame de Tourvel has received since her arrival here and every letter she writes from now on.

JULIE But, sir . . .

VALMONT Deliver them to Azolan by midnight tomorrow.

He stands, continuing to look at her for a moment, until she snatches at the sheet and covers herself. He brings a handful of gold coins out of his dressing-gown pocket and pours them on to the bed.

For your trouble.

INT. CORRIDOR OUTSIDE AZOLAN'S BEDROOM. NIGHT

Azolan is waiting outside the door. Valmont gives him his candle to hold, while he gathers up the train of his dressing gown. This done, he takes back the candlestick and begins his descent from the attic floor of the château.

INT. GRAND SALON IN MERTEUIL'S HOUSE. DAY

Cécile is playing the harp and singing an aria from Gluck's Paride e Elena, *accompanied on the harpsichord by Danceny. On the far side of the room, Volanges is a benevolent spectator. After a time, Danceny breaks off, hitting a note several times to indicate where Cécile's voice has gone wrong. They resume a few bars back; this time Cécile gets it right and Danceny nods in approval. They proceed until Cécile makes a mistake with the harp. Danceny, seeing that Volanges's back is now turned, crosses, takes Cécile's hands and adjusts them to the correct position. Then, he takes the opportunity to slip a piece of paper between the harp strings. She frowns and then unfolds it. It contains the message:* I LOVE YOU.

Merteuil arrives in the room, smiling hospitably at Volanges. Cécile darts a furious glance at Danceny. Then they resume playing and singing.

Merteuil winces, closing her eyes as if to blot out the cacophony.

INT. MERTEUIL'S BOX AT THE OPERA. EVENING

Merteuil and Cécile are attending a performance of Paride e Elena.*Cécile, evidently in some distress, turns to appeal to Merteuil.*

CÉCILE Would it be very wrong of me to answer Monsieur Danceny's letters?

MERTEUIL In the circumstances, yes.

CÉCILE In what circumstances?

Merteuil pretends to reflect before answering.

MERTEUIL It's not my place to tell you this, my dear . . . if I hadn't become so fond of you . . .

CÉCILE Go on, please!

MERTEUIL Your marriage has been arranged.

CÉCILE Who is it?

MERTEUIL Someone I know, slightly. Monsieur le Comte de Bastide.

CÉCILE What's he like?

MERTEUIL Well . . .

CÉCILE You don't like him.

MERTEUIL It's not that. He's a man of somewhat . . . erratic judgement. And rather serious.

CÉCILE How old is he?

MERTEUIL Thirty-six.

CÉCILE Thirty-six? He's an old man!

Merteuil smiles, as another thought galvanises Cécile.

Do you know when?

MERTEUIL In the new year, I believe.

She stares, unseeing, at the stage, lost in thought. Merteuil leans in closer to her.

Perhaps there is a way to let you write to Monsieur Danceny . . .

CÉCILE Oh, madame!

She's caught hold of Merteuil's hand, her eyes shining.

MERTEUIL If you were to let me see both sides of the correspondence, I could reassure myself . . .

Cécile throws herself into Merteuil's arms and embraces her. Merteuil's eyes glitter in the darkness. Then Cécile looks up at her.

CÉCILE I can't show you the letters I've already sent him . . .

She breaks off, realising she's given herself away, her expression apprehensive. But Merteuil's smile is indulgent. As the impassioned love duet on stage reaches a climax, she stretches out a hand to caress Cécile's neck and collarbone.

EXT. GARDENS OF ROSEMONDE'S CHATEAU. DAY

Tourvel moves down a path in a secluded part of the gardens.

She becomes aware, too late for evasion, that Valmont is approaching down a separate but intersecting path. He speaks as he intercepts her.

VALMONT I trust you slept well. I wish I could say that I had.

TOURVEL I thought the least I could hope for was that you would respect me.

VALMONT But I do, of course I do.

TOURVEL You've offended me deeply, it's unforgivable. This confirms everything I've been told about you. I'm beginning to think you may have planned the whole exercise.

She turns and moves briskly away, obliging him to hurry after her.

VALMONT I had no idea you were staying here. Not that it would have disturbed me in the slightest if I had known. You see. until I met you, I had only ever experienced desire. Love, never.

He has succeeded in stopping her with his eloquence. Now she moves away again, offended.

TOURVEL That's enough.

He pursues her, talking fast.

VALMONT No, no, you made an accusation, you must allow me the opportunity to defend myself. Now I'm not going to deny that I was aware of your beauty . . .

TOURVEL Monsieur.

VALMONT . . . but the point is, all this has nothing to do with your beauty. As I got to know you, I began to realise that beauty was the least of your qualities. I became fascinated by your goodness. I was drawn in by it. I didn't understand what was happening to me and it was only when I began to feel actual physical pain every time you left the room, that it finally dawned on me: I was in love, for the first time in my life.

Tourvel quickens her pace.

I knew it was hopeless, but that didn't matter to me; and it's not that I want to have you . . .

He succeeds in stopping her short.

. . . all I want is to deserve you. Tell me what to do, show me how to behave, I'll do anything you say.

TOURVEL Very well, then. I would like you to leave this house.

VALMONT I don't see why that should be necessary.

TOURVEL Let's just say you've spent your whole life making it necessary. And if you refuse, I shall be forced to leave myself.

VALMONT Well, then, of course, whatever you say.

TOURVEL Thank you.

She moves away again, leaving Valmont temporarily bested. He lets her go two or three steps, before setting off in pursuit.

VALMONT Perhaps I might be so bold as to ask a favour in return. I think it would only be just to let me know which of your friends has blackened my name.

TOURVEL If friends of mine have warned me against you, I can hardly reward them with betrayal. I must say you devalue your generous offer if you want to use it as a bargaining point.

VALMONT Very well, I withdraw the request. I hope you won't think I'm bargaining if I ask you to let me write to you?

TOURVEL Well . . .

VALMONT And pray that you will do me the kindness of answering my letters?

He follows her, weaving from side to side, confusing her.

TOURVEL I'm not sure a correspondence with you is something a woman of honour could permit herself.

VALMONT So you're determined to refuse my suggestions, however respectable?

TOURVEL I didn't say that . . .

VALMONT And you'd rather be unjust than risk showing me a touch of kindness?

TOURVEL I would welcome the chance to prove to you that what lies behind this is not hatred or resentment but . . .

VALMONT But what?

Tourvel seems unable to find a satisfactory answer to this. She moves away, leaving Valmont pensive and not wholly displeased with the encounter.

INT. CORRIDOR OUTSIDE AZOLAN'S ROOM. NIGHT

Julie comes up the attic stairs holding a bundle of letters. She knocks on the door and Azolan opens it. She hands him the letters and he lets her into the room. He makes a wry face and closes the door behind her.

INT. VALMONT'S BEDROOM. NIGHT

Valmont sits on his bed, inspecting one of the letters. Azolan stands beside him, holding a candle. his expression complacent.

VALMONT Listen to this: 'He knows exactly how far he may venture without risk and guarantees his own security by tormenting only the safest kind of victim: women.'

He turns the letter over and reads out the signature, nodding grimly.

VALMONT Madame de Volanges.

EXT. MAIN ENTRANCE TO ROSEMONDE'S CHATEAU. DAY

Valmont embraces Rosemonde as his big black carriage waits at the foot of a flight of outside steps.

VALMONT Goodbye, aunt.

ROSEMONDE Goodbye, dear boy.

He moves across to Tourvel, who waits nearby, kisses her hand and keeps hold of it a little too long. She speaks in an undertone.

TOURVEL Monsieur, please . . .

VALMONT I'll write soon.

To her alarm, he leans forward and kisses her on the cheek. Then he turns and moves down through lines of liveried servants towards his carriage.

INT. ÉMILIE'S BEDROOM. NIGHT

A sheet of writing paper is spread across the bare back of Émilie, a courtesan, lying on her luxurious canopied bed. Valmont perches a china inkwell on one of her buttocks and begins to write. Outside, there are occasional rumbles of thunder and flashes of lightning.

VALMONT 'My dear Madame de Tourvel . . . I have just come . . .'

Émilie laughs and turns to look back at him.

Don't move, I said . . . 'to my desk, in the middle of a stormy night; during which I have been . . . tossed . . .'

EXT. GARDENS OF ROSEMONDE'S CHATEAU. DAY

Tourvel sits on a bench, reading Valmont's letter.

VALMONT (*voice over*) '. . . from exaltation to exhaustion and back again; yet despite these torments I guarantee that at this moment I am far happier than you. . .'

The letter: a teardrop falls on to the paper, smudging the ink.

INT. ÉMILIE'S BEDROOM. NIGHT

Valmont lays aside paper, pen and inkwell and murmurs to Émilie.

VALMONT We'll finish it later, shall we?

He leans in to embrace her.

INT. GRAND SALON IN MERTEUIL'S HOUSE. DAY

Merteuil stirs her tea, listening attentively. Her guest is the Vicomte de Valmont. It's September now and there's a hint of autumn in the afternoon light.

VALMONT Your damned cousin, the Volanges bitch, wanted me away from Madame de Tourvel: well, now I am and I intend to make her suffer for it. Your plan to ruin her daughter, are you making any progress? Is there anything I can do to help? I'm entirely at your disposal.

MERTEUIL Well, yes, I told Danceny you would act as his confidant and adviser. I want you to stiffen his resolve, if that's the phrase.

Valmont frowns, not at all pleased.

I thought if anyone could help him . . .

VALMONT Help? He doesn't need help, he needs hindrances: if he has to climb over enough of them, he might inadvertently fall on top of her.

He shakes his head dismissively, and moves over to flop down beside her on the sofa.

I take it he hasn't been a great success.

MERTEUIL He's been disastrous. Like most intellectuals, he's intensely stupid.

Valmont enjoys this: he looks at Merteuil, shaking his head in admiration.

VALMONT I often wonder how you managed to invent yourself.

MERTEUIL I had no choice, did I? I'm a woman. Women are obliged to be far more skilful than men. You can ruin our reputation and our life with a few well-chosen words. So of course I had to invent: not only myself but ways of escape no one has ever thought of. And I've succeeded, because I've always known I was born to dominate your sex and avenge my own.

VALMONT Yes; but what I asked you was how.

MERTEUIL When I came out into society, I was fifteen. I already knew that the role I was condemned to, namely to keep quiet and do what I was told, gave me the perfect opportunity to listen and pay attention: not to what people told me, which was naturally of no interest, but to whatever it was they were trying to hide. I practised detachment. I learned how to look cheerful, while under the table I stuck a fork into the back of my hand. I became a virtuoso of deceit. It wasn't pleasure I was after, it was knowledge. I consulted the strictest moralists to learn how to appear, philosophers to find out what to think and novelists to see what I could get away with. And, in the end, I distilled everything down to one wonderfully simple principle: win or die.

VALMONT So you're infallible, are you?

MERTEUIL When I want a man, I have him; when he wants to tell, he finds he can't. That's the whole story.

VALMONT And was that our story?

Merteuil pauses before answering: the air is becoming increasingly charged with eroticism.

MERTEUIL I wanted you before we'd even met. My self-esteem demanded it. Then, when you began to pursue me, I wanted you so badly. It's the only time I've ever been controlled by my desire. Single combat.

Valmont slides down the sofa towards her; but a heavy silence is interrupted by the arrival of Merteuil's Majordomo, who murmurs into her ear.

MAJORDOMO Madame de Volanges.

Merteuil is delighted.

MERTEUIL Ah, Madame de Volanges.

INT. MAIN STAIRCASE. DAY

The Majordomo escorts an anxious-looking Volanges up the stairs.

INT. GRAND SALON. DAY

Volanges is shown into the great room. No sign of Valmont.

VOLANGES Your note said it was urgent . . .

MERTEUIL It's days now. I haven't been able to think of anything else. Please sit down.

Volanges subsides on to the sofa, thoroughly alarmed.

I have reason to believe that a, how can I describe it, a dangerous liaison has sprung up between your daughter and the Chevalier Danceny.

A pan reveals, in the other half of the room, behind a screen, Valmont, who is eavesdropping, bemused; he shakes his head, at a loss to understand Merteuil's tactics. Meanwhile, Volanges is confidently dismissing the suggestion.

VOLANGES No, no, that's completely absurd. Cécile is still a child, she understands nothing of these things; and Danceny is an entirely respectable young man.

MERTEUIL Tell me, does Cécile have a great many correspondents?

VOLANGES Why do you ask?

MERTEUIL I went into her room at the beginning of this week, I simply knocked and entered; and she was stuffing a letter into the right-hand drawer of her bureau: in which, I couldn't help noticing, there seemed to be a large number of similar letters.

Silence. Behind the screen, Valmont's mouth is open in admiration and amazement. Volanges rises to her feet.

VOLANGES I'm most grateful to you.

Merteuil rings, unable to resist a smile at the ease of it all. Volanges stands up, still in a state of mild shock.

MERTEUIL Would you think it impertinent if I were to make another suggestion?

VOLANGES No, no.

MERTEUIL If my recollection is correct, I overheard you saying to the Vicomte de Valmont that his aunt had invited you and Cécile to stay at her château.

Valmont stands on a chair to look over the screen at Merteuil and convey his displeasure at this turn of events.

VOLANGES She has, yes, repeatedly.

Merteuil shoots a warning glance at Valmont.

MERTEUIL A spell in the country might be the very thing.

Valmont has withdrawn; but now realises he is visible in one of Merteuil's enormous mirrors and is obliged to dive full-length to escape detection. The Majordomo hovers, waiting to show Volanges out; she turns back in the doorway, bowed down with care, her expression piteous.

VOLANGES Thank you.

She leaves, and Merteuil turns back to Valmont, triumphant. He is lost in admiration.

MERTEUIL You asked for hindrances.

VALMONT You are a genuinely wicked woman.

MERTEUIL And you wanted a chance to make my cousin suffer.

VALMONT I can't resist you.

MERTEUIL I've made it easy for you.

VALMONT But all this is most inconvenient; the Comtesse de Beaulieu has invited me to stay.

MERTEUIL Well, you'll have to put her off.

VALMONT The Comtesse has promised me extensive use of her gardens. It seems her husband's fingers are not as green as they once were.

MERTEUIL Maybe not. But from what I hear, all his friends are gardeners.

VALMONT Is that so?

MERTEUIL You want your revenge. I want my revenge. I'm afraid there's really only one place you can go.

VALMONT Back to Auntie, eh?

MERTEUIL Back to Auntie. Where you can also pursue that other matter. You have some evidence to procure, have you not?

Valmont doesn't answer for a moment. He approaches, reverting to the tone of just before Volanges's arrival.

VALMONT Don't you think it would be a generous gesture, show a proper confidence in my abilities, to take that evidence for granted . . .?

MERTEUIL I need it in writing, Vicomte.

He's close to her now, giving her his most charming smile. She leans her head back, unmoved. Their voices are intimate, his persuasive, hers amused.

And now you must leave me.

VALMONT Must I? Why?

MERTEUIL Because I'm hungry.

VALMONT Yes, I've quite an appetite myself.

MERTEUIL Then go home and eat.

He leans in to kiss her, but she turns aside, offering him her cheek.

In writing.

He gives up, smiling at her, still in admiration.

Long shot: the two of them move across the vast room, exiting by different doors.

INT. CÉCILE'S BEDROOM IN VOLANGES'S HOUSE. DAY

Cécile looks up with a start as Volanges storms into the room, goes straight to her bureau and opens the right-hand drawer. Her eyes widen in horror as Volanges brings out a handful of letters. Volanges opens one of them, reads a sentence or two and looks up at Cécile, outraged. Cécile crumples to the floor in a dead faint.

INT. GRAND SALON IN ROSEMONDE'S CHATEAU. DAY

Valmont is holding a sealed letter behind his back. He moves past Tourvel, who sits staring, ashen, at a book; he pauses by Cécile, who sits in a window seat, busy with her embroidery, and waves the letter at her, but she fails to understand and he is obliged to move on; past Volanges in the other window seat; finally drifting by Rosemonde, who is playing solitaire at her card table. Now he's back where he started, his eyes fixed on Tourvel, who glances up at him resentfully. Volanges arrives behind him, startling him as she snaps open her fan, but her position gives him another opportunity to display the letter to a still-puzzled Cécile.

ROSEMONDE You'll be pleased to hear, my dear, that Armand is on his feet again and back at work.

VALMONT Who?

ROSEMONDE Monsieur Armand, whose family you helped so generously.

VALMONT Oh, yes.

Rosemonde turns to address Volanges.

ROSEMONDE When my nephew was last staying here, we discovered quite by chance . . .

Valmont interrupts her, suddenly rising to his feet, looking across at Tourvel.

VALMONT Are you feeling all right, madame? I'm sorry to interrupt you, Aunt, it seemed to me all of a sudden that Madame de Tourvel didn't look at all well.

TOURVEL I'm . . . no, I'm quite all right.

By now, Rosemonde and Volanges are on their feet, converging on Tourvel.

VOLANGES Perhaps you need some air. Do you feel constricted in any way?

TOURVEL No, really . . .

VALMONT I feel sure Madame de Volanges is right, as usual. A turn around the grounds perhaps.

ROSEMONDE Yes, yes, a little walk in the gardens; it's not too cool, I think.

Valmont takes advantage of the confusion to throw the letter to Cécile, landing it neatly in her embroidery box, which she has the presence of mind to close. Meanwhile, Rosemonde and Volanges are shepherding a bewildered Tourvel towards the French windows.

Fresh air will do you the world of good.

VOLANGES The meal was somewhat heavy, perhaps . . .

ROSEMONDE I don't believe that was the cause . . .

During this exchange, Cécile has gathered up her shawl and made to follow the others. As she's spreading it across her shoulders, however, she's startled to find it tugged away from her by Valmont, who drops it on a chair, murmuring between clenched teeth.

VALMONT Come back for it.

She frowns at him for a moment, then follows the still-clucking ladies out into the garden. Valmont waits, by the window; presently Cécile hurries back into the room, not immediately seeing Valmont.

Mademoiselle: I've no wish to arouse suspicion, so I'll be brief. The letter is from the Chevalier Danceny.

CÉCILE Yes, I thought . . .

VALMONT Now, the handing over of such letters is a far from easy matter to accomplish. I can't be expected to create a diversion every day. So . . .

He produces a large key.

This key resembles the key to your bedroom, which I happen to know is kept in your mother's bedroom, on the mantelpiece, tied with a blue ribbon. Take it, go up now, attach the blue ribbon to it and put it in place of your bedroom key, which you will then bring to me. I'll be able to get a copy cut within two hours. Then I'll be able to collect your letters and deliver Danceny's without any complications.

He puts the key into Cécile's hand.

Oh, and in the cupboard by your bed, you'll find a feather and a small bottle of oil, so that you may oil the lock and hinges on the anteroom door.

He points towards the door.

CÉCILE Are you sure, monsieur?

VALMONT Trust me.

Cécile curtsies to him and begins to move away.

Believe me, mademoiselle, if there's one thing I can't abide, it's deceitfulness.

He watches her as she hurries away.

EXT. TERRACE. DAY

Valmont emerges from the French windows and pauses on the top step. Below, on the terrace, are Rosemonde, Volanges and Tourvel.

INT. VOLANGES'S BEDROOM. DAY

Cécile finds the key on the mantelpiece and begins grappling with the blue ribbon.

EXT. TERRACE. DAY

Valmont is now at the bottom of the steps. He calls out to Tourvel, who's walking away with Volanges.

VALMONT I trust you're feeling a little better, madame.

Rosemonde watches from a nearby bench, her expression shrewd, as Tourvel bears down on Valmont, speaking in a fierce undertone.

TOURVEL If I were ill, monsieur, it would not be difficult to guess who was responsible.

VALMONT You can't mean me. Do you?

TOURVEL You promised to leave here.

VALMONT And I did.

Valmont suddenly becomes aware that Volanges is heading purposefully back into the house.

Would you excuse me, madame?

He breaks away from her and hurries off up the stairs.

INT. GRAND SALON. DAY

Volanges bustles in through the French windows. Behind, unseen by her, Valmont follows, slipping across the room and out by a different door.

INT. VOLANGES'S BEDROOM. DAY

Cécile has almost finished tying the blue ribbon on to the second key, when she's startled by the sound of the creaking ante-room door. The key slips from her fingers and drops into a tall china vase in the grate. She drops to her knees to retrieve it, but the neck of the vase is too narrow to admit her hand. As she struggles with it, Valmont appears in the doorway.

VALMONT Quick. Your mother.

He hurries across to her, assessing the situation in a flash, picks up the vase and inverts it, emptying the key into Cécile's hands. Then, before she can hand it to him, he hurries away, just managing to dive behind the open door of Cécile's bedroom, as Volanges arrives.

VOLANGES What are you doing?

Behind her, Valmont tiptoes backwards across the opening between the two rooms. Meanwhile, Cécile gropes for an answer.

CÉCILE I just came up to fetch your shawl.

She picks up Volanges's shawl from a chair and hands it to her, giving Valmont the opportunity to make his escape across the ante-room.

INT. MAIN STAIRCASE. DAY

Volanges follows Cécile down the staircase. All of a sudden Cécile stumbles in shock, allowing her mother to overtake her.

What has caused her surprise is that Valmont has somehow arrived at the bottom of the stairs and is now approaching them.

As he passes he fumbles discreetly at Cécile's hand, but nothing happens. He grimaces in extreme annoyance, but Cécile has been more alert than he imagined possible; and the key is sitting there, left by her on the stone banisters. Valmont picks it up.

EXT. FORMAL GARDENS. DAY

Valmont bears down on Tourvel in a secluded corner of the rigidly manicured gardens. He perches on the end of the stone bench, where she's sitting.

VALMONT Why are you so angry with me?

TOURVEL All I can offer you, monsieur, is my friendship; can't you accept it?

VALMONT I could pretend to; but that would be dishonest. The man I used to be would have been content with friendship; and set about trying to turn it to his advantage. But I've changed now; and I can't conceal from you that I love you tenderly, passionately –

Tourvel gets up and moves away agitatedly, causing Valmont to change tack smoothly.

– and, above all, respectfully. So how am I to demote myself to the tepid position of friend? Not that you've even been pretending to show friendship.

TOURVEL What do you mean?

VALMONT Well, is this friendly?

And having worked himself up into a fine indignation, Valmont begins to stride away, until, as he's calculated, Tourvel stops him with her protest.

TOURVEL Why must you deliberately destroy my peace of mind?

Valmont turns and walks back to her, finally speaking with the greatest earnestness.

VALMONT You're wrong to feel threatened by me, madame. Your happiness is far more important to me than my own. That is what I mean when I say I love you.

TOURVEL I think we should end this conversation.

VALMONT I shall leave you in possession of the field.

He turns and walks away; then stops and addresses her again.

But look: we're to be living under the same roof at least for a few days. Surely we don't have to try to avoid each other?

TOURVEL Of course not. Provided you adhere to my few simple rules.

VALMONT I shall obey you in this as in everything.

Rather to her surprise, he bows formally and moves off.

TOURVEL Monsieur?

VALMONT What?

She looks at him for a moment, troubled; then shakes her head.

TOURVEL Nothing.

Valmont permits himself a private smile and disappears. Tourvel stands, not moving, locked in some private struggle.

INT. ANTE-ROOM TO THE VOLANGES'S BEDROOMS. NIGHT

The hinges no longer squeak as Valmont, in his dressing gown, carrying a candlestick, closes the door behind him, produces the key, crosses to another door, inserts the key in the lock, turns it, removes and pockets the key, opens the door and advances.

INT. CÉCILE'S BEDROOM. NIGHT

Cécile is fast asleep in the large bed. Valmont closes the door behind him and crosses silently to the bed. He stands for a moment, contemplating Cécile. Then he puts the candlestick down carefully, leans forward and very gently eases back the covers. Cécile stirs but still doesn't wake. Valmont passes his hand through the air, tracing the contours of her body. Finally, he puts his hand over her mouth. She wakes with a start, her eyes wide above his hand. Valmont smiles and speaks in a whisper.

VALMONT Nothing to worry about.

He removes his hand. She stares up at him, frowning.

CÉCILE Have you brought a letter?

VALMONT No.

CÉCILE Then what . . .

Instead of answering, he leans forward to kiss her. There's a brief, fierce struggle, in which Cécile successfully defends herself from the kiss, but is entirely taken by surprise when Valmont plunges a hand up inside her nightdress. Her eyes widen in horror, but her cry is instantly stifled as Valmont's other hand clamps down on her mouth. She writhes determinedly for a moment, succeeds in freeing her head and dives across the bed to reach for the bell-pull. Valmont leaps on to the bed, grasping her wrist just in time. She grapples with him for a moment.

VALMONT What are you going to tell your mother? How will you explain the fact that I have your key? If I tell her I'm here at your invitation, I have a feeling she'll believe me.

Cécile stops struggling, her eyes wide with fear. He's lying beside her on the bed.

CÉCILE What do you want?

VALMONT Well, I don't know. What do you think?

His hand goes back up inside her nightdress.

CÉCILE No!

VALMONT All right. I just want you to give me a kiss.

CÉCILE A kiss?

VALMONT That's all.

CÉCILE Then will you go?

VALMONT Then I'll go.

CÉCILE Promise?

VALMONT Whatever you say.

Cécile flops back on the pillow and closes her eyes.

CÉCILE All right.

Valmont leans in and gives her a long kiss, his hands roaming as he does so. After a while he pulls away.

All right?

VALMONT Very nice.

CÉCILE No, I mean, will you go now?

VALMONT Oh, I don't think so.

CÉCILE But you promised.

VALMONT I promised to go when you gave me a kiss. You didn't give me a kiss. I gave you a kiss. Not the same thing at all.

Cécile peers at him miserably. He looks back at her, calmly waiting.

CÉCILE And if I give you a kiss . . .?

VALMONT Let's just get ourselves more comfortable, shall we?

He leans over to reach the sheet and dispose it over them, as Cécile stares at him, transfixed.

INT. DINING ROOM. DAY

Rosemonde sits at the head of the polished table, with Cécile on her right and Valmont on her left. Further down, on Valmont's side, is Volanges; opposite her, Tourvel. It's breakfast time and the sideboard is groaning with beef and poultry and lamb cutlets. Valmont is eating heartily; Cécile, on the other hand, stares unseeingly at the proffered plate of cutlets. She looks up. Across the table, Valmont catches her eye and leers at her. As her distress mounts, he makes another unmistakably lascivious moue. *Immediately, she bursts into noisy tears, gets up and hurries out of the room. Consternation, except for Valmont, who, unperturbed, sips at his champagne.*

VOLANGES I'd better go and see what's wrong, if you'll excuse me.

ROSEMONDE Of course, my dear.

VALMONT I shouldn't worry, madame. The young have such miraculous powers of recuperation. I'm sure she'll soon be back in the saddle.

Volanges, on her feet already, acknowledges Valmont with a perfunctory smile, as she hurries out of the room. He catches Tourvel's eye and smiles at her, as she looks back at him, bemused.

INT. ANTE-ROOM. NIGHT

Valmont tiptoes in, carrying a candlestick. He reaches Cécile's door, brings out his key and turns it in the lock. The door does not yield. Valmont frowns, puzzled, and tries again.

INT. CÉCILE'S BEDROOM. NIGHT

The door is bolted on the inside. Cécile sits at her bureau, writing a letter, tears rolling down her face. She looks up at the sound of the key in the lock, then returns with an even fiercer concentration to her letter.

CÉCILE (*voice over*) 'Who else can I turn to in my desperation, madame?'

INT. DRESSING ROOM IN MERTEUIL'S HOUSE. DAY

Merteuil reads, her face concealed by Cécile's letter.

CÉCILE (*voice over*) 'And how can I write the necessary words?'

Merteuil lowers the letter to reveal a smile of sardonic relish.

EXT. MAIN ENTRANCE TO ROSEMONDE'S CHATEAU. DAY

A large and elegant carriage draws up outside the château. The head footman, a silver-haired veteran, passes down the steps through the ranks of servants, who wait at attention, opens the carriage door, lowers the steps and remains bowed in anticipation.

Presently the Marquise de Merteuil emerges from the carriage. Volanges hurries down the steps between the ranks of servants and mutters urgently to Merteuil as they embrace.

VOLANGES There's something going on, Cécile won't tell me, you must speak to her at once.

INT. DRAWING ROOM IN THE CHATEAU. DAY

Cécile kneels at Merteuil's feet.

MERTEUIL Tell me: you resisted him, did you?

CÉCILE Of course I did, as much as I could.

MERTEUIL But he forced you?

CÉCILE No: not exactly, but I found it almost impossible to defend myself.

MERTEUIL Why was that? Did he tie you up?

CÉCILE No. No, but he has a way of putting things. You just can't think of an answer.

MERTEUIL Not even 'no'?

CÉCILE I kept saying 'no' all the time; but somehow that wasn't what I was doing.

She looks up at Merteuil.

I'm so ashamed.

MERTEUIL You'll find the shame is like the pain.

She's on her feet now, crossing to the mirror, in front of which she removes her hat; and adds with a sudden melancholy.

You only feel it once.

She sits down again, turning back to Cécile.

You really want my advice?

Cécile gets up and goes over to sit next to her on the sofa.

Allow Monsieur de Valmont to continue your instruction. Convince your mother you have forgotten Danceny. And raise no objection to the marriage.

Cécile gapes at her, bewildered.

CÉCILE With Monsieur de Bastide?

MERTEUIL When it comes to marriage one man is as good as the next; and even the least accommodating is less trouble than a mother.

CÉCILE Are you saying I'm going to have to do that with three different men?

MERTEUIL I'm saying, you stupid little girl, that provided you take a few elementary precautions, you can do it, or not, with as many men as you like, as often as you like, in as many different ways as you like. Our sex has few enough advantages, you may as well make the most of those you have.

Cécile is fascinated: she looks at Merteuil with a kind of wild surmise.

And now here comes your mama, so remember what I've said and, above all, no snivelling.

Volanges arrives from the next room, anxiously looking at Cécile.

VOLANGES How are you feeling now, my dear?

CÉCILE Oh, much better, thank you, Maman.

VOLANGES You look so tired. I think you should go to bed.

CÉCILE No, really, I . . .

MERTEUIL I think you should do as your mother suggests. We can arrange for something to be brought to your room. I'm sure it would do you good.

CÉCILE Well. Perhaps you're right, madame.

And she leaves the room, turning back once to exchange a mischievous glance with Merteuil. Volanges doesn't see this, having turned gratefully back to Merteuil.

VOLANGES You have such a very good influence on her.

INT. GRAND SALON. EVENING

Rosemonde is entertaining members of the local nobility and everyone has made an effort to do justice to the occasion.

Valmont and Merteuil move through the crowd, resplendent, conversing in an undertone, as they acknowledge the greetings of their acquaintances. Valmont makes a particularly deep reverence to Volanges and Cécile, at which the former smiles in queasy response. Valmont kisses Cécile's hand before she moves off with her mother.

MERTEUIL I don't think I've congratulated you on your revenge.

VALMONT So you know.

MERTEUIL Oh yes. And I believe from now on you'll find her door unbolted.

Valmont is not best pleased by this. Merteuil has moved away and he sets off after her.

Where is she?

VALMONT Can't see her at the moment. Surely I've explained to you before how much I enjoy watching the battle between love and virtue.

MERTEUIL What concerns me is that you appear to enjoy watching it more than you used to enjoy winning it.

VALMONT All in good time.

MERTEUIL The century is drawing to its close.

Their travels have brought them back close to Volanges and Cécile, whom Valmont surreptitiously indicates.

VALMONT Isn't it a pity that our agreement does not relate to the task you set me rather than the task I set myself?

MERTEUIL I am grateful, of course: but that would have been almost insultingly simple. One does not applaud the tenor for clearing his throat.

As Valmont smiles at this sally, there begins the orchestral introduction to the aria 'Ombra mai fù' from Handel's Xerxes.

INT. GRAND SALON. NIGHT

As the music continues, Tourvel makes her way into the grand salon, where she arrives as the aria begins. The aria is sung in a pure and unearthly soprano by a man of melancholy aspect: a castrato. He stands on a dais in front of a small baroque orchestra, singing exquisitely, the veins standing out on his temples.

Tourvel pauses in the doorway. Among the audience are Valmont and Merteuil, Cécile, Rosemonde and Volanges, the latter somewhat bemused by the castrato.

As he continues, Tourvel, looking frail and exhausted, pauses again behind Merteuil and Valmont. Valmont watches her make her way along the row to an empty seat. Merteuil notices his preoccupation and follows his eyeline. Then she looks away.

Tourvel reaches her seat and sits. Along the row, Valmont is watching her, transfixed.

Merteuil turns back and becomes aware that Valmont is in another world. She frowns, disturbed.

Tourvel turns to look at Valmont.

At the other end of the row, Valmont continues to stare gravely at Tourvel; while Merteuil quickly looks away.

Tourvel smiles shyly at Valmont.

Valmont turns away sheepishly and kisses Merteuil's hand.

Tourvel can't resist looking at Valmont again.

And Valmont returns her gaze uneasily, as the aria comes to a close.

INT. UPSTAIRS CORRIDOR. NIGHT

Valmont, carrying a candlestick, leads Cécile along the corridor. They're both in dressing gowns. Below, a servant ascends the stairs. Valmont and Cécile hurry away.

INT. VALMONT'S BEDROOM. NIGHT

Valmont stands at the foot of the bed, taking off his slippers, as Cécile tugs at his shirt.

VALMONT As with every other science, the first thing you must learn is to call everything by its proper name.

CÉCILE I don't see why you have to talk at all.

VALMONT Without the correct polite vocabulary, how can you indicate what you would like me to do or make me an offer of something I might find agreeable?

CÉCILE Surely you just . . .?

Impulsively, Cécile is pulling off her nightdress; Valmont leans over to help her.

VALMONT You see, if I do my work adequately, I would like to think you'll be able to surprise Monsieur de Bastide on his wedding night.

CÉCILE Would he be pleased?

His task completed, Valmont lowers himself on to the bed with her.

VALMONT Of course, he'll merely assume your mama has done her duty and fully briefed you.

CÉCILE Maman couldn't possibly talk about anything of the sort.

VALMONT I can't think why. She was, after all, at one time, one of the most notorious young women in Paris.

CÉCILE Maman?

VALMONT Certainly. More noted for her enthusiasm than her ability, if I remember rightly. There was a famous occasion, oh, before you were born, this would have been, when she went to stay with the Comtesse de Beaulieu, who tactfully gave her a room between your father's and that of a Monsieur de Vressac, who was her acknowledged lover at the time. Yet in spite of these careful arrangements, she contrived to spend the night with a third party.

CÉCILE I can't believe that.

VALMONT No, no, I assure you, it's true.

CÉCILE How do you know?

Valmont looks down at her, a slow smile spreading.

VALMONT The third party was myself.

Cécile's jaw drops. For a moment she stares at Valmont, appalled. Then she bursts out laughing, her laughter abandoned. He lets her finish, then closes her mouth with a kiss.

You asked me if Monsieur de Bastide would be pleased with your abilities; and the answer is: education is never a waste.

He caresses her thoughtfully, and begins kissing her, his head travelling down her body. He plants a kiss on her stomach and looks up at her.

Now, I think we might begin with one or two Latin terms.

INT. PRIVATE CHAPEL. DAY

The Curé is intoning the mass, when Valmont arrives, late. He genuflects, pleased to notice that the seat next to Tourvel is empty, possibly even reserved for him by her. He sits, yawning and winking at Cécile. Tourvel looks up at him, welcoming.

EXT. GROUNDS OF THE CHATEAU. DAY

Valmont and Tourvel stroll through parklands, the château silhouetted on a ridge behind them, deep in conversation.

VALMONT (*voice over*) 'We go for a walk together almost every day: a little further every time down the path that has no turning.'

INT. DRESSING ROOM IN MERTEUIL'S HOUSE. DAY

Merteuil sits, in her négligé, reading a letter.

VALMONT (*voice over*) 'She's accepted my love; I've accepted her friendship.'

EXT. GROUNDS OF THE CHATEAU. DAY

Valmont and Tourvel continue to approach.

VALMONT (*voice over*) 'We're both aware how little there is to choose between them.'

They arrive within earshot.

I wish you knew me well enough to recognise how much you've changed me. My friends in Paris remarked on it at once. I've become the soul of consideration, charitable, conscientious, more celibate than a monk . . .

TOURVEL More celibate?

VALMONT Well, you know the stories one hears in Paris.

Tourvel can't suppress a smile. Long shot: the two of them moving through the autumn landscape.

(*voice over*) 'I feel sure that she is inches from surrender.'

INT. MERTEUIL'S DRESSING ROOM. DAY

Merteuil continues to read.

VALMONT (*voice over*) 'Her eyes are closing.'

She looks up, thoughtful.

INT. VALMONT'S BEDROOM. NIGHT

Valmont stands, still fully dressed, in his candlelit bedroom, his door slightly ajar, his eye to the crack in the door. A peal of thunder in the distance.

INT. CORRIDOR. NIGHT

Valmont's point of view, through the crack in the door: Tourvel, alone, arrives at the top of the stairs.

INT. VALMONT'S BEDROOM. NIGHT

Valmont straightens up and saunters out of his room.

INT. CORRIDOR. NIGHT

Valmont stops, as if surprised, and bows to Tourvel.

VALMONT Madame.

TOURVEL Where are you going, monsieur?

VALMONT To the salon.

TOURVEL There's no one there. The others have all decided on an early night.

He's following her along the corridor now, on the way to her room.

VALMONT I very much missed our walk today.

TOURVEL Yes.

VALMONT I fear with the weather as it is, we can look forward to very few more of them.

TOURVEL This heavy rain is surely exceptional.

VALMONT Oh, yes.

By this time, they've arrived at the door to her bedroom, which she's opened. She hesitates in the doorway and Valmont decides to take a chance.

May I?

TOURVEL Of course.

Trying to conceal his astonishment, he follows her into the room.

INT. TOURVEL'S BEDROOM. NIGHT

Valmont speaks, to cover his entrance into the room, which is similarly appointed to his own, though somehow far more sober in feeling.

VALMONT But, you see, within a week I shall have concluded my business.

Tourvel stops in her tracks, clearly affected by this news.

TOURVEL I see.

VALMONT Even so, I'm not sure I'll be able to bring myself to leave.

TOURVEL Oh, please. You must!

It's an involuntary exclamation; Valmont knows exactly how to capitalise on it.

VALMONT Are you still so anxious to be rid of me?

TOURVEL You know the answer to that. I rely on your integrity and generosity. I want to be able to be grateful to you.

VALMONT Forgive me if I say I don't want your gratitude. What I want from you is something altogether deeper.

She turns and begins to move away from him.

TOURVEL I know God is punishing me for my pride. I was so certain nothing like this could ever happen.

VALMONT Nothing like what?

TOURVEL I can't . . .

VALMONT Do you mean love? Is love what you mean?

He's pursued her and now they begin to circle one another as she tries to escape and the words come tumbling out.

TOURVEL You promised not to speak of it.

VALMONT Yes, of course, I understand, but I must know, I must know if . . .

TOURVEL I can't . . . don't you understand . . . it's impossible . . .

VALMONT . . . if you love me, you don't have to speak, you don't have to speak, just look at me.

Long silence. Finally, slowly, Tourvel raises her eyes to him.

TOURVEL Yes.

They're motionless for a moment. Then Valmont releases her hand and puts his arms around her. As he does so, her eyes suddenly go dead and she collapses sideways, obliging him to catch her. She sways in his arms for a moment, then comes to and jerks violently away from him, running halfway across the room. Then she bursts into tears. She stands for a moment, sobbing wildly, then rushes at Valmont, falls to her knees and throws her arms round his legs.

For God's sake, you must leave me, if you don't want to kill me. You must help!

Valmont, somewhat taken aback at first by her intensity, collects himself and lifts her to her feet. For a moment, they sway together in an ungainly embrace; then Tourvel's sobs cease abruptly and give way to chattering teeth and almost epileptic convulsions. Startled, Valmont gathers her up in his arms, carries her over and deposits her gently on the bed. The convulsions continue, her teeth are clenched, the blood drained from her face. He leans forward and loosens her bodice as she stares helplessly up at him. Slowly, her features return to normal. He looks down at her, perplexed. Her arms open, she relaxes, her lips part. He starts to lean towards her, then suddenly checks himself and looks away, something almost like shame darkening his expression. Her face begins to collapse. He looks back at her, gnawing at his lip. She begins to go into shock again and he straightens up. Her sobs drive him from the room.

INT. CORRIDOR. NIGHT

As Valmont steps into the corridor, Rosemonde's maid, Adele, comes hurrying up, struggling into her dressing gown.

VALMONT Fetch madame. Madame de Tourvel has been taken ill.

Adele hurries away and Valmont steels himself to step back into the room.

INT. TOURVEL'S BEDROOM. NIGHT

As Valmont appears in the doorway, Tourvel stretches out her hand to him. He crosses and takes it between both of his. He stands, massaging her hand, bemused and thoughtful. He lets go of her hand abruptly as Rosemonde appears, shepherded by Adele.

VALMONT I heard something as I was passing; she seemed to be having difficulty breathing.

ROSEMONDE Oh, my dear, whatever is it?

TOURVEL I'm all right now.

VALMONT I shall leave her in your capable hands, Aunt.

And still looking strangely abashed, he leaves the room.

ROSEMONDE We must send for a doctor, my dear.

Tourvel is roused from her rapt contemplation of Valmont's departure.

TOURVEL No, no, please, I don't need a doctor. I just . . . sit with me for a moment.

INT. CORRIDOR. NIGHT

Volanges hurries down the corridor, on her way to investigate the disturbance. She's blocked by Valmont, who grimaces at her, uttering a bizarre hiss to discourage her from entering Tourvel's room. She hesitates, then turns away, strangely unnerved.

As she recedes, Valmont looks again at Tourvel's door, then moves away and sinks on to a bench in the long corridor, completely mystified.

INT. TOURVEL'S BEDROOM. NIGHT

Adele finishes lighting the candles and leaves the room.

Rosemonde's kindly face looks anxiously down at Tourvel. They're holding hands. Tourvel speaks very quietly, controlling herself with enormous difficulty.

TOURVEL I must leave this house. I'm most desperately in love.

Rosemonde bows her head, unsurprised.

To leave is the last thing in the world I want to do, but I'd rather die than have to live with the guilt.

ROSEMONDE My dear girl. None of this is any surprise to me. The only thing which might surprise one is how little the world changes.

TOURVEL Well, what should I do? What's your advice?

ROSEMONDE If I remember rightly, in such matters all advice is useless.

TOURVEL I've never been so unhappy.

ROSEMONDE I'm sorry to say this: but those who are most worthy of love are never made happy by it.

TOURVEL But why, why should that be?

ROSEMONDE Do you still think men love the way we do? No. Men enjoy the happiness they feel; we can only enjoy the happiness we give. They're not capable of devoting themselves exclusively to one person. So to hope to be made happy by love is a certain cause of grief. I'm devoted to my nephew, but what's true of most men is doubly so of him.

TOURVEL And yet . . . he could have . . . just now. He took pity on me.

ROSEMONDE If he has released you, my dear child, you must go.

Tourvel looks up at her. Tears begin to cascade from the corners of her eyes.

INT. VALMONT'S BEDROOM. NIGHT

Azolan leans over Valmont, shaking him. Valmont comes up from the bottom of a deep sleep and wakes with a start.

AZOLAN Get up, sir, quick.

VALMONT What is it?

Azolan is already over by the window.

AZOLAN Over here.

Valmont, spurred by the urgency of his tone, scrambles out of bed and joins him at the window.

VALMONT What is it?

AZOLAN Madame de Tourvel.

Suddenly, Valmont is wide awake.

VALMONT What?

EXT. MAIN ENTRANCE. NIGHT

Below, a carriage pulls away and speeds down the entrance drive.

INT. VALMONT'S BEDROOM. NIGHT

Valmont issues his orders calmly and decisively.

VALMONT I want you to follow her, right now. Stay close to her. I want to know everything. Who she sees, where she goes, what she eats, if she sleeps. Everything.

He's fetched what looks like a great deal of money out of his desk. He throws it across the room to Azolan.

That's for bribes. Yours will come later.

AZOLAN Yes, sir.

VALMONT Now go. Go!

Azolan hurries out of the room. Valmont looks back towards the window, the shock beginning to show.

INT. TOURVEL'S DRAWING ROOM. DAY

Tourvel sits at her desk, writing a letter.

TOURVEL (*voice over*) 'Dear Father Anselme: try as I may I cannot see the necessity for the interview you suggest. However, since you insist, I propose you bring him to see me on Tuesday the 28th at six o'clock p.m.'

Julie passes by in the background.

INT. DRAWING ROOM IN VALMONT'S HOUSE. DAY

Valmont is reading the letter. Presently, he hands it to Azolan, who is standing nearby with a self-satisfied expression.

VALMONT This is excellent. Make sure Father Anselme receives it. What news?

He settles himself at his desk.

AZOLAN No visitors. There still hasn't been a single visitor since she got back.

INT. DRAWING ROOM IN TOURVEL'S HOUSE. NIGHT

Tourvel sits staring sightlessly into space; beside her, a tray of food, scarcely disturbed. There are dark circles under her eyes.

AZOLAN (*voice over*) Bit of soup last night but didn't touch the pheasant. Afterwards a cup of tea. Nothing else to report. Oh yes, there is. You wanted to know what she was reading.

INT. DRAWING ROOM IN VALMONT'S HOUSE. DAY

Azolan smiles complacently.

AZOLAN The book by her bed is *Christian Thoughts: Volume Two.*

Valmont, pleased, hands Azolan some gold coins.

VALMONT How's Julie?

AZOLAN Seems a bit keener than she was in the country.

VALMONT And yourself?

Azolan sighs, shaking his head gloomily.

AZOLAN Talk about devotion to duty.

Merteuil and Danceny are shown into the room. Valmont dismisses Azolan, speaking out of the side of his mouth.

VALMONT Off you go. Keep it up.

Valmont kisses Merteuil's hand, as Azolan leaves the room.

Madame.

MERTEUIL Vicomte.

She turns, making him aware of Danceny.

VALMONT Well!

He exchanges a pregnant glance with Merteuil, before crossing to Danceny.

What a pleasant surprise!

He embraces him, kissing him on both cheeks.

Danceny!

DANCENY Thank you, monsieur, for everything.

VALMONT I was afraid I'd been a sad disappointment to you.

DANCENY On the contrary, it's you I have to thank for keeping our love alive.

VALMONT Ah, as to love, Cécile thinks of little else. She and her mother are coming back to Paris in two weeks and she's longing to see you.

DANCENY I've had the most wonderful letter from her.

VALMONT Really?

DANCENY Not like any of her other letters. Somehow quite a different tone of voice.

Merteuil, watching in the mirror, has to disguise her laughter with a cough.

CÉCILE (*voice over*) 'My dearest Danceny . . .'

INT. VALMONT'S BEDROOM IN ROSEMONDE'S CHATEAU. NIGHT

Cécile is taking dictation from Valmont, pressing on his bare back.

CÉCILE '. . . I swear to you . . .'

VALMONT '. . . on my chastity, that even if my mother forces me to go through with this marriage, comma, I shall be yours completely. Your friend, the Vicomte de Valmont . . .'

INT. GRAND SALON IN MERTEUIL'S HOUSE. DAY

Merteuil is reading the finished letter.

VALMONT (*voice over*) '. . . has been very active on your behalf. I doubt if you could do more yourself.'

Merteuil smiles, folding up the letter.

INT. DRAWING ROOM IN VALMONT'S HOUSE. DAY

DANCENY I don't know how I can bear to go another two weeks without seeing her.

MERTEUIL We shall have to do our very best to provide some distraction for you. And now, if you'd be so kind as to wait in the carriage, there's a matter I must discuss with the Vicomte in private.

DANCENY Of course.

He bows to Valmont and pumps his hand heartily.

I don't know how I can ever repay you.

VALMONT Don't give it another thought, it's been delightful.

Danceny leaves the room and Valmont and Merteuil look at one another.

Poor boy. He's quite harmless.

MERTEUIL Sometimes, Vicomte, I can't help but adore you.

VALMONT I have a piece of news I hope you might find entertaining: I have reason to believe the next head of the house of Bastide may be a Valmont.

MERTEUIL What can you mean?

VALMONT Cécile is two weeks late.

Merteuil is startled; she frowns, assessing the implications.

Aren't you pleased?

MERTEUIL I'm not sure.

VALMONT Your aim was to revenge yourself on Bastide. I've provided him with a wife trained by me to perform quite naturally services you would hesitate to request from a professional and very likely pregnant as well. What more do you want?

MERTEUIL All right, Vicomte, I agree, you've more than done your duty. Shame you let the other one slip through your fingers.

Valmont's expression darkens.

VALMONT I let her go.

MERTEUIL But why?

VALMONT I was . . . moved.

MERTEUIL Oh, well, then, no wonder you bungled it.

VALMONT I have an appointment to visit her on Thursday. And this time, I shall be merciless.

MERTEUIL I'm pleased to hear it.

VALMONT Why do you suppose we only feel compelled to chase the ones who run away?

MERTEUIL Immaturity?

VALMONT I shan't have a moment's peace until it's over, you know. I love her, I hate her, my life's a misery.

Merteuil, not best pleased by this, pretends to suppress a yawn.

MERTEUIL I think I may have kept our young friend waiting long enough.

VALMONT I shall call on you sometime soon after Thursday.

MERTEUIL Only if you succeed, Vicomte. I'm not sure I could face another catalogue of incompetence.

VALMONT I shall succeed.

MERTEUIL I hope so: once upon a time, you were a man to be reckoned with.

She hurries away, leaving Valmont alone and troubled.

INT. ENTRANCE HALL IN TOURVEL'S HOUSE. EVENING

Tourvel's footman, Georges, and Father Anselme, by appearance an amiably dim-witted Cistercian, beckon Valmont in. Outside the drawing room, Valmont murmurs in Father Anselme's ear and the latter, after a moment's hesitation, sits down in the hall. Valmont drops to one knee, kisses Father Anselme's hand and steps into the room.

INT. DRAWING ROOM IN TOURVEL'S HOUSE. EVENING

Tourvel is sitting with her back to the door. As Valmont follows Georges into the room, she struggles to her feet, visibly trembling, ethereal with exhaustion. Georges is surprised to be dismissed impatiently with a gesture from Tourvel.

VALMONT I understand Father Anselme has explained to you the reasons for my visit.

TOURVEL Yes. He said you wished to be reconciled with me before beginning instruction with him.

VALMONT That's correct.

TOURVEL But I see no need for formal reconciliation, monsieur.

VALMONT No? When I have, as you said, insulted you; and when you have treated me with unqualified contempt.

TOURVEL Contempt?

VALMONT You run away from my aunt's house in the middle of the night; you refuse to answer or even receive my letters: and all this after I have shown a restraint of which I think we are both aware. I would call that, at the very least, contempt.

TOURVEL I'm sure you understand me better than you pretend, monsieur

VALMONT It was me you ran away from, wasn't it?

TOURVEL I had to leave.

VALMONT And do you have to keep away from me?

Tourvel nods miserably. Valmont moves away from her, speaking half to himself, it seems.

I'm as unhappy as you could ever have wanted me to be.

TOURVEL I've only ever wanted your happiness.

VALMONT How can I be happy without you?

He runs across to her, falling to his knees.

I must have you or die.

He buries his face in her lap. Cautiously, as if plunging it in boiling water, Tourvel allows her hand to rest for a few seconds on Valmont's head. Then she scrambles to her feet and retreats across the room. Valmont remains on his knees.

Death it is.

She looks back at him, distraught. He rises to his feet, calmer now.

I'm sorry, madame. All I wanted from this meeting was your forgiveness for the wrongs you think I've done you, so that I may end my days in some peace of mind.

TOURVEL I understood you approved of the choice my duty has compelled me to make.

VALMONT Yes. And your choice has determined mine.

TOURVEL Which is what?

VALMONT The only choice capable of putting an end to my suffering.

Tourvel's eyes are full of fear.

TOURVEL What do you mean?

Valmont puts his hands on her arms and almost shakes her.

VALMONT Listen. I love you. You've no idea how much. Just remember I've made far more difficult sacrifices than the one I'm about to make. Now goodbye.

He pulls away from her, but she clutches at his wrist.

TOURVEL No.

VALMONT Let me go.

TOURVEL You must listen to me!

VALMONT I have to go.

TOURVEL No!

During this exchange they have been struggling, he to free himself, she to hang on to him. Now she collapses into his arms and the struggle resolves into a long kiss. Then he sweeps her up in his arms, carries her across the room and gently sets her down on the ottoman. She bursts into tears and clutches on to him as if she's drowning. Eventually he speaks, his voice unusually tender.

VALMONT Why should you be so upset by the idea of making me happy?

Gradually she stops crying, looking up at him.

TOURVEL Yes. You're right. I can't live either unless I make you happy. So I promise. No more refusals and no more regrets.

He leans in and kisses her gently. Then he looks at her for a second and they begin tearing at one another's clothes, suddenly both equally ravenous.

INT. MAIN STAIRCASE AND LANDING IN MERTEUIL'S HOUSE. DAY

Valmont springs up the staircase, easily outpacing the puffing Majordomo.

VALMONT Success! Success!

INT. GRAND SALON IN MERTEUIL'S HOUSE. DAY

Merteuil is looking up with eager anticipation.

VALMONT I arrived about six.

MERTEUIL Yes, I think you may omit the details of the seduction, they're never very enlivening: just describe the event itself.

VALMONT It was . . . unprecedented.

MERTEUIL Really?

VALMONT It had a kind of charm I don't think I've ever experienced before.

Merteuil's facing away from him now, so he's unable to see – or discern from her voice, which remains icy – that for her, every word is like a dagger.

Once she'd surrendered, she behaved with perfect candour. Total mutual delirium. Which for the first time ever with me outlasted the pleasure itself. She was astonishing. So much so that I ended by falling on my knees and pledging her eternal love.

INT. DRAWING ROOM IN TOURVEL'S HOUSE. EVENING

Valmont and Tourvel, their faces close, their expressions rapturous.

VALMONT (*voice over*) And do you know, at the time . . .

INT. GRAND SALON IN MERTEUIL'S HOUSE. DAY

Close on Valmont, as he realises he's allowed himself, perhaps unwisely, to be carried away.

VALMONT . . . and for several hours afterwards, I actually meant it.

MERTEUIL I see.

VALMONT It's extraordinary, isn't it?

MERTEUIL Is it? It sounds to me perfectly commonplace.

VALMONT No, no, I assure you. But of course the best thing about it is that I am now in a position to be able to claim my reward.

Hooking his foot under her chair, he begins to draw it towards him; but she rises abruptly and moves away across the room, digesting all that's been said, her expression grim.

MERTEUIL You mean to say you persuaded her to write a letter as well, in the course of this awesome encounter?

VALMONT I didn't necessarily think you were going to be a stickler for formalities.

MERTEUIL In any case, I may have to declare our arrangement null and void.

Valmont gets up, puzzled by her sudden vehemence.

VALMONT What do you mean?

MERTEUIL I'm not accustomed to being taken for granted.

VALMONT But there's no question of that. You're misunderstanding me.

MERTEUIL And I've no wish to tear you away from the arms of someone so astonishing.

VALMONT We've always been frank with one another.

MERTEUIL And as a matter of fact, I have also taken a new lover, who, at the moment, is proving more than satisfactory.

VALMONT Oh? And who is that?

MERTEUIL I am not in the mood for confidences. Don't let me keep you.

She turns and moves decisively away from a startled Valmont.

INT. CORRIDOR OF MIRRORS. DAY

Valmont follows Merteuil, as she moves briskly along the corridor.

VALMONT You can't seriously imagine I prefer her to you?

MERTEUIL You may genuinely be unaware of this. But I can see quite plainly that you're in love with this woman.

Valmont stops in his tracks, shocked by the suggestion.

VALMONT No.

Merteuil turns back to him.

Not at all.

MERTEUIL Have you forgotten what it's like to make a woman happy: and to be made happy yourself?

VALMONT I . . . of course not.

MERTEUIL We loved each other once, didn't we? I think it was love. And you made me very happy.

VALMONT And I could again. We just untied the knot, it was never broken.

MERTEUIL Illusions, of course, are by their nature sweet.

VALMONT I have no illusions. I lost them on my travels. Now I want to come home.

He's reached her side now, and leans in to kiss her cheek tenderly. She softens, her eyes closing. Valmont straightens, his habitual expression back in place.

As for this present infatuation, it won't last. But, for the moment, it's beyond my control.

Merteuil's smile vanishes; she moves away from him and he leaves the corridor, shrugging off her obvious displeasure. Merteuil moves slowly along the corridor; then she hesitates and turns back, her preoccupied stance reflected and distorted in the mirrors. Then, purposefully, she opens the secret door.

INT. SPIRAL STAIRCASE. DAY

At the top of the stairs, Merteuil leans her forehead against the wall, collecting herself.

INT. MERTEUIL'S BEDROOM. DAY

Her smile now dazzling, Merteuil steps into the room and hurries over to an unidentified man.

EXT. STREET. EVENING

A large carriage passes, Merteuil's pale face at the window.
There's someone next to her in the shadows, unrecognisable.

MERTEUIL (*voice over*) 'My dear Vicomte: I'm obliged to go away for a couple of weeks, but I'm well aware of our arrangement.'

INT. VALMONT'S BEDROOM. DAY

Valmont lies in bed, re-reading the letter, a half-smile on his face.

MERTEUIL (*voice over*) 'On my return you and I will spend a single night together. We shall enjoy it enough to regret that it's to be our last; but then we shall remember that regret is an essential component of happiness. All this, of course, providing you are able to procure this famous letter.'

INT. VALMONT'S DRAWING ROOM. NIGHT

Valmont sits at his desk, writing.

VALMONT (*voice over*) 'It shall be done . . .'

INT. BEDROOM IN MERTEUIL'S SUBURBAN VILLA. EVENING

Merteuil, in her négligé, sits reading the letter. In the background, face down in the bed, a man stirs in his sleep.

VALMONT (*voice over*) '. . . but Paris is so tedious without you; and I am living like a medieval hermit.'

INT. VALMONT'S DRAWING ROOM. DAY

Valmont is deep in an embrace with Émilie, when Azolan arrives and murmurs in his ear. Whatever he says seems to be an unpleasant surprise to Valmont.

VALMONT All right, give me a moment.

He turns back to Émilie as Azolan leaves, indicating her champagne glass.

Drink up.

ÉMILIE What is it?

VALMONT Someone who may well not appreciate your presence.

ÉMILIE You mean a woman?

VALMONT A lady, we might even say.

ÉMILIE Oh, not the one we wrote that letter to?

VALMONT The very one.

ÉMILIE I enjoyed that.

VALMONT And you proved a most talented desk.

ÉMILIE I'd love to see what she looks like.

VALMONT Well, you can't.

Valmont is having some difficulty disentangling himself from Émilie. Finally he tears himself away and draws her to her feet. Suddenly, there is a strange, reckless excitement in his eyes.

On second thoughts, I don't see why you shouldn't.

INT. ENTRANCE HALL. DAY

Azolan receives Tourvel and sets off, moving very slowly, towards the drawing room.

INT. VALMONT'S DRAWING ROOM. DAY

Valmont still can't tear himself away from Émilie.

VALMONT Tell me: do you have plans for this evening?

ÉMILIE A few friends for dinner.

VALMONT And after dinner?

ÉMILIE Nothing firm.

He moves away at last, heading for his desk.

VALMONT Well . . .

INT. DOWNSTAIRS CORRIDOR. DAY

To Azolan's alarm, Tourvel manages, in her eagerness, to overtake him.

INT. VALMONT'S DRAWING ROOM. DAY

Tourvel hurries into the room and stops in her tracks, startled.

Her point of view: Valmont is handing Émilie some money.

This done, he kisses her on both cheeks. She looks at Tourvel, a sardonic smile on her face. Valmont watches, plainly enjoying himself. Tourvel lowers her eyes, miserably confused.

ÉMILIE I'll be there.

She walks towards Tourvel, staring at her with undisguised fascination. At the last minute, just as she's leaving, Émilie is suddenly convulsed with mirth. She vanishes, shaking with laughter, and Azolan withdraws, closing the double doors behind him.

VALMONT This is an unexpected pleasure.

TOURVEL I know that woman.

VALMONT Are you sure? I'd be surprised.

TOURVEL She's been pointed out to me at the Opéra.

VALMONT Yes, well, she is striking.

TOURVEL She's a courtesan. Isn't she?

VALMONT I suppose, in a manner of speaking . . .

He's moved over to cut off her exit: just in time, for she now makes a decisive effort to leave the room. He takes hold of her shoulders to block her and she struggles with him as her anger rises.

TOURVEL I'm sorry to have disturbed you.

VALMONT Of course you haven't disturbed me, I'm overjoyed to see you.

TOURVEL Please let me go now.

VALMONT No, no, I can't, this is absurd.

TOURVEL And you will never be received at my house again!

VALMONT Let's sit down . . .

TOURVEL I don't want your lies and excuses!

VALMONT Just hear me out, that's all I ask. Then you can judge.

He locks the door behind him and lets the key drop on to the floor. Then he forces her over to a sofa and sits her down. He settles himself on a nearby stool and begins to speak with unruffled calm. She watches him, transfixed.

Unfortunately, I cannot unlive the years I lived before I met you, and during those years I had a wide acquaintance, the majority of whom were no doubt undesirable in one respect or another. Now, it may surprise you to know that Émilie, in common with many others of her profession and character, is kind-hearted enough to take an interest in those less fortunate than herself. She has, in short, the free time and the inclination to do a great deal of charity work: donations to hospitals, soup for the poor, protection for animals, anything which touches her sentimental heart. From time to time, I make small contributions to her purse. That's all.

TOURVEL Is that true?

VALMONT My relations with Émilie have for some years now been quite blameless. She's even done a little secretarial work for me on occasion.

TOURVEL Why did she laugh?

VALMONT I've no idea.

TOURVEL Does she know about me?

VALMONT No doubt she made what, in view of my past, must be regarded as a fair assumption.

Tourvel seems almost convinced.

TOURVEL I want to believe you.

VALMONT I knew you were coming up, you were announced.

She looks at him, her eyes clear and candid.

TOURVEL I'm sorry.

Valmont flinches, a look of real guilt appearing. He takes her in his arms and she buries her face in his chest, weeping softly.

VALMONT No, no, it's I who must apologise. It was most insensitive of me.

INT. VALMONT'S BEDROOM. DAY

Tourvel lies in Valmont's arms. He looks down at her, profoundly contented.

VALMONT I didn't think it was possible for me to love you more, but your jealousy . . .

He breaks off, genuinely moved. Tourvel looks up at him, speaks with the utmost simplicity.

TOURVEL I love you so much.

Valmont draws her up so that she's lying on top of him; and kisses her, his expression uncharacteristically tender.

VALMONT When will you start writing to me again?

EXT. COURTYARD OF VOLANGES'S HOUSE. NIGHT

Valmont, wrapped up against the blustery wind and wintry rain, encounters the concierge in the courtyard. He hands over a sum of money and the concierge admits him by a side door.

MERTEUIL (*voice over*) 'My dear Vicomte: I don't believe this self-denial can be good for you: I hope it doesn't mean you're neglecting your little pupil.'

INT. CÉCILE'S BEDROOM. NIGHT

Valmont lies with Cécile in her large four-poster. They speak in whispers.

CÉCILE But where can Danceny be?

VALMONT I told you, I have all my people out looking: and no trace of him.

The door suddenly bursts open. Cécile suppresses a shriek. Valmont, who is nearer the door, gets up after a few seconds and tiptoes towards the gaping doorway. No one. He closes the door with a sigh of relief and locks it.

Only the wind.

He turns back to discover that Cécile has vanished.

Where are you?

There's a groan from the far side of the bed. Hurrying over, Valmont discovers that Cécile has jammed herself in her panic into the tiny space between the bed and the wall. He helps her up, smiling: but Cécile looks anguished.

Nothing to worry about.

CÉCILE Yes there is. I'm bleeding.

EXT. ENTRANCE AND COURTYARD OF MERTEUIL'S HOUSE. NIGHT

The same windy and rainy night. Merteuil's carriage turns in at the entrance and comes to a stop in the courtyard. The porter emerges from his lodge with a large open umbrella as footmen converge on the carriage.

Lurking in the archway which leads out to the street is Azolan. He moves so as to stay out of sight, peering into the courtyard to try to identify the occupants of the carriage. After a while, he reacts, with an expression of surprise and cynical amusement.

INT. CORRIDOR OF MIRRORS IN MERTEUIL'S HOUSE. NIGHT

The house is deserted. Valmont moves stealthily down the mirrored corridor, surrounded and apparently pursued by his reflections. He stops and hesitates, looking from one mirror to another. Then he remembers and applies pressure to one, opening it to reveal the spiral staircase.

INT. MERTEUIL'S BEDROOM. NIGHT

Valmont flicks back the curtains on Merteuil's four-poster to reveal Merteuil and her new lover lying on the bed. For a while the young man makes no move, hoping perhaps to escape identification: vainly, since he is quite clearly Danceny.

Merteuil has remained perfectly calm.

VALMONT Your porter seems to be under the impression you are still out of town.

MERTEUIL I have in fact only just returned.

VALMONT Without attracting the attention of your porter. I think it may be time to review your domestic arrangements.

MERTEUIL I'm exhausted. Naturally I instructed the porter to inform casual callers that I was out.

Valmont checks a retort and turns instead, smiling, to Danceny.

VALMONT And you here as well, my dear young friend. The porter would seem to be having a somewhat erratic evening.

DANCENY Oh, well, I, erm, yes.

VALMONT As a matter of fact, it's you I'm looking for.

DANCENY Is it?

VALMONT Mademoiselle Cécile returns to Paris after an absence of over two months. What do you suppose is uppermost in her mind? Answer, of course, the longed-for reunion with her beloved Chevalier.

MERTEUIL Vicomte, this is no time to make mischief.

VALMONT Nothing could be further from my mind, madame.

DANCENY Go on.

VALMONT Imagine her distress and alarm when her loved one is nowhere to be found. I've had to do more improvising than an Italian actor.

DANCENY But how is she? Is she all right?

VALMONT Oh, yes. Well, no, to be quite frank. I'm sorry to tell you she's been ill.

Danceny is horrified.

DANCENY Ill!

VALMONT Calm yourself, my friend, the surgeon has declared her well on the road to recovery. But you can well imagine how desperate I've been to find you.

DANCENY Of course, my God, how could I have been away at such a time? How can I ever forgive myself?

His voice trails away, as he becomes aware of Merteuil's withering glance.

VALMONT But, look, all is well now with Cécile, I assure you. And I shan't disturb you further.

He kisses Danceny on both cheeks and then produces a piece of paper from an inside pocket.

It's only that I have something to show the Marquise.

Merteuil looks up sharply: he's succeeded in catching her interest. He shows her the letter. She reaches for it but he pulls it away again. She looks at him for a moment, amused.

MERTEUIL Wait in my dressing room. It's through there.

VALMONT I know where it is.

He straightens up and begins to move away.

INT. MERTEUIL'S DRESSING ROOM. NIGHT

Merteuil finishes reading the letter. Its contents have obviously not pleased her, but she controls herself and looks up, her expression truculent.

MERTEUIL I see she writes as badly as she dresses.

Before Valmont can respond, she changes the subject.

Is it really true the little one has been ill?

VALMONT Not so much an illness, more a refurbishment.

MERTEUIL What do you mean?

VALMONT A miscarriage.

MERTEUIL Oh, Vicomte, I am sorry. Your son and Bastide's heir.

VALMONT Isn't there something else we should be discussing?

MERTEUIL I do hope you're not going to be difficult about Danceny.

VALMONT I know Belleroche was pretty limp, but I think you could have found a livelier replacement than that mawkish schoolboy.

MERTEUIL Mawkish or not, he's completely devoted to me. And, I suspect, better equipped to provide me with happiness and pleasure than you. In your present mood.

VALMONT I see.

He lapses into an injured silence. Then Merteuil smiles coquettishly.

MERTEUIL If I thought you would be your old charming self, I might invite you to visit me one evening next week.

VALMONT Really?

MERTEUIL I still love you, you see, in spite of all your faults and my complaints.

INT. GRAND STAIRCASE. NIGHT

Merteuil leads Valmont, holding his hand. At the top of the grand staircase, he turns to her.

VALMONT Are you sure you're not going to impose some new condition before you agree to honour your obligation?

Pause. Merteuil considers how best to respond. Finally, she sets off down the stairs, speaking with deadly precision and calm.

MERTEUIL I have a friend, who became involved with an entirely unsuitable woman. Whenever any of us pointed this out to him, he invariably made the same feeble reply: 'It's beyond my control,' he would say. He was on the verge of becoming a laughing-stock. At which point, another friend of mine, a woman, decided to speak to him seriously. She explained to him that his name was in danger of being ludicrously associated with this phrase for the rest of his life. So do you know what he did?

VALMONT I feel sure you're about to tell me.

MERTEUIL He went round to see his mistress and bluntly announced he was leaving her. As you might expect, she protested vociferously. But to everything she said, to every objection she made, he simply replied: 'It's beyond my control.' Goodnight.

She turns and leaves him. For a while he doesn't move, but stands deep in thought, his heart heavy.

INT. DRAWING ROOM IN TOURVEL'S HOUSE. DAY

There's a fire burning in the grate. Tourvel paces anxiously up and down. The door opens and Georges shows in Valmont.

She runs across to him, unable to conceal her delight, and buries herself in his arms. He embraces her, his expression strained and weary. He sinks to his knees, still clasping her tightly.

TOURVEL You're only five minutes late, but I get so frightened. I become convinced I'm never going to see you again.

VALMONT My angel.

TOURVEL Is it like that for you?

VALMONT Yes. At this moment, for example, I'm quite convinced I'm never going to see you again.

He's still holding her close and she fails to discern the edge in his voice. She laughs, still unconcerned.

TOURVEL What?

Valmont rises to his feet and breaks away from her. Now, his expression is icy and Tourvel feels an automatic stab of fear.

VALMONT I'm so bored, you see. It's beyond my control.

TOURVEL What do you mean?

VALMONT After all, it's been four months. So, what I say. It's beyond my control.

TOURVEL Do you mean . . . you don't love me any more?

VALMONT My love had great difficulty outlasting your virtue. It's beyond my control.

TOURVEL It's that woman, isn't it?

VALMONT You're quite right, I have been deceiving you with Émilie. Among others. It's beyond my control.

TOURVEL Why are you doing this?

Until this point, every word has been dragged from Valmont. Now, he turns on her to deliver the coup de grâce.

VALMONT There's a woman. Not Émilie, another woman. A woman I adore. And I'm afraid she's insisting I give you up. It's beyond my control.

Suddenly Tourvel rushes at him, fists flailing. They grapple silently and grimly for one moment, before she screams at him.

TOURVEL Liar! Liar!

VALMONT You're right, I am a liar. It's like your fidelity, a fact of life, no more nor less irritating. Certainly, it's beyond my control.

TOURVEL Stop it, don't keep saying that!

He hurls her across the room; she crashes to the floor against the ottoman.

VALMONT Sorry. It's beyond my control.

He closes his eyes and wills himself onwards.

Why don't you take another lover?

She bursts into tears, shaking her head and moaning incoherently.

Whatever you like. It's beyond my control.

TOURVEL Do you want to kill me?

Valmont strides over to her, takes her by the hair and jerks her head up.

VALMONT Listen. Listen to me. You've given me great pleasure. But I simply can't bring myself to regret leaving you. It's the way of the world. Quite beyond my control.

He lets her go and she collapses full-length, moaning and sobbing helplessly. He hurries from the room. She remains where she is, utterly distraught.

INT. ENTRANCE HALL. DAY

Outside the door Valmont has stopped. He can hear the sound of Tourvel's weeping. He closes his eyes and leans his head back against the door for a moment, his expression tormented and queasy. His hand reaches for the doorknob, but he overcomes the temptation and hurries away.

EXT. COURTYARD OF MERTEUIL'S HOUSE. NIGHT

Valmont's carriage clatters into the courtyard through swirling fog. Valmont jumps down from the carriage and calls up to the Coachman.

VALMONT Tomorrow morning, early.

COACHMAN My lord.

He flicks his whip and the carriage moves off. Valmont sets off towards the entrance, a black shape cutting through the fog.

INT. GRAND SALON IN MERTEUIL'S HOUSE. NIGHT

The two fires at either end of the great room reflect in the mirrored doors and sparkling chandeliers. Furniture has been drawn up round the fires, forming two islands of objects, leaving the centre of the room a bare arena. Merteuil, alone in the room, sits at a small escritoire, writing. Valmont, dishevelled, wigless, advances purposefully across the room, throwing his cloak to one side. Merteuil is unpleasantly surprised to see him, but overcomes her alarm.

MERTEUIL This is not your appointed night.

VALMONT That story you told me, how did it end?

MERTEUIL I'm not sure I know what you mean.

VALMONT Well, once this friend of yours had taken the advice of his lady friend, did she take him back?

MERTEUIL Am I to understand . . .?

VALMONT The day after our last meeting, I broke with Madame de Tourvel, on the grounds that it was beyond my control.

A slow smile of great satisfaction spreads across Merteuil's face.

MERTEUIL You didn't!

VALMONT I certainly did.

MERTEUIL But how wonderful of you.

VALMONT You kept telling me my reputation was in danger, but I think this may well turn out to be my most famous exploit, I believe it sets a new standard. Only one thing could possibly bring me greater glory.

MERTEUIL What's that?

VALMONT To win her back.

MERTEUIL You think you could?

VALMONT I don't see why not.

MERTEUIL I'll tell you why not: because when one woman strikes at the heart of another, she seldom misses; and the wound is invariably fatal.

VALMONT Is that so?

MERTEUIL Oh, yes; I'm also inclined to see this as one of my greatest triumphs.

VALMONT There's nothing a woman enjoys as much as a victory over another woman.

MERTEUIL Except, you see, Vicomte, my victory wasn't over her.

VALMONT Of course it was. What do you mean?

MERTEUIL It was over you.

Silence. Valmont's eyes are suddenly full of fear. Merteuil, on the other hand, has never seemed more serene.

You loved that woman, Vicomte. What's more, you still do. Quite desperately. If you hadn't been so ashamed of it, how could you have treated her so viciously? You couldn't bear even the vague possibility of being laughed at. And this has proved something I've always suspected. That vanity and happiness are incompatible.

Valmont is very shaken. He has to make an effort to be able to resume, his voice ragged with strain.

VALMONT Whatever may or may not be the truth of these philosophical speculations, the fact remains it's now your turn to make a sacrifice.

MERTEUIL Is that so?

VALMONT Danceny must go.

MERTEUIL Where?

VALMONT I've been more than patient about this little whim of yours, but enough is enough.

MERTEUIL One of the reasons I never remarried, despite a quite bewildering range of offers, was the determination never again to be ordered around. I must therefore ask you to adopt a less marital tone of voice.

VALMONT She's ill, you know. I've made her ill. For your sake. So the least you can do is get rid of that colourless youth.

He slaps her face with his glove; but she simply looks back at him, brimming with confidence.

MERTEUIL Haven't you had enough of bullying women for the time being?

Valmont's face hardens.

VALMONT I see I shall have to make myself very plain. I have come to spend the night. I shall not take at all kindly to being turned away.

MERTEUIL I am sorry. I've made other arrangements.

A grim satisfaction begins to enliven Valmont's features.

VALMONT Yes. I knew there was something.

Merteuil sits, her expression icy.

MERTEUIL What?

Valmont settles himself opposite her, taking his time.

What?

VALMONT Danceny isn't coming. Not tonight.

MERTEUIL What do you mean? How do you know?

VALMONT I know because I've arranged for him to spend the night with Cécile.

Silence. Valmont smiles.

Come to think of it, he did mention he was expected here. But when I put it to him that he really would have to make a choice, I must say he didn't hesitate. He's coming to see you tomorrow to explain; and to offer you, do I have this right, yes, I think I do, his eternal friendship. As you said, he's completely devoted to you.

Merteuil rises abruptly.

MERTEUIL That's enough, Vicomte.

VALMONT You're absolutely right. (*He gets up, throwing his hat and gloves on to the sofa.*) Shall we go up?

MERTEUIL Shall we what?

Valmont is taking off his coat, dropping it over the back of the sofa.

VALMONT Go up. Unless you prefer this, if memory serves, rather purgatorial sofa.

MERTEUIL I believe it's time you were leaving.

VALMONT No. I don't think so. We made an arrangement. I really don't think I can allow myself to be taken advantage of a moment longer.

MERTEUIL Remember I'm better at this than you are.

VALMONT Perhaps. But it's always the best swimmers who drown. Now. Yes or no? Up to you, of course. I merely confine myself to remarking that a 'no' will be regarded as a declaration of war. A single word is all that is required.

MERTEUIL All right.

She looks at him evenly for a moment, until he concludes that she has made her answer and stretches out his hand to her. But he's wrong. The answer follows now, calm and authoritative.

War.

She leaves the room and Valmont closes his eyes and lowers his head unhappily.

EXT. DRY MOAT. DAWN

There's snow on the ground: and the camera pans down towards the bare patch of earth under a bridge where Valmont and Danceny, épées in hand, circle one another in the grey dawn light. There are men in black on the bridge above; Azolan and the other seconds wait below. Valmont bears down on Danceny.

MERTEUIL (*voice over*) 'My dear Chevalier Danceny: I understand you spent last night with Cécile Volanges. I learnt this from her more regular lover, the Vicomte de Valmont.'

The duel begins, fierce and determined, Valmont's skill against Danceny's aggression. For a while they're evenly matched, with Valmont, clearly a talented swordsman, looking the more dangerous. Very soon, he inflicts a small wound under Danceny's arm. Then he turns away impatiently, throws aside his épée and takes another from the case Azolan holds open. Then he advances menacingly on Danceny, who retreats, until, under the bridge, Valmont fells him and has him at his mercy. However, overcome by a strange paralysis, he looks away.

INT. VALMONT'S BEDROOM. DAY
As before, Valmont draws up Tourvel, so that she's lying on top of him.

EXT. DRY MOAT. DAWN
Valmont moves away, looking surprised at himself: and Danceny scrambles up.

INT. PRIVATE ROOM IN THE CONVENT. DAY
The camera follows Volanges and Cécile as, led by a nun, their footsteps ring out on the stone flags of a high Gothic room. They approach a curtained bed, where Tourvel lies, deathly pale. As they arrive at the bed, Tourvel turns to look at Volanges.
TOURVEL I'm dying because I wouldn't believe you.

EXT. DRY MOAT. DAWN
Valmont returns to the attack: they cut and parry with immense energy. Then Valmont skids in the snow and Danceny, more by luck than good judgement, succeeds in wounding him in whichever is not his sword arm. Danceny immediately withdraws, according to the rules. Valmont looks down at the wisp of blood staining his torn sleeve.

INT. TOURVEL'S ROOM IN THE CONVENT. DAY
Tourvel groans and struggles, held down by nuns, who heat and apply cupping-bowls over the wounds produced in a cross-hatched pattern by the surgeon's scarifier.

EXT. DRY MOAT. DAWN
The duel continues: vicious thrust and parry, until Valmont, to Danceny's surprise, suddenly turns his back on him and moves away.

INT. VALMONT'S BEDROOM. DAY

As before, Tourvel, on top of Valmont, kisses him passionately.

EXT. DRY MOAT. DAY

Valmont turns back to Danceny and the next pass degenerates into a brawl, which ends as Danceny discovers Valmont's blade at his throat. But, once again, Valmont turns his back on Danceny.

INT. TOURVEL'S ROOM IN THE CONVENT. DAY

The surgeon's curved blade cuts at the vein on the inside of Tourvel's elbow and dark blood begins to flow into a small silver bowl.

EXT. DRY MOAT. DAY

Danceny drives Valmont back, but the effort brings him to his knees in the snow. Both are exhausted now and Danceny's shirt is stained and mottled with the blood from numerous flesh wounds. Valmont staggers away and leans against the cool stone wall rearing up from the moat. Danceny remains on his knees, gasping for breath. Close on Valmont: his hand slowly loosens its grip on the hilt of the épée until he's balancing it against the wall on one finger. He glances at Danceny out of the corner of his eye. He lets his sword drop and at the same moment turns quickly away from the wall, running on to Danceny's sword, which buries itself deep in his stomach. There's a moment of mutual shock and then Danceny withdraws his blade. Valmont slides down the wall, his face crashing into the snow.

Danceny shouts to his second.

DANCENY Fetch the surgeon.

VALMONT No, no.

DANCENY Do as I say!

The second hurries away as Azolan drapes Valmont's coat around him. Danceny stands alone, uncertain.

VALMONT A moment of your time.

Danceny reluctantly approaches.

Two things: a word of advice, which of course you may ignore, but it is honestly intended; and a request.

DANCENY Go on.

VALMONT The advice is: be careful of the Marquise de Merteuil.

DANCENY You must permit me to treat with scepticism anything you have to say about her.

VALMONT Nevertheless, I must tell you: in this affair, we are both her creatures.

Painfully, he reaches into his coat pocket and brings out a bundle of letters.

As I believe her letters to me will prove.

He hands Danceny the bloodstained package.

When you've read them, you may decide to circulate them.

DANCENY And the request?

VALMONT I want you somehow . . . somehow to get to see Madame de Tourvel . . .

DANCENY I understand she's very ill.

VALMONT That's why this is most important to me. I want you to tell her I can't explain why I broke with her as I did, but that since then my life has been worth nothing. I pushed the blade in deeper than you just have, my boy, and I need you to help me withdraw it. Tell her it's lucky for her that I've gone and I'm glad not to have to live without her. Tell her her love was the only real happiness I've ever known.

Close on Danceny: tears are rolling down his cheeks.

Will you do that for me?

DANCENY I will.

Danceny raises a hand to brush away his tears. Azolan looks over at him indignantly.

AZOLAN It's all very well feeling sorry now.

VALMONT Let him be. He had good cause. I don't believe that's something anyone has ever been able to say about me.

His head slumps to one side. He's dead. Overhead shot: Azolan and Danceny kneel on either side of Valmont's body. All around, the snow is red with his blood.

EXT. CONVENT. EVENING

Danceny strides through the cloisters.

INT. TOURVEL'S ROOM IN THE CONVENT. EVENING

Danceny leans over Tourvel, talking to her, unheard.

Volanges and Cécile wait in the background.

Tourvel raises a hand and Danceny stops speaking.

TOURVEL Enough.

She looks up at Danceny.

Draw the curtains.

Danceny rises and draws the curtains on her bed. Behind the curtains, Tourvel turns until her profile is silhouetted through the linen.

INT. TOURVEL'S ROOM IN THE CONVENT. NIGHT

The nuns close Tourvel's eyes.

INT. TOURVEL'S ROOM IN THE CONVENT. NIGHT

Cécile stands by the deathbed as the nuns light the candles at the corners of the bed.

INT. MERTEUIL'S DRESSING ROOM. DAY

A great cry of anger and frustration; and then Merteuil bursts into the room. She sweeps all her perfume boxes off the dressing table. Then she smashes everything in the room she can possibly break, ornaments, mirrors, glass jars. Finally, she crashes to her knees, tearing at her clothes. A number of maids have arrived: they hover in the doorway appalled and she looks up at them, furious.

MERTEUIL Get out. Get out, all of you.

They hurry away in something of a stampede. Merteuil kneels, desolate, in a field of glittering debris. Her head comes down again, contorted with misery and rage.

INT. MERTEUIL'S BOX AT THE OPERA. EVENING

It's before curtain-up and Merteuil moves to the front of the box to contemplate the house. Three boxes away a distinguished-looking middle-aged couple are doing the same thing. Merteuil bows to them. To her surprise, they turn away from her, ignoring her ostentatiously. She turns to look down at the orchestra, frowning; and becomes aware that the crowd below are murmuring to one another and pointing up at her. Gradually, the hum dies and there's silence in the theatre. Everyone in the stalls is looking up at her. Suddenly, there's a hiss and then, growing quickly in volume and intensity, a torrent of hissing and booing. Merteuil absorbs it for a moment, then turns on her heel, her face an impenetrable mask. She stumbles as she leaves the box.

INT. MERTEUIL'S DRESSING ROOM. NIGHT

Everything is back exactly as it was, leaving no trace of Merteuil's rampage. She sits at her dressing table, alone, removing her make-up. As it comes off, a new Merteuil seems for the first time to be revealed, weary, fragile, vulnerable almost. She looks at her reflection with the anxiety someone feels in the presence of their only friend: and the image slowly fades to black.

Carrington

For Laura

CAST AND CREDITS

Carrington was first shown at the 1995 Cannes Film Festival. The cast and crew included:

CARRINGTON	Emma Thompson
LYTTON STRACHEY	Jonathan Pryce
RALPH PARTRIDGE	Steven Waddington
GERALD BRENAN	Samuel West
MARK GERTLER	Rufus Sewell
LADY OTTOLINE MORRELL	Penelope Wilton
VANESSA BELL	Janet McTeer
PHILIP MORRELL	Peter Blythe
BEACUS PENROSE	Jeremy Northam
FRANCES PARTRIDGE	Alex Kingston
ROGER SENHOUSE	Sebastian Harcombe
CLIVE BELL	Richard Clifford
MAYOR	David Ryall
MILITARY REPRESENTATIVE	Stephen Boxer
MARY HUTCHINSON	Annabel Mullion
DUNCAN GRANT	Gary Turner
MARJORIE GERTLER	Georgiana Dacombe
NURSE	Helen Blatch
COURT USHER	Neville Phillips
DR STARKEY SMITH	Christopher Birch
PORTER	Daniel Betts
FLY DRIVER	Simon Bye
GONDOLIER	Marzio Idoni

Written and directed by	Christopher Hampton
Producers	Ronald Shedlo and John McGrath
Co-producer	Chris Thompson
Editor	George Akers
Director of Photography	Denis Lenoir

Executive Producers	Francis Boespflug
	Phillipe Carcassonne
	Fabienne Vonier
Production Designer	Caroline Amies
Casting by	Fothergill and Lunn Casting
Music by	Michael Nyman
Costumer Designer	Penny Rose

Caption on black screen:

ONE
LYTTON AND CARRINGTON 1915

EXT. LEWES STATION. DAY

The hiss and clatter of a steam train.

A small, dirty engine pulls its train into the deserted station, shabby from wartime neglect. One door opens and a man steps down on to the platform and deposits his luggage. The steam clears to reveal a bizarre and astonishing figure: Lytton Strachey. He's immensely tall and thin, his limbs unnaturally elongated and his face concealed behind a luxuriant reddish beard and steel-rimmed spectacles. He is wearing an elderly, shapeless tweed suit under a cloak, a Homburg hat and a very long tartan scarf, wound several times around his neck, the ends reaching his knees. It's 1915 and he is thirty-five.

He leaves the train door open and makes no attempt to advance down the platform: simply waiting by his suitcase until a very young porter appears through the steam. Lytton brightens perceptibly.

The porter rushes towards Lytton and picks up his case.

LYTTON Hello . . .

PORTER Sir . . .

The porter leads Lytton towards the taxi rank.

Taxi or a fly, sir?

LYTTON Well, I don't think we ought to make too hasty a decision, do you?

In the station forecourt are a couple of taxis and a row of small one-horse carriages. The porter stands, waiting for Lytton to make up his mind. The various drivers are milling around. Lytton scans them hastily and expertly, until his eye falls on one very handsome young man, who is standing alongside his fly.

I believe I'll take that one.

EXT. COUNTRY TRACK. DAY

The fly bounces along a narrow country track; as it approaches, it becomes clear that Lytton is flirting with the driver.

EXT. ASHEHAM HOUSE. DAY

A fine, simple Georgian house, set in a hollow among fields and elms, no other houses in sight. The fly pulls up outside the house. Lytton pays off the driver, tipping him, it would appear from the latter's pleased expression, rather generously.

The front door of the house opens and Vanessa Bell appears in the doorway. She's thirty-six, extremely beautiful, wearing an elegantly simple long dress, which is, however, none too clean.

Lytton approaches her, drops his suitcase and kisses her.

LYTTON Nessa, I'm dropping.

VANESSA The kettle's on.

Lytton walks straight past Vanessa, leaving her to pick up his heavy suitcase and umbrella.

INT. ASHEHAM HOUSE. DRAWING ROOM. DAY

Lytton sweeps into the house. He drops his hat and briefcase on to the floor, and shakes hands with Clive Bell.

CLIVE Ah . . .

LYTTON Clive.

CLIVE I'm afraid we're fending for ourselves this weekend. The servants are off till Monday.

LYTTON Oh, dear.

CLIVE We've put you in the front bedroom.

VANESSA There's a fire in the sitting room.

LYTTON Jolly good.

INT./EXT. SITTING ROOM. DAY

Lytton heads on into the sitting room, crossing directly to sit on a chair by the French windows; Vanessa follows him into the room.

VANESSA I'll get you a cup of tea.

LYTTON Oh, please. Oh . . .!

He fumbles in his breast pocket and produces a battered booklet.

I brought you my ration cards.

VANESSA Thanks.

Lytton's point of view: out on the lawn, Vanessa's children, Julian and Quentin, are playing football with a youthful, androgynous figure, who's running with the ball in the dying light, cheeks red, blonde hair flying.

LYTTON Vanessa?

VANESSA Yes.

LYTTON Who on earth is that ravishing boy?

Vanessa joins him at the window, looks out at the garden, momentarily puzzled, then smiles sardonically.

VANESSA I take it you're not referring to either of my sons.

LYTTON No. (*He gets up and points.*) Him.

Their point of view: the person he's watching kicks the ball and comes to a standstill. It's Dora Carrington: she's twenty-two, childlike, not beautiful but striking, large, melancholy eyes, round cheeks, pale skin, shoulder-length hair cut like a Florentine pageboy and an indefinable aura of fragility. Vanessa smiles, opens the window and calls out.

VANESSA Carrington!

A sharp intake of breath from Lytton.

LYTTON Good God.

VANESSA Someone I want you to meet!

EXT. GARDEN. DAY

Carrington's point of view: Vanessa at the window.

CARRINGTON Coming!

She runs over to let herself into the house.

INT. SITTING ROOM. DAY

Carrington steps through the French windows and hesitates, momentarily intimidated by Lytton's strange appearance.

VANESSA This is Lytton Strachey.

Carrington advances, her hand outstretched.

CARRINGTON Hello.

Lytton, still grappling with his confusion and disappointment, reluctantly accepts her hand in a limp handshake. Vanessa smiles, with a trace of malice, and slips out of the room.

VANESSA I'll fetch some tea.

LYTTON So. You're Carrington.

CARRINGTON Yes.

She's watching him coolly, a shade defiantly.

LYTTON Mark Gertler's friend.

CARRINGTON Well, I know him.

LYTTON Ah.

He can't think of anything further to say. He moves over to the well-stocked bookshelves and begins intently studying their contents. She moves over to the window.

The two of them. It's a sparsely furnished room, elegantly decorated and with a number of paintings by Vanessa and Duncan Grant. The log fire blazes. Carrington stares out into the garden. Lytton selects a book. Silence. Carrington gives it a moment longer and then returns to the garden.

INT. DRAWING ROOM OF ASHEHAM HOUSE. NIGHT

Lytton is sitting in the only comfortable armchair, next to the fire, a rug spread over his knees. He is knitting a scarf. Carrington sits in the window seat. Vanessa sits on a small sofa embracing her lover, Duncan Grant, thirty, an extremely handsome and dishevelled young man. Her husband Clive Bell, thirty-four, moves around the room, puffing at a cheroot, occasionally stopping to ruffle the hair of a young blonde woman, Mary Hutchinson, twenty-six, his mistress.

LYTTON They'll be bringing in conscription in a matter of weeks. We shall all be dragged in front of some appalling tribunal.

MARY You'll have to be conscientious objectors.

LYTTON I'd rather go to prison or down the mines. It'd be warmer and I'm sure you'd meet a much nicer class of person.

BELL Ottoline says she'll be able to help.

LYTTON Well, there must be some compensation for having friends in high places.

Carrington has been watching him. Now she speaks with scarcely disguised hostility.

CARRINGTON Don't you like Ottoline?

LYTTON I'm devoted to Ottoline. She's like the Eiffel Tower. She's very silly but she affords excellent views.

Carrington looks annoyed.

Do you think knitting scarves for the troops would be classified as essential war work?

Carrington seems about to say something, but checks herself.

One's so busy nowadays. I've been learning German as well. I must say, it's a most disagreeable language.

CARRINGTON Then why learn it?

LYTTON Well, my dear, I mean, suppose they win?

Bell is now behind Lytton, at the sideboard, where he opens a bottle of champagne. Lytton, startled by the pop, lets out a high-pitched shriek.

Ye gods: can you imagine what the war must be like?

Carrington's cheeks are red with indignation.

EXT. SUSSEX DOWNS. DAY

Clear, windy day. Clive Bell and Mary Hutchinson pass, arm-in-arm. Then, a few yards behind, Duncan Grant and Vanessa. Finally, some yards behind them, somewhat stiffly bringing up the rear, Lytton and Carrington. Lytton gestures towards the two couples ahead.

LYTTON I must say, as Nessa and Clive are both having affairs with cousins of mine, I can't help thinking theirs is a peculiarly civilised marriage.

Carrington glances at him, somewhat disapprovingly, and doesn't answer. He decides to try a different tack.

Do you really like to be called Carrington?

CARRINGTON Yes.

LYTTON Why?

CARRINGTON My first name is Dora.

LYTTON Ah, I see.

They stop for a moment to contemplate the view. Below them, deserted fields roll away to the coast. In the distance, the dull gleam of the Channel, iron-grey and flat. There's a strange sound in the air, a barely audible rumble, as of some remote thunderstorm.

CARRINGTON Can you hear them?

LYTTON What?

CARRINGTON The guns.

LYTTON Oh, yes.

They stand a moment, listening.

CARRINGTON I have three brothers over there.

LYTTON I can't tell you how angry it makes me feel.

CARRINGTON I'd have joined up, if I'd been a man.

LYTTON But surely you don't believe . . .

CARRINGTON Of course not, of course I don't believe in it. But I'd still have joined up.

The others have disappeared on ahead. Silence, except for the guns.

I wish I'd been born a boy.

Lytton is momentarily disconcerted by her intensity. Then, he smiles.

LYTTON You have such lovely ears.

Suddenly, Lytton puts his gloved hands round the back of Carrington's head, stoops and kisses her on the lips. She resists, violently struggling.

CARRINGTON Don't. Stop it!

Lytton releases her.

Would you mind not!

LYTTON Sorry.

They stand a moment longer, Lytton sheepish, Carrington furious. Then they turn more or less simultaneously and set off up the hill without a word.

INT. LANDING IN ASHEHAM HOUSE. DAWN

Carrington tiptoes along the landing. She carries a large pair of kitchen scissors.

She stops outside a door, hesitates, then opens the door with extreme care and lets herself into Lytton's bedroom.

INT. BEDROOM IN ASHEHAM HOUSE. DAWN

Lytton is in bed, asleep. He's lying on his back, his beard outside the covers.

Carrington tiptoes over to him. She leans over him, gently lifts his beard and tucks it in between the blades of the scissors; then, suddenly struck by something about him, she freezes in the very act of operating the scissors.

Lytton opens his eyes and smiles at her.

LYTTON Have you brought my breakfast?

CARRINGTON No, I haven't.

Lytton suddenly becomes aware of the scissors, exhibits a trace of alarm.

I was going to cut your beard off.

Lytton stares at her, perplexed, as she carefully withdraws the scissors.

LYTTON Why?

CARRINGTON To punish you.

LYTTON Oh, I see.

CARRINGTON Yes.

Lytton smiles. He seems to find the whole situation exhilarating. He plucks briefly at his beard. Carrington is still staring at him like a frightened rabbit.

LYTTON And do you still want to punish me?

CARRINGTON No. No, I don't.

Fade.

Caption on black screen:

TWO
GERTLER 1916–1918

EXT./INT. GERTLER'S STUDIO. NIGHT

Sounds of struggle. The studio consists of a strange passage-like glass structure erected against a wall and leading into a kind of garden shed which serves as Gertler's bedroom. Carrington and Gertler, apparently engaged in a kind of amorous dance, grapple the length of the studio.

INT. GERTLER'S BEDROOM. NIGHT

Gertler manhandles the struggling Carrington through the door and over to the bed, on to which they collapse and flounder around for a time. Gertler is an intense, slight, dark man of twenty-four, whose excessive energy gives off a strong whiff of banked-down violence.

CARRINGTON Enough. That's enough!

She smacks at his hand and sits up, straightening her dress. Gertler sighs impatiently.

GERTLER Why?

CARRINGTON I'll have to go soon, anyway.

GERTLER Why don't you stay the night?

CARRINGTON Look, let's not go through all this again.

GERTLER I'm only asking.

CARRINGTON It makes me think you're only interested in me sexually.

Gertler springs to his feet, enraged.

GERTLER You make me so angry. Of course I'm interested in you sexually. But I'm not *only* interested in you sexually. I can get that anywhere. I'm interested in you, your opinions, your work, what you think of me, so naturally I'm interested in you sexually as well. What do you expect? I did ask you to marry me, for God's sake.

CARRINGTON I know, Mark, but . . .

GERTLER I'd understand if you thought I was ugly. If you thought I was ugly, you wouldn't like me at all and you say you do.

CARRINGTON Of course I do.

GERTLER Well, then . . .

CARRINGTON It's you I like, not your body.

GERTLER I am my body.

CARRINGTON Goodnight.

Carrington picks up her coat, turns and opens the studio door, and hurries out into the night. Gertler calls after her.

GERTLER You can't expect to stay a virgin all your life.

INT. GERTLER'S STUDIO. DAY

Carrington sits, modelling for Gertler in a plain blue dress. Gertler applies the paint to his canvas with a delicate brush and a series of precise, almost finicky strokes. He looks up and frowns.

GERTLER What's the matter?

CARRINGTON I was just thinking about that disgusting old man with a beard.

GERTLER I really shouldn't brood about it if I were you. After all, he's a bugger.

CARRINGTON What?

GERTLER Lytton. He's a bugger.

CARRINGTON I never know what that means.

Gertler sighs, exasperated.

GERTLER He's a homosexual.

Carrington nods sagely; but she's evidently none the wiser.

INT. ANTE-ROOM IN HAMPSTEAD TOWN HALL

Lytton sits on a bench, isolated, his rug around his knees, waiting, lit from above through a municipal stained-glass window, reading a stout volume.

INT. COURTROOM IN HAMPSTEAD TOWN HALL. DAY

Carrington slips unobtrusively into the chamber in which the Hampstead Conscription Tribunal is in session. She sits on her own at the back of the gloomy room unnoticed by Gertler who sits at the front with Clive and Vanessa Bell, Duncan Grant and Mary Hutchinson, whose comparative youth and unconventional appearance seem at odds with the general atmosphere. The tribunal itself, its eight members seated behind a long table, includes the Mayor (in full regalia) and the uniformed Military Representative. In the main body of the room, a few elderly members of the general public. The usher is crossing to open the doors to the courtroom.

MAYOR (*voice over*) Call Mr Strachey!

USHER Giles Lytton Strachey!

It is not Lytton, however, who enters, but a dignified and impressive figure, formally dressed, carrying an uninflated light-brown air cushion. This is Philip Morrell, forty-six. The Mayor looks up at Morrell, shadow of a frown.

MAYOR Mr Strachey?

MORRELL No. Philip Morrell.

Impressive pause.

M.P. for Burnley.

He carefully sets down the air cushion on the empty chair in the centre of the room.

MAYOR Erm . . .

MORRELL I believe Mr Strachey is marshalling his documents.

At this moment Lytton blunders into the room, wearing his overcoat and carrying a tartan rug, a Homburg, an ancient briefcase, a volume of Gibbon and an umbrella. He walks through the court towards the empty chair. He hooks his umbrella on the back of the chair, drops his briefcase on the floor and folds the rug over the arm of the chair. He then takes off his hat, scarf and coat and lets them fall either side of the chair. Carrington is watching intently from the back of the room.

MAYOR Mr Strachey.

Lytton raises an enormously long finger.

LYTTON One moment.

He takes the air cushion from the chair, unscrews its stopper and proceeds, with some effort and far from silently, to inflate it. The Mayor and Members of the Tribunal watch him, transfixed. Lytton finishes inflating the cushion, puts it down on the chair and lowers himself cautiously on to it. Then he looks up.

I'm a martyr to the piles.

The Mayor's face is swept by contradictory emotions. He swallows, clears his throat, consults his papers.

MAYOR You are a . . . writer by profession, is that correct?

LYTTON It is. I am.

MAYOR Now, according to this report from the Advisory Committee, you've made a statement to the effect that you have a conscientious objection to taking part in the war.

He pauses. Lytton, however, doesn't answer.

Did you make such a statement?

LYTTON Yes.

The Military Representative, who has had difficulty in controlling his impatience, now intervenes.

MILITARY REPRESENTATIVE Mr Strachey.

LYTTON Yes.

MILITARY REPRESENTATIVE Are we to understand that you have a conscientious objection to all wars?

LYTTON Oh, no. Not at all. Only this one.

Silence. Then the Military Representative unleashes his prize question.

MILITARY REPRESENTATIVE Then, would you care to tell us what you would do if you saw a German soldier raping your sister?

Lytton considers a moment, then speaks with the utmost deadpan seriousness.

LYTTON I believe I should attempt to come between them.

Laughter in the court. The Mayor passes a hand in front of his eyes. He's caught by surprise as Lytton leans forward and speaks with a quiet intensity.

I will not assist, by any deliberate action of mine, in carrying on this war. My objection is based not upon religious belief, but upon moral considerations; and I will not act against these convictions, whatever the consequences may be.

There's a round of applause from his friends; and Carrington, somewhat to her own surprise, finds herself joining in.

EXT. HAMPSTEAD HEATH. DAY

Spring day. Gertler crosses the Heath with Lytton, swathed in coat, scarf, Homburg, gloves and galoshes, drained by the proceedings of the Tribunal.

LYTTON Well, after all that, the prospect of jail seems positively soothing.

GERTLER They'll never send you to jail. Too many of them went to school with you.

LYTTON I only hope you're right.

He darts a shrewd glance at Gertler.

Any luck with the famous Carrington conundrum?

GERTLER It's only ignorance. Fear and ignorance. But it's been going on for four years. I'm at my wits' end.

LYTTON Well, it's no good asking my opinion. I'm afraid when it comes to a creature with a cunt I'm always infinitely *désorienté*.

GERTLER All the same, I've decided, if anyone can help me, you can.

INT. GERTLER'S STUDIO. DAY

Lytton perches uncomfortably on a wooden chair, sipping a mug of tea, huddled up against a paraffin stove, having retained every item of clothing except his hat. Gertler is on his feet. On an easel, as yet unfinished, is Gertler's painting, 'The Merry-Go-Round', subsequently to become his most famous canvas, a harsh, stylised study of men, mostly uniformed, and women, astride wooden horses, frozen in sinister and joyless pleasure.

LYTTON I? How?

GERTLER Well, I don't know exactly. I mean if you just *be* with her a little. A man like you, she has no older friends, you see, she's bound to learn.

LYTTON Keats's letters, of course, are very poignant on the subject of virginity.

GERTLER And my work.

LYTTON What?

Gertler waves an arm at 'The Merry-Go-Round'.

GERTLER Take this, for example. This is a radical painting. This is my statement about the soulless mechanisms of war. She won't understand that. The harmonies, for example, they're like Bach, don't you agree?

Lytton contemplates the painting, alarmed, searching for an appropriate response.

LYTTON But, the critics . . . I mean, surely nowadays the papers are full of nothing but Gertler.

GERTLER That's no good to her. Someone must explain to her, someone she respects, that I'm an important artist.

LYTTON And you think if she realises that, she'll . . .

GERTLER I'm sure of it.

INT. CARRINGTON'S STUDIO AT 2 GOWER STREET. EVENING

Close on Lytton.

LYTTON To begin with, I'm still compelled, at my advanced age, to live in my mother's house, simply because I'm more or less *sans le sou.* You probably think of me as a man of letters, but all I've ever managed to publish is a few reviews and a slim volume of criticism. I can't write half the things I want to write; and if I did, I wouldn't dare publish them, for fear of killing my mother.

During this, the camera has tracked slowly back to reveal that Lytton is lying on a chaise longue, holding a large book. A tartan rug covers him. Carrington is eventually revealed at her easel; she's working on a portrait in oils, concentrating fiercely.

Furthermore, I now find myself, despite my great age and notorious health, being harassed by the government to go off and take part in some entirely ridiculous war they seem quite unable to grasp is resulting in large numbers of people dying. So I'm now reduced to the degrading task of writing pamphlets for the No-Conscription Fellowship which may very possibly land me in prison. In other words, I'm obscure, decrepit, terrified, ill-favoured, penniless and fond of adjectives.

Carrington looks up, smiling.

CARRINGTON Surely it's not that bad.

LYTTON No, no. You're quite right, looked at another way, I'm a perfectly respectable elderly bugger of modest means.

Carrington laughs, pausing in her work. She glances out of the window.

CARRINGTON I suppose you ought to be going soon, before it gets dark.

LYTTON Oh, no, no, no, I adore the blackout, the most thrilling encounters . . . you mustn't deny us our few simple pleasures, dear, after all, we've not much else to look forward to, except old age.

Carrington resumes painting. Silence.

LYTTON Dear God, can you imagine it? The rain, the loneliness, the regret.

CARRINGTON No, I can't imagine it.

LYTTON Well, you just wait till it's staring you in the face.

CARRINGTON How old are you, anyway?

LYTTON I'm thirty-six next birthday.

Carrington smiles, carries on painting.

Ottoline's invited me up to Garsington next weekend.

EXT. GARSINGTON MANOR. DAY

Beautiful spring day. The back of Garsington Manor house, a two-storeyed Jacobean mansion built of Cotswold stone, leading into two hundred acres of the Berkshire downs. The gardens, at present empty, except for two or three elderly gardeners and a sprinkling of guests on the croquet lawn, are spectacularly designed and maintained.

CARRINGTON (*voice over*) Me too.

LYTTON (*voice over*) Oh. I'll go if you go. Last time I was there, everyone was either deaf or French.

INT. LYTTON'S BEDROOM AT GARSINGTON. DAY

Lytton is dressing. He's almost finished putting on his trousers, when an extraordinary figure sweeps into the room without knocking. It is Lady Ottoline Morrell, a woman of strikingly eccentric appearance, swathed in an astonishing, trailing peach silk dress and wearing a preposterous matching hat. She's forty-two and her beaky nose and prognathous jaw give her face an alternately regal and ridiculous expression which is heightened by bizarrely and lavishly applied make-up. Lytton struggles with his fly buttons, exhibiting a faint trace of annoyance.

OTTOLINE Well? How is the campaign proceeding?

Lytton frowns, bemused. Ottoline has produced a humbug from somewhere, which she pops into her mouth and sucks noisily.

LYTTON Campaign?

OTTOLINE The Carrington matter. I take it you're still working on her.

LYTTON Really, Ottoline, must you put things quite so baldly? I prefer to think of myself as an educator rather than a . . .

OTTOLINE A what?

LYTTON A pimp.

OTTOLINE Now, don't be silly, you know as well as I do, it's a sickness with Carrington. A girl of that age, still a virgin, it's absurd.

LYTTON I was still a virgin at that age.

OTTOLINE But that's my whole point, don't you see, so was I. Is there to be no progress?

And with this, she sweeps out of the room.

EXT. FORMAL GARDENS AT GARSINGTON MANOR. DAY

Carrington moves disconsolately through the gardens in Ottoline's wake.

OTTOLINE Now I must have a serious talk to you before Mark arrives.

Despite the heat, Ottoline is entirely wrapped in a heavy black cloak and wears a three-cornered hat, so that she looks like some demented highwayman. She is attended by several snuffling pugs.

I know how difficult it is, my dear, to reconcile puritanism with a love of beauty. It's a consideration that's never far from my thoughts when I'm in Burnley.

Carrington opens her mouth to protest, but Ottoline surges on.

I mean, take this garden, for example. Surely it wouldn't be right to plant nothing but cabbages and cauliflowers? Or do you think it's wanton or wicked of us to love the bastard tulip or the Turk's Head lily?

CARRINGTON Of course not, no.

Ottoline interrupts her with a wagging finger.

OTTOLINE One can't have it all ways. Remember that! And I firmly believe it's high time you took the bull by the horns.

Carrington turns away and hurries along the grass path. Ottoline is unaware that Carrington is no longer following her.

We can't always live under glass like a cucumber. We have to engage with life!

EXT. GARSINGTON MANOR TERRACE. DAY

Carrington runs up the steps towards the terrace where she is unable to avoid being intercepted by Philip Morrell.

MORRELL Ah, there you are, Carrington. I was hoping to find an opportunity to talk to you in private before Mark's arrival.

Morrell takes her by the arm and leads her into the house.

CARRINGTON (*voice over*) And then, would you believe it, Pipsey harangued me for half an hour on the perils of virginity.

EXT. ROOF OF GARSINGTON MANOR. DAY

Lytton listens to Carrington, amused, propped against a gable. Below, oblivious, visitors move through the formal gardens.

CARRINGTON He got more and more breathy and the hairs in his nostrils became horribly agitated. Finally, he told me it was someone like me had driven his brother Hugh to suicide.

LYTTON Ah, semen. What is it about that ridiculous white secretion that pulls down the corners of an Englishman's mouth?

Silence. Carrington broods for a moment.

CARRINGTON You see, I'm not against it in theory. It's just the thought of Mark somehow.

LYTTON Well, I can't, of course, agree with you, but there we are.

EXT. WITTENHAM CLUMPS. DAY

A clump of old elms, surmounting a hill. Lytton sits up, leaning against one of the trees, his panama hat very straight on his head.

Beside him, Carrington is stretched out, lying on her stomach, chin in her hands, her long, cheap dress pulled up slightly to show her short white socks and child's shoes. The countryside is spread out below them. Silence.

CARRINGTON Lytton.

Lytton doesn't answer, turns his head to her. She reaches up and takes his hand.

I love being with you.

Again, Lytton doesn't answer, except for a vague smile.

You're so cold and wise.

Lytton frowns, slightly perplexed.

These last few months, whenever I know I'm going to see you, I get so excited inside.

Lytton watches her.

If you were to kiss me again, I don't think I'd mind at all.

Silence.

LYTTON You know, it's a strange thing, but I'd rather like to.

He leans down to her and kisses her briefly on the lips. His hat falls off. She smiles up at him and he stretches himself out and kisses her again.

CARRINGTON Your skin is like ivory.

She kisses him again, quickly, and then snuggles into the crook of his arm.

That day I came in, you remember, to cut your beard off. I knew then.

Lytton disengages his arm, sits up, puts his hat on, wraps his arms around his knees.

LYTTON I don't think this is what Mark had in mind at all.

CARRINGTON He's not to know.

LYTTON All the same, I can't help feeling rather shifty.

Longish silence. Carrington sits up on one elbow.

CARRINGTON What I knew was, was that I was in love with you.

Lytton looks down at her, surprised. Then he smiles at her, touched, and reaches across to stroke her cheek.

EXT. GARDENS AT GARSINGTON. EVENING

Towards sunset. Lytton and Carrington move hand in hand across the lawns. In the distance, the sound of a harmonium playing 'When This Lousy War Is Over'.

LYTTON I heard from the Military Doctors' Board this morning. They've rejected me. Medically unfit for any kind of service.

CARRINGTON But, Lytton, that's wonderful.

LYTTON Wonderful for me.

They pass through an archway in a hedge and stop. Lytton lets go of Carrington's hand. The harmonium modulates to a jaunty variation of the same tune.

Below them, on a sunken lawn not far from the house, Ottoline's party is in full swing. Morrell is pumping away at the treadle of the harmonium, sweating profusely in his high, stiff collar. All the other guests are dancing. Several of them have been kitted out with Oriental costumes from Ottoline's wardrobe. Ottoline herself is wearing an outrageous Bakstian costume with a turban to match. The dancing is strangely modern, the dancers in couples but moving independently to the music as the fancy takes them.

Lytton and Carrington stand, looking down at the tableau.

LYTTON Thousands of boys are dying every day to preserve this, did you know?

CARRINGTON Yes.

Lytton watches. A spasm of something very like passion contorts his face for a moment.

LYTTON Goddamn, blast, confound and fuck the upper classes.

The dancers leap and jig, lurid in the reddening light. Lytton shakes his head.

Let's see if we can't avoid all this, shall we, and go and read some Rimbaud.

They disappear back through the arch as the dancers pound on, oblivious.

EXT. LAKE AT GARSINGTON. DAY

Gertler, faintly ludicrous in a striped bathing costume, hauls himself out of the lake, his expression fierce and embittered, and flops down next to Carrington, going straight on to the attack as if pursuing some argument.

GERTLER You're the lady, I'm the Jew-boy from the East End, that's it, isn't it?

CARRINGTON Of course not.

GERTLER I don't know why you don't admit it!

CARRINGTON Because it's not true.

Gertler stares at her, unbelieving.

You don't understand. I need my freedom.

GERTLER Freedom? How can you have any freedom when you're frightened to use your body?

CARRINGTON You must have patience.

GERTLER What do you mean, patience? It is killing me all this, it is killing me.

CARRINGTON I'm sorry.

GERTLER Think how much your body has deteriorated in the past four years, all that time wasted.

CARRINGTON Keats's letters . . .

Gertler interrupts her, shouting.

GERTLER Don't talk to me about Keats, what the hell use is Keats to me?

Carrington maintains a stubborn silence as Gertler flounces away, throwing down his towel.

EXT. GARSINGTON MANOR TERRACE. DAY

Gertler sits on a low wall, sketching Lytton, who's taking his ease in a wicker armchair, nursing a glass of wine.

LYTTON I have a suggestion.

GERTLER What?

LYTTON I'm planning a couple of weeks' holiday in Wales. Why don't I take her with me?

Gertler looks up, surprised, a touch suspicious.

You see, I've been teaching her French. We're about to get on to the French poets, I've a feeling they may prove decisive.

Gertler frowns, still dubious.

EXT. WELSH COAST. DAY

Carrington stands on a hillock, facing out to sea, painting. She's wearing corduroy trousers and a green shirt. Presently Lytton appears round the hill: he looks dashingly eccentric and moves with an unwonted spring in his step. He comes up to Carrington and looks at her landscape for a moment.

LYTTON I've come to the sad conclusion there's no such thing as a beautiful Welsh boy. At any rate, I've seen nothing but the most unparalleled frumps.

CARRINGTON But wouldn't it be lovely to live in the country? I'm sick of towns.

LYTTON Yes. (*He reflects for a moment.*) Perhaps we should set up house together.

Carrington stops painting and looks up at him, surprised and delighted. Lytton is already regretting his impulsiveness.

CARRINGTON Do you really mean that?

LYTTON Well yes . . . I did . . . yes.

Carrington considers. Lytton watches her, in suspense.

CARRINGTON No, I don't think so.

Lytton looks unmistakably relieved.

LYTTON Probably just as well. Anyway, I couldn't afford it.

CARRINGTON I see.

LYTTON I'm sorry. I tend to be rather impulsive in these matters. Like the time I asked Virginia Woolf to marry me.

CARRINGTON She turned you down?

LYTTON No, no, she accepted. It was ghastly.

Silence. Carrington is hurt.

CARRINGTON And if I'd accepted, I suppose that would have been ghastly?

LYTTON No, I don't think it would.

INT. BOARDING HOUSE BEDROOM. NIGHT

A plain country bedroom with twin beds. Lytton sits up in his bed, taking pills and washing them down with a glass of water. Carrington is pulling on her pyjama bottoms, somewhat inadequately concealed by an open wardrobe door. Lytton pretends not to watch.

CARRINGTON What's that you're taking?

LYTTON Dr Gregory's Rhubarb Pills. I find them sovereign.

Carrington ties her pyjamas, starts off towards her bed, hesitates fractionally. Lytton smiles at her.

One bed is warmer than two.

Carrington crosses quickly to Lytton's bed and climbs in. He kisses her. Then he draws his head back and they look at each other. Carrington speaks very quietly.

CARRINGTON Anything you like, Lytton. Anything.

Silence. Then Lytton smiles apologetically.

LYTTON It's all very well . . .

He breaks off, strokes her cheek.

CARRINGTON It doesn't matter.

She turns her head away from him so he can't see her face.
Really it doesn't.
Lytton smiles again, wistfully, strokes her hair, leans over and tenderly kisses her ear. She thinks for a moment and puts her arm down under the covers. Lytton raises his eyebrows. Carrington's arm starts to move. Lytton closes his eyes.

INT. LYTTON'S STUDY AT 6 BELSIZE PARK GARDENS. EVENING
A rather formal, gloomy room. Lytton sits in his armchair by the fire, a rug over his knees and a glass of Sanatogen at his elbow. Carrington is moving around the room, worried and thoughtful.
CARRINGTON Mark's borrowed Gilbert Cannan's house at Cholesbury. He wants me to spend a few days with him.
LYTTON Then you must go.
CARRINGTON I'm not sure I want to.
LYTTON Then you mustn't go.
CARRINGTON Can't you see, Lytton, I'm asking you to help me.
LYTTON My dear, as we both know, I'm supposed to be bringing you together . . .

INT. DRAWING ROOM IN THE WINDMILL AT CHOLESBURY. NIGHT
Gertler sits alone, in front of a dying fire, waiting. He gulps down a glass of wine. Finally, he gets up and leaves the room, taking the oil lamp with him.
LYTTON (*voice over*) . . . but in these matters, in these matters above all, you really have to make your own decisions.

INT. STAIRCASE AND LANDING IN THE WINDMILL. NIGHT
Gertler climbs the stairs slowly, lighting his way with the lamp. He moves down the landing, comes to a halt outside a door which is slightly ajar. He waits a second before speaking.
GERTLER Ready?
Carrington answers, panic in her voice, from inside the room.
CARRINGTON (*off-screen*) It's too big, Mark, I can't get it in, I've tried and tried, but I can't.
Gertler starts to push the door open.
(*off-screen*) Don't come in!
Gertler goes in, closing the door behind him.

EXT. THE WINDMILL. NIGHT

The house, lit by moonlight. Deep silence. Then, inside the house, Carrington cries out.

INT. BEDROOM IN THE WINDMILL. NIGHT

The room is strangely lit by the oil lamp, which Gertler has left on the floor. He is making love to Carrington, violently.

Carrington's face is contorted with fear and disgust. Her eyes are tightly shut. Tears squeeze out of the corners of her eyes.

INT. QUEEN'S HALL. EVENING

Schubert's Quintet in C.

Carrington is in the audience, sitting next to Lytton. Tears run down her cheeks. She turns and whispers to Lytton.

CARRINGTON Lytton.

LYTTON Yes.

CARRINGTON What you said about us living together in the country.

LYTTON Yes.

CARRINGTON Did you really mean it?

Lytton is pensive a moment. Then he turns to her.

LYTTON Yes.

EXT. COUNTRY ROAD IN OXFORDSHIRE. DAY

Carrington cycles down a deserted country lane.

EXT. RECTORY IN BERKSHIRE. DAY

Carrington cycles up the front drive of a red-brick rectory.

EXT. SMALL MANOR HOUSE IN OXFORDSHIRE. DAY

Carrington scrambles up a bank to look over the gate at the Georgian house.

EXT. THE MILL HOUSE AT TIDMARSH. DAY

The back garden of the Mill House, a pleasant six-bedroom house, with the mill stream running under it. The garden is secluded and consists of a large lawn, an orchard, several yew trees, a greenhouse, a vegetable garden and an old shed. Lytton stands, looking up at the house, hands in pockets. Carrington is standing beside a small sunken bath, full of old leaves and debris at the moment, but kept fairly clear by the mill stream which flows through it.

LYTTON Yes, but a pound a week. I don't see how I can manage it.

CARRINGTON Our own Roman bath, look.

LYTTON Most hygienic.

INT. LARGE BEDROOM IN THE MILL HOUSE. DAY

Lytton stands in the middle of the room, which is entirely bare, looking suspiciously at the peeling walls. There's dust everywhere.

CARRINGTON And this will be your room.

Lytton's expression is profoundly dubious.

And electric light in every room, look.

LYTTON Yes, that is a blessing.

CARRINGTON Now, don't worry, by the time I've finished with it, you won't recognise it.

Lytton's on his way to the door, covering his mouth with his handkerchief.

LYTTON Hm.

INT. TOUR EIFFEL RESTAURANT IN CHARLOTTE STREET. EVENING

Carrington and Gertler face each other across a half-eaten meal.

GERTLER Are you going to live with him?

CARRINGTON No. I just felt I had to tell him I was in love with him.

GERTLER What did he say?

CARRINGTON He said he was sorry.

Gertler laughs incredulously.

GERTLER Is that all?

CARRINGTON Well, it's not his fault. What else could he say?

Silence. Gertler stares at her for a moment, speaks quietly.

GERTLER I never want to see you again. So would you mind if I left you directly after dinner?

CARRINGTON No.

Another pause. Then, suddenly, Gertler crashes his knife and fork down on the plate and shouts at her.

GERTLER I've always said life was a crooked business! To think after all these years . . . to fall in love with a man like Strachey . . . twice your age . . .

He breaks off, jumps to his feet and stumbles out of the restaurant.

CARRINGTON (*voice over*) I thought I'd better tell Mark, as it was so difficult going on.

LYTTON (*voice over*) Tell him what?

INT. CARRINGTON'S STUDIO IN GOWER STREET. NIGHT

Lytton sits in the armchair in front of the fire. Carrington paces up and down.

CARRINGTON That it couldn't go on. So I told him. I told him I was in love with you.

Silence. Lytton looks at her, dismayed.

LYTTON Aren't you being rather romantic? Are you certain?

Carrington smiles.

CARRINGTON There's nothing romantic about it.

LYTTON What did Mark say?

CARRINGTON He was terribly upset.

LYTTON It's all too incongruous. I'm so old and diseased, I wish I was more . . . able.

CARRINGTON It doesn't matter.

Carrington kneels in front of Lytton. Silence. Lytton is still perplexed.

LYTTON What do you think we ought to do about the physical?

CARRINGTON I don't mind about that.

LYTTON Ah. But you should.

Silence.

CARRINGTON All this is quite deliberate, you know.

Silence.

LYTTON I wish I was rich, then I could keep you as my mistress.

Carrington looks up at him, angrily.

CARRINGTON What difference would that make?

Silence. Then, Lytton gets down on his knees and takes her hands. She looks up at him a moment, then releases her hands, gets up on her knees, takes hold of his beard and kisses him passionately. They kneel there, swaying a moment, then break apart.

Will you stay?

LYTTON Well . . . I . . .

CARRINGTON Won't you spoil me? Just this once, tonight?

EXT. LONDON STREETS. NIGHT

Lytton strides through the darkness of the blackout, head bowed.

INT. CARRINGTON'S STUDIO. NIGHT

The half-finished portrait of Lytton, only just visible in the darkness: the sound of Carrington weeping. She's sitting alone on the chaise longue.

EXT. THE MILL HOUSE. DAY

Carrington is up a ladder, painting the window frames.

INT. LYTTON'S BEDROOM IN THE MILL HOUSE. DAY

Carrington is decorating Lytton's bedroom.

EXT. FRONT OF THE MILL HOUSE. DAY

There's a green pantechnicon pulled up outside the house and Carrington is supervising a number of workmen, who carry furniture in through the front door.

EXT. MILL HOUSE. DAY

Carrington runs to greet Lytton, who's just paying off a taxi, which pulls away, revealing two large suitcases and a cardboard box containing about twenty light bulbs. Having pecked Carrington on the cheek, Lytton, after the briefest hesitation, picks up his box of bulbs and sets off down the slope, leaving Carrington to struggle after him with both cases. He shows her the box of bulbs.

LYTTON I come bearing gifts.

CARRINGTON Oh! Globes.

LYTTON Looted from Mother's.

CARRINGTON What a hero. If I were bigger, I'd carry you across the threshold.

Lytton smiles, but he's clearly very apprehensive. He steps gingerly into the house.

INT. HALLWAY IN THE MILL HOUSE. DAY

Chaos. Dust sheets, paint pots, bookcases, a ladder. And so on. Lytton advances down the hallway with some difficulty.

LYTTON Well done!

He reaches for the handle of a closed door. Carrington, who's started off up the stairs, drops the suitcases in alarm.

CARRINGTON Don't go in there!

Lytton frowns briefly at her, then opens the door.

INT. DOWNSTAIRS ROOM IN THE MILL HOUSE. DAY

Lytton's point of view: an indescribable mess. Apart from anything else, the room is two inches deep in water.

INT. HALLWAY AND STAIRCASE. DAY

Lytton turns to look at Carrington, appalled.

CARRINGTON The pipes seized up. Then they burst.

LYTTON Good God!

CARRINGTON Come upstairs.

Lytton, his expression profoundly gloomy, plods across the hall and starts off up the stairs after Carrington, bumping his head on a low beam.

INT. LYTTON'S BEDROOM IN THE MILL HOUSE. DAY

Carrington has painted Lytton's room with a representation of the Garden of Eden. The huge figure of Adam faces, further down the wall, the only slightly less huge figure of Eve. There's a fire burning in the grate and the bedcovers have been turned back to accommodate three hot-water bottles. Carrington nervously shepherds Lytton into the room. He stands in the doorway, looking around the room in amazement. Carrington waits, his suitcases in her hands, on tenterhooks.

LYTTON It's remarkable!

Carrington, immensely relieved, finally puts down the suitcases.

INT. DINING ROOM OF THE HUTCHINSONS' HOUSE IN HAMMERSMITH. NIGHT

The room is crowded with guests, eating a buffet supper. In a corner of the room, Lytton has managed to secure a chair and sits, eating. Around him, squeezed into uncomfortable positions by the crowd, are Clive Bell and Mary Hutchinson. Carrington squats at his feet, eating.

LYTTON Yes, it seems that *Eminent Victorians* is about to burst upon an astonished world.

MARY That's marvellous, Lytton.

BELL And not before time.

LYTTON Chatto and Windus claim to find it enchanting. It's not absolutely the adjective I had in mind, but I . . .

He breaks off as a plate crashes to the ground. Gertler has appeared in the doorway, pale and haggard, and has barged into one of the guests. He, Lytton and Carrington are immediately aware of each other.

Ignoring the protests of the man he has bumped into, Gertler pushes over to the corner and, without a word, seizes Carrington's wrist, drags her up, upsetting her plate, and pulls her over to the door.

INT. HALL AND STAIRCASE IN THE HUTCHINSONS' HOUSE. NIGHT

Carrington struggles to free her wrist, but Gertler, his face grim and set, drags her across the hall and up the stairs. Guests stop in their tracks and stare, open-mouthed. At the top of the stairs Gertler stands for a moment staring at Carrington, panting slightly. His movements are unsteady.

Carrington watches him, tense but apparently calm.

GERTLER You're living with him!

CARRINGTON Yes.

Gertler explodes, shouting at her.

GERTLER How could you lie to me like that? Did you think I wouldn't find out?

CARRINGTON I didn't want to hurt you.

Gertler gives a snort of bitter laughter.

GERTLER Do you know, when I found out, just thinking about you and that half-dead eunuch, I vomited all night. You've poisoned my life. Haven't you any self-respect?

CARRINGTON Not much.

GERTLER But he's just a disgusting pervert.

CARRINGTON You always have to put up with something.

Despite the incongruity of this remark, she makes it with an odd dignity. She pulls away from him, walks down the stairs, crosses the crowded hallway, quietly and deliberately takes Lytton's hand and leads him away.

EXT. TOW-PATH. NIGHT

Moonlit night. A small front garden leads on to a towpath alongside the Thames, in the shadow of Hammersmith Bridge. The pavements are shiny with rain. Lytton walks arm in arm with Carrington along the tow-path.

LYTTON It's very bright tonight, do you think there'll be a raid?

Suddenly Gertler comes hurtling out of the house, grabs Lytton's sleeve, spins him round and smashes both fists into his face. Lytton goes down like a ninepin. Gertler hurls himself full length on top of him and gets hold of handfuls of his hair.

GERTLER Have you managed it yet? Have you?

Guests begin to drag him off and away from Lytton. He struggles violently. Lytton scrambles to his feet. Bell and Mary dust him down and lead him away.

Meanwhile, another three guests restrain Gertler with difficulty.

I'll kill him!

Lytton giggles nervously.

LYTTON That was all rather thrilling.

As he's led away, his voice rises again, a trifle hysterically.

Anything more cinematographic could scarcely be imagined.

Gertler is being led back towards the house, shouting incoherently; Lytton is being taken off down the towpath, giggling; alone now, by the river, rooted to the spot, frightened, looking first one way and then the other, is Carrington.

Fade.

Caption on black screen:

THREE
PARTRIDGE 1918–1921

CARRINGTON (*voice over*) Rex Partridge, the young man I was telling you about, is coming down to see us on Friday.

EXT. THE MILL HOUSE. DAY

Partridge, twenty-three, tall, powerfully built, blond, blue-eyed and pink-cheeked, wearing a Major's uniform, cycles down the slope towards the front door of the Mill House, singing, at maximum volume, 'La Donna e Mobile'.

CARRINGTON (*voice over*) After the war he plans to sail a schooner to the Mediterranean islands and trade in wine and dress like a brigand.

Partridge lets his bicycle drop and raps smartly at the door.

INT. DINING ROOM. DAY

Lytton's chair is pulled back from the table, so that his face is in shadow. He is staring silently and greedily at Partridge, who at the moment is demolishing an apple. Carrington sits opposite him, her expression somewhat agitated. Remains of lunch on the table.

CARRINGTON You mean that you enjoy it?

PARTRIDGE Well, no, it's not that I enjoy it, of course not, but it does seem a good deal more real over there. And it's a relief to get out of range of all those Bolsheviks and malingerers who spend all their time complaining about subjects they don't know the first thing about.

Silence. Carrington shoots a quick look at Lytton and sees he has no intention of saying anything.

CARRINGTON If you mean conscientious objectors . . .

PARTRIDGE I do. That's exactly what I mean. Only I call them skulkers.

CARRINGTON A lot of them are prepared to suffer for their beliefs, you know. Bertie Russell's in jail.

PARTRIDGE Best place for him, I dare say. Anyway, he's better off there than in the trenches, isn't he?

CARRINGTON That's not the point . . .

PARTRIDGE 'Course it is.

CARRINGTON What are you supposed to do if you're a pacifist, what, what would you suggest?

PARTRIDGE What would I suggest?

CARRINGTON Yes.

PARTRIDGE I'd suggest they were put up against a wall and shot, that's what I'd suggest.

Silence. Carrington is profoundly shocked. Lytton watches, silent.

INT. BATHROOM. NIGHT

Lytton is sitting up in his bath to allow Carrington to sponge his back. Absorbed and tender, she rinses off the soap.

CARRINGTON I'm so sorry.

Lytton looks up, surprised.

LYTTON What for?

CARRINGTON I thought you'd like him.

LYTTON What do you mean?

CARRINGTON I'm sorry he was so awful.

Lytton looks at her a moment, genuinely puzzled.

LYTTON But I thought he was wonderful.

EXT. GARDEN OF THE MILL HOUSE. DAY

Blazing sun. Lytton lies in the shade wearing a white Brahminical robe. He's surrounded by a sea of newspapers. Carrington sits nearby in the sun, sketching the mill race.

LYTTON (*flourishing* The Times) 'Thanks to the brilliancy of his style, *Eminent Victorians* is a fascinating book.' I suppose this is what must be meant by the phrase 'to wake up famous'. Chattos say the book is selling so well, they've been forced to consider a reprint, that's bad luck, isn't it?

Carrington smiles at him; he reaches for one of the newspapers.

I can't claim it was my intention to demolish Victorian values once and for all: but if that's what I've done, I'm not in the least sorry.

INT. LYTTON'S BEDROOM IN THE MILL HOUSE. NIGHT

Lytton and Carrington lie in bed in each other's arms. She is playing with his beard, curling it round her fingers. An atmosphere of profound contentment.

LYTTON It seems I'm in distinct danger of becoming a man of means.

On the bed is a copy of the Times Literary Supplement, *which he indicates.*

Terrible review by Gosse. I can't tell you what a relief it is to be denounced at last. It hasn't been easy, remaining calm in the face of hysterical praise from the *Daily Telegraph*.

Carrington pulls his face towards her and kisses his forehead.
The curse of it all is, I can't see how to get out of writing another book, can you?
She kisses him again.

INT. SITTING ROOM IN THE MILL HOUSE. DAY

Carrington brings Lytton a cup of tea and a scone, sets them down on his desk. He takes a sip of tea. She stands, looking down at him.

LYTTON I don't know why you're so good to me, it's a constant mystery.
Carrington picks up a penwiper from Lytton's desk. It's made of red and blue felt with ragged edges, and on it, embroidered in green, are the words 'USE ME'.

CARRINGTON That's how I feel, Lytton. You must always remember that. I'm your penwiper.

INT. FLAT IN THE ADELPHI. NIGHT

Armistice Day. The flat is packed with celebrating people. Most of the guests are very formally dressed, but the atmosphere is riotous, even slightly hysterical. Music and dancing. Seated at a table to one side are Lytton and Carrington, Ottoline and Partridge. The latter is still in uniform, while the others form a striking contrast to the tailcoats and ball gowns. Ottoline is in her most spectacular outfit, her hair vivid with henna.

LYTTON I know it was an obscene and ridiculous war, but I suppose it's quite convenient to have won.

OTTOLINE Now we shall see real progress, Lytton. We are on the threshold of a Golden Age!
Lytton smiles, a touch cynically, then is suddenly caught up in the spirit of the occasion.

LYTTON Do you know, Ottoline, given the circumstances, I really think we ought to dance.

OTTOLINE Very well.
They take the floor. Lytton jigs amiably up and down, completely out of time with the music; Ottoline's methods are more dramatic. They make a spectacularly peculiar couple. Carrington and Ralph join them on the dance floor. She is watching Lytton intently.

CARRINGTON I wish he'd worn his pullover.

PARTRIDGE I must say, to look at him, you wouldn't think he could have written that book.

CARRINGTON Why not?

PARTRIDGE I read it the other day, couldn't see what all the fuss was about.

Carrington frowns indignantly at him.

LYTTON (*voice over, reading from* The Duchess of Malfi)
'Cardinal: I'll leave you.
Ferdinand: Nay, I have done.
I am confident, had I been damned in Hell,
And should have heard of this, it would have put me
Into a cold sweat.'

INT. SITTING ROOM IN THE MILL HOUSE. EVENING

LYTTON
'In, in, I'll go sleep:
Till I know who leaps my sister, I'll not stir.
That known, I'll find scorpions to string my whips,
And fix her in a general eclipse.
Exeunt.'

Lytton, Carrington and Partridge: Lytton lays the book aside.

I've been meaning to tell you: I can't say I really approve of Rex.

PARTRIDGE What do you mean?

LYTTON As a name.

PARTRIDGE It's not my real name.

Lytton looks at him, waiting.

My real name is Reginald.

LYTTON Ah.

Silence.

Myself, I'm very much in favour of Ralph.

He pronounces it 'Rafe'. Partridge looks at him, frowning.

LYTTON Ralph Partridge. Ralph Partridge. It sounds very well, don't you agree? Ralph.

EXT. GARDEN OF THE MILL HOUSE. DAY

Partridge reclines, naked, smiling, in the long grass in a corner of the garden by the mill race.

Carrington is drawing him, concentrating, her tongue slightly protruding.

PARTRIDGE What's the matter?

She sighs, shakes her head, tears up the sketch.

CARRINGTON I don't know. I seem to be in rather a flux.

Partridge smiles knowingly.

EXT. ST EDMUND HALL BOAT HOUSE, OXFORD. DAY

Lytton sits alone on a canvas chair, patiently staring out at the river. Eventually, a boat appears. Partridge is one of the eight. He rows powerfully and rhythmically.

LYTTON (*voice over*) It's really not fair. Why aren't I a rowing blue, with eyes to match?

Lytton risks a little wave: as the boat speeds by, Partridge flashes a broad grin at him.

CARRINGTON (*voice over*) That's all very well, but his conversation is so dull. He's like some Norwegian dentist.

EXT. RIVER IN CORNWALL. DAY

A pool beside a small waterfall. Partridge and Carrington are swimming naked. He swims towards her as she floats on her back. She shrieks as he capsizes her.

LYTTON (*voice over*) I suppose your privileges give you the right to judge.

INT. CARRINGTON'S BEDROOM IN THE MILL HOUSE. NIGHT

Lytton is in bed with Carrington.

LYTTON I don't know what the world is coming to. Ladies in love with buggers and buggers in love with womanisers – and what with the price of coal . . .

Carrington laughs.

Do you think your Major would stay more often if you had a more comfortable bed?

CARRINGTON The bed's all right.

LYTTON Let me put it another way: I wish he would stay more often.

Mix to:

INT. CARRINGTON'S BEDROOM. NIGHT

Carrington and Partridge lie entwined in a huge new four-poster bed, brilliantly decorated by Carrington.

PARTRIDGE When you go up to London . . .

CARRINGTON Mm.

PARTRIDGE . . . who do you see?

CARRINGTON Nobody you know.

PARTRIDGE Yes, but who?

Silence.

CARRINGTON I like to keep a bit of privacy in my life, you know. And if you're going to cross-examine me all the time, that seems very much like jealousy, and I don't believe in that.

PARTRIDGE Well, if you don't believe in it, why should you mind telling me who you see when you go to London?

His tone is light, but Carrington isn't pleased. She turns away from him.

EXT. GARDEN OF THE MILL HOUSE. DAY

Blazing summer's day. Partridge, wearing only a dirty pair of white shorts, is feeding the ducks in the mill race.

Lytton, in dark suit and panama hat, sits in a deckchair, a book open on his knee, watching him. Carrington is watering the flower bed.

LYTTON Yes, but will I like him?

PARTRIDGE Gerald? I don't see why not. Long as you don't frighten him.

LYTTON I can't imagine what you mean.

PARTRIDGE Well, he's shy. I used to take him to the brothel in Amiens . . .

EXT. THE MILL HOUSE. DAY

Gerald Brenan advances slowly down the path towards the door which opens directly to the sitting room. He's twenty-five, compact, handsome and has a small moustache. His eyes are large and dreamy. His clothes – an open greyish shirt, an ancient sports jacket and grey flannels – are strikingly shabby.

PARTRIDGE (*voice over*) . . . but he always used to wait downstairs or slope off to look at the cathedral.

Brenan reaches the front door, hesitates and lifts a hand to knock. As he does so, he becomes aware that the leather patch on his elbow is flapping loose. He starts to adjust this, when the top half of the door is suddenly flung open by Carrington, startling him considerably. She's wearing a blue dress.

CARRINGTON You must be Gerald Brenan.

BRENAN Miss Carrington?

CARRINGTON Carrington.

BRENAN Rex . . . that's to say, Ralph . . . tells me you're a Bolshevik.

CARRINGTON He tells me you're an idealist.

They smile. They like each other.

INT. DINING ROOM. DAY

The remains of lunch on the table. Brenan is holding an apple, speaking excitedly. Carrington is next to him, Partridge opposite and Lytton at the head of the table, glaring at Brenan.

BRENAN I'm going to look for a house in Spain.

LYTTON Why?

BRENAN To educate myself.

LYTTON Unlikely reason.

BRENAN I'm too old to go to university now and I have to do something to repair my ignorance. So I'm eloping with two thousand books.

LYTTON Why Spain?

BRENAN Because it's hot and cheap.

LYTTON True.

BRENAN And the women are beautiful.

LYTTON Sounds worse and worse.

Brenan begins, carefully and fastidiously, to peel his apple. Next to him, Carrington is peeling an apple in precisely the same way. Partridge watches them for a moment. Then he reaches for an apple and removes almost half of it with a mighty bite.

EXT. WOODS NEAR TIDMARSH. DAY

Partridge, stripped to the waist, and Carrington manage to coax and negotiate Lytton along a log, fallen across a narrow stream.

Brenan brings up the rear. Once over the stream, Lytton strides on ahead with Partridge, a hand on his shoulder, while Brenan and Carrington follow at a more leisurely pace, some yards behind.

BRENAN You mustn't believe everything Ralph tells you about me.

CARRINGTON Why do you say that?

BRENAN He invents everyone he meets. You must have noticed. He gives them a character and a set of opinions so he can argue with them.

Carrington looks at him, impressed by this insight.

CARRINGTON I suppose you're right.

Silence. They walk on.

BRENAN I don't mean to attack Ralph. He's my closest friend. But he lives entirely by his instincts and I can't do that. I wish I could.

CARRINGTON Isn't going off to live in Spain following your instincts?

BRENAN Not really. I'd say it was very calculated. It has to be.

CARRINGTON You mean, money?

BRENAN I'm told you can rent a house there for five pounds a year.

They walk on a little further.

CARRINGTON Whereabouts in Spain are you going?

BRENAN No idea.

Carrington smiles and Brenan counters defensively.

I have a map.

Carrington laughs: they walk on.

CARRINGTON Well, I hope you'll write to me.

BRENAN Of course, I'll write to both of you.

CARRINGTON Separately.

Brenan smiles back, somewhat uncertain.

INT. SITTING ROOM IN THE MILL HOUSE. EVENING

Lytton sits in his armchair, reading Shakespeare. Carrington is writing a letter, scribbling away at great speed. On the old horn gramophone, hissing and scratching, is Schubert's Quintet. Late sun pours into the room. Carrington looks up.

CARRINGTON How d'you spell intangible?

Lytton spells it for her. Carrington looks at what she's written, frowning.

Oh, well, never mind.

INT./EXT. CARRINGTON'S BEDROOM IN THE MILL HOUSE. DAY

Carrington stands at her window, staring wistfully out across the fields. Lytton is sitting on a deckchair reading in the shade.

INT. SITTING ROOM IN THE MILL HOUSE. EVENING

Lytton moves around the room, clearly agitated and upset. Partridge watches him, waiting. The sound of distant thunder.

LYTTON Won't you be just some glorified typesetter?

PARTRIDGE No. And that's not really the point, is it?

LYTTON Oh, what is the point?

PARTRIDGE The point is, I shall have to live in London. And I want Carrington to come with me.

LYTTON Oh. I see.

PARTRIDGE We'll come back here every weekend. And the servants will look after you during the week.

LYTTON It's not the same: I shall miss you terribly.

PARTRIDGE It won't be so very different. All your gallivanting about, you know yourself you're only here about half the time, except when you're working, and then it'll be an advantage to be on your own.

Silence. Lytton reflects, morosely.

LYTTON Suppose she doesn't agree.

PARTRIDGE Then I think it would be best for me to make a complete break.

Lytton is shocked. He stares for a moment at the dominating figure of Partridge.

LYTTON My darling. I don't think I could face that.

INT. CARRINGTON'S BEDROOM. NIGHT

Carrington and Partridge are undressing, ready for bed. A few seconds' heavy silence.

CARRINGTON Why do you think I moved away from London in the first place? I hate London.

PARTRIDGE That's rather a selfish attitude.

CARRINGTON I can't just . . . abandon Lytton.

PARTRIDGE I think you'll find he doesn't quite see it in that light.

Carrington stops in the act of taking off her shoe and looks at Partridge, real fear in her eyes.

CARRINGTON What do you mean?

INT. CARRINGTON'S BEDROOM. NIGHT

Semi-darkness. Lytton, Carrington and Partridge are all in the four-poster bed, Partridge in the middle. Carrington is asleep. Lytton is stroking Partridge's hair, whispering to him.

LYTTON There are times when I feel like a character in a farce by Molière: *Le Bougre Marié.* (*He snuggles closer to Partridge.*) I do wish you weren't quite so single-minded, dearest. I mean, I have tried, I can't help it, women's bodies, I find, somehow, subtly offensive. Or reproachful, would it be? Something.

He leans forward to nibble at Partridge's ear. Partridge's expression is good-natured but by no means responsive.

EXT. BERKSHIRE DOWNS. DAY

Damp autumn landscape. Partridge and Carrington stride through the bracken.

PARTRIDGE Lytton said a strange thing last night.

CARRINGTON Oh, yes, what?

PARTRIDGE He told me he thought women's bodies were disgusting.

Carrington looks at him, shocked, as if she's just been slapped in the face.

INT. LYTTON'S BEDROOM IN THE MILL HOUSE. EVENING

Lytton is squeezing shut an old leather suitcase. Another lies on the floor, already packed. A knock at the door. He looks up, lets go the lid of the suitcase.

CARRINGTON (*off-screen*) Can I come in?

LYTTON Of course.

The door swings open and Carrington appears, both hands behind her back. Lytton smiles at her, mystified.

CARRINGTON Two indispensable items you've forgotten.

She brings one hand from behind her back and flourishes a pair of binoculars.

These. Very handy for boy-watching in Italy.

Lytton takes them, smiling. Then she brings out her other hand, in which she's holding the light-brown air cushion, limp and uninflated.

And.

Lytton takes it.

LYTTON You are wonderful. You think of everything. I shall give you a kiss.

He does so. Carrington smiles, although there is panic in her eyes. He notices.

CARRINGTON What am I going to do, Lytton?

LYTTON He's very determined, my dear. He tells me if you don't marry him he's resolved to go and live abroad.

CARRINGTON If only I wasn't so plural. Especially when people seem to want me so . . . conclusively.

LYTTON I'm sure you'll do the right thing.

His face is expressionless. She looks at him, frightened.

INT. SITTING ROOM OF PARTRIDGE'S FLAT. EVENING

Carrington and Partridge are in the middle of an argument.

CARRINGTON I can't see what possible difference getting married would make.

PARTRIDGE A great deal of difference.

CARRINGTON It's just a piece of paper.

PARTRIDGE For one thing, think how much easier it would be travelling abroad . . . and . . . and . . .

CARRINGTON And what?

Partridge leaps to his feet, enraged by the coldness in Carrington's voice.

PARTRIDGE Well, if that's the way you feel, there's only one thing for it.

He pauses, expecting a question which doesn't come.

I shall go to Bolivia.

CARRINGTON What?

PARTRIDGE A man I know in Oxford wants me to run a sheep farm in Bolivia.

Carrington looks at him a moment, then bursts out laughing.

I'm quite serious! I can't go on like this!

CARRINGTON Don't be ridiculous.

PARTRIDGE I will not be treated like a child!

He strides out of the room, slamming the door.

INT. WORKMEN'S CAFE. DAY

Carrington and Partridge face each other across the cheap wooden table. Congealing, untouched fried eggs and bread and butter in front of Partridge. A large china mug of milky tea in front of Carrington. Partridge looks grey and ill; Carrington exhausted, cornered.

PARTRIDGE If I go, he won't let you live with him any more, you know that, don't you?

CARRINGTON He's never said that.

PARTRIDGE I don't think he wants to see you again when he gets back from Italy.

Carrington is dumbfounded.

INT. LYTTON'S BEDROOM IN THE MILL HOUSE. DAY

Carrington stands beneath the Adam mural.

CARRINGTON (*voice over*) My dearest Lytton. There is a great deal to say and I feel very incompetent to write it today.

INT. PRIVATE APARTMENT AT I TATTI, FLORENCE. DAY

Lytton sits, marooned in a vast, palatially furnished room, reading a letter.

CARRINGTON (*voice over*) You see, I knew there was nothing really to hope for from you, well, ever since the beginning.

INT./EXT. CARRINGTON'S BEDROOM IN THE MILL HOUSE. DAY

Carrington stands at her window, as before, looking out across the fields. This time, Lytton's deckchair beneath the tree is empty.

INT. BATHROOM IN THE MILL HOUSE. DAY

Carrington slips into the bathroom, crosses to the bath, picks up Lytton's sponge and smells it.

CARRINGTON (*voice over*) All these years I have known all along that my life with you was limited. Lytton, you are the only person who I have ever had an all-absorbing passion for.

I shall never have another. I couldn't now. I had one of the most self-abasing loves that a person can have.

INT. PARTRIDGE'S FLAT IN GORDON SQUARE. DAY

Carrington stands at the window, craning to look at the square below.

CARRINGTON (*voice over*) It's too much of a strain to be quite alone here waiting to see you . . .

EXT. GORDON SQUARE. DAY

Lytton's panama hat appears, bobbing up and down above the hedge on the other side of the square.

CARRINGTON (*voice over*) . . . or craning my nose and eyes out of the top window at 44 Gordon Square to see if you were coming down the street.

INT. PARTRIDGE'S FLAT. DAY

Carrington reacts, delighted to see Lytton approaching.

INT. CARRINGTON'S BEDROOM IN THE MILL HOUSE. NIGHT

Partridge is making love to Carrington. She looks up at the ceiling, virtually expressionless.

CARRINGTON (*voice over*) Ralph said you were nervous lest I'd feel I had some sort of claim on you and that all your friends wondered how you could have stood me so long, as I didn't understand a word of literature.

INT. CARRINGTON'S BEDROOM. NIGHT

Later. Partridge is heavily asleep, Carrington silently weeps.

CARRINGTON (*voice over*) That was wrong. For nobody, I think, could have loved the Ballades, Donne, and Macaulay's essays, and, best of all, Lytton's essays, as much as I.

EXT. GARDEN IN THE MILL HOUSE. DAY

Carrington carries a cup of tea and some buttered toast across to Lytton's table, set up under a tree, facing the house. He looks up in pleasurable anticipation.

CARRINGTON (*voice over*) You never knew, or never will know, the very big and devastating love I had for you. How I adored every hair, every curl of your beard. Just thinking of you now makes me cry so I can't see this paper.

EXT. TERRACE AND GARDEN AT I TATTI. DAY

Lytton sits at a long wooden table on the terrace outside the villa; he puts aside Carrington's letter and takes up his pen.

CARRINGTON (*voice over*) Once you said to me, that Wednesday afternoon in the sitting room, you loved me as a friend. Could you tell it to me again? Yours, Carrington.

Close on Lytton: tears glisten in his eyes. He begins to write.

LYTTON (*voice over*) My dearest and best . . .

He breaks off and looks up, reflecting.

Long shot: Lytton is seated on the terrace, in the lea of the villa.

(*voice over*) Do you know how difficult I find it to express my feelings either in letters or talk?

INT. ST PANCRAS REGISTRY OFFICE. DAY

Partridge and Carrington stand in front of the registrar. Partridge pushes a narrow, plain gold ring on to Carrington's finger. She looks lost and unhappy.

LYTTON (*voice over*) . . . do you really want me to tell you that I love you as a friend? But of course that is absurd and you do know very well that I love you as something more than a friend, you angelic creature, whose goodness to me has made me happy for years. Your letter made me cry, I feel a poor old miserable creature.

INT. GRAND STAIRCASE TO THE ST PANCRAS REGISTRY OFFICE. DAY

Carrington moves slowly down the stairs, slumped on Partridge's arm.

LYTTON (*voice over*) If there was a chance that your decision meant that I should somehow or other lose you, I don't think I could bear it. You and Ralph and our life at Tidmarsh are what I care for most in the world.

EXT. SIDE CANAL IN VENICE. DAY

The handsome young gondolier beams at Lytton, who sits sideways on in the small upright armchair. Carrington and Partridge are side by side on the banquette; Partridge's arm is loosely draped around Carrington's shoulders.

LYTTON Well, I think I shall spend all my honeymoons here.
His eye falls on Carrington's left hand.
Shouldn't you be wearing a ring?

CARRINGTON I lost it. Somewhere in the Italian Alps.
She looks at Lytton, sitting opposite, expansive and contented.
Do you ever get terrified of dying?
Silence, except for the splash of the oar. Then the gondolier utters a melancholy cry and steers the gondola round a blind corner.
Fade.
Caption on black screen:

FOUR
BRENAN 1921–1923

On sound: the buzz and hum of an English summer's day.

EXT. WHITE HORSE HILL, UFFINGTON. DAY

Brenan lies on a rug, propping himself up on one elbow, close to a chalk indentation which forms part of the giant White Horse etched into the hillside. Above him, Carrington sketches: him and the vast tract of countryside spread out below. Remains of a picnic nearby. Two bicycles lie on the ground. Carrington puts down her sketch pad and moves down the hill to join Brenan.

CARRINGTON When you've been married as long as six weeks, you've no idea how pleasant it is to get away on your own.
Brenan smiles uncertainly, hesitates before speaking.

BRENAN I sometimes wish I'd met you before Ralph did.

CARRINGTON Yes.

BRENAN I don't suppose I'd have made much impression on you.
Instead of answering, Carrington leans forward and kisses him on the lips. Brenan's eyes register surprise and a touch of alarm. Then he submits. Long kiss. Then Carrington breaks away and smiles down at him. A long silence. Brenan sits, looking at her, completely bewildered.

INT. SITTING ROOM IN THE MILL HOUSE. EVENING

Sunset. Brenan sits in an armchair, reading. Carrington is moving round the room, putting flowers in vases and arranging them. As she finishes doing this, Brenan looks up from his book. Carrington begins to cross the room, stops for a moment in front of a window, through which the evening sun streams in. Brenan is watching her. His mouth is open and a look, almost of pained amazement, comes into his eyes. Carrington notices.

CARRINGTON What's the matter?

BRENAN I don't know . . .

He stops. They look at each other, transfixed. Suddenly, the door bursts open, startling both of them, and Partridge appears. He's wearing white shorts and a rowing vest and is in the best of spirits.

PARTRIDGE You know something, Gerald, you're mad. Why d'you have to go back to Spain so soon? Why don't you come and join us on holiday?

Silence. Brenan looks as if he's in pain.

BRENAN No, I couldn't.

EXT. DERELICT BARN. DAY

Carrington is painting a portrait of Brenan, concentrating intently, when Partridge appears, rod in hand.

PARTRIDGE Ready?

CARRINGTON This is going very well, do you mind awfully?

PARTRIDGE Not at all.

He waves his fishing rod as he leaves.

EXT. RIVER BANK. DAY

Partridge sits motionless on the banks of the river, fishing. He reaches absently towards a newspaper parcel, fumbles in it for a moment, fetches out a hard-boiled egg, which he cracks and peels dexterously with one hand, and starts to eat, never allowing his concentration to wander. The camera rises, pulling away from this scene to a high angle, to reveal, concealed from Partridge by a wall, the abandoned easel standing outside the rough stone barn.

INT. DERELICT BARN. DAY

Carrington and Brenan lie entwined in the hayloft, kissing passionately. Finally, reluctantly, he pulls away from her.

BRENAN I must tell Ralph.

CARRINGTON What?

BRENAN I must. I can't bear this deceit. After all, he is one of my oldest friends. I think I ought to go and tell him I love you, that he has nothing to worry about, that it's just like brother and sister . . .

He breaks off. Carrington is staring at him in some anxiety.

CARRINGTON I shouldn't.

BRENAN Why not?

CARRINGTON You'd upset him.

BRENAN But surely . . .

CARRINGTON You would, really you would. He's such a dear, it wouldn't be fair. I feel shittish enough about it as it is.

She reaches out and puts her hands on his cheeks, draws him down to her. They kiss.

BRENAN I want you to come back to Spain with me. Now. Today. And live with me.

CARRINGTON I can't, Gerald.

BRENAN Why not?

Carrington doesn't answer. Instead, she reaches for him and glues her mouth to his.

I feel as if I'm drowning.

EXT. COUNTRY ROAD NEAR WATENDLATH FARM. DAY

Sunny day. Partridge strides along the road, humming a folk song. Brenan, with his rucksack, and Carrington trail along behind, looking strained and tense, groping surreptitiously for one another's hand. They come to a fork in the road. Partridge stops.

PARTRIDGE Well, old chap, I think this is the parting of the ways.

BRENAN Yes.

Silence. Then Brenan and Partridge shake hands.

PARTRIDGE Take care of yourself.

BRENAN I will.

He stretches out his hand to Carrington, who takes it.

PARTRIDGE Oh, I think the lady and gentleman might be permitted a kiss, don't you?

Brenan leans forward and pecks at Carrington's cheek. Then he turns on his heel and hurries away. Partridge and Carrington stand, watching him go. She looks close to tears. Abruptly, she turns away and sets off down the other fork. Presently, Partridge catches her up.

I really don't understand you, a bit of effort.

CARRINGTON What do you mean?

PARTRIDGE Well, if you'd just tried to persuade him, I'm sure he'd have stayed another couple of days.

INT./EXT. CARRINGTON'S BEDROOM IN THE MILL HOUSE. EVENING

Carrington is working on the Brenan portrait. Lytton opens the door and hovers in the doorway.

LYTTON Do you know if Ralph's coming back this evening?

There's just the faintest hint of disappointment in his voice, which Carrington registers.

CARRINGTON He said he had some work to do in London.

Lytton moves into the room and shuts the door.

I don't know who it is, Lytton.

Lytton walks towards Carrington, looking at Brenan's portrait.

I've had three letters already this week.

Lytton looks at her shrewdly.

I miss him terribly.

LYTTON When is he coming back to England?

CARRINGTON He says he can't afford the fare.

Lytton considers this carefully for some time.

EXT. DOWNS ABOVE TIDMARSH. DAY

Brenan strides across the rolling hills. There's a rucksack on his back and a rolled-up rug across his shoulders.

INT. CARRINGTON'S BEDROOM. DAY

Carrington and Brenan are on their knees unrolling a handsome Spanish rug.

CARRINGTON It's lovely, Gerald, I shall always treasure it.

Suddenly, they're locked in a violent embrace, sprawling on the rug. Eventually, Brenan manages to extricate himself and pulls back. Carrington grabs at his wrist.

Look, this is silly. Ralph has mistresses, you know, I'm sure he's with one of them now; so I can't see the sense in it.

She pulls Brenan towards her and they kiss; then, once again, they're sprawling on the rug. Brenan starts to unbutton her dress.

INT. SITTING ROOM IN THE MILLHOUSE. DAY

Lytton is reading Gibbon. He looks up from the book at the sound of Carrington, crying out with pleasure.

INT. CARRINGTON'S BEDROOM. DAY

Carrington lies in Brenan's arms; he looks down at her tenderly.

BRENAN Now will you come back to Spain with me?

Carrington shakes her head gravely.

CARRINGTON You mustn't spoil things, Gerald.

BRENAN You want to stay in England with Ralph . . .

CARRINGTON No. Not with Ralph. With Lytton.

EXT. THE MILL HOUSE. NIGHT

Partridge stands in the garden, clutching an almost empty whisky bottle which he now proceeds to drain.

PARTRIDGE Carrington!

A light goes on upstairs. Partridge throws the whisky bottle against the wall, shattering it.

INT. LYTTON'S BEDROOM. NIGHT

Lytton wakes in alarm. As Partridge's voice rings out again, Lytton decides to stay where he is and let matters take their course.

EXT. THE MILL HOUSE. NIGHT

Partridge is lurching towards the front door, when it opens. Carrington stands in the doorway, blinking out into the night.

PARTRIDGE Where's Brenan?

CARRINGTON He's not here.

PARTRIDGE I said where is he?

CARRINGTON I told you. He's not here.

PARTRIDGE I'll kill him!

CARRINGTON Has somebody told you something? Who?

PARTRIDGE None of your business. Out of the way!

CARRINGTON He's gone to stay with his parents.

PARTRIDGE Will you get out of the way! I'm going to pull his arms off.

He storms past her and vanishes into the house.

INT. STAIRCASE AND LANDING. NIGHT

Carrington runs after Partridge as he bounds upstairs.

INT. CARRINGTON'S BEDROOM. NIGHT

Partridge bursts into the room. It's empty. As Carrington appears in the doorway, he's striding over to look under the four-poster bed.

PARTRIDGE Where is he?

INT. BRENAN'S BASEMENT ROOM IN LONDON. DAY

Grey day, poor light. The flat is poor and shabby; not much of anything. Partridge and Brenan sit, not looking at each other. They both look terrible, Partridge hung-over and unshaven, Brenan miserable and uncomfortable. Heavy silence.

PARTRIDGE So, you were in love with her?

BRENAN Yes.

PARTRIDGE And you're trying to tell me that you haven't been fucking her, do you expect me to believe that?

BRENAN Yes.

PARTRIDGE I know you're pretty feeble, Gerald, but what exactly is the meaning of this heroic self-restraint?

BRENAN I was always very aware that you're my friend and she's my wife, I mean, your wife.

Silence.

PARTRIDGE All right, let's go through this step by step, shall we? Now presumably you kissed her. I mean you must have kissed her.

BRENAN I suppose so, yes.

PARTRIDGE And did you, for example . . . did you ever put your hand down the front of her dress?

BRENAN No, I don't think so.

PARTRIDGE You don't think so. I'm asking you if you ever touched her tits?

BRENAN No. (*He shakes his head wearily.*) What's the point of all this?

PARTRIDGE The point is, the point of it is, this is all important information because I have to decide whether I ever want to see either of you again, that's the point of it.

Silence.

Another thing, you realise I can't possibly allow you to see or communicate with her ever again.

INT. DINING ROOM IN THE MILL HOUSE. DAY

Carrington and Brenan sit facing each other across the dining-room table. Lytton sits at the head of the table, chewing gravely. Funereal atmosphere. Brenan's hands are shaking, he seems to be in a state of shock.

BRENAN Having to lie to him, that's what I couldn't bear.

LYTTON We know that, Gerald, but you must understand it was essential.

BRENAN I suppose so, I don't know . . .

LYTTON I don't approve of jealousy any more than you do, but no doubt if one's afflicted with it, there's very little one can do about it.

BRENAN Yes, but he's so irrational . . .

LYTTON We must proceed with extreme caution. Let me see what I can do.

EXT. MILL HOUSE. DAY

The chrome grille of a gleaming four-seater 1922 Morris Oxford reflects a departing taxi and an approaching Partridge. He looks grey and exhausted. He hesitates in front of the car and looks up, puzzled, as Lytton joins him.

PARTRIDGE What's this? Visitors?

Lytton smiles. He's excited.

LYTTON No. It's by way of a present.

PARTRIDGE Who for?

LYTTON Well, since neither Carrington nor I drive . . .

INT./EXT. UPSTAIRS CORRIDOR. DAY

Carrington at the window, watching.

Her point of view: Partridge seizes Lytton and kisses him on both cheeks. Carrington turns wearily away from the window.

INT. BRENAN'S BASEMENT. EVENING

Brenan has obviously done everything in his power to tidy up the very shabby room. There are lilies in a bowl on the dining table, together with a bottle of wine and a small opened pot of caviar. The fruit bowl on the sideboard is full of fruit.

He's just starting to lay the table when there's the sound of a key in the lock and Carrington appears, crossing the small entrance hall. Brenan looks up, surprised, puts down his handful of knives and forks, crosses to Carrington and kisses her. She seems a little distant.

BRENAN I didn't expect you so early.

Carrington notices the preparations and smiles, slightly suspicious.

CARRINGTON What's all this? I thought we were going out.

BRENAN Well, I thought . . .

Carrington picks up the pot of caviar.

CARRINGTON Caviar? Gerald, you can't afford this.

BRENAN I know.

Silence. Carrington is looking at him, puzzled.

I thought I might induce you to stay the night.

CARRINGTON You know very well how careful we have to be.

BRENAN Otherwise it seems so sordid.

CARRINGTON Don't let's quarrel: there isn't time to quarrel.

She sets off across the room in the direction of the bed beneath the skylight, dropping her coat over a sofa on her way. By the bed, she slips off her waistcoat and starts to unbutton her dress.

Come on.

Brenan advances reluctantly towards her, taking off his jacket en route.

EXT. GARDEN OF THE MILL HOUSE. DAY

Lytton sits in a deckchair under the shade of a beach umbrella; Carrington sits at his feet in the sun.

CARRINGTON He keeps wanting me to go and live with him. Why is he so demanding?

LYTTON No doubt because he hasn't understood that people in love should never live together. When they do, the invariable result is that they either fall out of love or drive one another insane. Tell him.

CARRINGTON He wouldn't believe me.

LYTTON Idealists are nothing but trouble. You can never convince them there's no such thing as the ideal.

CARRINGTON I can't see what's going to happen. It's frightening me.

LYTTON Whatever happens, my dear, you're safe here.

She reaches up and takes his hand.

INT. GENNARO'S RESTAURANT IN SOHO. EVENING

Carrington and Brenan have just had dinner. They're drinking coffee. Carrington looks at her watch.

CARRINGTON I shall have to go in about five minutes.

BRENAN Aren't you coming back to the flat?

CARRINGTON I'd rather not tonight, if you don't mind very much.

BRENAN Then I shall just have to walk the streets until I find a whore.

CARRINGTON Yes, I expect you will.

Hostile silence. Then, all of a sudden, Carrington smiles warmly at Brenan.

Shall we have another picnic on the White Horse Hill? A sentimental pilgrimage?

Brenan, taken completely by surprise, can only smile and shake his head.

Come at ten on Sunday. I'll meet you there.

EXT. THE MILL HOUSE. DAY

The house stands, beautiful in the soft morning light.

LYTTON (*voice over*) I can't bear the thought of leaving this house.

INT. LYTTON'S BEDROOM IN THE MILL HOUSE. DAY

Carrington is in bed with Lytton.

LYTTON The orchard, the mill race, my wonderful room, the Garden of Eden.

He indicates Carrington's Adam and Eve mural.

CARRINGTON Yes, but the rheumatism, Lytton, the lumbago; the rising damp and the falling plaster; the rats in the wainscot.

LYTTON Very true.

CARRINGTON I keep thinking I've forgotten something, you know the feeling?

She shuts her eyes fiercely, and burrows into Lytton's arms.

EXT. WHITE HORSE HILL, UFFINGTON. DAY

Brenan is alone on the slopes of the hillside, the giant White Horse poised mockingly above him, his bicycle lying some way off in the grass. Cloudy day. He stops to look at his watch, then pivots on his heel, peering in every direction, before continuing to pace up and down. After a while, it comes on to rain.

Fade.

Caption on black screen:

FIVE
HAM SPRAY HOUSE 1924–1931

EXT. HAM SPRAY HOUSE IN HUNGERFORD. DAY

The camera approaches a doorway cut into a tall laurel hedge and tracks through it to discover the back of a large, low, interesting house, with irregular windows, unexpectedly placed.

As the camera stops to contemplate the house, Carrington rides through the gap in the hedge on her white horse, Belle. She dismounts, casually leaving the horse to graze on the large sunken lawn, climbs a few steps, crosses a kind of grass plateau, past a white iron table and chairs and steps into the house.

INT./EXT. GAMES ROOM. DAY

She's stepped into an empty room with ground sheets, ladders and a trestle. On the trestle are Partridge, standing, crowded against the ceiling, screwing in a rose to carry a light fitting; and a very pretty girl of twenty-four, Frances Marshall, who's whitewashing the ceiling. As Carrington exchanges greetings with them, Lytton comes into the room from the hallway with Roger Senhouse, a handsome student in his early twenties.

LYTTON Ralph? Ah, Ralph, this is Roger Senhouse, my young friend from Oxford.

Partridge stretches down to shake hands with him as Lytton continues his introductions.

Ralph Partridge; and this is his friend Frances Marshall. Oh, and this is Carrington.

Carrington shakes hands with him, concealing whatever affront she feels at Lytton's off-hand tone.

I'm sure there's a brush here for you somewhere.

ROGER Oh, do you think so? I'm horribly bad at it.

LYTTON Of course you are. Come, I'll show you the garden.

Lytton smiles at him indulgently and shepherds him out into the garden.

Carrington watches, through the window, slightly concerned as Lytton drapes a negligent arm around Roger's shoulders and Roger gently extracts a piece of food from Lytton's beard.

She turns and crosses the room, noticing as she leaves how Partridge, up on the trestle, playfully ruffles Frances's hair.

EXT. BACK GARDEN. DAY

Late afternoon. Carrington is sketching Lytton; her pencil flies across the paper.

CARRINGTON Good to be on our own again.

Lytton looks out across the Downs, not answering for a moment.

LYTTON I must say I find these new young people wonderfully refreshing. They have no morals and they never speak. It's an enchanting combination. (*He looks across at her, then continues in a low voice.*) I was standing outside a door, trying to pluck up courage to knock, when suddenly it swung open. I can scarcely believe it's happened.

CARRINGTON I thought you were looking rather sprightly.

LYTTON No, it's more than that; it was like being let into paradise.

Carrington looks up at Lytton, alarmed.

INT. DRAWING ROOM AT HAM SPRAY. EVENING

The room is half-decorated and still only provisionally furnished. Lytton sits in the only armchair, watching, as a quarrel rages between Carrington and Partridge.

CARRINGTON You wait until Lytton virtually bankrupts himself and then you announce you're not going to live here.

PARTRIDGE I didn't say that. I said my life would have to be in London with Frances.

CARRINGTON Why didn't you tell us this before?

PARTRIDGE It's only just happened, I told you, we've only just decided.

CARRINGTON How can you be so thoughtless? It's just not fair on Lytton.

She looks at Lytton, as if in appeal; but he says nothing and she turns back to Partridge in exasperation. Close on Lytton, as he watches.

It's not fair on any of us: to put our future in the hands of an outsider.

INT. ORIENTAL CLUB, LONDON. DAY

Frances Marshall makes her way across the cavernous reaches of the Oriental Club, startling various aged members as they doze or thumb absently through newspapers. She arrives in front of Lytton, installed in a colossal leather armchair. He looks up at her.

LYTTON How kind of you to come. I thought, of the four of us, you and I were the ones most likely to be able to discuss this sensibly. Do sit down.

She does so, smiling politely, nervous but unintimidated.

The fact of the matter is, if you and Ralph do plan to set up permanently in London, then I shall be forced to resell Ham Spray.

FRANCES I understand.

LYTTON You see, Ralph has become quite indispensable to us. We rely upon him for every practical decision.

FRANCES Well, I certainly have no intention of . . . stopping Ralph from . . . seeing Carrington or interfering in any way. It's just that we're . . .

LYTTON I know.

FRANCES Ralph told me, when they first got married, they used to live in London during the week and . . .

LYTTON Yes. It's a question of making a quite formal arrangement.

FRANCES Couldn't we do the same, come down every weekend? I mean, the last thing I want to do . . .

Lytton smiles, hugely relieved.

LYTTON I knew you were the right person to talk to. Can I get you some tea?

EXT. DECK OF THE TRAWLER 'SANS PAREIL'. DAY

At sea. Carrington grapples with the wheel, watched by a young man of twenty-six, Bernard (Beacus) Penrose. He stands with his hands on his hips, blond, handsome, his face burnt brick-red by sun and wind.

CARRINGTON (*voice over*) He likes to be called Beacus. He's not in the least curious, in fact rather remote, in other words, just what I need: and so beautiful. Lytton, the brass buckle on his belt . . .

INT. CABIN OF THE 'SANS PAREIL'. DAY

Penrose is stretched out on one of the bunks. Carrington, dressed, moves about the cabin making breakfast. As she passes, he reaches out and grabs hold of her skirt. She smiles and ruffles his hair. He takes her hand, quite roughly, and puts it to his lips. Then he puts two of her fingers in his mouth and nibbles at them. With his other hand, he lifts her skirt. She's wearing white stockings.

PENROSE Why don't you wear black stockings or dark brown? They show off a leg so much better than these things. And suspenders I like. Why don't you wear suspenders?

His hand roams around under her skirt.

INT. HALLWAY AT HAM SPRAY. DAY

Carrington crosses the hallway to answer the phone.

CARRINGTON Hello?

INT. ORIENTAL CLUB. DAY

Lytton stands in the panelled alcove which contains the club's telephone. Senhouse sits on a nearby sofa, reading.

LYTTON Hello, it's me . . .

INT. HALLWAY. DAY

Carrington stands, holding the receiver, listening.

LYTTON I shan't be able to get back this evening.

CARRINGTON Oh?

INT. ORIENTAL CLUB. DAY

Lytton is looking directly at Senhouse.

LYTTON As a matter of fact, I've done something rather impulsive . . .

Senhouse looks up, catches Lytton's eye and smiles.

INT. HALLWAY. DAY

Close on Carrington, as Lytton continues to speak. Her face gradually disintegrates into a mask of suffering.

LYTTON (*voice over*) . . . I've taken some rooms in Gordon Square. It won't make the slightest difference to our arrangements, don't worry: it's just a way of circumventing these impossible difficulties, means I shan't have to keep depending on friends, taking hotel rooms, skulking about.

CARRINGTON Sounds a very good idea.

She hangs up.

INT. ORIENTAL CLUB. DAY

Lytton frowns, shrugs and hangs up. Then, his expression emphatic, he fetches something from his waistcoat pocket and bears down on Senhouse. With a flourish, he produces a key. Senhouse frowns at him interrogatively.

LYTTON Your key.

Senhouse hesitates.

SENHOUSE Oh, no, Lytton, you know me. I'd only lose it. You keep it.

He smiles charmingly at Lytton, who puts the key back in his pocket, clearly disturbed, and turns back to his book.

EXT. FALMOUTH HARBOUR. DAY

The 'Sans Pareil' rides at anchor in the harbour.

INT. CABIN OF THE 'SANS PAREIL'. DAY

The camera slowly approaches to find Carrington leaning forward across the bunk as Penrose makes love to her, violently.

EXT. GARDEN AT HAM SPRAY. DAY

Long shot through the gap in the laurel hedge. Carrington spurs on her horse and gallops through the pouring rain towards the back of the house.

INT. HALLWAY. DAY

As Carrington emerges into the hall, drenched to the skin, Lytton comes out of the drawing room to intercept her.

LYTTON What can you be thinking of, going out in this weather?

CARRINGTON There's a reason for it, Lytton.

LYTTON What? What can it possibly be?

CARRINGTON *Je suis perdue.*

In the ensuing long silence, she sets off across the hallway and starts up the stairs. It's Lytton's voice, full of sympathy, which stops her.

LYTTON Are you sure?

Carrington nods.

And you're sure you don't want it?

CARRINGTON Oh, Lytton, I could never have a child.

She turns and carries on up the stairs, adding in an undertone.

Unless it was yours.

Lytton decides to ignore this, speaks again as she reaches the top of the stairs.

LYTTON Have you told Beacus?

CARRINGTON It's no good telling him, it'd only make him angry. I don't know why he puts up with me as it is.

LYTTON I don't know why you put up with him.

CARRINGTON Because he's the most exciting man I've ever slept with. And because I'm getting old.

She starts moving along the landing towards her room; Lytton speaks to her, stopping her in her tracks.

LYTTON Now you know what it feels like.

She looks down at him from the gallery.

CARRINGTON I always did.

Lytton watches as she disappears down the corridor.

INT. DRAWING ROOM AT HAM SPRAY. DAY

Carrington sits in front of an untouched cup of coffee, shivering, grey-faced. Lytton walks into the room with a piece of paper, which he puts down on the table in front of her. He speaks very decisively.

LYTTON Here's the address of a very good man in London.

INT. CARRINGTON'S BEDROOM AT HAM SPRAY. DAY

Carrington is in bed. Lytton advances into the room with a tray of lunch.

LYTTON Well, this makes a change.

CARRINGTON A very different pair of boots.

LYTTON How are you feeling?

CARRINGTON Rotten.

He hands her the tray. She takes it, looking up at him.

I know you don't like him, Lytton, or approve of him.

LYTTON It's not that.

CARRINGTON I'm sure he's as dim as a blind owl in a holly tree, but he never says anything, so you can't really tell.

She's beginning to cry. Lytton backs away and leaves the room.

EXT. GARDEN OF HAM SPRAY. NIGHT

A tracking shot, as before, passes through the opening in the laurel hedge.

It stops at Carrington and Lytton, who are standing by the tree stump in the middle of the lawn. Through the lighted window of the games room Penrose and Senhouse can be seen, playing table tennis. Distant clack of the ball. Next door, in the dining room, Partridge and Frances are moving around, clearing up. Lytton sighs.

LYTTON D'you suppose they're going to play that wretched game all night?

He sets off without waiting for an answer, goes into the house, passes through the games room in a meaningful way and out. Presently, the light goes on in the drawing room and he appears in the window, holding a newspaper, which he scarcely seems to be reading.

All this from Carrington's point of view: now she decides to sit on the tree stump and watch.

The light goes out in the dining room; Penrose and Senhouse finish playing; Senhouse goes to join Lytton in the drawing room for a moment; the light goes on upstairs in Partridge's bedroom and he and Frances appear; then Penrose appears in the next bedroom, pulling off his shirt as he crosses to the window; the light goes out in the drawing room.

Now, the camera slowly rises until it's at the level of the first floor: the light goes on in Lytton's bedroom and Senhouse appears in the window; Frances pulls the thin curtains, so that only her and Partridge's silhouettes can be seen as they move around the room and eventually embrace; Penrose continues to undress; Lytton comes up to Senhouse and stands with him in the window; Penrose reappears in his window, still bare-chested, wearing blue-striped pyjama bottoms; Lytton and Senhouse embrace.

The camera draws back to look at Carrington, isolated, unhappily watching, motionless on the tree stump.

Caption on black screen:

SIX
LYTTON 1931–1932

INT. LYTTON'S STUDY AT HAM SPRAY. EVENING

Lytton's study is a kind of comfortable upstairs library with a large desk. A portrait of Voltaire dominates the room, which at the moment is in darkness. Lytton sits at his desk, his face buried in his hands. The door opens, throwing a shaft of light into the room and Carrington appears. She's immediately aware that something is the matter and hurries over to Lytton.

CARRINGTON What's the matter?

Lytton looks up at her: his face is streaked with tears. He's holding a letter.

LYTTON I've had a letter from Roger. He's not coming down next week. He says I've let him mean too much to me. He says I've oppressed him.

Carrington puts her arms around him, struggling with her own pain.

He's right, of course. One doesn't intend to let it get out of hand; and then it does; and then there's this blackness.

He begins to sob uncontrollably. Carrington draws him to her and strokes his hair.

EXT. DECK OF THE 'SANS PAREIL'. DAY

Carrington is steering the boat and Penrose is winching in a sail.

CARRINGTON Sometimes . . .

She breaks off, but then can't prevent herself from saying it.

Sometimes I think you don't like me very much.

Penrose looks at her, expressionless.

PENROSE No, no. It's not that. I'm devoted to you, you know that. It's just . . .

CARRINGTON Go on.

PENROSE It's just you don't really attract me sexually. To be honest.

Carrington stares at him, horrified, the blood drained from her face.

INT. DRAWING ROOM AT HAM SPRAY. DAY

Lytton sits in the window, being painted by Carrington.

LYTTON That man from the London Group, who keeps offering you an exhibition: why don't you take him up on it?

CARRINGTON I've told you before, I don't want an exhibition. That isn't why I do it. I paint when I feel well and it makes me feel even better. I'm not interested in selling them. They're for us.

Silence.

LYTTON So, you're all right now?

CARRINGTON Yes, I am. At least it's been a great mercy, not being in the wrong this time.

LYTTON I've been thinking of giving you a little pension, just a hundred a year or so.

CARRINGTON Do keep still, you're causing havoc.

EXT./INT. DINING ROOM AT HAM SPRAY. EVENING

Seen through the window, Lytton and Carrington eat their dinner and drink their wine, bathed in a pool of gentle light.

EXT. GARDEN OF HAM SPRAY. DAY

Lytton sits in his deckchair, reading to Carrington, his voice unheard.

INT. LYTTON'S STUDY. DAY

Lytton and Carrington have been having tea. Now, Carrington makes a move to clear away.

CARRINGTON I'd better leave you to get on.

LYTTON Oh. God, no, please stay for a while. (*He sighs theatrically.*) I have heard rumours to the effect that there are people who actually enjoy writing. Can this be true? I loathe it. All that work and then at the end of it some slim volume, what's the point, I ask myself.

CARRINGTON Think of posterity.

LYTTON Why? What's posterity ever done for me?

They smile. Lytton reflects for a moment.

I've done my best to keep it quiet, but I'm an ambitious man. I thought if I could cut through all that atrocious fog of superstition that poisons so many people's lives, I might be able to do some good in the world. But the truth is, I've always been better at living than I ever was at writing.

CARRINGTON What's wrong with that? (*She looks at him for a moment.*) I don't think you have any idea how happy you've made me.

EXT. GARDEN OF HAM SPRAY. EVENING

Carrington, Partridge, Frances, and three or four other young guests are listening to Lytton in full spate. Drinks have been served and the sun is setting over the Downs.

LYTTON Anyway, I was about to speak to this black-haired tart in gumboots, when I suddenly noticed a much prettier tart, blond, in the gallery next door. So I abandoned the gumboots and began to sidle up to the blond, very fetching he was, pink and chubby. I was about to murmur something seductive into his delicious ear when suddenly the light fell on him and I realised who he was. (*He leans forward, stage whisper.*) The Prince of Wales!

General laughter. Then, completely unexpectedly, Lytton vomits. Carrington hurries over to him, concerned, and begins mopping up.

Oh, my God, I'm most terribly sorry.

INT. DINING ROOM AT HAM SPRAY. DAY

Carrington and Partridge sit at the kitchen table. Partridge is staring morosely at a piece of untouched toast and marmalade. Carrington speaks with a strange brittle cheerfulness.

CARRINGTON Oh, come on, Ralph, don't be so gloomy. There's nothing to worry about.

Partridge looks up at her, startled.

INT. LYTTON'S BEDROOM AT HAM SPRAY. EVENING

Lytton's bedroom is magnificently appointed, notably with a gold

Boris Anrep mosaic of a reclining hermaphrodite over the fireplace and Giotto angels on a wall painted Giotto blue by Carrington. A uniformed Nurse, grey-haired, bespectacled and forbidding, sits near the window, knitting in the half-light. Carrington pours cologne on to a damp handkerchief and dabs it on Lytton's forehead. He smiles feebly at her.

INT. DINING ROOM AT HAM SPRAY. EVENING

Carrington, Brenan and Partridge are sitting in silence, sipping soup. At the head of the table is Lytton's empty chair. Carrington raises her spoon towards her mouth, but can't quite bring herself to eat.

INT. LYTTON'S BEDROOM AT HAM SPRAY. EVENING

Carrington comes into Lytton's dark bedroom, leading Brenan by the hand. Partridge brings up the rear. They stand by Lytton's bedside. He's looking perceptibly thinner and weaker. He smiles at them.

LYTTON Well, my dears, shall we go to Malaga in the spring?

EXT. HAM SPRAY HOUSE. DAY

The camera tracks through the laurel hedge. The lawns are white with frost. Cloudless sky.

INT. LYTTON'S BEDROOM AT HAM SPRAY. DAY

Lytton lies in bed. He opens his eyes and looks over at Carrington, who is standing, looking out of the window.

LYTTON Carrington. Where's Carrington?

Carrington turns, surprised.

CARRINGTON I'm here.

LYTTON Why isn't she here? I want her.

Carrington hurries to the bedside and takes his hand.

CARRINGTON Here I am.

LYTTON Where is she? I love her. I always wanted to marry Carrington and I never did.

He sinks back, exhausted. Carrington stands holding his hand for a long moment.

The door opens. The nurse comes in. Carrington lets go of Lytton's hand and hurries across to her, speaks in an urgent whisper.

CARRINGTON Is there any chance he'll live?

The nurse looks at her, momentarily surprised. Then she answers, not unkindly.

NURSE Oh, no, I don't think so. Not now.

EXT. COURTYARD OF HAM SPRAY. NIGHT

Moonlight. Carrington creeps out of the back door and across the courtyard, her breath rising in the cold night air. She passes the stable door, where Belle's white head is visible, and presses on the garage door. At first she can't get it open. She tugs at it with increasing desperation.

INT. LYTTON'S BEDROOM AT HAM SPRAY. NIGHT

Lytton suddenly jerks convulsively and gasps for breath. Partridge, who's been sitting with him, is on his feet immediately and the nurse, who has been dozing, comes to. She hurries over to Lytton. Partridge stands a second, then leaves the room, moving quickly.

INT. UPSTAIRS CORRIDOR AT HAM SPRAY. NIGHT

Partridge runs along the corridor, opens the door of Carrington's bedroom.

INT. CARRINGTON'S BEDROOM AT HAM SPRAY. NIGHT

Partridge switches the light on. Carrington's room is empty. Partridge frowns, puzzled. Then a terrible thought strikes him.

EXT. COURTYARD OF HAM SPRAY. NIGHT

Partridge dashes across the courtyard, grapples desperately with the garage door and wrenches it open.

INT. GARAGE. NIGHT

The interior of the car, a green 1928 Sunbeam, is an island of light. Partridge, coughing and spluttering, rushes to the car door, opens it, reaches in and turns off the ignition. Then he leans across the back seat, grabs hold of Carrington and tugs at her body. She's unconscious. He struggles to get her out of the car, tears streaming down his face.

INT. CARRINGTON'S BEDROOM AT HAM SPRAY. DAY

Carrington grapples fiercely with Partridge, who's holding her down on the bed, so that the doctor, Dr Starkey Smith, who's hovering in the background, can administer an injection. Carrington is screaming at them.

CARRINGTON No! No! Go away! Go away!

STARKEY SMITH Now, Mrs Partridge . . .

CARRINGTON Go away!

He succeeds in giving the injection. Carrington goes limp and Partridge gathers her up in his arms and kisses her feverishly. He looks shattered.

PARTRIDGE How could you do it?

INT. LYTTON'S BEDROOM AT HAM SPRAY. DAY

Carrington, deathly pale and unsteady on her feet, Partridge and the nurse stand in a semi-circle at the foot of the bed.

After a while, Lytton speaks, scarcely more than a whisper, but clearly audible.

LYTTON If this is dying, then I don't think much of it.

Hint of a smile. He is so pale as to be almost transparent.

Partridge's face is contorted with an almost unbearable strain.

Carrington looks greenish, desperate.

They wait. Gradually, Lytton stops breathing. Long silence. Then the Nurse steps forward, puts her hand on his heart, waits and shakes her head. She moves away. The others stand in shocked silence. Then, Carrington moves forward. She touches Lytton's forehead, then recoils, drawing her hand away involuntarily.

CARRINGTON You're so cold.

Partridge lowers his head.

Fade.

INT. SITTING ROOM OF GERTLER'S FLAT AT 22 KEMPLAY ROAD. DAY

Gertler, now forty, still youthful, but with the watchful expression of a man long used to suffering, is opening a parcel. With him is his wife, Marjorie, a rather beautiful woman of thirty.

GERTLER It's a wedding present. From Carrington.

He's unwrapped three plates of her design. Marjorie smiles.

MARJORIE Only two years late, do you suppose that's a record?

But Gertler is disturbed. He turns over one of the plates, considering.

GERTLER Strange.

EXT. TERRACE AT GARSINGTON. DAY

Ottoline, fifty-eight now, battered but still grandiose, a chiffon scarf wound around her neck, her make-up as strikingly erratic as ever, is sorting through her morning mail. One letter in particular strikes her attention. She opens it and a number of sepia photographs spill out on the table.

CARRINGTON (*voice over*) Dear Ottoline, It is to you I owe the happiness, probably, of my life with Lytton. I thank you for those days at Garsington when I grew to love him. Yours, Carrington.

Ottoline stops looking through the photographs, lays them aside and looks away, moved.

EXT. GARDEN OF HAM SPRAY. DAY

Carrington is planting bulbs under the trees.

INT. DRAWING ROOM AT HAM SPRAY. DAY

Partridge stands at the window, looking anxiously out at Carrington. Frances joins him.

FRANCES What's she doing?

PARTRIDGE Planting bulbs.

FRANCES Well, that's surely a good sign, isn't it?

PARTRIDGE Yes. Yes, it is.

INT./EXT. DINING ROOM AT HAM SPRAY. DAY

Carrington stands at the window; behind her Partridge and Frances eat lunch in silence.

Carrington's point of view: a couple of rabbits are jumping about on the lawn.

EXT. FRONT DRIVE OF HAM SPRAY. DAY

Carrington drives the Sunbeam up to the front of the house and pulls up.

Partridge can be seen at the window, on the telephone. Now, he replaces the receiver and comes hurrying out of the house.

Carrington gets out of the car, awkwardly. She's carrying a double-barrelled shotgun. Partridge intercepts her and she straightens up to face him, her expression defiant.

PARTRIDGE What the hell are you doing with that?

CARRINGTON I borrowed it from Bryan. It's for the rabbits.

PARTRIDGE Now, look here . . .

Carrington disappears into the house, calling back to him.

CARRINGTON It's for the rabbits!

INT. DRAWING ROOM AT HAM SPRAY. EVENING

Carrington and Partridge. He looks ragged with exhaustion: she, calm, almost serene.

CARRINGTON Look Ralph, it's no good going on like this.

PARTRIDGE I can't leave you!

CARRINGTON You know perfectly well I'm going to France next week, it's all arranged, the tickets are bought . . .

PARTRIDGE Yes, I know . . .

CARRINGTON And now, I want to be on my own for a bit, that's all. I can't stand the strain of worrying about you worrying about me.

PARTRIDGE Listen . . .

CARRINGTON I must be on my own.

EXT. FRONT DRIVE OF HAM SPRAY HOUSE. DAY

Carrington kisses Frances, who gets into the passenger seat of the Sunbeam. Then, Carrington and Partridge stand for a moment looking at each other.

CARRINGTON Don't worry. I'll be all right.

PARTRIDGE Yes.

He puts his arms round her and she lets him kiss her. Then, just as he's about to break away, she kisses him quite fiercely.

CARRINGTON I want you to be very happy.

She lets him go. He stands there a moment, shocked by the implications of what she's just said, his face racked by contradictory emotions. Then, abruptly, he breaks away, gets into the car, starts it up and drives away. Frances waves; Partridge doesn't look back. Carrington stands, a hand raised in farewell, caught in suddenly emerging sunlight, beatific. On sound, the Schubert Quintet.

EXT. COURTYARD OF HAM SPRAY. DAY

A ferocious clatter, as Carrington empties her tubes of paint and brushes into the metal dustbin.

EXT. GARDEN OF HAM SPRAY. DAY

Carrington stands by a blazing bonfire, a pile Of Lytton's old clothes beside her, which she feeds one by one into the fire. Finally, glinting at the bottom of the pile, are his spectacles. She picks them up, holds them for the briefest moment and then throws them in the fire. The frames curl and buckle in the heat.

CARRINGTON (*voice over*) No one will ever know the utter happiness of our life together.

INT. DRAWING ROOM AT HAM SPRAY. EVENING

Carrington is lying motionless on the sofa. Draped across her body is one of Lytton's tweed jackets and spread out on her face, covering it, is one of his initialled handkerchiefs.

CARRINGTON (*voice over*) It is impossible to think that every day of my life you will be away.

INT. LYTTON'S STUDY. EVENING

Pan slowly round the bookshelves and along one shelf of Lytton's books, all beautifully bound in a uniform edition. Finally the camera reaches Carrington. She is sitting on the floor in a corner of the darkening room, arms wrapped round her knees, holding Lytton's binoculars, staring into space, eyes dead.

CARRINGTON (*voice over*) I write in an empty book. I cry in an empty room.

INT. LYTTON'S BEDROOM AT HAM SPRAY. NIGHT

Carrington opens Lytton's wardrobe. It's now empty except for his purple silk dressing gown. She slips it off the hanger and strokes her cheek against it.

CARRINGTON Oh, my very darling Lytton.

INT. CARRINGTON'S BEDROOM AT HAM SPRAY. DAWN

Carrington wakes. It's still almost dark. The purple dressing gown is lying across the foot of the bed. She gets out of bed and puts the dressing gown on.

INT. DINING ROOM AT HAM SPRAY. DAWN

Carrington has eaten an apple.

She puts down The Times *for 11 March next to two or three opened letters, neatly stacked. She takes a sip from a half-empty mug of tea, puts it down and rises, calm and decisive, to her feet. She leaves the room.*

INT. HALLWAY AND STAIRCASE. DAWN

The camera follows Carrington across the hallway, up the stairs and back along the upstairs landing.

INT. CARRINGTON'S BEDROOM. DAWN

Carrington walks into the room, moves to the wardrobe, reaches in and brings out the shotgun.

She pushes the wardrobe shut and crosses to the cheval mirror, standing on Brenan's rug.

She puts the butt of the gun against the floor, tucks the barrel in under her heart and checks her position in the mirror.

Then, she leans forward, closes her eyes and pulls the trigger.

Nothing.

She opens her eyes and lifts the gun. A moment, before she realises. She has forgotten to release the safety catch.

She does so, puts the gun back in position. Long silence. She looks in the mirror. She smiles. She closes her eyes and slowly bows forward over the shotgun.

EXT. HAM SPRAY HOUSE. DAWN

The camera tracks through the doorway in the laurel hedge and stops, as the second movement of the Schubert Quintet comes to an end. The house. Five seconds. Explosion. Darkness.

Mary Reilly

CAST AND CREDITS

MARY REILLY	Julia Roberts
DR JEKYLL/MR HYDE	John Malkovich
MR POOLE	George Cole
MARY'S FOTHER	Michael Gambon
MRS KENT	Kathy Staff
MRS FARRADAY	Glenn Close
BRADSHAW	Michael Sheen
ANNIE	Bronagh Gallagher
MARY'S MOTHER	Linda Bassett
HAFFINGER	Henry Goodman
SIR DANVERS CAREW	Ciaran Hinds
YOUNG MARY	Sasha Hanau
YOUNG WOMAN	Moya Brady
YOUNG WHORE	Emma Griffiths Malin
DOCTOR	David Ross
VICAR	Tim Barlow
SCREAMING GIRL	Isabella Marsh
SCREAMING GIRL'S MOTHER	Wendy Nottingham
SCREAMING GIRL'S FATHER	Richard Leaf
INSPECTOR	Stephen Boxer
POLICEMAN	Bob Mason

Director	Stephen Frears
Screenplay by	Christopher Hampton
Baded on the Novel by	Valerie Martin
Producers	NedTanen
	Nancy Graham Tanen
	Norma Heyman
Co-Producer	Iain Smith
Executive Producer	Lynn Pleshette
Director of Photography	Philippe Rousselot, ASC
Production Designer	Stuart Craig
Editor	Lesley Walker
Costume Design by	Consolata Boyle
Musis	George Fenton
Casting	Leo Davis, Juliet Taylor

EXT. RIVER THAMES. DAWN

In the grey pre-dawn light, the camera moves, fast and low, following the curves of the river, not more than a few inches above its turbid, brownish surface, under bridges, past moored boats, unstable pontoons and long, blackened coal barges on their way downstream. The year is 1886.

After a while the camera stops, abruptly, and turns ninety degrees to contemplate a large, plain Georgian house set on a corner, four windows and a door with a fanlight on the ground floor, five sash windows on the two upper stories and three dormer windows just visible at roof level. Beside the house, a steep side road moves upwards, between a row of more sombre Georgian houses on one side and a row of discreetly prosperous shops on the other. The road is spanned by a kind of Bridge of Sighs with leaded windows, which forms (as will become apparent) part of the property. In front of the house is a paved area fringed by flower beds, enclosed by railings and a wrought iron gate, a tow path, a wall interrupted by a watergate and a landing stage. The house, which in its classic simplicity of design somewhat resembles a child's drawing, is flanked by much more modest, run-down, higgledy-piggledy buildings, red-brick, opposed to the warm brown bricks of the house. These buildings separate the house from the corner of another side road which leads down to the towpath; down this side-road a hansom cab is slowly approaching. One further detail: a uniformed under-housemaid is on her knees in front of the house, scrubbing the front steps.

The cab comes to a halt at the end of the side road and a gentleman descends and pays. He's in full evening dress, with an opera cloak, a top hat and a silver-knobbed ebony cane. He moves down to the river wall. As the cab turns and pulls away, he stands for a moment, looking out across the river.

As he turns and begins to approach the house, the camera begins, very slowly this time, to travel towards him. The maid, unaware of his approach, continues to scrub. The camera, as it moves closer to the river's edge, where the retreating tide has left an irregular deposit of jetsam, observes a significant number of well-fed rats fossicking through the garbage, then passes on, across the tow-path, to join the gentleman as he moves lightly through the gate and up the front path. The maid, absorbed in her task, has not heard him, and, as she is blocking the doorway, he comes to a halt behind her, looking down at her. He's a silver-haired, distinguished-looking man of about fifty; while she, once we are able to see her properly, turns out to be a surprisingly ethereal pre-Raphaelite beauty of twenty-two: Mary Reilly.

Mary finishes scrubbing, rises to her knees and puts the brush in the pail of dirty water, still unaware of the man, who waits patiently above and behind her. Eventually, he speaks, his voice soft and attractive.

MAN Mary.

Mary, who has been dreaming for a moment, comes to with such a start, she almost overturns the bucket. She looks up at him, blushing in confusion.

MAN It's all right, I'm not going to bite you.

MARY I'm sorry, sir, it's just you gave me a fright.

MAN Then I'm sorry. You're up very early.

MARY I'm generally up by five, sir, otherwise I get behind.

The man nods, digesting this; Mary moves her donkey-stone and bucket aside to give him free access to the front door, which is slightly ajar.

MAN Tell Poole to bring me some luncheon at one o'clock. I don't want to be disturbed before then, I need to sleep.

MARY Very good, sir.

The man's shoes, which make an incongruous contrast to his evening clothes, are thick with mud; he uses the boot-scraper to take some of it off.

MAN Takes it out of me, a night on the tiles, I suppose I must be getting old.

MARY I wouldn't say so, sir.

MAN When I was your age, I could stay up all night and suffer no ill effects whatever. Ah, well.

He sweeps on into the house. When he's gone, Mary reaches across for the boot-scraper, takes the thick, wet mud off with her hands and drops it into the water in the bucket. She rinses her hands in the dirty water, dries them on her pinafore, picks up the wooden pail and empties it into one of the flower beds. Then she cleans out the bucket with a little water from a jug and pours some more water into it. She takes out of her wooden housemaid's box a stoppered glass vessel marked with a skull and crossbones, containing oxalic acid, a little of which she pours into the water. She replaces the stopper carefully, then reaches for a piece of flannel, which she gingerly dips into the mixture she's prepared. Then she applies the piece of flannel to a square brass plaque and begins to rub. The plaque reads as follows:

DR HENRY JEKYLL
M.A., D.C.L., LL.D., F.R.S.

EXT. COURTYARD. DAY

The back of the house, by contrast to the front, is surprisingly irregular. A rounded wall incorporates a pair of tall bay windows, one above the other, the upper containing some panels of stained glass. There are buildings on two sides of the rather cheerless courtyard: various domestic offices leading from the house (sculleries, larders, coal stores, laundry rooms etc.) while at right angles to these, at the far end of the courtyard, is a self-contained block, where a dark door is set into a blank, windowless, high wall, a door which leads to an old operating theatre and Dr Jekyll's laboratory beyond.

The camera approaches a window in the servants' block.

INT. BOOT ROOM. DAY

Through the window: Bradshaw, the footman, a sprightly-looking, slight twenty-five-year-old, is vigorously cleaning one of Jekyll's shoes, polishing the sole under the instep. Behind him rears a huge boot stand, which supports dozens of pairs of shoes and a row of tall boots, standing at attention.

Mary is also in the plain, whitewashed room, her back to Bradshaw, engaged in some task; and as the camera closes up to the window, we can see what it is: she's ironing the shoelaces with a heavy flat-iron. She finishes one and hands it to Bradshaw, who takes it without comment and begins to thread it into the shoe he's just finished cleaning.

INT. DRAWING ROOM. DAY

The drawing room is a long room which runs the whole width of the house and looks out on to the river. Mary, on her knees, finishes emptying the ash from one of the two coal fires into the cinder sifter, which rocks on its base and retains reusable fragments of coal on a grille. Then she turns to begin the gruelling task of blackleading the grate. She dips the heavy-bristled brush into the blacklead mixture and begins applying it to the still hot, elaborately ornate fireplace. Close on her hands as she scrubs: she's been doing other fires and her arms are black to the elbows so that a network of fine scars on her hands and wrists are thrown into relief.

INT. KITCHEN. DAY

The kitchen is a large room full of pinewood – tables, shelves and a dresser and a huge cast-iron range (a 'kitchener') with two ovens and a high-pressure boiler. Mrs Kent, the cook, a stoutish, red-faced party, with wisps of hair escaping anarchically from under her bonnet, is standing opposite Mary. Each of them holds a flat-ended wooden spoon in her right hand and one end of a kind of woollen hammock full of vegetable matter in her left hand. They are engaged in tammying the soup, which is to say they are grinding the cooked vegetables with the spoons until the juice strains through the cloth into the soup dish below. This is in fact a ferociously demanding task, their arms move like pistons in a rhythmic exchange, backwards and forwards, and their foreheads are beaded with sweat. They grind on, silent and concentrating.

INT. HALL. DAY

Poole, the butler, a dauntingly formal figure, a man in his fifties with the demeanour of a senior diplomat, waits at the foot of a broad staircase in the entrance hall, a comfortable room with polished flagstones, an open fire and a number of imposing oak cabinets. Presently, Mary appears from the back of the house with Dr Jekyll's lunch, several dishes concealed under silver lids and a decanter of claret on a large tray with lowerable sides; she hands the tray to Poole, who accepts it without comment and sets off up the stairs.

INT. LIBRARY. DAY

The library is the upper room with panels of stained glass in its bay window.

Mary has paused in her task of dusting the desk in the window to look at some of the books piled up there. She moves aside a German text, Mendel's Versuche über Pflanzenhybriden, *and picks up the book underneath. It's by Darwin and it's called* The Descent of Man and Selection in Relation to Sex.
She begins to leaf through it and pauses on a page with a number of elaborate line-drawings of the heads of chameleons. Then she turns back to a chapter headed 'Descent of Man from some Lower Form' and begins to read.
Another angle reveals that, unbeknownst to her, Dr Jekyll is standing in the doorway looking at her. After a while, he half-smiles, turns away and quickly carries on down the stairs. Mary reads on, still unaware she's been observed.

INT. JEKYLL'S BEDROOM. DAY
The windows are open, the heavy wine-coloured curtains are drawn back, the fire is burning and the bed is stripped; it's a big, heavy bed with a headboard elaborately carved with fruit and flowers and a plain oak footboard balanced on cameleopard feet. Mary has finished folding the sheets, now she empties Jekyll's washbasin and his chamber pot into a slops bucket and rinses them out with a little hot water from a heavy jug.

EXT. COURTYARD. DAY
It's late afternoon and the light is beginning to fail. Mary, seen through the window, her arms full of linen, moves from one laundry room to another.

INT. LAUNDRY ROOM. DAY
Mary puts the linen (which has been washed) down on a table and turns to the one piece of furniture which dominates the small room: a giant cast-iron mangle. She takes a sheet from the top of the pile, adjusts the tin tub below, introduces the sheets between the rollers and begins, with great effort, to turn the handle to crank the sheet through. When it's passed through, she reaches for the next item, a handkerchief, with the initials HJ stitched in blue.

INT. KITCHEN. EVENING

Mary and the kitchenmaid, Annie, a pasty, exhausted-looking girl of about sixteen, struggle across the kitchen with a huge stockpot, boiling and bubbling, straight off the range. The kitchen is a regular inferno now, in the run-up to dinner. Mrs Kent is attending to the joint of beef suspended in the centre of the open meat-hastener, in front of the open fire. The meat hangs from a rotating bottle jack which clicks and chatters as it's turned by its clockwork mechanism, now being rewound by Mrs Kent. She turns to shout above the noise.

MRS KENT Mary, you'll find an eel in the fish pantry. Fetch it in for me, will you?

Mary hands the dishcloth she's been using to protect her hands to Annie and heads for the door.

INT. CORRIDOR. EVENING

In the half-light of dusk, Mary moves down the corridor of the servants' wing, passing the doorways of a series of increasingly small whitewashed rooms; the larder, full of barrels and glass jars of preserves; the meat larder where whole hams and half a lamb's carcass hang from hooks; the game larder, where hens and pheasant dangle upside down; and finally the fish pantry, much the smallest room, into which Mary turns.

INT. FISH PANTRY. EVENING

The fish are laid out on blocks of ice on draining boards: a pair of speckled rainbow trout, an enormous, yellowish carbuncled turbot, and, in the corner, dark against the ice, the serpentine shape of the eel. Mary approaches and picks it up firmly in both hands. It's about three feet long.

INT. CORRIDOR. EVENING

Close on the eel's head as Mary carries it down the gloomy corridor. Its eye suddenly flutters.

Mary gasps in shock as the eel begins to wriggle and thrash in her hands. She grips it tight and hurries on.

INT. KITCHEN. EVENING

Mary comes in still grappling with the eel. Annie draws back, but Mrs Kent seems quite unperturbed.

MARY It's alive.

MRS KENT Warmth of your hands, that'll be: revived him.

She indicates a deal table in front of her, rubbed down with a little flour.

Put him here.

Mary does so. Mrs Kent, meanwhile, is rummaging through a drawer at the end of the table.

Difficult buggers to kill is eels. Keep a hold of his tail.

And so saying, she takes a long spike out of the drawer, holds the eel's head down with her other hand and drives the spike through its neck, pinning it to the table. Then, she fetches out a sharp kitchen knife and delicately slices through the skin in a ring just below the spike. Mary hangs grimly on to the lashing tail. Mrs Kent puts down the knife, turns, leans in, inserts her fingers between skin and flesh and pulls with all her might. At the third or fourth attempt the whole skin peels off like a glove. Moving fast now, Mrs Kent picks up the knife, cuts off the head and chops the body into chunks approximately six inches long. Mary has let go the tail and now steps back, extremely shaken. Mrs Kent glances at her.

What's the matter with you?

MARY I'm all right.

MRS KENT You're as white as a sheet.

MARY I'm sorry.

MRS KENT Well, fetch me that big saucepan off the range.

Mary hurries to do as she's told. She picks up the saucepan and starts off back with it. She gets halfway and then stops in her tracks.

On the table, each chunk of eel still quivers with independent life. Mrs Kent pulls out the spike and throws away the head, ignoring the twitchings of the flayed sections.

Mary still hesitates, deathly pale.

INT. HALL. EVENING

The gas lamps are burning now as Mary emerges, backwards, through the green baize door at the top of the basement stairs. She's carrying a tray of food. She crosses the hall and hands the tray to Bradshaw, stationed at the dining-room door.

INT. DINING ROOM. EVENING

Mary's point of view through the door gives a glimpse of the dining room. Bradshaw makes his way towards the sideboard where Poole waits, impeccable in tails and white gloves. Dr Jekyll, dressed for dinner, sits at the end of a long, polished table, surrounded by silver candlesticks, crisp napery, dazzling crystal, cutlery, fruit bowls, épergnes, a book propped open in front of him on a silver stand. The great bay window behind him overlooks the courtyard.

INT. HALL. EVENING

Mary turns to make her way back towards the green baize door.

INT. FRONT PARLOUR. NIGHT

Dr Jekyll stands at a lectern in the formal front room conducting evening prayers. The servants, Mary, Annie, Mrs Kent, Poole and Bradshaw, are all present, kneeling in front of their upright chairs, resting their elbows on the seats and burying their faces in their hands.

ALL . . . and lead us not into temptation, but deliver us from evil. For thine is the kingdom, the power and the glory, for ever and ever. Amen.

Dr Jekyll opens his eyes and looks up.

JEKYLL Good night to you.

SERVANTS Good night, sir.

They rise to their feet and begin to file out. Mary catches Dr Jekyll's eye. He half-smiles at her. She blushes and turns away, shuffling with the others towards the door which leads out into the hall.

INT. MARY'S BEDROOM. NIGHT

Mary shares an attic room with Annie, sleeping with her in a rudimentary double bed tucked in under the steep angle of the roof. There's a plain candle in a saucer by the bed and moonlight streams in the uncurtained window. Annie is already in bed and Mary, in her nightgown, is drying herself after using the heavy china washbasin. This done, she folds the towel and climbs into bed.

MARY Shall I leave the candle awhile or do you want to sleep?

ANNIE I always want to sleep. I can't understand why it should take so much effort to look after one man.

MARY I don't mind hard work.

ANNIE Well, I do.

MARY I've been in service since I was twelve and this is by far the best place I've had. He's a kind man, the doctor, anyone can see that.

ANNIE If he was that kind, he'd let me sleep in till six.

Mary smiles at her.

MARY Goodnight, then.

She reaches over to pinch out the candle, once more revealing the network of scars on her wrist and hand.

The room is now lit only by the window. Mary settles alongside Annie but she's clearly not yet ready for sleep.

I feel safer here is all.

Her eyes glitter in the darkness.

INT. KITCHEN. NIGHT

The kitchen is deserted. The gas lights flicker, and there's a glow from the fire. Everything has been tidied away. The room looks oddly distorted, larger than before. And on the deal side table the chunks of eel-flesh wriggle in involuntary spasm. Over this, two curious sounds: first, footsteps, one foot dragging a little to make an easily recognisable dissonance. Then, after a while, as the camera moves slowly in towards the twitching lengths of eel, a strange scrabbling and squeaking.

INT. MARY'S BEDROOM. NIGHT

Mary wakes with a start and sits up as straight as the ceiling angle allows. Annie breathes with heavy regularity. Mary listens, her face white above her white nightdress. Is there a light, irregular footstep on the wooden staircase outside the room? If so, it disappears almost at once. Mary continues to listen, frowning with concentration. Fade.

INT. DRAWING ROOM. DAY

Grey day. Dr Jekyll sits in his deep leather armchair, a scientific journal open on his lap. But he's not reading: he's staring, quite fixedly, across the room.

His point of view: Mary is on her knees in the fireplace, her back to him. She's finished blacking the grate and is now picking lumps of coal from the scuttle to complete her setting of the fire.

Eventually, Jekyll speaks, startling her. She turns to look up at him.

JEKYLL I never imagined you would be able to read, Mary.

MARY Oh yes, sir, Mrs Smith, the housekeeper at my last position, she learned me, sir.

JEKYLL So you weren't just looking at the illustrations?

MARY I'm sorry, sir, I know I should have been working, I didn't mean to displease you.

JEKYLL I'm not in the least displeased. On the contrary, you're very welcome to borrow any book in the library that takes your fancy.

INT. STAIRCASE. DAY

Outside the room, Poole, hearing the sound of voices, pauses on the staircase, frowns and continues on his way.

INT. DRAWING ROOM. DAY

MARY Well . . . thank you, sir: I wouldn't want the others to think I was getting above myself.

JEKYLL I'm sure they wouldn't think anything of the kind.

In the ensuing pause, Mary rises to her feet, picks up her housemaid's box and sets off towards the door.

JEKYLL Just a moment.

Mary, stops where she is, apprehensive.

Scars, Mary; I notice you have some quite deep scars on your wrists and hands.

MARY I do, sir.

JEKYLL Would you mind if I examined them?

MARY Now, sir?

She stands, plainly reluctant, still holding the box.

JEKYLL Not if you would find it an imposition.

MARY It's not that, sir, it's I don't like to come close, my arms is black as your hat and it do travel.

Jekyll smiles: he contemplates her thoughtfully for a moment.

And there is another thing.

JEKYLL What's that?

MARY I don't want to keep Mr Poole waiting, he has his eye on me today.

JEKYLL You think he might object to your following my instructions?

MARY He wouldn't do that, sir, but he likes to tell me what you want and he's not so fond of the other way about.

Jekyll nods, acknowledging the logic of this.

JEKYLL Well then, how's this? Poole is going round to the chemist's this afternoon to fetch some prescriptions for me. Couldn't you perhaps bring me my tea in the library?

MARY I don't see why not, sir.

JEKYLL Good.

She's about to set off again, but Jekyll springs to his feet and crosses to her.

There are some on your neck as well.

Below her right ear are four symmetrical small scars. Jekyll reaches out to touch them and, as he does so, the blood rushes to Mary's face.

They look almost like . . . teeth marks; the bites of some animal.

MARY That's, yes . . . that's what they are, sir.

Jekyll frowns, perplexed. Mary holds his gaze for a moment, then starts to move off; and, this time, Dr Jekyll lets her go, watching her all the way out of the room.

INT. SERVANTS' HALL. DAY

Mary enters the dark room, where Poole and the other servants are eating their breakfast at a long, scrubbed pine table.

POOLE You were in the drawing room with the Master some considerable time, Mary. I hope you haven't been making a nuisance of yourself.

MARY No, sir.

POOLE What were you saying to him?

Conversation has stopped; needless to say, the others are all riveted by this question. Mary makes her way rather shakily to sit next to Annie on the wooden bench: she knows she's going to have to say something.

MARY We talked about doing something with the garden.

POOLE The garden?

MARY It's that gloomy out there, I thought we could plant out a flower bed or two.

POOLE Who's going to do all that?

MARY I would. I don't mind.

POOLE Aren't we finding enough work for you?

MARY I could do it on my afternoons off.

Poole grunts sceptically; he seems displeased, but for the moment is unable to devise any further objections.

MRS KENT My last place in the country –

POOLE I think we're familiar with your reminiscences, Mrs Kent.

Mrs Kent ignores him, surging unstoppably on.

MRS KENT – the Master used to send for one of the housemaids every morning at nine, regular as clockwork. In the end, of course, she fell in the family way and was dismissed without a reference. I often wonder what become of her.

BRADSHAW I expect now she entertains gentlemen all hours of the day . . .

POOLE Bradshaw!

BRADSHAW Yes, Mr Poole?

POOLE Save your breath to cool your porridge.

BRADSHAW Yes, Mr Poole.

But he doesn't look particularly repentant; and Annie is having the greatest difficulty suppressing a fit of the giggles.

INT. LIBRARY. DAY

The loaded tea tray is on Jekyll's desk; but he is leading Mary by the hand towards a small table where an oil lamp burns. It's already almost dark outside. Jekyll begins to examine Mary's hands. The right hand is more scarred than the left, the white tracks and indentations spread across her palm and down to her wrist; and Jekyll focuses on this, moving her thumb gently back and forth.

JEKYLL These go very deep. Did they never affect the use of your fingers?

MARY I couldn't move my thumb for a while, but in the end, gradually, you know, it came back to working.

JEKYLL Does it still cause you any pain?

MARY Gives me a bit of gyp when the weather's damp, otherwise it's right as rain.

Jekyll goes on examining her hands, looking at them for longer than seems necessary: finally, he looks up at her, releasing her hands.

JEKYLL What did this?

MARY I can't rightly say as I saw it, sir, it were dark as sin in there.

JEKYLL In where?

MARY The little cupboard under the stairs.

JEKYLL And what were you doing in there?

MARY It were a punishment, sir.

Dr Jekyll's eyes gleam with a sudden spark of interest.

JEKYLL Why don't you sit down . . .?

MARY Oh no, I couldn't, sir.

JEKYLL Yes, do: and I will. I want you to tell me the whole story.

He settles himself at his desk and reaches for his cup of tea. Mary hesitates a little longer, then chooses a hard, straight-backed chair, perching on the very edge of the seat. She doesn't seem to know where to begin and, after a time, Jekyll prompts her gently.

Off you go.

EXT. SLUM COURTYARD. DAY

The low, dingy houses face each other across a narrow, cobbled strip with an open drain running down the middle. Tattered clothes and sheets hang on poles sticking out of upstairs windows. At the far end of the courtyard an entrance through to the next street admits a rectangle of light, grey but bright by comparison with the blackened plaster and slimy cobblestones. Rising above the distant, regular street noises are the sounds of blows and the whimpering of a child.

MARY (*voice over*) He took his belt off to us near enough every day.

JEKYLL (*voice over*) Who was that?

INT. SLUM HOUSE. DAY

The room which constitutes the ground floor of a tiny house. A table, two wooden chairs, a straw mattress in the corner, an empty fireplace. A red-faced, sweating, unshaven man in threadbare clothes is buckling back on a broad and dog-eared leather belt. A child of about ten, a girl in a shabby print dress, cowers on the floor, her body convulsed with sobs.

MARY (*voice over*) My dad.

The child looks up at him, she's making a great effort to control herself.

TEN-YEAR-OLD MARY I'm sorry, sir, really I am.

FATHER You will be. Yes. You will be.

He looks around the room, considering.

MARY (*voice over*) But on this particular day I done something really terrible. I dropped one of our cups. And it broke.

Mary's Father comes to a decision. He crosses to the child, reaches down to seize hold of one of her ears, pulls her up, takes her over to the stairs, unlocks the tiny cupboard under the stairs and pushes her in. It's so small, she can only fit with her knees drawn right up under her chin.

INT. CUPBOARD. DAY

The small triangle of light disappears and there's the sound of the key turning in the lock. The dim outline of the child is only just visible in the darkness.

MARY (*voice over*) So he locked me in the little cupboard under the stairs.

INT. SLUM HOUSE. DAY

Mary's Father crosses the room and places the key carefully near the edge of the table. Then he sits in one of the chairs and stares at the triangular cupboard door. Eventually, there's the smallest sound of a stifled sob.

MARY (*voice over*) But even that wasn't enough for him.

INT. LIBRARY. DAY

Mary looks up so that the light catches her eyes.

MARY He knew there was one thing frightened me more than anything else in the world.

INT. SLUM HOUSE. DAY

Mary's Father has been rummaging about in the corner. Now he finds what he's looking for and gives a grunt of satisfaction. It's a coarse hopsack bag with a drawstring top. He crams a battered top hat on his head and sets off towards the door.

INT. CUPBOARD. DAY

The child's body shifts uneasily at the sound of the house door slamming shut.

INT. LIBRARY. DAY

Close on Dr Jekyll; he's so fascinated, he's hardly daring to breathe.

MARY (*voice over*) So he went looking for it.

INT. CUPBOARD. DAY

The shape of the child, barely discernible in the darkness.

MARY (*voice over*) He was away some time.

The child stiffens at the sound of the front door. Various other sounds ensue: the clink of a bottle, the rattle of a drawer, the striking of a match.

MARY (*voice over*) He had a strange way of walking, not exactly a limp, but his footsteps . . . well, I always knew it was him, it was like every step was calling my name.

And now, again, the two sounds from Mary's dream: the light footsteps, one foot dragging behind the other; and a frantic squeaking and urgent scrabbling.

MARY'S FATHER (*voice over*) You still there?

TEN-YEAR OLD MARY Yes, Father.

The sound of the key in the lock: and a triangle of light appears, as the door to the cupboard swings open. Seen from Mary's point of view at a nightmarish angle, the image consists of a few terrifying elements: her Father's red, leering face, his hat, bent to one side, tilted; his giant shadow, thrown against the far wall in the flickering lamplight; and in his hand the hopsack bag, violently shuddering and twitching, uttering high-pitched squeaks.

FATHER I didn't want you getting lonely, so I found summat to keep you company.

TEN-YEAR-OLD MARY Don't.

He leans in and deposits the bag in her lap with exaggerated care. Then he closes the door and the key turns in the lock. The child whimpers as the bag in her lap begins to thrash and twist.

MARY (*voice over*) I knew what it was soon as he put it in with me.

INT. LIBRARY. DAY

Dr Jekyll is listening intently, the tip of his pink tongue peeping between his lips.

JEKYLL It was a rat.

MARY (*voice over*) You guessed it, sir.

She sits, perched rigidly on the edge of the chair.

He knew the way I felt about them. He knew I couldn't abide even the idea of them.

INT. SLUM HOUSE. EVENING

Mary's Father sits at the table, waiting.

MARY (*voice over*) And he knew, sooner or later, it was going to bite its way through that bag.

Suddenly, there's a terrible scream from inside the cupboard.

INT. CUPBOARD. EVENING

A frenzied impression of thrashing limbs and the darting, panic-stricken rodent. The child screams and screams.

INT. SLUM HOUSE. EVENING

Mary's Father pours gin into a cracked cup and sits back to drink it, his expression a picture of unruffled satisfaction, as the screaming continues.

INT. LIBRARY. DAY

Mary is silent for a moment, remembering. Then she goes on talking.

MARY My mum didn't get back from work till late.

INT. SLUM HOUSE. NIGHT

Mary's Father is asleep, his head on the table next to the empty gin bottle. He doesn't stir when the door opens and Mary's Mother appears. She's a thin, exhausted-looking woman. She's in her late twenties, but looks nearer fifty. She immediately senses something is wrong and her eye falls on the cupboard key. She picks it up and hurries to the cupboard. She unlocks the door. The second the door opens, the rat scurries out, vanishing into the shadows of the room: then the child, unconscious, tumbles out sideways. There's blood on her neck and her hands and her wrists are a bleeding mass of wounds.

MARY (*voice over*) When she saw what had happened, she took me away from there that very night.

Mary's Mother drags the child out and picks her up in her arms. There's blood on the child's ankles and shins as well. She rocks her to and fro, but the child doesn't regain consciousness.

INT. LIBRARY. DAY

The light is fading fast. Dr Jekyll sits in shadow, his eyes bright.

MARY Soon after that she put me into service; and I never seen him again from that day to this.

Long silence. Finally, Jekyll stirs. His voice is slightly thick with emotion.

JEKYLL Thank you for being so . . . candid with me, Mary. You may go.

Mary rises stiffly to her feet and curtsies.

MARY Very good, sir.

JEKYLL I shan't forget this.

INT. KITCHEN. NIGHT

Mary and Annie are finishing the day's last batch of washing-up. Mary washes and Annie dries.

MARY He's a solitary one, isn't he, the doctor?

ANNIE Year or two back he used to have dinner parties regular; then he just stopped.

MARY Shame.

ANNIE Oh, no, best thing that ever happened: think of the washing-up.

Mary smiles, hands her a milk saucepan to dry.

MARY And he's never had any sort of a lady friend?

ANNIE Never a woman stepped in the front door, not since I been here.

MARY Strange.

ANNIE Bradshaw says he goes to houses.

MARY What do you mean?

ANNIE You know . . . houses.

MARY No.

She thinks about it for a moment.

No, I can't believe that.

INT. JEKYLL'S BEDROOM. DAY

Dr Jekyll is in bed and Mary advances across the darkened room with his breakfast on a tray. He looks pale and preoccupied.

MARY Good morning, sir.

He watches her as she settles the tray across his knees.

JEKYLL I've been thinking a great deal about that story you told me yesterday, Mary.

Mary pulls back one of the heavy curtains and a pale shaft of light tumbles into the room.

Your father, you must really have hated him.

MARY I don't know, sir . . .

JEKYLL But he was a monster.

MARY When I was little and he was in work down at the docks, he wasn't so bad then. It was the drink that did it.

JEKYLL You think it was only the drink?

He's asked the question with such quiet intensity that Mary gives it her most serious attention.

MARY You can't never tell with drink. It makes some people loud and cheerful and others just want a fight. But my dad, what he liked, was to see us suffer; he took his pleasure in hurting; the drink turned him into a different man.

JEKYLL A different man?

MARY Yes, he even looked different. It was like he carried this beast inside him and the drinking brought it out.

JEKYLL Or maybe . . . set it free.

He's spoken very softly, almost sorrowfully and so strangely that Mary is completely at a loss as to how to react. His eyes slide away from her; and she curtsies hurriedly and goes to slip out of the room.

EXT. COURTYARD. DAY

A strange, reflected, moving and jolting image of part of the courtyard, accompanied by sighs and grunts of effort, into which the uniformed mid-section of Mary presently appears. Another angle shows the image to be a reflection in a large cheval mirror which Poole and Bradshaw are struggling to carry across the yard, as Mary bobs alongside them. Now they reach the door in the blank wall of the operating theatre and pause.

POOLE It's here in my left-hand pocket, Mary.

Mary reaches into Poole's jacket and produces a large key. She hurries to the door, inserts the key and fumbles ineffectually with it.

Come along, hurry up, this weighs a ton.

MARY It's a bit stiff, sir. I haven't used it before.

The door yields, Mary heaves it open and the building swallows up her, the men and the mirror.

INT. OPERATING THEATRE. DAY

The room, lit by huge skylights, is dominated by the grim, oversize operating and dissecting table, bolted to the floor, still furnished with frayed leather straps and restrainers, centred so as to be visible from all the seats, which rise in three rows behind desktops as in a lecture room. There's a stale, unused feel about the room, the window panes are murky. There are cabinets in corners and half-empty crates of equipment and chemical supplies litter the recesses. The men's footsteps resound on the grimy flagstones. At the far end is a staircase leading up to a red baize door. Poole jerks his head in its general direction.

POOLE Key's hanging up by the door.

Mary hurries ahead of them across the room and up the stairs. She unhooks the key and unlocks the red baize door.

INT. LABORATORY. DAY

The room Mary lets herself into is clearly divided into two sections: a cosy, domestic section with an armchair drawn up to the fireplace, a kettle on the hob, a large rug, a tea table and bookshelves floor to ceiling; and, at the other end, the laboratory itself, three tall windows behind a window seat, letting the light in on a huge architect's table, covered with tubes and retorts, mortars, pestles, scalpels, sets of scales and all manner of strange instruments. Against the wall, at right angles to the table, are three tall glass presses, each of the many drawers carefully labelled, standing on the bare flagstones.

Mary stands, wondering at all this, as Poole and Bradshaw come puffing into the room. They set up the cheval mirror in the domestic end of the room, looking across at an angle to the laboratory table. Poole tests the mirror, checking its ability to swivel on its hinge.

BRADSHAW Wonder what he wants this for, eh?

POOLE Ours not to reason why.

Mary is staring dreamily across at the mirror.

Wake up, Mary. Holiday's over.

EXT. COURTYARD. DAY

Poole is about to lock the door to the operating theatre behind him, when he becomes aware of Dr Jekyll hurrying purposefully across the courtyard towards him. He pauses, waiting for Jekyll to arrive.

JEKYLL Mirror in place?

POOLE Just where you indicated, sir.

JEKYLL No dinner this evening, I don't think. Tell Mrs Kent, if you'd be so kind. Just leave a bowl of soup outside the door.

POOLE Very good, sir.

He hands Jekyll, who has reached him now, the two keys. Then he takes the opportunity to speak, an edge of malice in his voice.

Mary was telling us you'd been holding a discussion with her about the garden.

Mary suppresses a gasp, but can't prevent a blush: Jekyll, on the other hand, is almost instantly in control of his surprise.

JEKYLL Quite right. Remind me what conclusion we arrived at, Mary.

MARY Flower beds there and there, sir, and a herb garden over there by the wall.

JEKYLL The very thing. Just what we need. Splendid.

He pauses in the doorway of the operating theatre.

I feel very optimistic today. I think I may be on the verge of a great breakthrough. Wish me well.

And he succeeds in directing a wink towards Mary, before disappearing into the theatre.

INT. MARY'S BEDROOM. NIGHT

Mary lies asleep next to Annie: but suddenly, she wakes with a violent start, her eyes instantly wide open. A pale, pre-dawn light, bright enough to see her clearly. She listens.

Outside, on the wooden stairs, a floor-and-a-half below, unmistakable this time, the sound of the strange footsteps, one foot dragging behind the other.

Mary is transfixed with fear, unable to move, until a door closes downstairs and the sound of the footsteps is swallowed up. She continues to listen intently, trembling slightly.

INT. DRAWING ROOM. DAY

It's a bright day for once and sunlight streams in through the tall windows, while reflections from the surface of the river ripple on the room's high ceiling. Dr Jekyll looks up eagerly, as Mary enters with the breakfast tray.

JEKYLL This is very welcome, Mary: I'm ravenous.

She puts the tray down on the table next to him and he snatches at a piece of toast and takes a substantial bite from it.

MARY I'm not surprised, sir. Cook says you didn't touch your soup last night.

JEKYLL I dare say I didn't.

MARY And I don't suppose you've had much sleep, either.

JEKYLL None at all, to be perfectly honest.

MARY And did you make your breakthrough?

Jekyll stops chewing. He looks up at Mary, his eyes glittering.

JEKYLL Oh yes. Last night all the barriers fell before me.

MARY Well, then, I'd say you deserve a rest, sir.

She turns to leave the room, but Jekyll stops her in her tracks.

JEKYLL Mary.

MARY Yes, sir?

JEKYLL Did I do well, about the garden?

MARY I'm sorry, sir, Mr Poole wanted to know why I'd been talking to you so long, yesterday morning.

JEKYLL Well, as we're already fellow-conspirators and partners in crime, perhaps you'd agree to do something for me in strictest confidence?

MARY I will if I can, sir.

JEKYLL Is tomorrow your afternoon off?

MARY That's right, sir.

JEKYLL Then will you be able to deliver this letter for me?

He picks up a sealed envelope and holds it out to her. She takes it and looks at the address, reacting to it with a trace of alarm.

Do you know where that is?

MARY I do, sir, it's in Soho.

JEKYLL There'll be no reply. Just a yes or a no.

MARY Very good, sir.

JEKYLL So you'll do it for me, will you?

MARY If you want me to, sir.

JEKYLL Thank you, Mary.

They look at each other for a moment: Mary is troubled, but somehow rooted to the spot. Jekyll watches her with his big, melancholy eyes.

Haven't you ever wished for a completely new life, Mary?

MARY No, sir, what good would that do?

JEKYLL I mean, suppose you were able to do absolutely whatever you wanted, with no consequences and no regrets, then what?

Mary considers gravely: Jekyll awaits her answer, perched with great concentration on the edge of his seat.

MARY I don't believe there is such a thing as actions without consequences.

This doesn't seem to be at all the answer Jekyll is hoping for: he grunts noncommittally and returns to his toast. Mary curtsies and begins to withdraw.

EXT. WEST END STREET. DAY

Mary, in crinoline, cloak, bonnet and gloves makes her way through the bustle of a West End thoroughfare, alive with vendors, carriages, horse-drawn omnibuses. It's been raining so the air is fresh, but there are puddles everywhere. Mary's expression is purposeful but apprehensive.

EXT. STREET IN SOHO. DAY

The atmosphere has turned sinister, rowdy and hopeless. The street is narrow, fetid, thick with mud and the passers-by are preoccupied, unresponsive to the beggars, whores and street urchins who lounge against the dripping walls. A strange bluish light gives the whole neighbourhood the aspect of a kind of slimy aquarium. Mary stops to give a penny to a pinched, solemn flower-girl, who looks uncannily like Mary herself at the age of ten, and accepts from her a bunch of violets. The child is barefoot.

Mary turns a corner and finds herself in front of a slightly less decrepit row of houses with front steps raising them above the layer of scum and viscous mud coating the sidewalk. One of these houses has a red door. Mary checks the envelope in her hand, hesitates, then pounds on the door.

Presently the door is opened by a ferocious-looking woman with dyed red hair. The deep lines around her eyes and the creamy bosom showing above her unexpectedly low-cut dress give out conflicting messages about her age. She stares down at Mary from the height of the step, coldly assessing her.

MRS FARRADAY Strictly speaking I've no vacancies at the moment, but we might be able to come to some arrangement.

MARY Are you Mrs Farraday?

MRS FARRADAY Who wants to know?

MARY I have a letter for Mrs Farraday from Dr Jekyll.

MRS FARRADAY Oh, Harry Jekyll, eh?

Before Mary can stop her, she's snatched the letter and broken the seal.

MARY Are you . . .?

MRS FARRADAY Yes, yes, yes. I'm Farraday, keep your wool on.

She opens the letter, deftly extracts two large banknotes which vanish into her bodice and reads. As she does so, a young woman accompanied by a much older man in a morning coat and top hat, pushes past Mary and disappears into the house behind Mrs Farraday without either acknowledging or being acknowledged by her. Mrs Farraday finishes reading.

Good old Harry, ever the good Samaritan. And I'll say something else for him. He may ask for a few special services, but he doesn't mind paying the price.

MARY So am I to say your answer is yes?

MRS FARRADAY My answer's always yes.

She smiles mirthlessly at Mary.

I have my obligations, so it'll take me at least a week to clear the place out. Then I'll need another week to make the . . . alterations he's asking for.

MARY Two weeks' time, then, I'll tell him, shall I?

MRS FARRADAY Tell him what you like. Tell him if he gets impatient, he'll have to make do with you.

And she slams the door in Mary's face.

INT. JEKYLL'S BEDROOM. DAY

Mary carries the breakfast tray into the room. Dr Jekyll is lying on the unslept-in bed in his dressing gown. He looks pale, waxy from exhaustion. He scarcely reacts as Mary approaches with her tray and settles it across his knees.

JEKYLL I'm not sure I can manage any of this.

Mary doesn't answer: she continues disposing the tray, avoiding his eye.

Did you deliver my letter, Mary?

MARY I did, sir.

JEKYLL What was the answer?

Mary looks him in the eye for the first time, a trace of indignation in her expression.

MARY She said yes. But she said she needs two weeks to get it ready.

JEKYLL Two weeks?

MARY Yes, sir.

JEKYLL Well, I suppose that'll have to do.

He looks up at her with a weary smile.

JEKYLL Thank you, Mary.

MARY Very good, sir.

Her answer is coldly formal: now she curtsies and hurries out of the room.

EXT. COURTYARD. DAY

Mary drives a garden fork into the hard earth and begins to turn it over. She jabs at the earth again, working with a contained violence, her face set in an almost angry expression.

INT. FRONT PARLOUR. NIGHT

Once again, the household at prayer: the Lord's Prayer comes to an end and Dr Jekyll looks up.

JEKYLL If you'd please all sit for a moment, I have an announcement to make.

This causes slight consternation, but Jekyll's manner is immediately reassuring.

Nothing to worry about, Mrs Kent, I assure you.

They settle themselves and Jekyll beams down at them from the lectern.

As you may be aware, the pressure of my work has increased considerably of late. Consequently, I have decided to take on an assistant.

He pauses. Mary looks across at Poole, who's frowning, unable for the moment to conceal his displeasure.

His name is Mr Edward Hyde, and I intend to give him the run of the house. Of course, his work will mainly be confined to the laboratory, but I wanted to establish that when he does have occasion to step over here, you will treat him with the respect you've always shown toward me.

POOLE You may rely upon it, sir.

MRS KENT Will the gentleman be taking his meals here, sir?

JEKYLL Not as a rule, no. And I'll be sure to inform you if anything out of the way is required.

MRS KENT Very good, sir.

JEKYLL One other thing: these extra demands on my time will make it difficult for me to conduct regular evening prayers from now on. Perhaps you would be good enough, Poole, to take over this duty for me?

POOLE By all means, sir.

JEKYLL Thank you. I knew I could count on you all. Goodnight to you.

SERVANTS Goodnight, sir.

He leaves the room and the servants rise to their feet amidst a pregnant silence.

BRADSHAW You'd think he'd have brought him in and introduced him to us.

POOLE As is often the case, Bradshaw, you'd be better off minding your own business.

Mary follows Mrs Kent out of the room, lost in thought.

EXT. COURTYARD. DAY

Mary, on her knees, works with fork and trowel, turning the earth conscientiously, much calmer now. A wider angle reveals that three beds have now been prepared, pretty much in the positions she indicated to Jekyll. She rocks back on her heels for a moment, clearing her hair out of her eyes with the back of her hand. Suddenly, however, in mid-gesture, she tenses, having caught sight of something.

EXT. BRIDGE OF SIGHS. DAWN

Her point of view: above, obscured by the mist and the poor light, and distorted by the old glass in the windows, someone with long hair and a strange, irregular gait is crossing the Bridge of Sighs: evidently not Jekyll.

EXT. COURTYARD. DAWN

Mary frowns, peering up at the bridge.

EXT. BRIDGE OF SIGHS. DAWN

Her point of view: the man pauses for a second, looking down at her, the white globe of his face behind the lozenge-shaped window panes, no features recognisable: then he moves on and vanishes.

EXT. COURTYARD. DAWN

Mary looks at the laboratory building for a moment, inexplicably disturbed. The lights go on. Then she rises to her feet and sets off back towards the house.

EXT. KITCHEN. DAWN

Mary arrives in the kitchen as Mrs Kent bustles in through the other door, her baskets full from the market and a rectangular box of small flowerpots containing pansies, pinks and herbs. She puts everything down on the table, at the same time bursting out with the news she's dying to pass on.

MRS KENT I seen him.

MARY Yes, he just crossed the bridge.

Mrs Kent is not at all pleased. She starts unpacking the shopping, her jaw set.

But I couldn't really make him out; what was he like?

Mrs Kent looks up at her, immediately mollified.

MRS KENT Well . . .

EXT. SIDE STREET. DAWN

Mrs Kent, her baskets full, moves down the hill towards the corner; the street is practically deserted. She looks up, her attention caught by something.

EXT. SIDE STREET. DAWN

Her point of view: moving up the street on the other side, approaching the shadow of the bridge, is a man in black. He has a curious, distinctive gait and his coarse black hair spills over his collar.

MRS KENT (*voice over*) He moves funny.

INT. KITCHEN. DAWN

Mary is listening intently.

MRS KENT Not exactly a limp, more of a shuffle. And he's sort of stooped.

MARY Did you see his face?

EXT. SIDE STREET. DAWN

Close on Mrs Kent, she's frowning and squinting across the street, inquisitive but uncomfortable.

MRS KENT (*voice over*) No.

EXT. SIDE STREET. DAWN

Mrs Kent's point of view: the man stands in the darkness underneath the bridge, fumbling for a key in his pocket.

He finds it; but just before he opens the battered little door, its dsrk paint peeling and defaced with graffiti, which opens on to a staircase leading up to the Bridge of Sighs, he turns to look at her, his eyes glittering with malevolence.

MRS KENT (*voice over*) Just his eyes.

INT. KITCHEN. DAWN

Mrs Kent shakes her head, a trace of fear in her expression.

MRS KENT He came out of the dark, like he was made of it.

She comes to herself abruptly, as Poole surges into the room, eyes narrowed.

POOLE What's this then, a mothers' meeting?

MRS KENT No, Mr Poole.

She busies herself unpacking her shopping and Mary goes to help her, reaching for the box of plants.

EXT. COURTYARD. DAWN

Mary steps up into the mist-shrouded courtyard, carrying the box of plants and a trowel. She crosses to one of the flower beds and puts the box down, dropping to her knees beside it and beginning to dig. As she does so, the door to the operating theatre suddenly emits a groaning creak and swings open.

Mary straightens up, peering into the mist; for the moment whoever's emerged into the courtyard is only indistinctly visible. Then, quite unexpectedly, he trips and falls heavily; and the voice that rings out is Jekyll's.

JEKYLL (*voice over*) Damn!

Mary springs up and hurries over to him. He's lying full-length on the ground.

MARY Oh, my Lord, sir, have you hurt yourself?

JEKYLL I'm very much afraid I may have sprained my ankle at the very least.

MARY Shall I go for Mr Poole?

JEKYLL No, just help me off with my shoe. It's this one.

He indicates his right foot. Mary unlaces the boot carefully and eases it off, causing Jekyll to gasp with pain.

MARY Should I fetch a doctor, sir?

JEKYLL I think there's one here.

Mary laughs.

MARY Sorry, sir, I wasn't thinking.

JEKYLL Rest my heel in one of your hands, and very gently move the foot in a circle.

She does so, until Jekyll responds with a pained intake of breath.

JEKYLL Yes, it's only a sprain. But I shall need help to get into the house.

MARY Shall I get your assistant?

JEKYLL What?

He's spoken so sharply, that Mary is confused.

MARY I just thought . . .

JEKYLL He's not there.

MARY Oh, I . . .

She breaks off and the moment passes. Jekyll makes an effort to lighten the atmosphere.

JEKYLL If you'll agree to lend me your support, I'm sure the thing can be accomplished.

He sits up and, with Mary's help, manages to scramble to his feet.

Then he puts an arm round her and, leaning on her heavily, starts to hop towards the house.

JEKYLL I shan't keep you too long from your flowers.

MARY That's all right, sir.

JEKYLL You're a great comfort to me, Mary.

Close on Mary as she helps him hobble towards the house. She's glowing with satisfaction.

INT. SERVANTS' HALL. NIGHT

The meal is proceeding in a silence which is interrupted by the sudden buzzing of a bell. Poole looks up at the indicator on the wall to confirm his suspicion that it's the bell from Dr Jekyll's bedroom and it rings again.

BRADSHAW Would you like me to go, Mr Poole?

POOLE I think in the circumstances I should go myself. I'll ring again if I require you.

He rises from the table and glides out of the room. When he's gone, the atmosphere immediately lightens. Mrs Kent leans forward confidentially.

MRS KENT I still can't puzzle out why he said his assistant wasn't there, when I saw him with my own eyes not minutes before.

BRADSHAW You sure you didn't imagine the whole thing, Mrs Kent?

MRS KENT I saw him clear as I can see you.

BRADSHAW And you say he was a dwarf?

MRS KENT I said no such thing, I said he was a bit crouched like: and funny-looking, with his long black curly hair. That's all.

The bell buzzes, abruptly. Bradshaw sighs.

BRADSHAW No peace for the wicked.

He stuffs in another mouthful and sets off, chewing furiously.

Mrs Kent, Mary and Annie are left at the table. Mary's looking up, concerned.

MARY I hope the Master's all right.

INT. DINING ROOM. NIGHT

Mary is putting the silver away in the canteen by the light of a single candle, when a movement catches her attention. She crosses to the large bay window.

EXT. COURTYARD. NIGHT
Mary's point of view: Poole and Bradshaw, one on each side, support the hobbling Dr Jekyll across the courtyard in the direction of the door to the operating theatre.

INT. DINING ROOM. NIGHT
Through the window, her face lit from below by the candle so that it looks like a moon in the dark expanse of glass, Mary peers anxiously out into the night.

EXT. RIVER THAMES AND SIDE ROAD. NIGHT
It's the middle of a moonlit night and the ten-year-old Mary, conspicuous in a white dress, is hurrying nervously along the towpath which leads past Dr Jekyll's house. She looks over her shoulder: there's a sound of brisk, heavy footsteps, one leg dragging somewhat, apparently following her, although there's no one in sight. The child increases her pace; but the footsteps seem to be gaining on her.
Panicked, she breaks into a run. Still the sound of the footsteps. Now she's running as fast as she can go, still looking back over her shoulder at the deserted towpath, fast approaching the corner of the side road which leads down to the river.
At the corner, she runs smack into a little man in a tall hat; clearly, he is the instigator of the footsteps, the sound of which must have been misplaced by atmospheric conditions. He is unbalanced, but she goes crashing full-length on the sidewalk. She looks up, terrified, from the ground. A face looms into frame above her; it's her Father. She screams. His lip curls back into a snarl and he raises a foot in a heavy boot.
Overhead shot: Mary's Father, in a savage frenzy tramples on the little girl in a white dress.

INT. MARY'S BEDROOM. NIGHT
Once again, Mary comes awake with a start, and once again she can hear the strange, dragging footsteps on the stairs. This time, she swings swiftly out of bed, crosses the room and reaches for her cloak, which hangs from a hook on the back of the door. Annie stirs and groans but doesn't wake. Mary glances at her, then lets herself very quietly out of the room.

INT. LANDINGS AND STAIRCASE. NIGHT

Mary flits across the landing in her bare feet. She hesitates at the top of the back stairs, then decides to move across the landing to where the main staircase arrives at the top of the house; and starts cautiously down.

Halfway down the first flight she becomes aware that there's someone moving around in the library below. Lamplight spills through the open door on to the stairs. She carries on down until she reaches the half-landing off which a couple of the main bedrooms are situated; and tucks herself into a kind of alcove from which she can look straight down on to the library door.

Whoever is in the library clears his throat: a hoarse, almost animal sound. There's a sound of tearing paper and then the rays of light begin to move erratically as the oil lamp is picked up.

Mary makes sure she's deep enough in the alcove to remain invisible.

Mr Edward Hyde emerges from the library. He's wearing evening clothes and an opera cloak. He's not so much small as tensed like a coiled spring and his strange loping gait is more like stalking than limping. He suddenly stops dead. His face is in shadow, so the curious sound he's making is not immediately identifiable. Then his face comes up into the light.

Mary shrinks back, pressing herself as hard as she can into the wall.

Hyde's looks are quite striking in a wolfish sort of way, his coarse features framed by his long, thick, black hair; and what he's doing is sniffing the air. He's an instantly terrifying figure, not for any obviously definable reason, but because of the sense of energy and danger which flows around him like an electrical field. He now looks straight at Mary, his nostrils still quivering. It's quite clear that he's smelled her.

In the darkness, Mary's hand goes up to her mouth. She's trembling with fear.

Hyde has the oil lamp in one hand and a piece of paper, a cheque, in the other. Now he comes to himself, his eyes hooded as he stares at Mary's hiding place with the faintest of sardonic smiles; and he sets off down the stairs, the lamplight bobbing away until silence and darkness fall.

Mary lets out a strangled gasp as she begins breathing again. For a few seconds longer, she's nailed to the spot; then she breaks and hurries down the stairs to the library.

INT. LIBRARY. NIGHT

The moonlight streams in through the stained-glass windows, casting strange pools of colour on the desk, where drawers stand open and papers are strewn around in disarray. Mary takes this in and sees that upppermost on the desk is Dr Jekyll's large chequebook, bent open, the ink still wet on the stub, where a coarse, bold hand has recorded the disbursement of a hundred pounds. Mary moves the chequebook out of the pool of reddish light in which it lies, straightening it on the desk; then, clearly puzzled, she turns to hurry away.

INT. STAIRCASE AND LANDING. NIGHT

Mary climbs back up the staircase, two steps at a time.

INT. MARY'S BEDROOM. NIGHT

Mary enters the room and crosses swiftly to the side window.

EXT. SIDE ROAD. NIGHT

Far below, seen from Mary's point of view, a small group is gathered in the street, near the entrance to the Bridge of Sighs, around the body of a small girl, who lies beneath a street-lamp, her white dress blotched with dark stains.

The group reacts as Hyde emerges suddenly from the side entrance. He hands over the cheque to a man dressed in working clothes. Then he stands for a moment, his posture somehow truculent, before beating a retreat from the growing indignation and hostility of the group of onlookers and vanishing back into the laboratory.

INT. MARY'S BEDROOM. NIGHT

Mary's face at the window.

Fade.

INT. DRAWING ROOM. DAY

Mary is cleaning the carpets with tea leaves, vigorously brushing them in. Bradshaw appears in the doorway behind her and startles her when he speaks.

BRADSHAW The Master's come in in a bad way, Mary. You'd best leave that and light the fire in his bedroom.

Mary puts the brush down and hurries out after Bradshaw.

INT. JEKYLL'S BEDROOM. DAY

Mary follows Bradshaw into the room and stops in the doorway, shocked by what she sees: Poole is on his knees in front of Jekyll, who lies back in his armchair, his clothes and hair in disarray, his face pale and twisted in pain. Poole has almost completed the business of cutting off his sock with a pair of scissors; he peels it away to reveal an ankle bruised and swollen to twice its normal size.

MARY Oh, Lord, sir, what have you done now, is it broken?

Poole looks up at her, scandalised by her spontaneous outburst.

POOLE Hold your tongue and light the fire.

JEKYLL It's all right, Poole: no, it's not broken, I just put my weight on it too soon.

Mary, blushing, hurries over to the fire and drops to her knees to finish setting it. Meanwhile, Poole and Bradshaw help Jekyll to his feet and move him over to the end of the bed, where he stands on one leg, holding on to the footboard, as Poole and Bradshaw begin to undress him.

There are some supplies I need urgently from the chemist's, Poole.

POOLE If you mean materials for your work, sir, I respectfully suggest you should stay here in bed for a day or two.

JEKYLL There are things I can't do without, Poole: I need them today and you're the only man I can rely on.

POOLE Very good, sir.

Poole is glowing with satisfaction as he helps Jekyll off with his shirt. Mary has the fire under way by now. She glances back over her shoulder, to see Jekyll, balanced on one foot, his skin creamy, his frame wiry, as Bradshaw goes to fetch his nightshirt from under the pillow; then she becomes aware of Poole's icy glare and turns hurriedly back to continue working on the fire, in some confusion.

INT. BUTLER'S PARLOUR. DAY

Poole's room is small, austere and astonishingly tidy. There's a desk, net curtains, masking the view of the well of the basement and a leather armchair, in which Poole sits, reading his copy of The Times. *He grunts in response to a knock at the door and Mary enters. She waits as he carefully refolds his newspaper, his expression black with disapproval. Finally, she nervously breaks the silence.*

MARY Mrs Kent said you wanted to see me, sir.

Poole looks up at her, maintaining, for longer than is comfortable, a freezing silence.

POOLE Dr Jekyll is all too benevolent an employer, so it falls to me to draw attention to occasions on which I feel members of the household are failing in their duties. It is also my task, may I remind you, to dismiss those of the staff who persistently overstep the mark.

MARY Yes, sir.

POOLE Have you any idea to what I may be referring?

MARY I spoke out of turn when I was in the Master's bedroom, sir.

POOLE Quite so. Now: help me on with my Ulster; the Master requires certain supplies from the chemist's.

He takes a baggy overcoat from a hook behind the door and hands it to her, continuing to speak as she helps him into it.

Naturally, all of us are concerned when Dr Jekyll is unwell, but we are hardly likely to improve his condition by drawing attention to our own entirely insignificant opinions.

He reaches for his bowler hat and heads for the door.

INT. HALL. DAY

Mary follows Poole across the hall towards the front door.

POOLE You must be aware that there are a great many young women in straitened circumstances, who would be able to fill your position *and* observe a few elementary regulations.

By now she's holding the front door open for him, as he settles his bowler on his head.

Remember that.

EXT./INT. JEKYLL'S HOUSE. DAY

Poole sets off, moving purposefully down the front steps.

A reverse shot: Mary stands for a moment in the doorway, shaken, but, at the same time, relieved at her reprieve.

INT. JEKYLL'S BEDROOM. EVENING

The fire glows red now with the colours of several hours' burning. There's a knock at the door and Mary lets herself in with the supper tray. Jekyll sinks back into his pillows, plainly disappointed.

JEKYLL Is Poole not back?

MARY Not yet, sir.

JEKYLL I suppose he must be running all over London for those . . . supplies of mine.

MARY I expect so, sir.

JEKYLL Send him up as soon as he returns.

By this time, Mary has put the tray on the bedside table: she looks at Jekyll, concerned.

Oh, God, Mary, I'm so cold. My hands are freezing.

Mary reaches out and takes one of his hands. From her reaction, it's clear he has not exaggerated. She chafes his hand between hers, then takes the other and rubs it as well.

MARY You must take some broth, sir. Hold the bowl and get some warmth into you. I'll bank up the fire.

She gives him the bowl of soup and he holds it a moment before taking a half-hearted sip from it as she pokes the fire and adds fresh coal.

JEKYLL Can you do something for me, Mary?

MARY Of course, sir.

JEKYLL On the desk, in the library, I believe you'll find my chequebook.

Mary suppresses a jolt of shock.

Would you mind bringing it to me? There's something I want to look at.

MARY Yes, sir.

She turns to leave the room.

INT. LIBRARY. EVENING

The strewn papers and chequebook are as they were on the desk. The stained-glass window throws strange patterns on the floor in green and gold and red. Mary crosses to look at the chequebook.

Inset: The stub has been filled out in a bold scrawl. It says: BLOOD MONEY, £100–0–0.

Mary contemplates this for a moment. Then she almost jumps out of her skin as a pigeon suddenly flaps loudly past the window. She moves towards the door, holding the chequebook.

INT. JEKYLL'S BEDROOM. EVENING

Dr Jekyll has put aside the unfinished soup and fallen asleep. Mary stands for a moment, looking at him, concerned. Then, she puts the chequebook on his bedside table. Finally, greatly daring, she leans across and brushes back a lock of hair which has fallen over one eye. He doesn't stir. She stands for a moment, looking down at him tenderly. Fade.

EXT. COURTYARD. DAY

It's a beautiful, late-autumn day and Mary is outside weeding one of the flower beds. The two flower beds, now full of blooms, have transformed the courtyard into a garden. Mary looks up to see Dr Jekyll emerging from the house. He's limping and leaning on a stick, but clearly in a much-improved condition. Mary looks away quickly and transfers her attention back to the weeds.

When she looks up again a moment later, Jekyll has paused beside her, supporting himself on an elegant ebony cane with an elaborate silver dog's head for a handle.

JEKYLL I must congratulate you, Mary; you've completely transformed the feel of this dreary yard.

MARY Thank you, sir: Cook helped choose the plants.

JEKYLL But you've done the work.

MARY More than I bargained for, sir, with these old weeds: I don't know where they come from and they're ever so strong.

JEKYLL Why do you suppose that is?

MARY Well, sir, being wild, they probably have a much greater will to life.

Jekyll closes his eyes; he suddenly looks queasy and tormented.

JEKYLL I don't know, Mary: why is it you strike me as you do?

MARY Are you all right, sir? Perhaps you shouldn't be going back to work so soon.

JEKYLL My work is not all positive, as yours is, Mary: it's dangerous and unconventional and may in the end be of no benefit whatsoever to mankind. But I have to go on with it.

He looks away for a moment, lost in thought.

I have to.

He moves off towards the operating theatre, his expression grave.

INT. MARY'S BEDROOM. DAWN

Mary wakes at an insistent knocking on the door. Even Annie, next to her in the bed, comes to this time. There's the palest grey light in the room. Before Mary can get out of bed, the door opens. Dr Jekyll is in the doorway, his eyes staring, his manner distraught. This is something which has never happened before and Mary's expression conveys her shock and alarm at this breach of domestic etiquette.

MARY What is it, sir?

JEKYLL Will you get dressed, Mary, there's something I urgently need you to do for me. I'll wait for you in the library.

He's blurted this out, his voice ragged with strain. Now, abruptly, he disappears. Mary doesn't hesitate, she scrambles out of bed.

INT. LIBRARY. DAWN

Dr Jekyll sits at his desk, finishing a letter. He folds it, puts it in an envelope and, as Mary steps into the room, he tears off a cheque and adds it to the envelope before sealing it.

JEKYLL I'm afraid this may not be a very pleasant errand, Mary.

MARY Is it to Mrs Farraday?

Jekyll looks round at her, surprised at her percipience.

JEKYLL It is. And I can't tell you how important it may be.

MARY What should I tell Mr Poole?

JEKYLL Nothing. I'll deal with him. You just go.

MARY Will there be a reply?

JEKYLL I'm afraid there may well be. I want you to bring it to me the moment you return.

He holds out the letter to her. Her hand closes over it.

EXT. STREETS. DAY

The fog is so thick, the streets are a different, disorienting world. Figures loom unexpectedly out of the mist. Sounds are distorted, so that the tap of Mary's footsteps echoes back to her as if she has an unseen follower. She holds the letter tight and edges along a sweating brown wall, feeling her way. There's a sudden violent clatter of hooves and before she can do more than press herself against the wall, the edge of a carriage slices by, inches away from her.

EXT. STREET IN SOHO. DAY

The fog has lifted slightly as Mary wades through the mud in the direction of the red door: which suddenly opens to disgorge an obvious whore of not more than seventeen. Mary slows down. The girl, whose crudely applied make-up is blotched and running, is sobbing helplessly, dabbing at her nose and eyes with a rouge-stained handkerchief. Mary stops at the door to watch the girl, as she moves away, crying noisily; and is thus caught completely off her guard, when the door bursts open, a hand grabs her arm and Mrs Farraday appears, hissing at her furiously.

MRS FARRADAY Get in here, you!

INT. HALL DAY

Mary is dragged bodily into a surprisingly well-furnished hallway, a little garish, but recently and expensively decorated. Mrs Farraday, who appears to be trembling with rage, slaps her hand against the letter that Mary is clutching.

MRS FARRADAY He won't slip out of this one with a few quid and a smarmy letter.

MARY All the same you'd better read it.

Mrs Farraday snatches the letter, turns her back on Mary, breaks the seal, examines the cheque and reads the letter. All this seems to calm her considerably. She turns back and considers Mary for a moment.

MRS FARRADAY He ought to have had the courage to come here hisself and clean up after that mad dog of his.

MARY He said there might be a reply.

Mrs Farraday looks at Mary: then an idea seems to strike her and, for a second, a wintry smile enlivens her expression.

MRS FARRADAY And so there might. Come with me.

She turns and sets off up the narrow staircase.

INT. STAIRCASE AND LANDING. DAY

Mary follows Mrs Farraday up the stairs with a growing sense of dread.

Mrs Farraday crosses the dark landing and throws open a door.

MRS FARRADAY In you go.

INT. BEDROOM. DAY

Mary steps across the threshold. As she takes the room in and Mrs Farraday comes in and closes the door behind her, her face crumples with horror.

Mary's point of view: the luxuriously furnished room is a shambles. One of the posters at the head of the large bed is broken and the canopy tilts at a drunken angle. A frayed piece of rope hangs from the other poster. The camera approaches very slowly to reveal, gradually, that where the blankets have been dragged back, the sheets are drenched with blood.

Mary takes a step back; her hand flies to her mouth.

The camera slews, taking her point of view again. There are bloody palm marks on the new wallpaper, dragging away into smears, which trail down towards the floor, on which is a ripped and bloodstained white nightdress.

Mary looks up, appalled; then sharply takes in a breath.

Her point of view again: there's blood on the ceiling.

MARY What . . .?

MRS FARRADAY Don't even ask.

Mary turns to her, her features working, desperately distressed.

Now you're a good housemaid, I can see that. How long would it take, in your professional opinion, to get this place looking shipshape?

MARY What was the message?

MRS FARRADAY Tell him no need to panic, I'll do everything he wants.

She bends, picks something up and, all in one fluid movement, presses it into Mary's hands.

And take this home with you to Harry Jekyll.

Mary looks down. What she has in her hand is one of the familiar handkerchiefs, with the initials HJ stitched in blue: and it's soaked in blood.

MARY And what should I . . .?

She breaks off, her eyes widening.

Mary's point of view: what she's seen on the floor, streaked with blood, its head stove in, is the corpse of a white rat.

MRS FARRADAY Oh, yes, it takes all sorts.

Mary is speechless with terror. Mrs Farraday leans in close, to murmur in her ear.

You tell Harry Jekyll this is such linen as even his old friend Mrs Farraday cannot clean for him.

INT. KITCHEN. DAY

Mary hurries into the room, where Mrs Kent is attending to various huge pots steaming on the kitchener. She's red in the face and frazzled-looking.

MRS KENT He's in the laboratory: he wants you to go and see him directly.

MARY Where's Mr Poole?

MRS KENT He's to the chemist's again: he's like the rest of us, he don't know if he's coming or going.

EXT. COURTYARD. DAY

Mary hurries across the courtyard, which is shrouded in fog.

INT. OPERATING THEATRE. DAY

The room is so tall and cavernous that strips of fog have seeped in through the skylights and hang motionless over the operating table. As Mary hurries across the room, she's aware of a series of rustlings and squeakings. She stops to investigate. Across the room, in a recess, are a number of small box cages. She takes a step or two towards them, then freezes: a whole row of the cages is occupied by white rats. She turns away, shuddering, and hurries up the stairs to knock on the red baize door.

INT. LABORATORY. DAY

Dr Jekyll is slumped in his armchair, staring into the fire. He looks up at the door. There's a glass of wine in his hand.

JEKYLL Yes?

Mary appears in the doorway, closes the door behind her and advances hesitantly into the room. Jekyll's eyes are haunted.

Was Mrs Farraday at home?

MARY She was, sir.

JEKYLL And what did she say?

MARY She said she'll do everything you want her to.

Jekyll visibly relaxes: but he tenses again as Mary brings the blood-soaked handkerchief out of her pocket.

MARY But she said this is such linen as even she cannot clean.

Jekyll is catapulted out of his chair. He snatches the handkerchief from Mary, turns and throws it on the fire. They watch it as it slowly catches fire, unfolding as it does so. When it's fully ablaze, Jekyll turns back to face Mary. His eyes are full of tears, his voice, however, indicates a successful struggle for self-control.

JEKYLL How did she seem?

MARY Very angry, sir.

JEKYLL On the rare occasions a woman like Mrs Farraday is not at fault herself, she is liable to experience a rush of righteous indignation. Tell me what she said.

MARY She said you should have gone yourself, sir. Instead of sending me.

JEKYLL Yes. But I couldn't.

Silence, as he sits and pours himself another glass of wine from the decanter on the table by his chair. Eventually, he looks up at her.

I know you're afraid of rats, Mary, you once told me: but what else are you afraid of?

MARY I don't know, sir, bad dreams, horses in the street.

JEKYLL I see.

He's spoken rather coldly and looks away, as if disappointed by her answer. She's aware of this and tries again.

MARY Confined spaces.

JEKYLL Yes, of course.

He looks at her, sympathetic once again.

And yet, when we spoke, you refused to say that you hated your father.

MARY I don't. He put a dark place in me and I can't forgive him for that; but it's part of me now and I can't regret what I am. Even though it often makes me sad.

JEKYLL Oh, well, sadness, yes, that can't be helped, that comes in like the tide.

He looks at her for a moment, frowning in concentration.

But what you're saying is, Mary, you're never afraid of yourself.

MARY No. I didn't say that.

JEKYLL You are afraid of yourself?

He waits, on tenterhooks, as Mary considers the question.

MARY Yes.

JEKYLL I thought so.

He seems relieved. He half-smiles at her, his eyes weary.

Because that's what frightens me the most: the dark places in me.

INT. LIBRARY. EVENING

Mary has finished her work in the library; there's a fire burning in the grate and, as dusk is falling outside the tall windows with the stained-glass panels, she's now lighting the lamps. As she does so, her eye falls on the desk where a huge medical book lies open; something about it puzzles her and when she finishes with the lamps, she moves over for a closer look.

Close on Mary as her look of curiosity changes to a frisson of alarm. The book is one of those manuals which largely consist of elaborate anatomical plates, in colour, illustrated in the most realistic detail. The plate displayed at the moment is of a male body, flayed to reveal the muscles, tendons and ganglia, largely painted in an angry red. What has caught Mary's attention, though, is the fact that certain additions or defacements have been made to the illustration in the same bold black ink she found on Jekyll's cheque-stub: thus, for example, the flayed body sports an eye-patch and a large phallus. She turns a page. Next is a pair of illustrations captioned DISEASES OF THE MOUTH*: here, one of the heads has been supplied with a cigar; while the second, mouth wide open to display lesions in a range of startling colours, has been labelled* TRUE BEAUTY LIES IN CORRUPTION.

Mary turns another page. Here, the plate features a foetus, sitting in its mother's womb: it's been embellished with a top hat, a moustache, and a glass of champagne. The added caption reads: PAIN BEGINS IN UNDERSTANDING.

A third page illustrates the eye, its connection to the brain and its contents in cross-section. Here there's no caption: instead a couple of extremely disturbing sketches in the margin of naked, disembowelled women.

Mary inspects these, absorbed and alarmed; so that the hoarse, breathy voice, when it comes, almost makes her jump out of her skin.

VOICE Mary Reilly.

She spins round and is face to face with Edward Hyde.

HYDE What do you think?

MARY I'm sorry, sir, I didn't mean to . . .

HYDE I've always had an artistic temperament. I know I owe my existence to science but I've never been able to whip up too much enthusiasm for it. Do you know who I am?

MARY You're Mr Hyde, sir. Master's assistant.

HYDE Yes, you might say so.

He smiles at her in an entirely unamiable way, looking her up and down so blatantly, that she shrinks back a little, into her window embrasure.

Strange, the thoughts that come unbidden, don't you find?

MARY If you mean, we are not always in control of our ideas, sir . . .

HYDE Why should we want to be, that's the question. I've never been in favour of control.

He moves a step or two towards her and she has to make a supreme effort not to shrink away from him.

By all accounts, your father was no paragon, when it came to controlling himself.

Mary is so shocked by this, she can't conceal the hurt which registers on her face. Hyde grins.

Men will chatter amongst themselves, you know.

He moves a little closer.

But what I didn't find out was how much further it might have gone between your father and yourself.

Mary draws herself up, fear giving way to anger.

MARY I've finished in here now, sir, so I won't disturb you any more.

She moves firmly in the direction of the door, but Hyde swiftly intercepts her.

HYDE If you've finished your work, perhaps it might amuse you to spend the evening with me?

MARY I don't know what you mean.

HYDE You've heard the expression 'painting the town red'? I had something of the sort in mind.

MARY I'm not at liberty to go out in the evenings, sir.

HYDE Even if you were, I don't suppose you'd agree to spend them with me.

MARY No, sir, I don't suppose I would.

Hyde nods: he seems amused by her defiance. He steps aside to let her pass.

HYDE Then I must continue my researches unchaperoned.

She shoots a look at him.

Researches into what, I sense you wondering. My subject is animal behaviour, its extremes and its limits.

Mary is held, hesitating reluctantly in the doorway.

Most of my experiments are designed to test those limits; but I feel that so far I have scarcely . . . scratched the surface.

They look at each other for a moment: then Mary makes a supreme effort, breaks the spell and leaves the room.

INT. MARY'S BEDROOM. NIGHT

For once, Mary is alone in her room. She lies on the bed in her nightdress. She looks frightened and sad; and, after a while, tears spill out of her eyes and begin to roll slowly down her cheeks.

She stands up and moves over to look into the plain mirror which is hung on the back of the door. She wipes the tears from her face, then, impulsively, takes off her nightdress, drops it beside her on the floor and stands, examining her body in the mirror.

INT. JEKYLL'S BEDROOM. DAY

Mary advances towards Jekyll's bed with the breakfast tray. He's awake, but the curtains are still drawn and the room is in semi-darkness.

JEKYLL Good morning, Mary.

MARY Morning, sir.

She's mumbled the reply and avoids his eye as she arranges the tray across his knees.

JEKYLL Is there something the matter?

Mary's first instinct is to deny that there is; but then she's unable to prevent herself from answering honestly.

MARY I thought, sir, when I spoke to you of private matters, those were confidences you would never repeat.

Jekyll doesn't seem at all surprised by this reproach: he nods understandingly.

JEKYLL I'm afraid you've been upset by my assistant.

MARY No, sir, I was more upset by you. That you told him.

Jekyll looks at her for a moment, interested.

JEKYLL As a doctor, I've always been in the habit of taking notes after any kind of consultation. I'm afraid my young man is less . . . scrupulous than he should be. He read my notebook.

MARY Oh, I see, sir; well, in that case, I . . .

She breaks off, evidently much relieved.

JEKYLL I do apologise. But I would like you to find it in your heart to forgive him. His manners are rough, but I've learned to look beyond that. He means a great deal to me.

MARY I hope he'll have no reason to complain of me, sir.

Jekyll lifts the silver lid to look at his breakfast, then sighs and replaces it.

JEKYLL Mrs Kent is so partial to kippers herself, it tends to slip her mind that I can't abide the things.

MARY Oh, let me . . .

JEKYLL No, no.

He starts to butter a piece of toast.

I was rather hoping you might be able to do something for me this afternoon: accompany my assistant on a scientific errand. That is, if you can see your way to overlook his offensive behaviour.

MARY Well, sir, I . . .

She breaks off, obviously in two minds about accepting Jekyll's proposition.

JEKYLL I'll send Bradshaw if you prefer; but I thought Hyde might show you the form, and then you could help me when he's engaged on other work. You see, I'm inaugurating a new line of research and I'm going to need various supplies from time to time. It might make an occasional break from this perpetual housework.

MARY Of course I'll go, sir, if you'd like me to.

JEKYLL Thank you.

Mary lowers her head and begins to move towards the door. Jekyll's soft voice checks her.

Mary.

MARY Yes, sir.

JEKYLL From what he has said to me, I think my assistant likes you very much. I see no reason why you shouldn't end up the best of friends.

INT. UNDERGROUND PLATFORM. DAY

The underground has not been functioning for very long and still uses steam trains, one of which is pulling up with a great hiss and roar, amplified by the narrow funnel. Mary hesitates, somewhat overawed by the train, but Hyde, dapper in black, an old black leather Gladstone bag in one hand, takes her firmly by the arm.

HYDE There's nothing whatever to be afraid of.

And so saying he marches her on to the train.

INT. TRAIN COMPARTMENT. DAY

Mary sits opposite Hyde, aware of his sardonic gaze, but avoiding his eye. Eventually, he speaks.

HYDE Unless I miss my guess, you have rather a soft spot for our employer.

MARY The doctor's been very kind to me.

She's embarrassed, aware of having spoken very stiffly. Hyde, on the other hand, appears to be enjoying himself.

HYDE He's too old for you, of course.

MARY I don't know what you mean.

HYDE Just as you like.

He looks out of the window for a moment, into the blackness, then turns back to her.

No doubt monogamy is a commercially convenient arrangement, but I can't see that it makes sense in any other way. Why would you choose deliberately to deprive yourself of all the qualities your partner lacks?

The question hangs in the air as Hyde turns away again to gaze out of the window.

EXT. THE JAGO. DAY

Mary follows Hyde, hurrying to keep up, down a dark and sinister East End street: mud, refuse, blank walls, occasional dangling chains to allow merchandise to be lowered from the warehouses to the street. What makes the street so eerie is the strangely echoing, panic-tinged distress calls of various farm animals, the bleat of lambs, the lowing of cattle. It's raining lightly and Hyde suddenly gives an involuntary shudder.

HYDE I hate the rain: not a single drop but I don't feel it sizzle.

He hurries on and turns the corner, stops for a moment. Mary arrives next to him, looks down the new street and suppresses a gasp.

EXT. SLAUGHTERHOUSE STREET. DAY

Mary's point of view: this street, relatively short but teeming with movement, is where the offal of the slaughterhouses is discarded. Consequently the street is crawling with beggars, searching for edible scraps, competing with the wild dogs and rats, often not scrupling to eat anything viable on the spot.

Mary is appalled: Hyde stands beside her, contemplating the scene with a jaundiced eye.

HYDE Would you guess that we were standing at the very centre of the greatest and wealthiest empire in history?

MARY Indeed not, sir.

He moves forward again and she follows him.

HYDE Surely, in the face of this vast indifference, there's something noble about individual wickedness. It shows someone is taking the trouble, don't you agree? And at least it's *personal.*

EXT./INT. MEAT MARKET AND SLAUGHTERHOUSE. DAY

A flock of lambs is being led into the cavernous, hangar-like space, at the front of which butchers in bloodstained aprons stand ready to make their wholesale deals. Mary decides to linger on the threshold, as Hyde moves in to speak to one of the butchers, a colossus, whose apron is marked with clear bloody handprints. Somewhere, far in the back, almost out of sight, animals thrash in their death throes, screaming with fear.

Mary watches Hyde, as he opens his Gladstone bag and extracts a long-bladed, gleaming knife. He hands it to the butcher. They lean over a freshly flayed ox corpse. Mary watches Hyde watching the butcher leaning over, slitting open the stomach, reaching in and operating with the knife again.

Mary looks away, distressed. After a time, she looks back, aware that Hyde is approaching with some object wrapped in bloody newspaper which he eventually, just as he joins her, pops into his Gladstone bag, grimly satisfied.

INT. NATURAL HISTORY MUSEUM. DAY

The Natural History Museum in South Kensington is a brand new Victorian monument, adjacent to and joined with the Science Museum, another recent innovation. Hyde leads Mary across the cathedral-like expanse which contains the reconstructed skeletons of the largest dinosaurs. Hyde hesitates for a moment beside the bones of the Tyrannosaurus Rex; he glances up at the towering edifice of the skeleton, lit in shafts of cold light from high windows; and with a swift, involuntary smile of complicity he reaches out to pat a gigantic femur.

INT. MUSEUM BACK CORRIDOR. DAY

The no man's land where one museum blends with the other. Strange abandoned artefacts, stuffed birds, glistening chunks of meteorite, a bottled foetus. Mary follows Hyde, who comes to a halt by a curious swing-door, the top half in frosted glass, behind which can be heard a susurration of voices.

HYDE Wait here.

He passes forcefully through the swing door. Mary, waiting outside, cannot help but catch glances into the room behind, three or four snapshots as the door continues to swing.

What she sees, unmistakably, are images of the last stages of an autopsy: serious bearded figures, four or five medical men in black waistcoats and shirtsleeves, clustered around the greenish corpse of a middle-aged man. The final swing of the door reveals a number of banknotes changing hands between Hyde and one of the doctors.

INT. DR JEKYLL'S OPERATING THEATRE. DAY

Two transparent containers, half-full of brine, wait on the operating table: we remain close on them as Hyde decants into them first the large, discoloured ox's liver; and second, a smaller, smooth and regular human liver.

Another angle reveals Mary watching, riveted despite herself.

MARY What does he want them for?

HYDE The doctor's notion is that there may be a way to replace worn-out organs with healthy organs from cadavers or even perhaps from animals. It sounds absurdly far-fetched to me . . .

He looks up at Mary for a moment: for once his eyes are full of melancholy and the habitual harshness of his voice softens noticeably.

. . . although, God knows, the ways of science are strange and twisting enough.

Mary frowns, unable to take her eyes off him, fascinated by the glimpse of another persona, which vanishes as, businesslike again, he gathers up the containers.

Wait here.

He sets off up the stairs, carrying the containers, and pushes open the red baize door. Mary stands below, watching him.

Afternoon, Doctor: a visit from the butcher.

He cocks his head, as if listening.

What's that?

After a moment he turns back to Mary.

He can't think why, Mary, but he suddenly feels peckish. Tea and sandwiches.

MARY For two, sir?

Hyde grins broadly.

HYDE Why not?

He turns and disappears into the room.

INT. KITCHEN. EVENING

Mary walks into the kitchen. Mrs Kent is busy at the kitchener; Annie is peeling potatoes; and Bradshaw is washing his hands, black with boot polish, at the sink. Mary picks up the big kettle and goes to fill it at the tap.

MARY Dr Jekyll and Mr Hyde would like some tea.

BRADSHAW How'd you get on with that Mr Hyde? He manage to keep his hands to hisself?

MARY You shouldn't judge everyone by your own standards, Mr Bradshaw.

Bradshaw makes a mock-deferential face, soaping his hands.

BRADSHAW I hope Hyde was politer to you than he was to old Poole.

MARY What do you mean?

BRADSHAW Just before you went off, he sends for Poole, tells him to get on the train and go off to some chemist's way out in the country; then when Poole says is there anything else I can do for you, sir, he says yes, mind your own business; and slams the door in his face.

Mrs Kent and Annie can't help laughing; and Mary's smiling as well.

MRS KENT He was that upset. I wouldn't cross him in the next day or two, if I was you. He said to me doesn't matter how well he speaks, Mr Hyde, no one could ever mistake him for a gentleman.

ANNIE Who is he, then?

BRADSHAW Ask me, he's got one over on the doctor. Spot of blackmail. Or, tell you what, perhaps he's a souvenir of the doctor's student days. Sort of a grown-up wild oat. They do look a bit alike.

Mrs Kent is hooting with scandalised amusement; but Mary, as Bradshaw quickly notices, is no longer smiling.

BRADSHAW Mary doesn't like to think the doctor's ever had any fun in his life.

INT. STAIRCASE AND LANDING. EVENING

Mary struggles up the stairs with a full coal scuttle.

INT. DRAWING ROOM. EVENING

Mary comes into the room and puts the scuttle down inside the fender of one of the fires. The lamps are burning in the room, but there's no fire in the grate. As she notices this, something else catches her attention: a brandy balloon stands on a small circular leather-topped table next to a large wing chair; and someone's foot is visible in the shadow in front of the chair. Mary makes a natural assumption.

MARY Can I make you a fire, Doctor?

But it's Hyde who leans forward and peers at her round the wing of the chair, his expression of contemptuous ferocity fully back in place.

HYDE I'm very sorry to disappoint you, but he isn't back yet. And no, I do not want a fire. It's altogether too damned stuffy in this house. I prefer to devise other methods of keeping warm. So you can refill my glass if you've a mind to.

MARY Very good, sir.

She fetches the decanter and pours some brandy into his glass.

HYDE Economising, is he?

MARY I don't understand.

HYDE What I mean is, has your master issued instructions to serve particularly short measures?

As he speaks, he's risen to his feet, taken the decanter from Mary, poured a more generous shot of brandy and thrust the decanter ungraciously back at her.

MARY No, sir.

HYDE I should think not. He must be one of the richest men in London.

Mary doesn't answer: instead, she replaces the decanter and starts to move towards the door. Meanwhile, Hyde drinks the brandy in a couple of gulps. Mary pauses in the doorway.

MARY Will there be anything else, sir?

HYDE Yes. Come here.

Mary hesitates: but there's something compelling in his tone and, as if under hypnosis, she slowly crosses the room until she's a couple of steps away from him. He's watching her, his eyes burning. He looks at her for a while, apparently finding it difficult to say what he wants.

There's something I've been trying to say to you all day: I want to apologise for the remarks I made yesterday.

MARY That's . . .

HYDE Yes. They were . . . unnecessarily offensive and . . .

He breaks off. Mary steals a glance at him. Something seems to be boiling around his eyes. Suddenly, there's a crunching sound. It's the brandy glass, as he crushes it between his hands. Shards break off and tumble to the carpet. Mary watches Hyde, transfixed.

Now look what you've made me do.

He opens his hands to reveal his bloodied palms. There's a large sliver of glass deeply embedded in his left palm. He pulls it out and it comes free with a slight sucking sound. Mary looks at him, paralysed with terror. He smiles mirthlessly. He dabs the blunt index finger of his right hand into the bloody gash, stretches out a hand

and smears blood on Mary's cheek. She closes her eyes, tears spilling out. He dips two fingers in the blood and smears her again, this time pushing his index finger into her mouth. He leans in to whisper hoarsely in her ear.

Don't you know who I am?

Close on Mary, her eyes tightly closed, her cheek stained with blood. After a moment, she opens her eyes, ready to run out of the room. Another angle reveals that Hyde has vanished. She's on her own.

INT. OPERATING THEATRE. DAY

Mary, carrying a tea tray with tea and cucumber sandwiches, climbs the staircase towards the red baize door. The lunch tray, still untouched, sits outside on the floor. Mary redistributes the weight of her tray and knocks at the door.

JEKYLL Who is it?

MARY Mary, sir.

A moment's hesitation, then:

JEKYLL Come in.

Mary pushes open the door.

INT. LABORATORY. DAY

Jekyll is at his architect's table, in shirtsleeves, intently absorbed in some chemical experiment. The remains of one of the livers sits in a kidney bowl leaking dark blood. Retorts bubble and test tubes fizz. Mary advances to put the tray down on the table in the domestic half of the room.

MARY I don't know why I'm bringing tea, sir, when you haven't even touched your lunch.

JEKYLL Since it's you who brought it, I will take some tea, Mary. Would you like to pour it for me?

He finishes what he's doing while she pours the tea. As he does so, he speaks, perhaps a fraction too casually.

I understand from my assistant that everything passed off very smoothly yesterday.

MARY Yes, sir.

She hesitates, steeling herself to continue.

But in future I'd be much obliged if you'd ask Bradshaw to accompany him.

JEKYLL I understand: but it won't always be such ghoulish business.

MARY It wasn't that, sir.

JEKYLL You don't care for Mr Hyde?

MARY It's not exactly even that, sir. It's just . . .(*She breaks off, trying to find the clearest way of putting it.*) . . . he troubles me.

Jekyll has stopped what he was doing to look at her. Now he crosses towards the tea table, his expression grave.

JEKYLL Yes: one of us is not altogether in his right wits. The question I can never decide is whether it be he or I.

MARY Are you making fun of me, sir?

JEKYLL No. No, no: I would never do that.

He takes a cucumber sandwich and nibbles at it reluctantly.

Is it tomorrow, your afternoon off?

MARY Yes, sir.

JEKYLL What are your plans?

MARY I generally just go for a walk in the park, sir.

JEKYLL With your young man?

MARY Oh, no, sir. At my last place, one of the maids used to take me dancing; she'd dance with one fellow after the other, but somehow they hardly ever used to ask me. Must be I'm not made for that.

JEKYLL I find that very hard to believe. You've certainly never struck me as a wallflower.

He's looking at her; she blushes and turns away.

MARY Drink your tea while it's hot, sir.

She begins moving away as Jekyll stands watching her, motionless.

EXT. KENSINGTON GARDENS. DAY

A corner of the park much frequented by domestic servants, most conspicuously nannies, supervising their charges at the edge of the round pond or pushing elaborate perambulators. Winter sun. Mary sits on a bench, engaged in some embroidery. She seems relaxed, smiles as she watches a boy in a sailor suit playing with his model boat, yawns, closes her eyes.

Mix to: later, as Mary wakes with a start. The park is now almost deserted, fog has begun to form and the low sun is as red as a blood orange.

Another angle, through the railings, shows Mary, in the distance, near the pond, her back to the camera. A small, coarse, man's hand, unusually hirsute, comes into frame, gripping the spearhead of one of the railings.
Mary sits up. She senses she's being watched, but can't quite bring herself to turn around. She folds up her embroidery, puts it away in her bag. Then she hesitates, her expression increasingly fearful.
From behind the bench: slowly, Mary stands up. She's still for a moment, then suddenly spins round on her heel.
Her point of view: a figure on the other side of the railings, scarcely visible through the fog, a small man with a tilted top hat, slips quickly out of sight.
Mary turns back and starts walking, fast, towards the gates.

INT. KITCHEN. DAY

Mary and Mrs Kent are preparing the tea tray, when Poole comes into the room holding a grubby envelope, which he hands to Mary without comment. She looks at it, puzzled, then steels herself to make a tentative request.

MARY May I open it, Mr Poole?

POOLE Very well; be quick about it.

She opens it and reads. Mrs Kent, watching her, sees how the blood drains from her face.

MRS KENT What is it, Mary, is it bad news?

MARY My mum's passed away.

Mrs Kent wipes her hands on her apron and fetches a kitchen chair.

MRS KENT You sit down a minute; I'll make you a nice cup of tea.

MARY This is from her landlord, it says she owes him money for the rent.

MRS KENT Now, don't you worry: Mr Poole will speak to Master, won't you, Mr Poole?

POOLE When I take him up his tea.

MRS KENT And you can go and see to things in the morning.

POOLE Are there no other relations?

MARY No, sir, only me.

POOLE I'm sorry to hear it, Mary.

MARY I've got my savings. Nearly eight pounds. Would that be enough to pay for a proper funeral?

MRS KENT Oh, yes, dear. That should do it easy.

POOLE She may have made some provision herself.

MARY I don't think so, sir. She had a job getting enough to eat.

There's a silence: Poole makes final arrangements to the tea tray, groaning with scones and sandwiches and sponge cake. Mrs Kent pours a cup of tea for Mary. Mary gnaws at her lip, staring across the room, remembering.

INT. LIBRARY. DAY

Dr Jekyll looks up from his desk, as Mary appears to collect the tea things. He watches her for a moment before speaking. He looks grey and oppressed.

JEKYLL I'm sorry to hear about your mother, Mary. Of course you must take whatever time off you may need.

MARY Thank you, sir.

JEKYLL Had she been ill?

MARY I don't know, sir, the landlord didn't say. I think he was more interested in the money.

JEKYLL And there really is no one else in your family? Not even . . .?

MARY I don't think so, sir.

Jekyll looks away. Sweat is breaking out on his forehead. Mary gathers up the tray. Jekyll looks back at her and speaks in a quite different tone.

JEKYLL You weren't afraid of him, were you?

MARY Afraid of who, sir?

He looks away again, his eyes suddenly blurred with tears.

INT. BASEMENT STAIRS AND BASEMENT IN HAFFINGER'S LODGING HOUSE. DAY

Double doors are thrown open at the top of the stairs and Mr Haffinger appears, a grubby little man with ginger hair, mittens and an air of ingratiating attentiveness. Mary's behind him, following him as he sets off down the rickety wooden stairs.

MARY Why isn't she in her room?

HAFFINGER Well, you see, I've a heavy demand for my rooms, a long waiting list, you see . . .

MARY Where have you put her?

HAFFINGER She's quite comfortable, you know, very snug really . . .

A reverse shot shows the ruined basement, a good deal of which is under water. There's a constant dripping from somewhere.

Don't you worry, it's dry as a bone, where she is.

He reaches the foot of the stairs and eases round the corner, avoiding the puddles. Mary, meanwhile, forces herself to continue down the stairs. Haffinger pulls open the creaking, triangular door to a cupboard under the stairs.

As he does so, Mary, who's more or less caught up with him, stays back, suppressing a gasp; this is because a large rat has darted out of the cupboard and run away from them, hugging the wall.

Mary's Mother's corpse is crammed into the cupboard, much as Mary herself was when she was punished by her father. Her body is frail and yellowish, dressed in a once white, now grey shift. She sits with her knees up under her chin; her mouth has dropped open, giving her an expression of alarm.

Mary stretches out a hand to touch her hand; it's obviously cold as ice and Mary jerks away, shocked. Close on her as she stands, looking down on her Mother, her eyes full of sadness. Then Haffinger closes the cupboard and straightens up, his tone cheerily businesslike.

Now, the parish will provide the expenses of the burial.

MARY No, I want her to have a proper funeral; I can pay.

HAFFINGER Oh, well, then, you must let me take you to a first-class undertaker of my acquaintance. Very competitive rates.

MARY Thank you, I prefer to make my own arrangements.

She turns to him, controlled anger in her voice.

MARY And did you say you were also owed money?

HAFFINGER Ah, no, I took the liberty of selling off her few bits of furniture and crockery and clothes.

He's rummaging in the depths of a capacious pocket.

Which I'm pleased to say cleared off her debt completely and, let me see . . .

He succeeds in fishing out a coin, which he drops in Mary's hand.

. . . yes, a shilling over.

Mary looks down at the small coin in her palm.

MARY A poor wage for a lifetime's drudgery.

HAFFINGER Very true, miss, this is a vale of tears.

EXT. SIDE STREET. DUSK

Mary, on her way back towards the Jekyll house, appears over the crest of the steep hill which leads down to the corner.

Close on Mary: as she starts down the hill, she's aware of the sound of fast-moving, but unequal footsteps. Involuntarily, she increases her pace, but the sound of the running footsteps grows louder.

Mary's about halfway down the hill, when a figure bursts over the top of the hill behind her. She glances over her shoulder and keeps going, pulling instinctively in towards the lee of the shopfronts. She looks back again.

Her point of view: the figure in its top hat and opera cloak, looms through the mist, now running pell-mell. His giant shadow, thrown on to the blank boundary wall of Jekyll's property, seems to pursue him like some great predator. And now there's another rapidly increasing sound: hoofbeats clattering on the surface of the road.

The fugitive is Hyde: in a moment, he's drawn level with Mary, skidded to a halt, guided by some animal instinct, taken her arm and drawn her swiftly into the shadow of the Bridge of Sighs.

HYDE I must crave your indulgence for a moment.

As he speaks, he's slipped off his cloak, taken off his top hat and dropped them on the ground in the shadows. Above, two mounted constables appear on the skyline and gallop down the hill. Hyde seizes Mary in his arms, turns his back to the road and buries his face in her neck. The constables ride by, scarcely sparing Hyde and Mary a glance. As they pass, Hyde's head comes up and half-turns.

Hyde and Mary's point of view: the constables reach the corner at the bottom of the hill, round it and disappear.

As Hyde turns back to Mary, she notices that his hand and sleeve are streaked with blood.

MARY What have you done?

Hyde ignores the question and smiles at her, not letting her go.

HYDE Thank you: you have a wonderful knack for being in the right place at the right time. Why are you about at this hour of the evening?

MARY My mother died, I've been . . .

HYDE Oh, yes, I heard about it. Well . . .

He leans in close to her.

She's not the only one.

He's fetched a key out of his pocket.

And now I must make good my escape.

He gathers up his cloak and top hat and opens the strange little door to the spiral staircase. Then, on a sudden impulse, he leans back towards her, puts a hand round the back of her head and kisses her, hard. Afterwards, he takes a step back and grins at her, insolently.

I don't suppose you'll ever see me again.

He sniffs the air, as if catching some pleasant scent, turns abruptly and vanishes through the door, slamming it behind him.

Mary moves out of the shadow of the bridge, down towards the corner. Then she looks up and back.

EXT. SIDE STREET. DUSK

Her point of view: Hyde's unmistakeable, hunched shape goes flitting across the Bridge of Sighs.

EXT. JEKYLL HOUSE. DUSK

Mary hesitates on the threshold. The front door is ajar and something is evidently amiss.

INT. HALL DUSK

Mary steps into the house. There's a uniformed policeman in the hall. He moves in on her, before she has time to compose herself.

POLICEMAN Are you the housemaid? Miss Reilly?

MARY Yes.

POLICEMAN This way.

He leads her across to the dining-room door, which he opens.

INT. DINING ROOM. DUSK

The lamps are lit in the dining room, where two plain-clothes men sit at the table, flanked by a couple of standing uniformed policemen. Poole sits opposite the Inspector in charge of the proceedings, with Mrs Kent, Bradshaw and Annie lined up behind him. All their faces turn to the door, as Mary steps into the room.

INSPECTOR Mary Reilly?

MARY Yes, sir.

INSPECTOR Where have you been?

MARY My mother's died, sir. I had some arrangements to make.

The Inspector nods brusquely, as if to acknowledge that this fits in with his information. Then he unexpectedly changes tack.

INSPECTOR And when did you last see the doctor's assistant, Mr Edward Hyde?

MARY Er, some time ago, sir.

INSPECTOR Not in the last twenty-four hours?

Mary's eyes have fallen on an object lying on the table in front of the Inspector: it's the broken-off top of Dr Jekyll's dog's-head ebony cane. The silver handle is black with congealed blood. She manages to answer, but her voice is not much more than a whisper.

MARY No, sir.

INSPECTOR Another question: are you acquainted with a friend of the doctor's, a Member of Parliament, Sir Danvers Carew?

Mary looks at the Inspector for a moment, het expression steady.

EXT. RED-LIGHT DISTRICT. NIGHT

The portly figure of Sir Danvers Carew leaves Mrs Farraday's, a young child-prostitute on his arm. Almost at once, Hyde steps out of the shadows, grasps the child's forearm, drags her away from Sir Danvers and makes some evidently contemptuous remark. Sir Danvers flushes with indignation and begins to remonstrate, although again no dialogue is heard, his jowls wobbling and his mouth opening and shutting furiously. Hyde hardly puts up with this for any time at all: decisive as a snake, he raises his cane and brings it down with shattering force on Sir Danvers's head. As Sir Danvers staggers back, it's clear that the silver dog's-head has penetrated his cheek; and Hyde has to exercise considerable strength to prise it out. All this has happened very quickly.

MARY (*voice over*) I don't believe so, sir.

INT. DINING ROOM. DUSK

The Inspector looks up at Mary, his expression beady.

INSPECTOR But I understand he was a regular dinner guest here at the house.

EXT. RED-LIGHT DISTRICT. NIGHT

To the horror of the child and the others standing in the street, Hyde continues to rain vicious blows on Sir Danvers's head. One of them lands near his eye and causes a spurt of blood to splash out on to Hyde's sleeve and cuff. Finally, his expression bewildered, Sir Danvers slowly keels over like a felled ox. As he's on the way down, another violent swipe with the cane causes the dog's-head handle to embed in his skull and the cane snaps in half. Sir Danvers crashes to the ground without dislodging the top half of the cane, which continues to stick out of his head at an unlikely angle. Meanwhile, deprived of his weapon, Hyde commences to let fly at the prostrate body and face with his steel-tipped boots.

POOLE (*voice over*) In point of fact, Reilly is the most recently engaged member of the domestic staff, and I don't believe Sir Danvers has dined here since her arrival.

INSPECTOR (*voice over*) I see.

EXT./INT. DINING ROOM. DUSK

Mary is still staring at the broken-off top of Jekyll's cane. She closes her eyes briefly, trying to dismiss the hideous images passing through her head.

INSPECTOR And now, if you'll oblige us, Mr Poole, we'd like to search the doctor's laboratory.

Mary's eyes open wide in shock.

MARY I don't think there's anyone out there, sir.

POOLE Will you not interfere in matters which don't concern you?

They're all looking at her now, which means she is the only one to see, across the courtyard, the door to the operating theatre open to reveal Dr Jekyll.

MARY You'd best ask the doctor yourself.

They all turn to the window. The Inspector rises to his feet and, a moment later, Poole moves over to open the French door to admit Jekyll, pale and dishevelled, but apparently perfectly composed.

JEKYLL May I be of some assistance, gentlemen?

INT. MARY'S BEDROOM. NIGHT

Mary wakes. The moonlight which pours through the dormer window shows that Annie's side of the bed is empty. Mary looks around, puzzled.

MARY Annie?

No answer. Mary gets up, crosses the tiny room, opens the door, listens. Nothing. She turns, closes the door, moves back towards the bed, frowning. She sits on the edge of the bed and turns; and is even more surprised to see the familiar bulging shape under the covers.

Well, I don't know. For some reason I thought . . .

She breaks off, not wanting to waken Annie, climbs back into bed and turns her back to Annie, whispering as she does so.

Goodnight.

Slowly a head comes up from under the covers; but it isn't Annie's: it is Hyde's. Very carefully, he leans towards Mary, who lies on her side with her back to him. His long tongue slips out between his lips. He pulls her nightdress down over her shoulders, puts his tongue between her shoulder blades and runs it very deliberately up to the nape of her neck. Then he buries his face in her neck, murmuring hoarsely as he does so.

HYDE Mary Reilly.

Suddenly, Mary comes to with a shock. She tries to get away from him and a short, violent struggle ensues, which ends with him lying on top of her, her nightdress torn, pinning her down on the mattress. He murmurs in her ear.

I'm sorry, there must be some misunderstanding. I thought you invited me here.

Mary looks into his eyes, inches way from hers. She's quite still now. Eventually, she answers.

MARY I did.

Hyde grins. He leans down to kiss her.

INT. MARY'S BEDROOM. NIGHT

Suddenly, Mary wakes up with a jolt. Annie is lying beside her with her eyes open. Mary raises her head off the pillow.

ANNIE What's the matter with you?

MARY I'm sorry. Bad dream.

ANNIE Didn't sound too bad.

Mary lies back on the pillow, her expression troubled.

INT. STAIRCASE. DAY

Mary is climbing the stairs, a bundle of sheets and blankets in her arms, when Jekyll suddenly appears in the doorway of the library.

JEKYLL Mary.

MARY Yes, sir.

JEKYLL I meant to ask you, I trust your sad mission was successful yesterday.

MARY Yes, thank you, sir, the funeral's to be on Thursday.

JEKYLL Then you must have the day off, of course.

MARY Thank you, sir.

JEKYLL Now would you step in here a moment. I want to speak to you.

MARY Mr Poole is . . .

JEKYLL Never mind Mr Poole.

He vanishes and, after a second's hesitation, Mary follows him into the room.

INT. LIBRARY. DAY

Jekyll stands in the window, his back to her. He glances over his shoulder.

JEKYLL Put those down.

Mary puts the sheets down on a chair as Jekyll turns, steeling himself to speak to her.

You saw him, yesterday.

MARY I did, sir.

JEKYLL And yet you told the police you hadn't. Why was that?

MARY I don't really know, sir.

JEKYLL You know what you've done has made you an accessory to murder? Like me. In a case like this, not telling the police everything you know is a criminal offence.

MARY I know that, sir.

JEKYLL Danvers Carew: I was at school with him, you know. He was corrupt and frivolous, but he didn't deserve that. And it was completely gratuitous. Just some vicious impulse. You see, he'd begun to think he was invulnerable, Hyde. But this was an important man, not someone you could sweep under the carpet. Not like the others.

Mary looks at him, shocked.

MARY What others, sir?

Jekyll looks away, out of the window, staring blankly out towards the laboratory.

What others?

JEKYLL There have been others.

He shakes his head, closing his eyes, oblivious to Mary's horrified expression. A moment passes, then Mary speaks, almost involuntarily.

MARY Where is he?

Jekyll opens his eyes and looks up at her, surprised by something in her tone.

JEKYLL Last night he walked in on me, bold as brass. He wanted money, so he could make good his escape. I made him promise to disappear and never show his face again. We're free of him. He's gone for ever.

The blood drains from Mary's face: she puts out a hand to steady herself.

What is it?

MARY Nothing, sir.

But Jekyll knows what it is. He looks at her and his eyes fill with tears.

JEKYLL My poor Edward. It's marvellous how much he loves his life.

MARY And his victims, sir. Did they not love theirs?

He makes an enormous effort to pull himself together and look up at her.

JEKYLL Forgive me, Mary.

MARY For what, sir?

He doesn't answer. He looks away and puts a hand to his forehead. Mary is also strongly affected. He turns back to her.

JEKYLL We're very grateful to you. Both of us. But the dream is over.

He seems on the verge of tears. He looks away, controlling himself with an effort.

JEKYLL Will you stay with me for a while?

MARY As long as you like, sir.

JEKYLL Thank you.

Silence. He looks at her.

Oh, Mary, I have had such a lesson.

She meets his eye to find he's looking at her strangely, with some intensity. After a while, as the silence lengthens, he rises to his feet and begins to move over to her. Finally he speaks, a curious hoarse note in his voice.

Your face is very dear to me, Mary.

He takes half a step towards her, stretching out a hand but not quite daring to touch her.

My life would be a sad thing if I couldn't . . .

He breaks off, grits his teeth and seems to find some momentary difficulty in getting his breath. Mary looks at him, all of a sudden very troubled. Some kind of seismic disturbance seems to be taking place under the skin of his face. Involuntarily, he turns to check his appearance in the mirror above the mantelpiece. Then he turns back to her, reaches out and seizes her wrist with his right hand. A moment later, however, he winces and turns his left hand palm upwards. As Mary, frightened now, looks on, a thin gash like a razor cut opens up in his palm and blood starts to spread and gather in his hand.

MARY What is it, sir? What's the matter?

Jekyll lets go of her wrist and pulls a white handkerchief out of his pocket; he wraps it roughly round his left hand. It also has a set of initials stitched in blue in one corner; only on this handkerchief the initials are EH. As blood begins immediately to soak through the linen, Jekyll notices the initials; and, looking up, notices that Mary has also noticed. She's staring at the handkerchief, transfixed. Without saying a word, grunting slightly, Jekyll turns and rushes out of the room. Mary stands there for a moment, then in her turn hurries to the door.

INT. STAIRCASE. DAY

Mary stops in the doorway. She can hear Jekyll clattering downstairs as fast as he can go. She waits a moment and turns back into the library.

INT. LIBRARY. NIGHT

Mary hurries across to the window.

EXT. COURTYARD. NIGHT

Mary's point of view: below, Jekyll moves swiftly across the courtyard in the direction of the operating theatre. He's moving strangely, somehow crouched, almost hobbling, although at some speed, until the darkness swallows him up.

Fade.

EXT. GRAVEYARD. DAY

Bleak, foggy day. The plumed black horses paw the ground, the hearse behind them is empty. The camera tracks towards a narrow grave over which an arthritic vicar, hunched against the cold, is concluding the burial service in a hasty mumble. The only mourners are Mary, neat in black, and Haffinger, in a tall, outmoded top hat, and a frock coat shiny with age. Two sextons wait nearby, somewhat impatiently, spades in hand.

As the vicar finishes, Mary steps forward, picks up a little trowel and throws some earth on top of the coffin, which lies in the grave no bigger than a child's coffin.

As she steps back, a little old man in a very worn but respectable dark suit and a tilted top hat, suddenly materialises at her elbow.

OLD MAN Sad day.

MARY Yes.

OLD MAN I'm glad I found you; I wanted to make a contribution towards the expenses of the funeral.

He's overcome by a violent coughing fit. When he recovers, he produces a gold sovereign from his pocket and holds it out to Mary, who's looking at him with mounting apprehension.

MARY Who are you?

OLD MAN Don't you even recognise your own father?

Mary gasps: and indeed, it is her Father, aged almost beyond recognition, wizened, white-haired and red-nosed. He doubles up, once again racked with coughs. Mary makes a supreme effort to control herself.

MARY Keep your money.

His coughing fit over, Mary's Father looks at her again, choosing to ignore what she's said.

MARY'S FATHER You're looking well; and settled. In service in some big house, so I was told.

MARY Who told you?

MARY'S FATHER Your mother.

MARY When?

MARY'S FATHER I seen a bit of her, this last couple of years. She wasn't one to bear a grudge.

His voice drops to a more intimate note, as he leans in towards her.

I was hoping we might be able to get together again sometime.

MARY No.

MARY'S FATHER Doctors tell me I ain't likely to live through the winter.

MARY I'm sorry.

Another burst of coughing, as if to illustrate his point; but Mary turns away and begins to move off. He stops coughing, flourishing the coin in his hand.

MARY'S FATHER My money's good as anyone's.

MARY Goodbye.

She accelerates; but the old man stumbles after her, his footsteps scraping in the old, recognisable way.

MARY'S FATHER Haven't you got a heart at all? I'm your father. Don't you feel anything for me?

Mary increases her pace: now a vile, lascivious, crooning note comes into her Father's voice.

We had our good times, didn't we? We had some good times. Don't you remember? You remember.

By now, Mary is breaking into a run, to escape from the terrible, wheedling voice and the sound of his irregular gait. She hurries away through the fog, which lies like a pall above the tombstones.

INT. STAIRCASE AND LANDINGS. DAY

Mary moves upstairs, a little unsteady, so that the teacup clatters on the breakfast tray. She arrives at the door to Jekyll's bedroom and knocks at the door.

INT. JEKYLL'S BEDROOM DAY

Mary advances into the room, towards the dark, motionless shape in the bed. She leans over to settle the tray, but at the last minute gasps and lets go of it, so that the crockery rattles and cutlery slides off on to the coverlet. This is because Hyde suddenly sits up, large as life and twice as alarming, brash and insolent as ever.

HYDE Did you miss me?

Mary pulls herself together with commendable speed.

MARY You promised the Master you'd go away.

HYDE Easier said than done, as it turns out.

MARY What have you done to him?

HYDE Better if you asked what he has done to me. The truth is, I *am* your master.

MARY What do you mean?

HYDE I mean that I am the bandit. He is merely the cave in which I shelter.

Mary starts to move back, but Hyde grips her wrist, moving quick as a snake.

Where are you going?

MARY To raise the alarm.

HYDE Last week you saved my life: now you want to send me to the gallows. Can you explain?

Mary hesitates fatally and Hyde's reaction is to release her wrist. He looks up at her.

Can you?

Mary meets his gaze and looks back at him, unflinching.

MARY No.

HYDE I feel differently with you, why should that be? You still the rage.

MARY Where does it come from, sir, this rage?

HYDE How would I know? It comes in like the tide.

Mary frowns, remembering Jekyll's use of the same phrase. But the thought is driven out of her head as Hyde reaches out to take back her wrist.

Show me.

He looks down at the network of scars on her wrist. Then he inclines his head, his long tongue emerges and he runs the tip of it around the white indentations in the flesh. Then, gently, he draws her towards him. She half-inclines, and then shakes her head, disengaging her arm.

Why not? We both know it's what you want.

MARY We all want things we can't have. Even a child knows that.

Hyde's eyes cloud; but for some reason he decides to control himself.

HYDE As always, you've taken the wise decision. When they say yes, I always have to kill them.

Mary's still looking at him, appalled and fascinated.

Go on.

Mary tears herself away and hurries out of the room, closing the door behind her.

INT. LANDING. DAY

Mary, profoundly shaken and relieved to be away from Hyde, sighs and leans her head back against the door.

All of a sudden, it bursts open and Hyde is there in the doorway with a knife in his hand, breathing hoarsely in her ear.

HYDE All right, here's another request: and this one you had better not refuse.

Mary jolts away, as if to make a run for it; but his free arm goes round her throat.

For years now the doctor has been suffering from a serious illness. From time to time, he would find ways to keep it at bay, but sooner or later it would return, more acute than ever. Finally, this year, he distilled two drugs, tested them and understood that he had found the cure, which took an unexpected form.

MARY What form?

HYDE Me. I was the cure.

Silence. Mary stares at him; her intuition tells her that what he has said makes sense, but her intelligence still finds it incredible.

The first formula transformed him into me; the second, which he always refers to, rather insultingly I can't help feeling, as the antidote, turned me back into him. Lately, I have found a way to escape from him, to become myself without having to wait for the injection.

MARY How?

HYDE Presumably because I am the stronger.

He breaks off for a moment, before resuming in a more businesslike tone.

Now listen very carefully: I want you to go to the glass presses in the doctor's laboratory. From the column of drawers marked 'E' I want you to take out the fourth drawer from the top, which is also the third drawer from the bottom, bring the whole drawer back here and push it inside the door. Is that understood?

MARY Yes.

HYDE Afterwards you may call the police, denounce me in the servants' hall, whatever you please. But unless you do as I ask, now, I guarantee you will never see your precious master again, alive or dead. Here is the key to the operating theatre. Now, go.

He's released her and handed her the key. She looks at him, her expression full of anger and contempt.

MARY You're an evil man.

HYDE Perhaps. But you don't mind that as much as you should, Mary. Unless my sense of smell deceives me.

He grins wolfishly and disappears back into the bedroom, leaving Mary frightened and confused.

INT. SERVANTS' HALL. DAY

Poole sips at a cup of tea; Bradshaw and Annie are still eating their breakfast and Mrs Kent is at the stove. Mary enters the room and starts crossing towards the back door, moving as unobtrusively as she can. Poole, however, alert as ever, stiffens as she approaches the door.

POOLE Where are you going, Mary?

MARY The . . . Master has asked me to bring him something from the laboratory.

POOLE I'll take care of that, you have your breakfast.

MARY He particularly asked that I should do it myself.

POOLE I will do it.

MARY You don't know what it is he wants, so please don't interfere.

Poole's jaw drops; the other servants are hanging on every word, riveted. By now, Mary has the back door open.

And he's not to be disturbed for the rest of the morning.

She leaves the room; Poole is aghast, the others scrupulously avoiding his eye.

INT. CABINET. DAY

Mary lets herself into the room and hurries over to the presses. She opens the door to the third press; the left-hand column of drawers is marked 'E'. She slides out the fourth drawer down; it contains a number of bottles, mostly almost empty, some with powders, some with liquids; a glass mixing-phial; a hypodermic in a kidney bowl; a number of fresh needles; a length of rubber piping; a battered notebook and a hand mirror.

INT. LANDING. DAY

As Mary arrives at Jekyll's bedroom door, it opens and the drawer is snatched from her hand. Before she can speak, Hyde has slammed the door.

INT. KITCHEN. DAY

Poole is still looking shaken and nursing his cup of tea and there's an oppressive silence in the room, broken only by the sound of Bradshaw chewing at some especially tough morsel. Annie and Mrs Kent look up expectantly as Mary comes into the room.

POOLE Mary.

MARY Yes, Mr Poole.

POOLE I want you to go and wait in my parlour. I have something to say to you.

MARY Yes, Mr Poole.

She turns to leave the room and then gasps; her hand flies to her mouth, Dr Jekyll, pale and drawn, holding the drawer in his hand, is standing in the doorway.

JEKYLL Poole: there you are.

POOLE Yes, sir, I . . .

JEKYLL I want you to pay very close attention to what I say. You must make another visit to John Bell and Croyden . . .

POOLE I'm very much afraid they won't be able . . .

JEKYLL Will you listen to what I'm saying before you start raising objections?

Poole's face falls: he looks as if all the stuffing has been knocked out of him. Jekyll has put his drawer down on the kitchen table: now he brings out a bottle containing a fairly small amount of red liquid and a test tube, into which he decants a few drops of the liquid. Then he corks the test tube and holds it up.

Three or four months ago they prepared this at my instruction. There must have been some impurity in the compound, because since then, neither they nor any of the other chemists have been able to reproduce it. You must ask them to analyse this precisely and wait on the premises until they succeed in reconstituting it. Is that clearly understood?

POOLE Yes, sir.

Jekyll hands the test tube to Poole, who takes it gingerly.

JEKYLL Tell them this is a matter of the greatest urgency. Life and death.

POOLE I will, sir.

JEKYLL And you come with me, Mary. At least there's someone in this house I can rely on.

He turns to leave the room, still clutching his drawer. Mary glances at Poole, whose head has sunk under the humiliation of this final body-blow, and then hurries after Jekyll.

INT. STAIRCASE. DAY

Mary follows Jekyll up the stairs. As soon as she's sure she's out of earshot, she murmurs to him.

MARY I didn't know if I could believe what he was saying. But it's true, isn't it?

JEKYLL It's true.

INT. HALL. DAY

Jekyll leads Mary out into the hall, stops and turns to her, suppressing a shudder.

JEKYLL Why didn't you guess? I kept thinking you must know we were the same man.

MARY How could anyone know such a thing? How could anybody possibly guess?

JEKYLL Yes.

He makes an effort to pull himself together.

Now: I want you to make me up a bed in the cabinet at once. I shall need to spend most of my time there from now on.

MARY Why's that, sir?

Jekyll looks at her, momentarily surprised; then he gives in to the question with a shrug.

JEKYLL Because it's where the final act must be played out.

Mary is unable to control a stab of fear; but she makes a great effort and reaches out for the drawer.

MARY Shall I take this over with me, sir?

Jekyll grabs at it, his expression panicky.

JEKYLL No, I need to keep it by.

He starts to move towards the stairs, but Mary's question stops him.

MARY He said you had an illness, sir. What kind of an illness?

Jekyll turns back to look at her, his expression haunted and crushed.

JEKYLL You might call it a fracture in my soul. Something which left me with a taste for oblivion.

Mary watches him as he shuffles away up the stairs.

INT. CABINET. NIGHT

A single bed has been brought in and made up, the room has been thoroughly cleaned and polished and a fire blazes in the grate. Mary's adding more coal to it, when Jekyll appears in the doorway, carrying his drawer of chemicals. He stands there a moment, looking at the transformed room, pale and unsteady.

JEKYLL Thank you, Mary.

He advances into the room, putting his drawer down on the architect's table. Mary straightens up and turns to face him. Slightly to her surprise, he bears down on her, moving closer and closer. She gathers a stray piece of hair and pushes it back under her cap in a nervous gesture. He's almost touching her before he speaks.

JEKYLL I'm afraid of what comes next.

MARY Isn't there any way to . . .?

JEKYLL He's taking over. He's waiting for me to sleep so he can return; or he may even be able to break through in my waking hours. The antidote is running out and, as you've seen, Poole's been everywhere and nobody can reproduce it. And he hates me now; he's in there, waiting to destroy me.

He breaks off, looking at her for a moment; then he stretches out a hand to touch the small scars on her neck, below her ear.

I love your eyes, Mary, their greenish light.

Mary leans towards him and he takes her in his arms. She stands close to him for a moment, her face on his chest, peaceful. Then she looks up at him. They're both aware of the proximity of the freshly made bed.

MARY Anything, sir; I'll do anything for you.

JEKYLL Yes, I know that now.

However, to her surprise, he breaks away from her. He reaches into his pocket and takes out an envelope.

There is something you can do for me.

MARY What, sir?

JEKYLL There's a hundred pounds in this envelope. It's for you. Leave this house tonight, go, don't look back . . .

MARY I can't leave you!

JEKYLL You must: because if you're here when he returns, he's going to kill you. Believe me: I know his mind.

She throws herself into his arms; he takes her face between his hands and covers her with kisses.

MARY Let me stay with you, sir.

JEKYLL No.

MARY Why not?

JEKYLL Because whenever you're close to me, I feel him kicking at the door.

He steps back from her.

Goodbye. Go quickly.

Mary seems about to say something; but can't. Instead, she turns and hurries away, crossing the room without looking back.

INT. SERVANTS' HALL EVENING

Mary, Mrs Kent, Bradshaw and Annie are eating supper, while Mr Poole's chair at the head of the table remains empty. Mary's lost in thought, not touching her food.

Close on Mary, as the other servants' voices run on in the background.

BRADSHAW (*off-screen*) I seen him shuffling across the courtyard like a little old man, holding on to that drawer, like he thought someone wanted to take it off him.

MRS KENT (*off-screen*) And poor Mr Poole, run off his feet, he's not looking very well on it either . . .

She breaks off as the door opens and Poole steps into the room, white-faced. He takes his seat and, as Annie gets up to serve him, he turns to Mary.

POOLE Mary, I'm afraid the Master has been put out of patience. As I feared, his new consignment of medicine was not at all satisfactory. There are a number of broken bottles in the operating theatre.

MARY I'll go and clear up, Mr Poole.

Poole looks at her for a moment, then shakes his head hopelessly.

POOLE No. Never mind. Leave it till the morning.

He looks baffled and defeated; a broken man.

EXT. JEKYLL HOUSE. NIGHT

The house rears up, monumental in the moonlight.

INT. COURTYARD. NIGHT

The courtyard is still, wintry. Light spreads upwards from the skylights of the operating theatre. It's the dead of night.

INT. MARY'S BEDROOM. NIGHT

Mary's dressed now and wearing her cloak. She tucks the envelope of money into her suitcase and closes it quickly, looking across at Annie to make sure she's still asleep. Annie doesn't stir and Mary eases herself out of the room.

INT. LANDING AND STAIRCASE. NIGHT

Mary hurries purposefully down the stairs, suitcase in hand.

INT. HALL. NIGHT

Mary's almost reached the front door, when second thoughts begin to overwhelm her. She sets down her suitcase, stands for a moment in the dark, closes her eyes; and then, impulsively, turns and moves towards the dining room, leaving her suitcase where it is.

EXT. COURTYARD. NIGHT

Mary emerges from the dining-room French doors. It's cold and foggy and, as she hurries across the courtyard, her breath rises on the air.

INT. OPERATING THEATRE. NIGHT

Mary lets herself into the huge room, weirdly lit by a lamp left standing on the floor, which is covered with shards of glittering broken glass. She advances cautiously towards the red baize door, ajar at the top of the stairs.

INT. CABINET. NIGHT

This room is also strangely lit, mostly by firelight, although a lamp burns in a recess. The bed is open and empty; and the room is apparently deserted, although Mary jumps as she suddenly catches sight of herself in the cheval mirror. Finally, noticing that the door in the far corner is open, Mary crosses to it.

INT. CORRIDOR. NIGHT

Mary follows the corridor round to the entrance of the Bridge of Sighs, moving cautiously through the gloom. She's about to cross the bridge to investigate the staircase beyond, when some infinitesimal sound spins her round.

Leading from the Bridge of Sighs to the door which gives directly back on to the operating theatre is a strange kind of catwalk suspended above a void. What it does is span the shell of the unused part of the building at the level of the cabinet, although in the darkness the floor one storey below is invisible. Mary begins to move across the catwalk. She's halfway across when another odd, metallic sound, from much closer at hand, stops her in her tracks. She looks round. Nothing. She frowns, puzzled.

MARY Master?

Silence. She decides to proceed. However, at the instant she turns to resume her progress, a hand comes up from beneath the catwalk and grabs her by the ankle.

She cries out in shock; and suddenly Hyde swings up from under the catwalk and pinions her roughly. His open shirt hangs down over his trousers, his feet are bare and his hair is tangled and dishevelled. For a moment Mary struggles helplessly in his arms.

HYDE I thought he told you to go.

MARY I didn't want him to suffer alone.

HYDE You should have listened to him.

By this time he's dragged her over to the door which leads back to the operating theatre, opened the door and bundled her through it.

INT. OPERATING THEATRE. NIGHT

When Mary reaches the bottom of the stairs, Hyde manhandles her in the direction of the operating table, striding through the broken glass in his bare feet. There's a short struggle, during which he drags off her cloak and drops it on the ground and then forces her back on to the table. He wrenches at her dress, exposing one shoulder, and runs a finger thoughtfully along her collarbone, his expression murderous. She look up at him; and when she speaks it's with a genuine quiet authority.

MARY Tell me something.

HYDE What?

MARY When you do this, must it always lead to killing?

HYDE It always has.

He's spoken quickly, unnerved by her candour. Now he paces up and down for a moment, leaving bloody footprints on the flagstones. She watches him, making no attempt to climb off the table. Finally, he strides back, snatches her arm, leans down and bites with all his strength into the area of her wrist where the scars are most plentiful. Somehow, despite the pain, Mary manages to prevent herself from crying out.

Hyde's head rises into frame: his mouth is slightly open. Blood runs between his front teeth down over his lower lip.

Mary looks up at the terrifying blood-spattered figure.

MARY Will this calm the pain?

HYDE For a while. Afterwards, I'll dig a hole in one of your flower beds and lie down in it.

He leans in over her. She makes no move to rise. Hyde takes off his shirt. Then he bends, cups a hand behind her head and kisses her on the mouth, a long, voluptuous kiss. He straightens up and looks down at her. She meets his gaze evenly, with no apparent trace of fear. He hesitates for a long moment, frozen in a kind of paralysis.

Contradictory impulses chase each other across his features. Finally, his face drops and he moans aloud. Then he looks up, breathless, agonised.

I always knew you'd be the death of us.

He moves round the operating table to a long laboratory bench in the corner. He bends and brings the drawer from the glass press up from the floor. With his other hand, he sweeps a quantity of equipment off the table and puts the drawer down. The bottle with the red liquid is almost empty; he empties it to the last drop into a graduated glass.

From another bottle he adds some white powder, also running very low, and from a third he tops up the mixture with a colourless liquid. He puts down the glass and watches as the mixture seethes, effervesces noisily and changes colour, first to purple, then to the palest green. He takes the length of rubber piping and wraps it tightly around his upper arm. Then he fills the hypodermic with the liquid from the glass, taps at a vein until he causes it to protrude and injects himself.

For a moment, nothing happens. Then his body is seized with a series of violent convulsions. He hangs on to the table, gasping. His face blackens. His limbs begin to spread and lengthen, splitting his clothes. His skin loses hair and begins to age. His face grows pale again and his features begin to melt and reassemble.

Mary watches, transfixed. Only when the process is complete does she break down and begin to sob. As soon as Jekyll comes to himself, he hurries over to take her in his arms

JEKYLL Even he couldn't bring himself to harm you.

He brings one of his initialled handkerchiefs out of his trouser pocket, sits her up, cleans and binds her wound. Then he leans forward and kisses her in the crook of her arm. She rests her other hand on the back of his head. Suddenly, he shudders, gripped by some internal convulsion. He moves back to the drawer to fetch out the hand mirror and check his appearance.

MARY What's the matter?

JEKYLL That was the last of the antidote. When I change back, I shall be Hyde for ever.

MARY What can be done for you, sir?

JEKYLL Nothing.

MARY And what did he mean, I'd be the death of you?

Jekyll looks down at the drawer and fetches out a bottle of colourless liquid. He considers it for a moment and then drinks straight from the bottle. He puts it down and moves back towards the operating table.

JEKYLL Can I lie down with you, Mary? This is very fast-acting.

He stretches out on the table beside her: she's looking down at him, appalled.

MARY What have you done, sir?

JEKYLL Only what I had to do.

She takes him in her arms and clings on to him, desperately.

Do you think we could have been happy together, Mary?

MARY Yes.

JEKYLL Yes, I expect we could.

He shudders again.

Is it very cold?

Mary gathers up her cloak and wraps him in it.

It was your goodness saved you.

MARY And it has killed you.

JEKYLL No. This was inevitable from the moment I found the way to achieve what I'd always wanted.

MARY What was that?

JEKYLL To be the knife as well as the wound.

He looks at her for a moment.

I can still taste your blood.

He takes her face between his hands and kisses her on the lips. Then his body arches., racked by another terrible convulsion. A spasm of fear crosses his features.

Has my face changed?

MARY No. Oh, no.

He takes her face between his hands again and looks at her, his expression now one of absolute serenity.

JEKYLL I wanted the night, you see. And here it is.

His head lolls back. He's dead. Mary takes him in her arms and holds him to her in a long embrace.

EXT. COURTYARD. NIGHT

The other servants, led by Mary, make their way across the fog-strewn courtyard; their night-clothes and the pools of light thrown by their lamps make an image like some Japanese print.

INT. OPERATING THEATRE. NIGHT

High angle as the party makes its way into the great room. Poole and Bradshaw hurry over to the operating table, followed, at a discreet distance, by Annie and Mrs Kent. Mary hangs back, moving reluctantly in their wake.

Poole touches the shoulder of the corpse, tipping it on to its back; his hand goes to his mouth and he gasps in horror.

The body is that of Edward Hyde, his teeth bared in a grimace which looks very like amusement.

The camera closes slowly in on Mary's face: her unutterable sadness.

A Bright Shining Lie

Caption against black screen:

SYRACUSE, NY, MAY 7, 1959

EXT. VANN HOUSE IN SYRACUSE. DAY

Fade up on a drowsy suburban afternoon: a battered green Ford pulls up in front of a large red-brick house.

John Paul Vann jumps out of the car. He's a man in the uniform of an infantry Major. His slight, tense body radiates waves of purposeful energy, which make him, under normal circumstances, a kind of red alert personified, an impression reinforced by his ruddy complexion and reddish hair teased into an aggressive quiff. However, at the moment he looks uncharacteristically uncertain and hesitates on the sidewalk, before eventually squaring his shoulders and setting off towards the front door.

INT. LIVING ROOM OF THE VANN HOUSE. DAY

His wife, Mary Jane Vann, is a compact, pleasant-looking woman of thirty-one. She's been sewing and at the moment is in the process of sifting through a big box which contains several hundred buttons. She looks up, surprised to see Vann in the doorway.

MARY JANE Hi, what are you doing?

He doesn't say anything and Mary Jane frowns.

What's the matter?

Vann closes the door behind him.

VANN Trouble.

MARY JANE What kind of trouble?

Vann looks away for a moment, then back at Mary Jane.

VANN Statutory rape.

Mary Jane reacts, startled, but not as surprised as one might expect.

MARY JANE Helga?

VANN Christ, no, that was years ago, and she was seventeen.

MARY JANE Then who?

Again, Vann looks away. Finally, he mumbles a word.

VANN Barbara.

Mary Jane screams. She hurls the box of buttons at him. It misses; buttons shower all over the room.

MARY JANE How could you?

VANN I'm sorry.

MARY JANE She's so horrible and fat and ugly!

VANN The Army isn't interested in is she going to win any beauty competitions. All the Army's interested in is she was fifteen.

MARY JANE What did you tell them?

VANN I told them she was lying.

Tears are rolling down Mary Jane's face now.

MARY JANE You deserve this, you asked for it, you're such an animal!

VANN She came up one day, when you were out with the kids. She had nothing on under her robe.

MARY JANE Get out!

Vann hesitates a moment; then he leaves the room. Mary Jane puts a hand in front of her face. Then she controls herself, crosses to pick up the box, goes down on her knees and begins to gather up the buttons.

INT. VANN'S OFFICE AT CAMP DRUM, NY. NIGHT

Vann's desk is covered with books and technical literature about the polygraph or lie detector. He himself is sitting behind a desk in the deputy comptroller's office in his undershirt. He's preparing to measure his own blood pressure, wrapping the rubber ligature round his arm, tightening it by squeezing air from the attachment, making a reading on the sphygmomanometer. This done, he jots a note and, looking at his watch laid out on the desk, takes his pulse.

Another angle reveals Mary Jane, facing him, perched anxiously on a hard chair, holding a sheet of paper fastened to a clipboard.

Vann finishes what he's doing, makes another note and looks up at Mary Jane.

VANN OK, read the questions.

MARY JANE Were you ever alone with Miss Devine in your apartment in Fort Leavensworth?

VANN Yes.

MARY JANE On more than one occasion?

VANN Yes.

MARY JANE Why?

VANN Miss Devine was very unhappy at home and she was having affairs with a couple of older men. She came to me for advice.

MARY JANE And on any of these occasions, did you and Miss Devine ever have intercourse?

VANN No, sir.

MARY JANE Did you ever at any time have intercourse with Miss Devine?

VANN No, sir, I didn't.

He begins wrapping the rubber ligature round his arm again. Mary Jane looks away, disturbed and unhappy.

INT. VANNS' BEDROOM. NIGHT

Mary Jane sits up in bed in her nightdress. Vann, in his underwear, sits by the dressing table facing her; the papers in his hand are ruffled by the breeze from a small fan set up beside him.

VANN Describe what happened.

MARY JANE Well, I came in from the kitchen and she was on the phone, I don't exactly know how to say this, talking dirty.

VANN And who was she talking to?

MARY JANE She told me afterwards it was this married man; her lover.

VANN What did you do about this?

MARY JANE I wasn't sure what to do, I told my husband about it when he came home.

VANN What was his response?

MARY JANE He told me not to allow Miss Devine to use our phone any more. I don't know if I can do this.

Vann looks up at her, suppressing a flicker of annoyance.

VANN Sure you can, this is easy, I'm the one has to beat the lie detector.

MARY JANE I know, John, but . . .

VANN The Army is my life. You going to tell me what I'm going to do, they throw me out? You any idea what kind of job

I could get with a dishonourable discharge? I don't have your daddy's fancy East Coast connections.

MARY JANE I just meant I don't know if I'm going to be able to remember it all.

VANN Don't think about me, think about the kids.

Mary Jane nods, making a visible effort to overcome her misery.

VANN OK, just a few more questions. (*He looks down at his papers.*) You knew of Miss Devine's visit to Dr Schultz, a gynaecologist in Leavenworth, Kansas?

INT. CONFERENCE ROOM IN 1ST ARMY HQ, FORT JAY, NY. DAY

Mary Jane, neat in a blouse, jacket and tweed skirt, sits facing the Investigating Officer at the Article 32 proceeding in Fort Jay. Vann, in uniform, sits at an angle; and only a couple of other officers are present, the atmosphere far more low-key than that of a courtroom.

MARY JANE Well, yes, sir, Dr Schultz was my gynaecologist. I recommended him to her mother.

INVESTIGATING OFFICER Dr Schultz has affirmed that Miss Devine told him she thought she might be pregnant by your husband.

MARY JANE I knew she was afraid she was pregnant. But she had told me who she thought, which of her lovers she thought was most likely to be responsible and it was not my husband.

INT. POLYGRAPH ROOM AT FORT JAY. DAY

Vann is hooked up to the machine. A bored-looking polygraph operator in a white coat perches on a stool, facing him.

OPERATOR Do you happen to know what day it is today, Major Vann?

VANN August 23rd, I believe.

Close on the polygraph pen, as it flows across the graph paper: the line continues, unbroken. The operator holds up a piece of card.

OPERATOR What colour is this?

VANN Blue.

Again, the polygraph line registers only the minutest variation.

OPERATOR Did you ever have sexual intercourse with Miss Barbara Devine in Fort Leavenworth?

VANN No, sir, I did not.

The polygraph pen: it moves, only just perceptibly, up and down, then resumes its straight path.

EXT. VANNS' HOUSE NEAR CAMP DRUM. DAY

A rambling farmhouse in upstate New York, on the shore of Lake Ontario. A crisp, winter day; snow and sun. The sound of a telephone.

INT. VANNS' SITTING ROOM. DAY

Vann answers the phone as best he can in the chaos of Christmas decorations. Mary Jane is decorating the tree with the help or hindrance of all five of her children: Patricia, thirteen; John Allen, eleven; Jesse, nine; Tommy, five; and Peter, four. They're making a tremendous noise. Vann puts his hand over the receiver.

VANN Quiet!

The noise subsides somewhat and Vann listens for a moment, murmuring into the phone. Finally, he speaks, crisply.

Thank you.

He puts the phone down and turns to his daughter.

Patty, look after the boys, OK? Your mom and I are going for a walk.

EXT. LAKESIDE. DAY

Vann bounds along beside the frozen lake and does a cartwheel. Mary Jane is wrapped up against the cold, but he has no jacket. She smiles and hurries up to him.

MARY JANE What is it? Aren't you going to tell me?

Vann looks at her for a moment, an expression of profound satisfaction on his face.

VANN Charge dismissed.

MARY JANE Oh, thank God.

VANN How about that? I beat the goddamn machine.

He utters an ear-splitting whoop.

You know something, this has been the worst six months of my life.

MARY JANE Yes.

VANN And I know it's been bad for you as well, I want to thank you, you've been terrific.

Mary Jane takes his arm and they walk on for a moment in silence.

MARY JANE Do you think you've learned your lesson?

VANN You bet. Next time I'll make sure the girl's old enough.

He turns and runs up a slope, gathering speed on the hard snow. Mary Jane watches him, troubled, her eyes narrowed against the low sun. Vann does a backflip, turns and smiles down at her.

INT. VANNS' BEDROOM. NIGHT

Mary Jane lies in Vann's arms: he smooths her hair out of her eyes.

VANN No more worrying.

MARY JANE I guess not.

VANN Then what is it?

MARY JANE I lied. I wish I hadn't done that. I swore on the Bible and then I told a lie.

VANN I know. I'm sorry you had to do that. But it was the lesser of two evils. There's such a thing as lying in a good cause.

Mary Jane looks up at him, her eyes wide in the darkness.

MARY JANE A lie's a lie.

Fade.

MAIN TITLE SEQUENCE

White on black. At the end of the sequence, another caption:

THIRTEEN YEARS LATER
NHATRANG, VIETNAM, JUNE 10, 1972

INT. KITCHEN IN VANN'S HOUSE IN NHATRANG. DAY

Fade up on a domestic tableau. A slim, petite, fragile-looking woman of twenty-three, Vann's Vietnamese girlfriend Annie, puts a bowl of fried rice in front of their four-year-old daughter, Thuy Van. The child picks up the bowl and chopsticks and begins to eat, as Annie idly opens her (Vietnamese) newspaper.

On the inside page is a large photograph of Vann. Annie starts, reads for a few seconds and then faints, collapsing to the floor. Thuy Van stops eating, her face puckers into a mask of misery as shock begins to give way to fear.

EXT. CAMBODIAN JUNGLE. DAY

An old-fashioned loudspeaker, secured to a tree, blasts out a newscast, uttered in the inspirational, urgent tones of Liberation Radio, Hanoi. Again, Vann's name can be recognised.

Below, in a clearing, chained to a tree, a man listens: he's Doug Ramsey, a thirty-seven-year-old American civilian, dreadfully emaciated, unshaven, ill, one of half a dozen American prisoners, all in a similar condition, guarded by black pyjama'd NVA troops.

Subtitles which read:

OUR HEROIC ARTILLERYMEN IN THE CHU PAO PASS
HAVE SCORED A MAJOR SUCCESS IN SHOOTING DOWN
AND KILLING ONE OF THE MOST DANGEROUS
OF ALL AMERICAN WAR CRIMINALS,
COLONEL JOHN PAUL VANN, CHIEF ADVISER
TO THE PUPPET FORCES IN THE SO-CALLED
II CORPS AREA AROUND THE CENTRAL HIGHLANDS

Ramsey reacts to this news: as the newscaster rants on, his face collapses and he draws the back of his hand across his eyes.

INT. BEDROOM IN LEE'S HOUSE IN SAIGON. DAY

Lee is a buxom woman of twenty-seven, much fuller in the figure than most Vietnamese. She lies in bed, sipping a cup of coffee, watching TV, a newscast in Vietnamese. All of a sudden a photograph of Vann comes up on the screen. Lee sits up with a shock, gasping as if winded, spilling her coffee.

EXT. ARLINGTON CEMETERY. DAY

Close on Mary Jane: her face is smudged with tears, her eyes puffy behind dark glasses. She's forty-four now; and as the camera pulls away, we see she's supported by her eldest son John Allen, now twenty-five, and encircled by her other sons: Jesse, twenty-two, whose blond hair flows down over his shoulders; Tommy, eighteen; and Peter, seventeen. The camera continues to pull back slowly, revealing the extraordinary size of the distinguished congregation, the solemnity of the occasion, the long line of limousines parked in the background.

John Vann's coffin, shrouded in a flag, is lowered by eight pall-bearers, sergeants in dress blues, on to a caisson trimmed with black bunting and drawn by six grey horses, which have been waiting outside the red-brick chapel in the summer heat. The last notes of the organ voluntary drift through the open doors of the chapel. Saluting as the coffin is lowered, resplendent in his white summer uniform, is General William Westmoreland, fifty-eight, whom we shall meet again.
The Drum Major's silver mace rises high and the band strikes up with the 'Colonel Bogey March'. The band leads off, followed by the colour-bearers, the honour guard, the actual and the official pall-bearers (including Westmoreland) and the chaplain. The horses drawing the caisson are next and these are followed by the large crowd of mourners.

INT. OVAL OFFICE. DAY

Mary Jane, still wearing her dark glasses, frowns in an effort to control her emotions; meanwhile we hear the unctuous cadences of a familiar voice.

NIXON (*voice over*) Soldier of peace and patriot of two nations, the name of John Paul Vann will be honoured as long as free men remember the struggle to preserve the independence of South Vietnam.

Another angle, over the President's shoulder, reveals that Mary Jane is part of a small audience, including her family, Vann's half-sister, Dorothy Lee Cadorette, a bespectacled, overweight woman, aides, reporters and a TV camera and crew. Nixon's cheek is caked with make-up.

NIXON His military and civilian service in Vietnam spanned a decade, marked throughout by supreme dedication and personal sacrifice. A truly noble American, a superb leader, he stands with Lafayette in that gallery of heroes who have made another brave people's cause their own.

He looks up expectantly, a little uneasy. John Allen steps forward to collect the Presidential Medal of Freedom.

INT. SITTING ROOM OF THE VANN HOUSE IN LITTLETON, COLO. NIGHT

Mary Jane kneels on the floor in a pool of light. In front of her, padlocked, is a battered wooden footlocker, painted a drab brown.

She takes a deep breath, unlocks the padlock and tips back the lid of the box.
One by one, she begins to lift out its contents: on top are Vann's medals, a Bronze Star and a Distinguished Flying Cross, nestled in silk, resting on a number of scrolls and citations. Under these is an old photograph album.
The first photograph shows Vann as a small boy looking up at a woman in her twenties, incongruously dressed in a grey-squirrel coat: this is Myrtle, his mother. His hand is stretched up towards her; but she ignores him, holding on to her handbag with both gloved hands, smirking at the camera. Then, as Mary Jane turns the page, more photographs, scenes from Vann's poverty-stricken childhood in Norfolk, Virginia: he stands barefoot in front of a single-storey frame house; he looks uncomfortable in ill-fitting, reach-me-down jacket and tie; he stands surrounded by younger, laughing half-brothers and sisters, his expression dreamy and remote. Tucked in the back of the album is a large formal wedding photograph of himself and Mary Jane, with a copy of the wedding invitation, printed in elaborate Gothic type, carefully clipped to it.
Mary Jane puts these aside and moves on to the next layer: a framed photograph shows Vann shaking hands with Kissinger; a golf ball has been autographed, 'In friendship, Richard M. Nixon'; and there's a round silver cigarette box, with the following inscription:

TO LT. COL. JOHN PAUL VANN
GOOD SOLDIER, GOOD FRIEND
FROM HIS ADMIRERS IN THE AMERICAN PRESS CORPS

Mary Jane puts the cigarette box on the floor: she's come to the bottom layer now. She reaches into the footlocker and comes up with a handful of Polaroid photographs. These are all of women, mostly Asian, a good many of them naked and striking provocative poses. Finally there's one in which Vann, also naked, stands behind a smiling, naked Vietnamese girl, his arms wrapped around her.
Mary Jane slowly lowers the photograph and lets it slip from her fingers. She closes her eyes, fighting off the waves of pain.
Fade.

EXT. MEKONG DELTA. DAY

A thin ribbon of tarmac road unfurls between flooded rice paddies, the green shoots of the new rice just visible above the surface of the water.

An open jeep is the only vehicle on the road.
A caption:

TEN YEARS EARLIER
THE SAIGON–MY-THO ROAD, MAY 21, 1962

Another angle on the jeep reveals that the driver is Vann, now a Lieutenant-Colonel, his cotton khakis newly starched, his green peaked cap set back on his head. He's in the highest spirits, whistling the 'Colonel Bogey March', as he speeds through the landscape.
Over this comes the voice, a gruff, Texan drawl, of Colonel Daniel Boone Porter, chief adviser to III Corps region (the Mekong Delta).

PORTER (*voice over*) Can you give me one good reason why I should make you chief adviser to the Infantry Division?

INT. COL. PORTER'S OFFICE IN MACV HQ, SAIGON. DAY

Porter, a tall, lean Texan, squints across the desk at Vann, who can hardly keep still he's so bursting with enthusiasm.

VANN There's nowhere sees more action than the Delta: it's the best assignment in the country.

PORTER You've only been out here two months. Why shouldn't I give it to a senior man?

VANN Because I'd do it better, Colonel. If President Kennedy wants us out of here by Christmas, you need a man who can get things done.

Porter considers him for a moment, amused by his presumption.

EXT. ROAD. DAY

Vann slows the jeep to allow an old peasant in a conical hat to lead a buffalo across the road. Then he accelerates, passing a construction team, supervised by US engineers, to whom he waves as he drives by. Bulldozers complete the filling in of paddies around the half-erected communications installation, bristling with antennae. The air is thick with dust, the buildings are an ugly blot on the serene landscape.

PORTER (*voice over*) All right, Frank Clay has six weeks to run down there . . .

VANN (*voice over*) I know, sir.

PORTER (*voice over*) You can go down right away, on probation: in a month's time I'll ask Frank how he feels about you.

VANN (*voice over*) Thank you, Colonel. You won't regret it.
Vann speeds away from the construction site, heading for open country.

EXT. BRIDGE. DAY

Vann has to stop the jeep at the approaches to the bridge, which is guarded by two ARVN soldiers. The bridge is a one-lane structure made out of Eiffel steel, guarded by concrete blockhouses, each protected by a sprawl of barbed wire. At present a truck is inching its way across the bridge towards him. Vann jumps down from the jeep, shows his pass to the guard, who scarcely bothers to glance at it, and buys from a peasant child a slice of fresh pineapple sprinkled with coarse-grained salt. A certain tension in the air.

PORTER (*voice over*) You going to drive down alone?

VANN (*voice over*) Sure.

INT. COL. PORTER'S OFFICE. DAY

Porter frowns across his desk at Vann, his tone earnest.

PORTER You be careful, John. We've lost going on twenty Americans already over here since this thing started. Some of them in ambushes.

VANN I'll be careful.

EXT. SEMINARY. DAY

The seminary is a two-storey L-shaped building in the French colonial style, backing on to a narrow river, with a large courtyard in front, now used as a parking lot for military vehicles and surrounded by a red-brick wall. The Vietnamese guard opens the tall iron-grillwork gate to let Vann's jeep into the courtyard. He parks it close to the main entrance on the ground floor of the building, which has now been turned into offices. He sits for a moment, looking up at the incongruously solid building, surmounted by its two big white crosses.

PORTER (*voice over*) Frank Clay will take you over to see his and your Vietnamese counterpart.

EXT. COLONEL CAO'S HOUSE. DAY

The house is a modest, two-storey, whitewashed building in My-Tho, nestling in a small compound shaded by flame trees. Colonel Huynh

Van Cao, thirty-four years old, an immaculate, slightly overweight figure, stands waiting at the top of a low flight of steps leading up to the porch, a gleaming swagger stick under one arm. He watches as a jeep pulls up containing Vann, Lt. Col. Frank Clay and Capt. Richard Ziegler. Vietnamese guards spring forward to open the doors of the jeep and, as the three Americans emerge, Cao snaps to attention and salutes them.

PORTER (*voice over*) His name is Huynh Van Cao. Colonel. Loyal to Diem. Catholic. Seven kids. He's the guy you have to try to get along with. Frank's been having some problems.

By this time, Vann has reached Cao, who pumps his hand enthusiastically, taking it in both of his.

INT. STAIRCASE. DAY

Cao leads the way up the curving staircase, followed by Vann, Clay and Ziegler and a number of Vietnamese officers. At the top of the stairs, with a flourish, Cao throws open double doors and steps proudly to one side.

INT. WAR ROOM. DAY

Vann pauses on the threshold, startled by the lavish scale of the large room, the polished table, the contoured maps, the Empire furniture, the podium at one end, the bank of radio receivers. Cao is beaming at him. He speaks English well, with a slight French accent.

CAO What do you think?

VANN Well, it's . . .

CAO Yes, an exact replica of Napoleon's map room, you know.

VANN Really?

CAO Sit down.

He barks an order and an aide begins fixing Scotch on the rocks, as the American officers settle at the table. Cao paces the room proprietorially.

You're going to be here during the operation tomorrow.

VANN I was kind of hoping to go out into the field.

CAO No, no. You should be here. A Commanding Officer has to direct from the nerve centre, where he can feel the flow of the battle. Of course, Frank doesn't see it that way.

CLAY You're in charge. I'm just an adviser.

Cao fetches a book down from one of the shelves and brings it over to Vann.

CAO A small gift for you. My novel.

VANN Oh.

CAO As you can see, it's in Vietnamese, so you won't be able to read it.

VANN Well, thank you, it'll be an incentive to learn.

Cao has opened the front cover of the book.

CAO I have written a dedication to you.

VANN Well . . .

CAO Its title, the translation, I mean, is *He Grows Under Fire.*

He hands it to Vann, turns away and begins to approach one of the maps, brandishing his swagger stick. Meanwhile, Vann catches Ziegler's eye and they have a hard time keeping a straight face.

EXT. ROAD TO THE SEMINARY. DAY

Vann, his face brick-red in the evening sun, is half-turned in his seat, to listen to what Clay and Ziegler, in the back seat of the jeep, are saying.

CLAY See, this is our first operation in weeks. He's been refusing to take our advice.

ZIEGLER So we told him he couldn't use the helicopters.

CLAY I said to him, what the hell use is having advisers if you don't listen to the advice? Then you get some diplomatic shit about our two great countries and give them the aid and they can do the job.

ZIEGLER He's real polite. But he just hates to be without those choppers.

VANN And doesn't he ever go out himself on operations?

CLAY Last time he did he asked the artillery to stop firing because it was giving him a headache.

Vann flourishes his copy of Cao's novel.

VANN *He Grows Under Fire*, huh?

ZIEGLER Yeah. Only problem is, he shrinks in the shower.

INT. WAR ROOM. DAY

Cao sits near the podium, looking out at a hive of activity. Radio operators pass on information continuously, which is translated into symbols superimposed on maps or model pieces shifted on the battlefield simulation. Vann and Ziegler are the only Americans in the room. Vann watches as Cao beams at a Lieutenant, who's relaying information to him in Vietnamese. Eventually, Cao turns to Vann.

CAO Estimated sixty enemy casualties already. None on our side.

VANN Wonderful.

CAO This is a great day.

VANN I'm convinced this is only the beginning, Colonel. We've been working on a new concept in Saigon. Joint planning. And because the Seventh is the most efficient and successful and important division in the country, we thought we should start here.

CAO Joint planning?

VANN The idea is that every one of your officers has a counterpart, the way I'm your counterpart. Captain Ziegler here would work with your planning officer and we'd appoint counterparts for your G-1, your intel and your logistics chief.

CAO Doesn't sound like joint planning, sounds like taking over . . .

He breaks off as someone hands him a note. Meanwhile, Vann and Ziegler exchange a worried glance, interrupted by Cao's horrified reaction to the note.

Oh, God!

VANN What is it?

CAO Colonel Clay has been wounded.

VANN Seriously?

CAO Oh, my God, this is terrible.

Vann, though concerned, is also puzzled by the devastating effect the news has had on Cao, who now looks completely poleaxed.

INT. SICK ROOM AT THE SEMINARY. DAY

Colonel Clay's hands are wrapped in bandages and his face is starred with an ugly cluster of wounds. It's clear, however, from his vigorous demeanour that the wounds are only superficial. He gestures energetically at his face, addressing Vann and Ziegler, who stand by his bed in the rudimentary sick room.

CLAY Fucking plexiglass, sprays everywhere.

VANN Thank Christ none of it went in your eyes.

CLAY They're taking me out of here this evening. Up to Saigon. So you're in at the deep end, John. I already told them I have every confidence in you.

VANN Thanks.

CLAY How'd you get on with Cao?

VANN When he heard about you, he looked like he was going to faint.

CLAY He hates to take casualties. He's real obsessional about it.

VANN Listen, Frank, I have a question. Have you ever sent out night helicopter attacks?

CLAY Jesus, nobody does night attacks. And Cao wouldn't ever . . .

He breaks off and smiles exhaustedly at Vann.

CLAY Well, I don't know, John, it's all yours.

EXT. LZ IN THE PLAIN OF REEDS. NIGHT

A fleet of sixteen Marine H-34 Choctaw helicopters comes roaring down towards the LZ, their navigation lights blinking in the darkness.

INT./EXT. CHOCTAW. NIGHT

Below, as the helicopter dips towards it, the LZ is marked out by stars of flame.

EXT. LZ. NIGHT

Vann and Ziegler stand beside one of the blazing buckets (containing sand soaked in oil) which mark the perimeter of the LZ, amid the screaming roar of the descending helicopters. Three assault groups of ARVN troops are divided into squads of a dozen men, lined up at intervals, one to each helicopter. Vann's and Ziegler's group is last; and now, as the first helicopter lands, the furthest squad rushes forward to scramble aboard.

EXT. CHOCTAW. DAWN

Vann's Choctaw is travelling alone now in a pre-dawn half-light, flying low over the reed fields, having peeled away from the other Choctaws in the final group.

INT./EXT. CHOCTAW. DAWN

Vann is shouting into the headset attached to his helmet. He's behind the pilot, between Ziegler and the door-gunner. In the back, sitting on the floor are the ARVN Rangers. Nearest the front is their commander, Captain Thuong, a Cambodian, much taller and darker-skinned than the Vietnamese, a sinister, overweight figure in tinted glasses.

VANN Buffalo, will you confirm no repeat no enemy contact?

The reply crackles through his earphones. He turns to Ziegler, incensed.

Your intel said there was a battalion down there.

ZIEGLER That's right.

VANN Well, where the hell are they? A battalion doesn't just disappear.

He's interrupted by the pilot, who's pointing down at the ground.

PILOT Nine o'clock.

Vann looks out of the side of the helicopter.

EXT. PADDY FIELD. DAWN

Silhouetted against the pearly light, a patrol of seven Viet Cong, crossing a dike between rice fields, scatters as the helicopter swoops towards them.

INT. CHOCTAW. DAWN

As the helicopter plunges towards the ground, the pilot calls back to Vann.

PILOT I can't set down here.

VANN OK, go in, we'll unass, make a pass, come back in five.

PILOT Roger.

The door-gunner opens fire with his M-60, the red tracer bright in the pale light.

EXT. PADDY FIELD. DAWN

Three of the scattering Viet Cong are wounded. One of these, clearly a patrol leader, calls out an order. Another, about to fire at the helicopter, lowers his rifle. As the helicopter hovers three feet above the paddy and Vann and the ARVN begin to jump out into the shin-high water of the field, the patrol leader rises to his feet, raising his hands in surrender.

INT./EXT. CHOCTAW. DAWN

The pilot looks down to see, below, the ARVN Rangers in an irregular group and the VC prisoners, forming a straight black line.

EXT. PADDY FIELD. DAWN

Vann and Ziegler confer, watching Thuong, who moves up and down in front of the line of prisoners, talking to them in a low, menacing voice.

VANN What's he saying?

ZIEGLER Asking where the rest of the battalion is, telling them they better give him some answers, stuff like that.

VANN They may not know, do you think they're with the 504th . . .?

He breaks off, because Thuong has begun to raise his voice and now draws from a scabbard on his belt a glistening Bowie knife with a fifteen-inch blade. For a moment, Vann and Ziegler watch, apprehensive but mesmerised, as Thuong works himself up into a frenzy. Suddenly, his arm shoots out, he grabs a prisoner by the hair and cuts his throat. As the prisoner drops, he resumes talking, quietly again. The ARVN Rangers look on, indifferent. Vann is so startled he takes a moment to respond: then he shouts at Ziegler.

VANN Will you tell him to cut that shit out!

ZIEGLER He's famous for it.

The prisoners are terrified now. Thuong stops in front of a young prisoner, who is literally belching with fear; and seeing Vann begin to move towards him out of the corner of his eye, Thuong swiftly cuts the young prisoner's throat. As he collapses, Vann grabs hold of Thuong's arm, white with rage.

VANN Goddamn you, I said to cut that shit out!

By now, the helicopter has returned and is settling into its final position, hovering a couple of feet above the water. In the noise and confusion, Thuong manages to struggle free, grabs another prisoner and cuts another throat. Vann raises his Armalite and points it at Thuong. Thuong looks at him and there's a frozen moment of confrontation between them, as the helicopter straightens up, furrowing the waters of the reed-bed, and the third victim writhes and chokes. Finally Thuong yells at him.

THUONG You want 'em? Take 'em.

He turns away, wiping the blood off his knife against his thigh, signals to the Rangers and leads them back on to the helicopter. Vann signals to the VC patrol leader to get his surviving men aboard. The patrol leader issues an order and the three prisoners step forward, supervised on to the Choctaw by Ziegler. Then the patrol leader himself steps forward, winces as his thigh wound takes the weight and overbalances. Vann helps him up and finally lifts him, moving forward to pass him into the helicopter. Then he scrambles in himself. The helicopter jerks, losing its equilibrium for a moment and tips the patrol leader and Vann back into the water. Vann lands heavily, the patrol leader on top of him. The patrol leader rises to his feet. Then he leans, picks up Vann, and puts him bodily into the helicopter. Vann, lying on the floor of the helicopter, looks into the patrol leader's eyes. There's some measure of understanding between them. Then the patrol leader climbs into the helicopter. Vann gestures to the pilot and the Choctaw finally lifts off.

INT. CHOCTAW. DAWN

As the helicopter pulls up and Vann rights himself, the pilot turns back to him.

PILOT One of our FACs has made visual contact with the enemy. Here.

He hands him a sheet of paper on a clipboard, which Vann digests almost instantly. Then he turns and shouts back at Thuong.

VANN I told you there was no need for that shit, you were just wasting our time.

Thuong looks away, deliberately ignoring Vann, who now speaks rapidly into his headset.

Hello, Napoleon, this is Topper Six, do you read?

INT. WAR ROOM. DAWN

Cao stands at the bank of radio receivers. Behind him, the room seethes with activity.

CAO Read you, Topper Six, come in.

INT. CHOCTAW. DAWN

Vann speaks fast and decisively.

VANN You have information of L-19's contact with Victor Charlie, Napoleon?

The radio squawks in inaudible reply.

VANN OK, here's what we do. Call up a strike, co-ordinates Willie Sierra 645875, that's Willie Sierra 645875; refuel the H-34s and the H-21s; I'm going over to observe.

EXT. PLAIN OF REEDS. DAY

The sun is up, burning the mist off the wilderness of reeds not far south of the Cambodian border. A force of several dozen Viet Cong is pushing north in some disarray, either in small sampans which hold no more than six men or on foot, struggling through the water, which is about two feet deep here. The atmosphere of panic is no doubt brought on by the drone of approaching aircraft.

INT./EXT. CHOCTAW. DAY

Vann stands in the doorway of the Choctaw, looking down. The helicopter is accompanying a flight of propeller-driven AD-6 Skyraiders, flying in a V-formation, which now begin to loose their rockets.

EXT. PLAIN OF REEDS. DAY

A sampan takes a direct hit and disintegrates in a welter of bodies, wood and water.

INT./EXT. CHOCTAW. DAY

Vann's point of view: the Skyraiders are replaced by the next wave of aircraft, T-28 Trojan trainers. Below, the water is a patchwork of explosions and frenzied guerrillas. Great silver canisters begin to slide out of the leading Trojan.

EXT. PLAIN OF REEDS. DAY

The canisters erupt in a great marigold blaze of napalm. One such explosion engulfs a group of half a dozen Viet Cong. At the periphery of the fireball, a smaller column of fire detaches itself: an individual soldier. He falls full-length into the water, which boils and bubbles and emits greasy black smoke; for a while the flames are visible underwater, then the soldier rises to his feet again, still unquenchably ablaze.

INT./EXT. CHOCTAW. DAY

Vann turns back to look at the pilot with an expression of grim satisfaction. He gestures at him to turn back. Ziegler leans forward to talk to Vann.

ZIEGLER The whole battalion's going to head for the Cambodian border.

VANN Then we should drop in a task force, head them off. The hammer and the anvil.

ZIEGLER Cao won't do that.

VANN What do you mean?

ZIEGLER He loves strikes, he doesn't give a shit who's under the bombs, so long as they beef up the body count. But he doesn't like ground-fighting. Frightened of taking casualties.

VANN We better go to work on him.

INT. WAR ROOM. DAY

Vann stands with Cao in front of the big wall-map. Ziegler hovers in the background.

VANN How do we stop the battalion just retreating three, four miles into Cambodia? What do you think, Colonel?

Cao looks at the map, pensive. Then he stabs a finger at the border area.

CAO Suppose we drop in a blocking force, cut them off?

VANN Jesus, what a great idea.

CAO You think so?

VANN The hammer and the anvil!

CAO It's a classic strategy.

Vann catches Ziegler's eye, but presses on shamelessly.

VANN Now I know why they call you the Tiger of the Delta.

CAO They do?

VANN Absolutely.

He winks at Ziegler, unobserved by Cao, who is glowing with self-satisfaction.

CAO You enjoy your day in the field, John?

VANN I wanted to talk to you about your Captain Thuong. What kind of a fucking animal is he?

CAO He's a Cambodian.

He giggles, but Vann is not to be diverted.

VANN He killed three prisoners in front of me today. What is he, insane?

CAO I tell him not to let you see that again.

VANN Shouldn't you tell him not to do it again?

Cao doesn't answer. He gives a tight smile and moves off to issue a brusque order in Vietnamese. Vann exchanges a glance with Ziegler, then decides to move in on Cao again.

VANN You sending in the blocking force, Colonel?

CAO Well, no, perhaps it is not such a good idea.

VANN Of course it is, what do you mean, how can you let three hundred sitting duck VC stroll back into Cambodia?

CAO This is already a big victory for the commander of the Tenth Regiment. He will not want to share.

Vann gapes at him for a moment; then he explodes.

VANN Well, tough shit!

CAO I think maybe you don't understand yet our country.

VANN I understand you're letting a whole battalion of the enemy escape. I know what that smells like to me.

CAO I am the commander here. You are my adviser.

Vann bites back a retort and looks away, furious. But Cao is smiling blandly.

Don't worry, John. Saigon will be very pleased about today. You'll see.

EXT. NATIONAL ASSEMBLY IN SAIGON. DAY

Colonel Cao, garlands round his neck, his swagger stick under his arm, a baseball cap on his head, stands in the back of the slow-moving jeep. The roads are lined with cheering crowds in their best clothes. The jeep is crawling towards the main square outside the National Assembly building (a former opera house), where a platform has been set up to display a variety of captured Viet Cong arms. It's a full-scale Victory Parade.

Another angle reveals a platform, the ultimate destination of Cao's jeep, at the centre of which waits the Defence Minister at the heart of a large reception committee. Vann waits on the fringes of this group, his expression disgruntled, next to Colonel Porter, who turns to murmur in Vann's ear.

PORTER Looks like I was right to follow my hunch and send you down to My-Tho.

VANN Glad you think so, sir.

PORTER What's the matter? You pissed at something?

VANN Long story.

He looks down at the fifty-eight-year old American General standing next to the Minister in his impeccable dress uniform. This is General Paul Harkins, Commander-in-Chief of Military Assistance Command in Vietnam. He bears a fleeting resemblance to John Wayne.

VANN Could you get me in to talk to General Harkins?

PORTER On a weekend?

EXT. GOLF COURSE AT THE SAIGON SPORTING CLUB. DAY

General Harkins, elegant in his pressed white trousers and sport shirt, drives the ball off the tee and stands for a moment, looking after it in some satisfaction. Vann and Porter, who have just arrived, wearing their uniforms, wait: then they follow as Harkins sets off after his ball, handing his club to his slight Vietnamese caddy, who struggles after them, bowed down by the weight of the golf bag. Harkins beams at Vann.

HARKINS Well, Colonel, you and your counterpart are shaping up to be just about the best damn team we have.

VANN Thank you, sir.

HARKINS Over a hundred and thirty enemy killed for the loss of two men. My.

VANN Our allies tend to be a little optimistic when it comes to body counts.

HARKINS Well, it may be. Even so, this is still the biggest single kill of the whole war.

VANN What concerns me, sir, is we let upwards of three hundred enemy walk out of an open door.

HARKINS What do you mean?

VANN My counterpart refused to complete an encircling manoeuvre. He said it might compromise the success of one of his majors.

HARKINS I see.

VANN Now maybe the major is President Diem's tennis coach or his cousin or his connection, but I don't think it's a great way to prosecute a war.

HARKINS I need to study the after-action reports on this, Colonel, but certainly what you say is disturbing.

VANN I'd also like to speak to you about the calling of air strikes in my area, sir.

Harkins frowns: the interview is beginning to make him uncomfortable. He fits a cigarette into a long white holder, before speaking.

HARKINS Go on.

VANN I think the bombing and napalming of hamlets just on the say-so of individual officers is counter-productive.

HARKINS The Vietnamese request the strikes, we provide them. Someone says to me they have intelligence of a VC arms factory, I say, blast it off the map.

VANN Except it usually isn't an arms factory. It's usually two peasant hootches may have given some rice to a VC patrol. And if you kill them, you're wiping out neutrals and if you don't kill them, you're right away creating VC supporters.

HARKINS You don't have to lecture me, I do check these requests, I always ask, are you sure these targets don't contain ordinary people?

Silence. Porter clears his throat.

PORTER I agree with the Colonel, our ally is not always as scrupulous as he might be.

VANN I also have documentation, sir, about the torture and murder of VC prisoners.

By this time they've drawn level with Harkins's ball and Vann waits as Harkins selects a club and addresses the ball. He muffs the shot. He looks up, clearly irritated: and speaks a sentence obviously intended to bring the interview to a close.

HARKINS I'm certainly grateful to you for drawing these matters to my attention, Colonel. (*He sounds precisely the contrary.*) But, after all, it is their war.

VANN Well, if it's their war, why don't we get the fuck out and let them lose it their way?

There's a horrified silence, which Porter breaks with a snort of laughter; this gives Harkins the chance to smile in an attempt to defuse the situation. But Vann's expression remains undiplomatically grim, as Porter begins to hustle him away.

EXT. DOWNTOWN SAIGON. DAY

The city has, at this date, a spacious Colonial appearance, its broad avenues not too cluttered with traffic, its bustling crowds purposeful and relaxed. A blue Chevrolet moves smoothly down the boulevard and turns into the Rue Catinat.

EXT. BROTHEL. DAY

The car pulls up in front of a cream stucco-covered building with bright-green shutters. Vann emerges, a camera over his shoulder, and saunters into the house, nodding familiarly to the doorman.

INT. BROTHEL PARLOUR. DAY

Vann has made his selection, a demure-looking girl in a colourful ao dai. *The Mamasan, a plump, older woman, watches him shrewdly.*

MAMASAN Maybe you like two girls today, M'sieur Vann.

Vann hesitates, checking his watch.

VANN I got a press conference in just over an hour.

He catches the eye of a second girl, who's smiling at him shyly.

OK, what the hell.

He stretches out a hand to the second girl, as the Mamasan issues instructions in Vietnamese.

INT. PRESS ROOM AT MACV HQ. DAY

Colonel Porter watches uneasily as Cao, on his feet, finishes briefing a roomful of journalists and photographers. Vann sits on the other side of Cao, impassive.

CAO So in one day I kill one hundred thirty-one Viet Cong. This is why they call me the Tiger of the Delta.

He sits, triumphant. A hand goes up in the crowd. It belongs to David Halberstam, the New York Times *correspondent, an enormous man, twenty-eight, six-foot-two, dark, square-jawed and short-sighted with thick, heavy-rimmed spectacles. Despite his youth, he radiates an air of authority.*

HALBERSTAM Halberstam, *New York Times.* I'd like to ask Colonel Vann what particular qualities made this an especially successful operation?

Porter looks across at Vann, apprehensive: but the answer comes out smooth as butter.

VANN Timing, I think, David, the landings were beautifully co-ordinated and exactly on schedule; and surprise. Looks as if, for once, we caught the VC completely off-guard.

HALBERSTAM No special problems?

VANN We do have a problem, David, and it's hard to know what we can do about it.

Porter stiffens, once again alarmed. But Vann's next remark causes him to sink back into his chair, relieved.

It's the VC: we just can't get them to stand and fight.

EXT. L-19 SPOTTER PLANE OVER AP BAC. DAY

1963. The L-19 'Bird Dog' observation plane is a single-engine, two-seated Cessna, unarmed, flimsy and precarious. Vann sits in the rear observer's seat, with the pilot, Captain O'Neill, in front of him. They communicate through their headsets. Vann also has a portable field radio wedged between his legs.

VANN OK, we'll make another pass. This time take her down as low as you can get.

EXT. TREELINE AND PADDIES WEST OF AP BAC. DAY

The paddies stretch out to a dike, the further and higher bank of which is protected by a line of trees. Behind this, the villages of Ap Bac and Tan Thoi can be glimpsed. A ground fog has almost been burned away by the sun. It's ten a.m.

The L-19 flies very low, more or less at tree-top level, past the treeline.

VANN (*voice over*) I know they're in there. I can feel it in my water. Come on, you bastards, take a shot, give us a sign.

As the plane passes out of frame, the camera closes in to reveal, at the end of the treeline, a brilliantly camouflaged .20 calibre machine-gun emplacement. The Viet Cong gunner has the plane in his sights, but the officer with him discourages him from firing with a gesture. The camera tracks back in the opposite direction: the entire bank of the dike below the trees is honeycombed with foxholes, each brimming with alert Viet Cong troops.

VANN (*voice over*) I just got an instinct: today's the day.

EXT. L-19. DAY

The plane pulls up steeply. Vann's point of view: down to the south-east a convoy of helicopters is approaching: ten troop-carrying Shawnees ('Flying Bananas') and six escorting HU-1 Iroquois ('Hueys'), led by another L-19. Vann talks to O'Neill.

VANN Speak to the FAC, will you? He should tell them to set down out of range of that treeline, minimum of three hundred yards, all right?

EXT. BANK OF THE DIKE. DAY

All along the dike, Viet Cong soldiers prepare, as the thunder of the approaching helicopters rises to a crescendo.

EXT. PADDY FIELDS. DAY

The helicopters come in low over the trees and prepare to put down in pairs in the paddy fields.

EXT. TREELINE. DAY

A Viet Cong officer issues quiet instructions to his troops and machine-gunners, all of whom are preparing to fire.

EXT. L-19. DAY

Vann leans down perilously to watch the incoming helicopters. Suddenly he jerks upright.

VANN Jesus Christ! What are they doing? They're setting down in range!

O'NEILL I told them three hundred.

INT. SHAWNEE. DAY

The American adviser, Sergeant Arnold Bowers, a strong, wiry twenty-nine-year-old, is poised to leap out of the first Flying Banana as soon as it lands. He looks considerably more enthusiastic than the dozen or so ARVN troops he's attached to.

EXT. TREELINE. DAY

The Viet Cong officer has waited until the helicopters are about fifty feet above the ground: now he gives the order to fire. All his troops swing their arms to aim a few yards in front of the descending Shawnees.

EXT. L-19. DAY

Vann's point of view: as he looks down at the treeline, a tremendous volume of rifle and machine-gun fire suddenly erupts from it.

VANN Oh, my God.

INT. SHAWNEE. DAY

The Shawnee is coming in to land. Suddenly, it's hit by a hail of fire. Several ARVN troops duck as bullets begin to penetrate the skin of the aircraft. Sergeant Bowers takes a firm grip on his M-2 carbine.

EXT. PADDY FIELD. DAY

The first Shawnee lands in the shallow water of the paddy. It's taking a number of hits, but not quite as many as its partner helicopter, which is absorbing long lines of green machine-gun tracer.

As the helicopter is landing, Bowers and his companions on board burst from it, jumping down into the paddy and charging towards the treeline.

The camera goes with Bowers as he moves as fast as he can through the ankle-high water, firing his carbine as he advances. After a while, he glances to one side, does a double-take and comes to a halt, bullets zinging around him.

He's alone, isolated between helicopter and treeline: the ARVN troops have vanished. Bowers turns and runs back. He finds that the ARVN troops have all taken cover in a paddy dike about fifteen yards from the helicopter. He bears down angrily on the ARVN Lieutenant, who is pressed down against the side of the dike, clearly terrified amid the roar of engines and bullets.

BOWERS We have to attack. If we stay out here, they'll cut us to pieces.

LIEUTENANT I no understand.

BOWERS No understand shit. You graduated Fort Benning.

LIEUTENANT I no understand.

EXT. L-19. DAY

Vann looks down from his plane on a scene of chaos. The ARVN company is floundering hopelessly in the paddy field, frantically taking cover, bodies dropping under the scything fire.

Meanwhile, the H-21s are taking off and the Huey gunships are firing rockets and red tracer at the treeline, without appreciable effect.

One of the Shawnees is left behind when the others take off, clearly incapacitated. A second H-21 turns back and flies in again to rescue the crew.

VANN Jesus, tell him he's landing the wrong side!

O'Neill starts trying to raise the pilot on his radio, but it's too late. The second Shawnee, which has approached between the downed helicopter and the treeline, takes an enormous pounding and is forced to make a crash landing.

Immediately, one of the Hueys peels away from bombarding the treeline and flies in to the rescue. This time, the pilot is thoughtful enough to circle round behind the two crippled Shawnees, but as he's coming in to land, a VC bullet hits the rotor and the Huey tips over on its side and crashes, its engine screaming, out of control.

OK, no more rescue attempts, got that? I'm going to bring in the M-113s.

As O'Neill starts broadcasting to the helicopter pilots, Vann activates his own radio.

Hello, Walrus, this is Topper Six.

EXT. WEST FLANK. DAY

Captain Robert Mays, a tall, thirty-two-year-old Texan, is adviser to a company of thirteen M-113s, armoured personnel carriers, each with a .50 calibre machine gun mounted in the turret. The M-113s are stationary and the company of ARVN troops are standing or sitting around in the vicinity. The rattle of gunfire is faintly audible. Mays's radio is the loudspeaker type. Vann's message crackles out of it.

MAYS Topper Six, this is Walrus, over.

VANN (*voice over*) Listen good, I have three repeat three choppers down and a rifle company pinned in the paddies due south-east of you at X-ray Sierra three-zero-niner-five-three-niner, do you read?

MAYS I read you, Topper Six.

By this time, Mays has been joined by his counterpart, Captain Ly Tong Ba, thirty, a strikingly handsome man, taller than the average Vietnamese, radiating the self-assurance of his wealthy background.

VANN (*voice over*) Tell your counterpart to get his tracks over here, fast as he can. Make sure he understands, this is urgent.

Mays looks up at Ba, who looks steadily back at him, expressionless. Mays presses the button on his microphone.

MAYS Roger.

EXT. L-19. DAY

Vann barks into his microphone.

VANN Out.

He looks up and switches to speak to O'Neill.

Take me down, I want to get a closer look.

O'NEILL Not safe.

VANN Do it!

O'Neill banks the plane and goes in low over the downed helicopters. Bullets and tracer hurtle past them, but Vann is concentrating on the scene below; dead bodies, cowering ARVN troops, and Bowers, staggering away from the disabled Huey and its still screaming engine, having pulled out the pilot, whom he is supporting, as they weave their way towards the nearest cover.

EXT. WEST FLANK. DAY

Captain Mays and Captain Ba stand by one of the M-113s, just as before. Mays speaks into the microphone.

MAYS Topper Six, this is Walrus, over.

VANN (*voice over*) Come in, Walrus.

MAYS We got a problem.

He looks up at Ba, who stares back at him coolly.

My counterpart refuses to move.

EXT. L-19. DAY

The L-19 is still pulling up from the battlefield. Below, the troops around the helicopters are pinned down by mortar fire.

VANN Goddamn it, this is an emergency! Doesn't he understand that?

EXT. WEST FLANK. DAY

Ba takes the microphone from Mays and speaks calmly into it.

BA I don't take orders from Americans.

EXT. L-19. DAY

Vann suppresses a wave of rage: he leans forward to press the button on his radio transmitter and replies with an almost equal calm.

VANN Roger, Walrus. I'll get right back to you.

He changes frequencies as quickly as he can.

Hello, Tiger, this is Topper Six.

INT. WAR ROOM. DAY

Colonel Cao and Captain Ziegler stand by the bank of transmitters.

ZIEGLER Come in, Topper Six.

VANN (*voice over*) I got some goddamn insubordinate sonofabitch captain refusing to advance the M-113 company, do you read that?

Cao smiles indulgently and leans in to answer.

CAO Relax, Topper Six. I give him the order.

VANN (*voice over*) And another thing, just where in hell are the Civil Guards? They're supposed to be marching up in support.

Cao says nothing, his expression impassive.

EXT. L-19. DAY

The little plane flies over a reserve company of Civil Guards, south of Ap Bac, facing a treeline which runs at right angles to the VC foxholes. Nothing is happening in the sector; indeed, the Civil Guards appear to be sunbathing, smoking or eating their rations. Vann stops looking at them and activates his transmitter.

VANN Tiger, this is Topper Six.

There's the crackle of an answer in his headset.

I'm just overflying your Civil Guards, Task Force Alpha. How would it be if you told them to get off their asses, there's a battle going on?

INT. WAR ROOM. DAY

Cao receives this message, quite expressionless. The radio crackles on.

VANN (*voice over*) And did you talk to that chickenshit captain yet? Over.

CAO Oh, yes, no problem. The M-113s are going in.

EXT. CANAL BANK. DAY

The M-113s are drawn up, stationary, along the bank of one of the many canals which criss-cross the paddy fields, within sight of their previous position. Mays and Ba stand on top of the leading vehicle. Beyond the canal, also blocking their way, is a second canal.

Mays looks up, alarmed, at the buzz of the approaching L-19.

Presently, his radio sputters into life.

VANN (*voice over*) That's right, Walrus, it's me again, Topper Six. Over.

Mays presses the button on his microphone.

MAYS Come in, Topper Six.

VANN (*voice over*) Would you mind explaining to me just exactly what the fuck is happening?

MAYS Yes, Topper Six, my counterpart feels it's going to take an hour to cross each of the canals between here and the objective.

VANN (*voice over*) So?

BA So you should find someone else who could reach there more quickly.

EXT. L-19. DAY

Vann's expression is icy.

VANN Did you or did you not receive direct orders from Colonel Cao to advance?

EXT. CANAL BANK. DAY

Ba is quite calm, as he answers the question.

BA Yes, I did receive orders to advance.

VANN (*voice over*) OK, just get off the line, I want to speak to Captain Mays.

MAYS Go ahead, Topper Six.

VANN (*voice over*) Can you personally take the company down there?

Mays frowns, puzzled by the question, not answering for a moment.

EXT. L-19. DAY

Vann's face is suffused with sudden rage.

VANN Answer the question, goddammit!

EXT. CANAL BANK. DAY

Mays, still puzzled, is nevertheless galvanised into answering.

MAYS Well, I could, yes, affirmative, Topper Six.

VANN (*voice over*) OK, here's what you do. You take out your service pistol, you put it in your counterpart's ear and you blow his fucking head off.

Mays and Ba look at each other, appalled.

EXT. L-19. DAY

Vann is warming to his theme.

VANN Then you throw him in the canal and drive over him. You got that?

EXT. CANAL BANK. DAY

Mays and Ba are still looking at one another, paralysed. Finally, Mays manages to croak out a reply.

MAYS Roger, Topper Six.

VANN (*voice over*) Alternatively, I'll help you to find the best places to ford these canals and you'll get down to the combat zone as fast as you can, what's it to be?

A moment's pause: then Ba nods, capitulating.

MAYS Sir, my counterpart would like to take up your second offer.

VANN (*voice over*) No kidding.

EXT. L-19. DAY

Vann is calm now, his features enlivened by a certain grim satisfaction.

VANN OK, about five hundred yards south of you, those two canals merge, so you only have one to cross. So move your ass. I got to go refuel. I want to see real progress when I get back. Out.

INT. WAR ROOM. DAY

Vann stands, with Cao and Ziegler, in front of the operations map. South of the block which represents the Viet Cong, who occupy the villages of Ap Bac and Tan Thoi, is a square representing the Civil Guards. Vann taps it with his finger.

VANN So the goddamn Civil Guards still haven't moved, why not?

CAO I decided they should stay where they are.

VANN What the hell for? I thought they were supposed to be hot shit.

CAO Yes, they are President Diem's elite.

Vann looks at Cao for a moment, trying to work out the implications of this. Cao returns his gaze, his expression bland. Finally, Vann frowns, as if he's understood something and turns away abruptly.

VANN I'm going back up.

EXT. PADDY FIELD. DAY

The final canal is about five hundred yards from the downed helicopters. Three of the M-113s have got across. The canal has been filled in at the crossing point with brush and chopped-down trees. One of the M-113s is now towing a fourth across the canal with a cable. Mays watches, then looks up at the sound of the L-19, which passes overhead, flying low.

MAYS Jesus.

Immediately, the loudspeaker crackles into life.

VANN (*voice over*) Well, Hallelujah, Walrus, a whole mile in less than three hours.

MAYS Thank you, Topper Six.

EXT. L-19. DAY

Vann's point of view: the M-113s lined up at the crossing point, the downed helicopters and, in the distance, the treeline.

VANN The two of you home free could go in and evacuate the wounded, OK?

EXT. PADDY FIELD. DAY

Mays and Sergeant Bowers finish loading the wounded into one of the M-113s under a withering hail of rifle and machine-gun fire from the treeline, covered by the thumping .50 calibre guns mounted on the M-113s. An inferno of noise. Mays shouts up to the driver.

MAYS OK, take it away.

He hears the L-19 passing overhead again and hurries to his radio receiver, which is already transmitting Vann's harsh tones. He crouches in the lee of the second M-113, yelling into the microphone.

MAYS Go ahead, Topper Six.

EXT. L-19. DAY

Vann's point of view: below, as one M-113 begins to withdraw, two others are driving up to reinforce.

VANN There are two more M-113s on their way to you. When they arrive, attack the treeline. How many casualties, over?

EXT. PADDY FIELD. DAY

Mays yells back against the rising cacophony.

MAYS We have two, repeat, two crewmen dead and . . .

A hail of bullets hits the M-113. The machine-gunner is instantly killed, blown right across the back of the vehicle; and another bullet hits the radio receiver, severing the aerial.

EXT. L-19. DAY

Vann knows immediately what has happened.

VANN Hello, Walrus, do you read? Come in, Walrus, talk to me. Over. Shit.

EXT. TREELINE. DAY

The Viet Cong foxhole. The formidable ugly shapes of three advancing M-113s trundle inexorably forward, despite the concentration of fire.

INT. M-113. DAY

The inside of the M-113 has space for ten soldiers facing each other in two rows. On a higher level are the driver, the machine-gunner and the commander, in this case Captain Mays. There's very little light and the sound of bullets bouncing off the armour like a swarm of bees. The vehicle stops. The rear clamshell hatches drop and Mays leads the troops out of the back.

EXT. PADDY FIELD. DAY

The troops string out and advance steadily, firing from the hip. Ahead of them, the M-113s advance, also firing. But they're attracting a hail of concentrated fire from the treeline and first one, then another soldier drops. Mays can see that it's hopeless.

MAYS OK. Back.

The ARVN troops scamper back at top speed, abandoning the wounded. Mays drags one, screaming and cursing until the other is reluctantly collected. When Mays scrambles back into the M-113, he's the last exposed man.

INT. M-113. DAY
Chaos inside the vehicle. One panicked soldier puts his boot on a wounded man's face. Mays pushes him aside and passes through.

EXT. M-113. DAY
Mays emerges to find the gunner on his knees, not looking where he's firing, spraying the tops of the trees. Mays grabs his collar and hauls him up.
MAYS Get up, goddammit, aim, you bastard.

EXT. L-19. DAY
Vann's point of view: although the leading three M-113s are stalled, four more are coming up on the right flank.
VANN All right, now we're in business.

EXT. TREELINE. DAY
In the thunder of the camouflaged foxhole, a Viet Cong squad leader looks across at the seven approaching M-113s and checks the grenades on his belt.

EXT. L-19. DAY
Vann's point of view: one by one, four of the M-113s sputter to a halt under the intensity of the barrage. Only one is close to the treeline, a machine with a different-shaped turret.
VANN Good, that's right, great.
The turret houses a flame-thrower. The M-113 stops eighty yards from the treeline, the cannon-like tube swivels and a spout of flame flares out. However, it travels no more than twenty yards and dies out almost immediately. Vann groans, horrified. Now, below, only two M-113s remain in contention.

EXT. PADDY FIELD. DAY
The leading M-113 is now only about twenty yards from the treeline. Suddenly, a Viet Cong squad leader bursts from the trees, followed by his squad. He pulls the pin on a grenade and waits for what seems an

insane length of time, before lobbing it towards the towering M-113. The grenade explodes in mid-air just above the M-113, seriously damaging its turret. Meanwhile the rest of the squad is firing rifle grenades at the second M-113. Several VC go down as the gunner of the second M-113 cuts a swathe with his machine gun.

EXT. L-19. DAY

Vann's point of view: the two leading M-113s turn and begin to retreat. In the aircraft, Vann throws up his hands in despair, speaking to no one in particular.

VANN They keep learning, we keep making the same fucking mistakes.

EXT. TREELINE. DAY

The Viet Cong squad has been decimated by machine-gun fire and shrapnel. Nevertheless, a ragged cheer goes up as the M-113s turn away.

EXT. L-19. DAY

Vann's point of view: below, harrassed by renewed Viet Cong fire, all the M-113s are now in retreat, trundling back towards the downed helicopters. Vann adjusts the frequency of his transmitter.

VANN Hello, Tiger, Topper Six, over.

The crackle of an acknowledgement.

First time ever, the VC have repulsed our M-113s. This is turning into the biggest fuck-up since Little Big Horn. I'm on my way back.

INT. WAR ROOM. DAY

Vann hurries into the busy room to be greeted by Colonel Porter. In the background Ziegler and Cao argue in front of a large map supported on an easel.

VANN Glad you're here, sir.

PORTER I heard there was some trouble. Now we got more. Our master-strategist wants to drop in reinforcements.

VANN That's what I was going to suggest.

PORTER Yes, but he wants to drop them in to the west of Bac.

Vann stares at Porter, incredulous. Then, abruptly, he strides over to Cao and Ziegler.

VANN I hear you're going to drop reinforcements to the east. Good thinking.

CAO No, no. To the west. That is more prudent.

Vann turns to the operations map: it shows the Viet Cong in the villages of Ap Bac and Tan Thoi, threatened by friendly forces from the north, west and south. Vann indicates each force in turn.

VANN OK. Here's the Seventh. Stalled by the VC in Tan Thoi. Here's our M-113s. And here's the Civil Guards, still taking a goddamn vacation.

Now he points to the empty space, east of the two villages.

You have to put them in on the east and close the box. It's the only chance we have to turn a defeat into a victory. Surround the enemy forces.

Cao points to the west, behind the M-113 company.

CAO No, no, they must go here. To reinforce.

VANN Reinforce what? The defeat? You have to put them there.

He stabs the map to the east of the combat area with his finger, so violently that the entire easel topples over. Ignoring the slight confusion which follows this, Vann blows his top.

Or do you want the VC to escape again? Are you scared to fight? What the fuck's going on here?

Cao looks at Vann, his expression glacial.

CAO Thank you for your advice. I must consider my options.

EXT. L-19. DUSK

Vann's face, set in an expression of grim, cold anger.

VANN (*voice over*) Well, you better consider fast, you got around ten minutes, because if you make your drop too close to sunset, you'll be dropping them in deep shit.

The little plane is passing over the downed helicopters and the company of M-113s to the west of Ap Bac. The sun is low on the horizon. A distant droning sound. The pilot glances back at Vann.

O'NEILL Here they come.

Up from the south comes a flight of whale-shaped C-123 Provider transport planes. Vann watches their approach, his expression bleak. Then he frowns, puzzled. Then his face clears.

VANN They passed the point. They're not going to jump. Thank Christ for that.

But almost immediately, parachutes begin to flower from the leading aircraft. Vann jerks to life, galvanised.

Talk to the pilots, Jesus!

He presses the button on his transmitter. Meanwhile, O'Neill begins shouting instructions into his headset.

Tiger, this is Topper Six. Abort parachute drop, do you read me, abort drop, drop is coming in too close to enemy lines, do you read, acknowledge, out!

He waits, anguished.

Do you read me, Tiger? This is Topper Six!

Evidently, there's no response. The sky is now full of parachutes. The green tracers are already beginning to arch towards them from the Viet Cong lines. Silhouetted against the setting sun, the Paras make an easy target. Hit by enemy fire, one or two of the parachutes blossom into flame.

EXT. PADDY FIELD. DUSK

A parachutist splashes into the paddy, landing awkwardly. The parachute canopy flutters down and settles around his body. Immediately the silk begins to stain with bright, arterial blood. The unearthly beauty of the landscape only emphasises the horror of the scene.

EXT. L-19. DUSK

Up above in the little spotter plane, Vann groans and buries his face in his hands.

INT. TENT BY TAN HIEP AIRSTRIP. DAY

General Harkins lights a cigarette and carefully inserts it into the long white holder. He's in the process of giving a statement to a group of a dozen or so journalists, among them Halberstam. His swagger stick lies on the lectern in front of him; he's immaculate in a short-sleeved shirt with four silver stars on each collar tab, light tropical trousers and street shoes. On either side of him, seated, are Colonel Porter and Cao, the latter wearing a fatuously complacent smile. Vann is off to one side, his expression grim.

HARKINS I realise this is getting monotonous, boys, but I have to announce to you yet another notable victory, the first of 1963, the year in which we intend to get this whole Vietnam thing over and done with.

The distant boom of artillery makes him pause and look up.
And this time, gentlemen, you are in at the kill. We have them in a trap, our artillery is softening them up, and in half an hour, we're going to spring that trap. So, if you'll excuse me, I have business to attend to.

HALBERSTAM General Harkins?
Harkins's eyes narrow, his expression suddenly cautious.

HARKINS David.

HALBERSTAM The casualty figures would appear to suggest that if this is a victory, it's been extremely costly, would you agree?

HARKINS We're about to take the objective. I'd call that a victory. Thank you, gentlemen.
He sweeps from the tent, followed by Cao and Porter. Vann hangs back for a moment and Halberstam moves swiftly to his side.

HALBERSTAM Any comments, John?
Vann looks at Halberstam for a moment; then, he looks away.

VANN Yes. The enemy gave a good account of themselves. They're brave men.
He looks back at Halberstam, who's intrigued by this answer.
I have to go to a briefing. You want to come see me at the Seminary tonight?

HALBERSTAM Sure. Just one more question. The General said he'd call this a victory. Would you call it a victory?
Again, Vann pauses before answering.

VANN No. I'd call it the most miserable fucking performance I've ever seen in my life.
He hurries out of the tent, leaving Halberstam flabbergasted.

EXT. TAN HIEP AIRSTRIP. DAY

Vann moves fast towards a second, larger tent. He pauses a moment, listening to the crump of the artillery, then pushes into –

INT. OFFICE. DAY

– a temporary office, where Harkins and Porter sit at a table, papers spread in front of them.

VANN Where is that maniac?

HARKINS Who?

VANN My counterpart, sir.

HARKINS He's directing the barrage.

VANN Why? Who the hell is he shelling? Water buffaloes? He knows as well as I do, the enemy walked out last night through the door he so carefully left open. The VC is out of there. Long gone.

HARKINS Colonel Cao has assured me –

VANN Believe me, sir, Colonel Cao will always assure you whatever it is he thinks you most want to hear. It's no different from you telling those press guys that yesterday was a victory.

HARKINS But it was a victory.

VANN A maximum of three hundred and fifty VC with obsolete weapons held off a force of over fifteen hundred men supported by air strikes, artillery, gunships and M-113s. They shot down five helicopters and killed close to a hundred men; then they escaped scot-free. This is a victory?

Before Harkins, who is beginning to look enraged, can comment, Vann plunges on.

It's taken me a long time, but I finally figured out what's going on. It was when President Diem's elite Guards refused to advance yesterday. It's not that they're cowards. Not at all. It's that they, and Cao as well, are under direct orders from Diem not to lose a single man or M-113 or tank or anything he might need to put down a rebellion. It's not the VC that scares them: it's their own people.

HARKINS I see.

He turns to Porter, trying to make a joke of it.

VANN And what's your opinion of this theory, Dan?

PORTER Sounds mighty plausible to me.

HARKINS Oh, does it?

He picks up from the table in front of him a map of the Northern Mekong Delta area, which is divided into zones coloured red and blue, the former somewhat predominating.

Well, fortunately we're not here to discuss Colonel Vann's political hunches. We're here because I need the answer to a simple question. This map claims that there are more areas under enemy control than there were last month.

He indicates the red areas of the map.

Why is that?

VANN I've been trying to explain, sir –

HARKINS Our information indicates precisely the contrary.

VANN Information from whom?

HARKINS Colonel Cao.

VANN Sir, except for yesterday's operation, which you instigated yourself, for the last three months Colonel Cao has only sent troops into areas where he knows for certain that there are no enemy forces. It's been driving us crazy. In the same period, he's refused us authorisation to follow up hard information and make contact with the enemy on forty-five different occasions.

HARKINS I can see you have a problem with your counterpart, Colonel. I'm not sure what bearing that has on our map here.

VANN Sir, the map is accurate.

HARKINS I don't think so.

Silence. They look at each other for a moment.

In a few weeks, John, your time in Vietnam is up and you rotate back home. Are you sure you want the record to show that this very important area under your supervision is the only place in the country where our allies are slipping back? Difficult thing to put in a progress report, don't you think?

Vann continues to look at him, his eyes cold. Harkins slides the map across the table to him.

So take another shot at this, John. See what you can come up with. Maybe you'll decide you like the look of this one better.

He slides another map out of an envelope, on which the proportions of red and blue are reversed. Vann looks down at it, astonished.

INT. VANN'S OFFICE IN THE SEMINARY. NIGHT

The maps are in front of Halberstam, sitting across the desk from Vann, and now it's his turn to look astonished. Halberstam looks up from the maps. His tape recorder is running.

HALBERSTAM Jesus Christ, John, these are dynamite.

VANN I know.

HALBERSTAM Listen, I'll get confirmation for this and of course I'll keep your name out of my story, but they're going to know this has to have come from you. You could be in big trouble.

VANN I'm aware I'm sworn not to reveal classified information: on the other hand, don't I have a duty as an American citizen?

HALBERSTAM I think you do. But that's easy for me to say.

VANN If I have to resign, I'll resign.

He pauses for a moment, then looks up at Halberstam, his expression candid.

It isn't that I care so much about lying, as a matter of fact I'm very good at lying, I've lied to you often and you've bought it.

HALBERSTAM Why should I believe you this time? I mean, I do, but why should I?

VANN Because I lie consciously, with a clear objective. That asshole with the cigarette holder tells lies as well; the difference is he doesn't know it. Most of the time he believes he's telling the truth. And that's really dangerous. Don't you see, if the people running the war keep kidding themselves, it turns this whole expedition into one big, bright, shining lie.

HALBERSTAM I guess it does at that.

Halberstam closes his notebook and glances at his watch.

I'll protect your ass the best I can, John. I really appreciate this.

VANN Somebody had to do it. It was time.

EXT. TAN SON NHUT AIRFIELD. DAY

A small crowd surrounds Vann as he makes his way across the tarmac towards the waiting aircraft. At the foot of the steps leading up to the plane, he turns to shake hands with Porter, Ziegler, Mays, Sergeant Bowers, even Colonel Cao. Finally he shakes hands with Halberstam, indicating as he does so the round silver cigarette box he holds in his left hand.

VANN Thanks for this.

HALBERSTAM It's for showing us the way.

VANN I'm going to miss this place. Crazy, isn't it? You're just starting to figure it out, they send you home.

HALBERSTAM I'll be in Washington next month.

VANN See you there.

HALBERSTAM You make them sit up at the Pentagon, OK?

EXT. PENTAGON. DAY

Seen from above, the small figure of Vann makes its way into one of the Pentagon's main entrances, a briefcase under his arm.

INT. PENTAGON OFFICES. DAY

Vann, immaculate in freshly pressed uniform and gleaming shoes, bustles into the outer office of General Earle Wheeler, Chief of Staff of the Army, extracting a document from his briefcase and slapping it down on the desk in front of a youngish captain, aide to the General.

VANN Good morning, I'm Colonel Vann, I'm briefing the Joint Chiefs this afternoon, here's a copy of the briefing for General Wheeler.

AIDE We already have a copy.

VANN Are you sure? I only just delivered it to General Krulak.

AIDE He sent it right over.

VANN Oh, OK.

AIDE And I have some news for you, buddy.

Vann pauses in the act of putting the document back in his briefcase.

AIDE Your briefing is cancelled.

VANN What do you mean?

AIDE I just removed your name from the agenda.

Abruptly, Vann circumvents the desk and plunges into the inner office, ignoring the aide.

AIDE Hey, wait a minute!

INT. GENERAL WHEELER'S OFFICE. DAY

General Wheeler, a trim, handsome man of fifty-five, looks up from what he's reading with considerable surprise, to find Vann standing in the doorway.

VANN Sir. why has my briefing been cancelled?

WHEELER You must be Colonel Vann.

VANN Yes, sir.

WHEELER Let me ask you a question, Colonel: why did you not issue copies of your briefing until this morning?

VANN I was afraid it would not be approved.

WHEELER Well, you were right. The Chairman has decided he doesn't want to hear this; and, judging by what I've read of it so far, I'm inclined to agree.

VANN But it's the truth.

WHEELER I don't think you have any reason to complain, Colonel. As I understand it, you've been giving unofficial briefings all over the Pentagon ever since you arrived; and I don't think there's a newspaperman in the country hasn't heard your opinions.

VANN I've been in the Army for twenty years, sir. I thought the best way I could repay what I owe was to let you know exactly what's happening over there.

WHEELER Well, Colonel, I appreciate your sentiment; but the Army's just going to have to get by without your advice.

He looks calmly at Vann, staring him down.

INT. DINER IN WASHINGTON. NIGHT

Vann sits across the table from Halberstam, whose expression is full of concern.

HALBERSTAM So what are you doing to do?

Vann finishes his mouthful of hamburger, savouring the drama of the pause, before his blunt reply.

VANN Resign.

HALBERSTAM Jesus, but that's terrible.

VANN I don't see what choice I have.

Silence. Halberstam shakes his head, reflecting.

HALBERSTAM I'm sure it isn't any consolation, but I had to threaten to resign as well. The *Times* was very unhappy about our story and the State Department has been leaning hard on us ever since. The paper makes me fight for every line, they really don't want to print this kind of news.

VANN Maybe they're hoping to lose the war without anybody noticing.

HALBERSTAM No, you opened our eyes and showed us what to look for and nobody's going to be able to con us from here on in. So whatever the army says, I know you've done a very important job for your country. It won't be forgotten.

Vann looks pleased; Halberstam hesitates before going on.

HALBERSTAM I just hope what's happened isn't completely our fault.

Vann looks up at him with a small tight smile.

VANN You never hurt me any more than I wanted to be hurt.

INT. LIVING ROOM OF THE VANN HOUSE IN CHESAPEAKE BAY. NIGHT

Vann, slumped on a sofa, his expression indignant, looks up at Mary Jane, who stands above him in her dressing gown.

VANN Chrissake, Mary Jane, all you ever say is why don't I come home? Now I find a good job, good money, you like Denver, it'll be great for the kids and you start telling me not to take it.

MARY JANE I just don't see you out of the Army, it's your life, John, that's what you always said. Just because the Joint Chiefs –

VANN I'm not taking retirement because of those assholes in the Pentagon. I'm leaving because I've gone as far as I can go. They'll never make me a general.

MARY JANE Is that so terrible?

VANN Means I either have to spend the rest of my time as some goddamn glorified clerk in Washington or taking dumb orders from guys who don't know shit. I had enough of that in Vietnam.

MARY JANE How do you know they won't make you a general?

Vann hesitates before speaking very quickly.

VANN Because of the statutory rape.

MARY JANE But . . . you were acquitted.

VANN It's on the record. It's a doubt. When they make a man a general they can't afford doubts.

Mary Jane thinks about this, frowning.

MARY JANE You must have known about this for years.

VANN How do you think I was able to shoot off at the mouth to all those goddamn reporters?

MARY JANE And they believed you.

VANN Sure they believed me. I was telling them the truth.

Mary Jane digests this: then she stretches out a hand.

MARY JANE Come to bed.

Vann takes her hand, springs to his feet and takes her in his arms.

VANN I'm just trying to think of what's right for you.

EXT. MARTIN MARIETTA AEROSPACE COMPLEX, DENVER. DAY

1964. Vann's small Triumph sedan pulls into a parking space outside the glass-and-steel colossus of the Martin Marietta Aerospace company. It's around nine o'clock and large numbers of employees are streaming into the building. It's a clear spring day.

INT. TRIUMPH. DAY

Vann sits at the wheel, not moving. He's wearing a grey suit, white shirt, blue tie. Eventually, with a considerable effort, he forces himself to take the keys out of the ignition and leave the car.

Slowly, increasing in volume as the montage develops, we hear the sounds of Vietnam: the buzz of insects, the voices of children in the streets of Saigon, the feathery stutter of distant helicopters, the stridulation of cicadas at dusk, the laughter of women – not the sounds of war, but those of everyday life.

INT. VANN'S OFFICE. DAY

Vann sits behind his desk, his jacket off and his tie loosened. For a moment he stares into the distance: then he resumes his task, attempting, with great seriousness, to land a series of crumpled sheets of paper in a distant waste-paper basket.

EXT. GARDEN OF THE VANN HOUSE IN LITTLETON, COLO. DAY

Vann, his expression intent, plays volleyball with his four sons, now aged between sixteen and ten, and two or three of their schoolfriends, in the early evening.

INT. CONCERT HALL IN DENVER. DAY

Vann sits on the platform at a rally of Republicans for Johnson. As the MC finishes his introduction, Vann springs to his feet and approaches the microphone.

INT. SITTING ROOM IN THE VANN HOUSE. NIGHT

Members of the family pass to and fro; the TV is on in a corner, relaying a news bulletin connected with the Johnson election. But Vann sits on a sofa with his feet up, staring into space, lost in another world.

EXT. VANN HOUSE IN LITTLETON. DAWN

1965. The sounds of Vietnam have faded away. Now, the pre-dawn silence is hardly dented by the arrival of Vann's Triumph, which glides up into the driveway.

INT. BEDROOM. DAWN

Mary Jane wakes instantly from a troubled sleep.

INT. SITTING ROOM. DAWN

Vann comes in from the kitchen with a glass of milk. He slips out of his jacket and slumps on to the sofa. He's unshaven and red-eyed, but doesn't seem especially tired. He takes a sip of milk, then senses a presence and looks up to find Mary Jane in the doorway.

MARY JANE I'm not even going to ask where you've been.

VANN Sit down for a minute.

MARY JANE Do you realise, you haven't had a meal at home for ten days?

VANN I have to talk to you.

Mary Jane sits at the table in an upright chair, watching him as he tries to formulate his thoughts.

There's a problem I've been having with everyday life in this country: nothing matters. And I got to thinking it wasn't so much the Army I was missing: it was Vietnam. See, I understood what was going on down there, better than the generals, better than anyone. Because I loved it. The others were just in for a year, tourists, kill a few gooks, then back to the world. But I loved the country, I loved . . .

MARY JANE The war.

VANN No, not the war, the people. The life. So I've been asking everybody. Said I was prepared to do anything and go anywhere. And finally the Far East Bureau came up with something.

MARY JANE I see.

VANN It's a lousy job, an ordinary province pacification officer, you know, I build schools, I give out food, I look after refugees, it's a province runs from Saigon to the Cambodian border, a real Siberia assignment.

He looks up at her. Her eyes are full of tears.

It's where I belong.

INT. BEDROOM. NIGHT

Mary Jane lies in Vann's arms in the darkness.

MARY JANE There's been like a wall between us ever since you got back from over there. I know how badly you've been missing it. I can see it's eating you alive. So I'm not even going to ask you not to go.

By this time, the tears are streaming down her face.
But where does that leave our marriage, John?

VANN I get thirty days' leave a year. I'll take it at Christmas. Hell, isn't it better to have some real quality time together than this kind of half-life?

MARY JANE The kids are going to miss you.

VANN No, you're doing a great job with them. And I'll be a much better example when I'm doing something I can believe in.
Close on Mary Jane, her face on his chest, her eyes wide open.

VANN (*voice over*) See, if I was to stay home, Mary Jane, well: the marriage would be over.

EXT. ROUTE I, SOUTH VIETNAM. DAY

A station wagon hurtles down the road, heading towards the Cambodian border, passing between fields of sugar cane. It's the only vehicle on the road.

Over this, Vann's voice, as he argues with the motor-pool officer at US Operations Mission.

VANN (*voice over*) Sure I'm going to drive, why the hell shouldn't I?

INT. OFFICE IN USOM, SAIGON. DAY

The officer, who looks harassed behind his cluttered desk, looks irritably across at Vann.

USOM OFFICER It's too dangerous, nobody's driven into Hau Nghia province, even in convoy, not for months.

VANN I always drove everywhere.

USOM OFFICER I guess things have changed a lot in two years.

INT. STATION WAGON. DAY

Vann brakes sharply and hauls on the wheel.

INT./EXT. ROUTE I. DAY

Vann's point of view: the remains of a jeep, tilting crazily on the rim of a mine crater. The corpse of the ARVN driver is still slumped across the wheel; parts of another, dismembered corpse lie to the right of the jeep. Vann pilots his station wagon carefully, dipping briefly over the edge of the crater. Then, he accelerates away and, apparently in high good humour begins humming a tune to himself: Woody Guthrie's 'This Land is Your Land'.

INT. USOM OFFICE. DAY

Vann stares insolently across at the USOM officer.

VANN OK, you going to give me a helicopter?

USOM OFFICER I'm not authorised to do that.

INT./EXT. STREETS OF CU CHI. DAY

Vann drives slowly through the crowded streets of Cu Chi. He's aware of a hostile atmosphere, people pointedly ignoring his presence or staring coldly at him. He turns off Route 1 on to a narrower road and begins to leave the centre of town behind him.

VANN (*voice over*) Then I'll drive.

EXT. ROAD TO BAU TRAI. DAY

The road, narrow and rutted, runs between rice fields: the low afternoon sun turns their waters into a fiery lake. The station wagon is still travelling too fast and Vann's voice floats through its open window.

VANN

This land is your land,
This land is my land,
From the DMZ
To the Gulf of Thailand . . .

INT. STATION WAGON. DAY

Vann sings out, in the grip of a genuine exhilaration.

VANN

. . . From the Mekong Delta
To the Central Highlands,
This land was made for you and me.

EXT. BAU TRAI. DAY

The province capital is little more than a hamlet, ramshackle and rundown. The station wagon pulls up beside two ARVN soldiers, who are lounging by the side of the road, drinking beer. Vann leans out to speak to them.

VANN Bau Trai?

The ARVN soldiers exchange glances. Finally one replies, his expression truculent.

ARVN SOLDIER Bau Trai.

VANN US Operations Mission?

The soldier points, indicating an unmade-up lane, running off the main street. Then, he turns away, raising the bottle to his lips. Vann frowns in annoyance, then decides to drive on.

EXT. USOM OFFICE. DAY

The station wagon pulls up outside a long, low warehouse, built of cement with a tin roof. Vann jumps out and vanishes into –

INT. USOM OFFICE. DAY

– the warehouse. It's a vast, gloomy space like a hangar, but there's hardly room to move. Total chaos. Sacks of corn and bulgur wheat and cement everywhere: and innumerable piles of miscellaneous items: mattresses, chairs, shovels, paint, lengths of iron, clothing and so on. None of this is systematically arranged; and in the middle of it all is a harassed, balding, middle-aged man wandering aimlessly from one pile of goods to another, jotting the occasional note on the pad clamped to his clipboard. He doesn't notice Vann's approach.

VANN Mr Pye?

Pye gives a start: then he peers at Vann suspiciously. Vann advances on him, extending his hand.

VANN I'm John Paul Vann.

Pye accepts his handshake with evident reluctance.

VANN Your successor.

PYE Ah. Welcome to the office.

VANN Office?

Pye points to a distant table, covered with dust and papers.

PYE Over there in the corner. We do the best we can.

Vann looks around, plainly horrified by the disorder.

EXT. SIDE STREET. DAY

Vann follows Pye down the muddy, narrow lane, carrying his grip.

VANN Do you have intelligence about troop dispositions in the province?

PYE Ours?

VANN Well, ours and theirs.

PYE That's not really our department, you know . . .

VANN By the way, how large is the province, how many square kilometres?

PYE Well, let's see now . . .

It's clear he has no idea; he breaks off with some relief to indicate a new but already shabby bungalow, surrounded by scraps of trodden-down barbed wire. Garbage is strewn around the muddy front area. Pye points at it sheepishly.

Here it is, home sweet home.

Vann follows him to the front door.

INT. USOM BUNGALOW. DAY

Pye leads Vann into the main room, which is as chaotic as the warehouse, overflowing with crates and sacks, every surface stacked with files, papers and dirty crockery. The atmosphere is evidently fetid.

PYE We'll have to share a few days, I hope you don't mind. I'm out of here on Tuesday.

VANN Good. Do you have air-conditioning?

PYE Air-conditioning? Hell, we don't even have electricity.

Vann drops his grip on the floor, glancing around in dismay.

VANN I guess we should have a conversation about the budget; would that be easiest to have in the office?

PYE What's the rush?

VANN There's a budget meeting tomorrow morning.

Pye looks at him wide-eyed, starting to panic.

PYE There is?

At this point, a very tall, dark man of about thirty lets himself into the room. This is Doug Ramsey; he has a shy, engaging smile.

RAMSEY Hi, I'm Doug Ramsey, I'll be your assistant.

He shakes hands with Vann, who's clearly relieved to meet him.

VANN You been out here long?

RAMSEY About a month.

PYE You starting to get hungry?

VANN Is there a restaurant in town?

PYE Jesus, you can't eat there. We eat in the mess.

VANN I thought if I was going to do this job right, I ought to try to live with the Vietnamese.

RAMSEY I'll take you to the restaurant.

Pye is clearly a little put out by this; but he rallies and addresses Vann, somewhat effusively.

PYE It's not too difficult here, I think you'll find. The main job is to distribute the bulgur wheat. I go round to each village, I make the distribution and I have a speech I make, you know, where I explain to them how they'll never get bulgur wheat from the VC. I'll be happy to leave you a copy of the speech.

He turns to Vann, hoping for a reaction, but there is none.

INT. VIETNAMESE RESTAURANT. NIGHT

Ramsey and Vann are the only Americans in the crowded restaurant.

RAMSEY The moment he leaves the village, they feed the bulgur wheat to the hogs.

VANN Is that so?

RAMSEY Vietnamese can't stand bulgur wheat. Of course, neither can we, that's why we give it away.

A waiter arrives with two plates of noodles. He bangs one of them down in front of Vann, dislodging a cloud of flies. Ramsey speaks to the waiter in fluent Vietnamese.

Vann watches; eventually, the waiter nods and leaves.

VANN You speak the best Vietnamese of any American I've met.

EXT. HAMLET OF SO DO. DAY

A canary-yellow International pick-up pulls up in the centre of the hamlet and Vann and Ramsey emerge from it. Ramsey leads Vann towards some large buildings in the south-east corner of the square. He points to one of the buildings; it's unguarded, the front door open.

RAMSEY One of the Ranger companies uses this as a base.

VANN Great security.

RAMSEY And there's the school.

He points towards the sound of chanting schoolchildren.

EXT. SCHOOL OF SO DO. DAY

Another angle shows why the children are so audible: the school has no walls. It simply consists of a roof made of aluminium sheets, supported by beams. Some of the children sit at tables, as does the teacher, a lively-looking middle-aged Vietnamese woman; but most of the children are sitting on the ground. The teacher, beaming, comes over towards Ramsey and Vann, greeting Ramsey by name.

RAMSEY Madame Tu. This is . . .

TU Yes, you must be Mr Vann.

VANN Madame.

They shake hands; as they do so, Vann looks up, aware of a jagged hole in the roof.

TU Shrapnel.

VANN Right. Don't let us interrupt. Maybe you'd like to give out some of these later.

He hands her an enormous bag of M and Ms, then turns to the children, smiling.

VANN Hi, children.

Mme Tu says something in Vietnamese and the children chant back a greeting. Vann's eye falls on a small girl in the front row, who quickly puts a hand over her mouth. Vann squats, taking a stick of gum out of his pocket. He gently takes the child's hand and puts the gum in it, revealing that she has a harelip. He smiles at her and looks up at the older children sitting at a nearby table. One of the boys also has a harelip. He straightens and turns back to Mme Tu.

VANN Got many of these kids? Kids with harelips?

TU Five or six maybe.

VANN We have a Filipino surgical team assigned to us in Saigon. I'm going to take these kids in in a couple of weeks, all right? It's a very simple operation.

TU Yes, that would be good.

EXT. USOM HOSPITAL, SAIGON. DAY

Vann completes the handover of half a dozen children with harelips, waves goodbye to them and climbs back into the yellow pick-up.

INT./EXT. PICK-UP CAB. DAY

Vann drives North through Saigon, moving into a residential area, alert as ever, chewing gum, his jaw working overtime. Something attracts his attention.

EXT. STREET IN SAIGON. DAY

Standing on the sidewalk, on the lookout for a taxi is Lee, dressed simply in a red sweater and short skirt, her long black hair flowing over her shoulders. She's twenty now and strikingly attractive.

Vann slows to a halt about ten yards beyond Lee. He watches her for a moment in the rear-view mirror. Then, moving decisively, he takes his gum out of his mouth and sticks it on the bottom of his shoe.

EXT. STREET. DAY

Lee notices Vann as he steps down from the truck and, miming annoyance, scrapes his foot on the kerb. She watches as he checks the sole of his shoe, hopping once to keep his balance. He looks up suddenly, catches her watching and smiles broadly.

VANN Hi. Do you speak English?

LEE I hope so. I make my living teaching it.

VANN Can I give you a ride home?

She turns and points to a substantial house, set back from the road.

LEE That's where I live.

VANN Oh.

LEE But you can drive me to school if you like. Save me cab fare.

VANN Sure. Delighted.

INT. PICK-UP CAB. DAY

Lee sits next to Vann, watching him, her expression quizzical.

VANN So. You're a teacher at this school?

LEE Not exactly. It belongs to me. I'm the principal.

VANN I see. Gee, you look way too young to be a principal.

LEE There's a big demand now for English speakers.

Vann negotiates a bend, then turns to her.

VANN I'm back in town on Sunday. Will you have dinner with me?

She looks at his hand, resting lightly on the wheel, registering the wedding ring.

LEE You married, yes?

VANN Separated.

Silence. Then Lee smiles to herself.

LEE OK.

INT. NIGHTCLUB. NIGHT

A Saigon nightspot with a mostly American clientele. The band, however, is Vietnamese, as are the hostesses discreetly deployed around the dance floor. Vann reaches across the table to fill Lee's wine glass. She looks at his hand.

LEE Where's your wedding ring?

VANN I don't always wear it.

LEE Do you have children?

VANN No. We wanted to, but my wife had some problems, it just wasn't possible.

LEE How long since you lived together?

VANN Let's see, I came over here three years ago. I guess about a year before that.

LEE So are you lonely?

VANN Sometimes. Sometimes I am. You want to dance?

He leads her to the dance floor and takes her in his arms.

I've been looking for someone like you.

They dance in silence for a moment: then Lee looks up at him.

LEE I'm taking the day off from school on Wednesday. You know why?

VANN Why?

LEE It's my twenty-first birthday.

VANN Well; I could take the day off myself.

LEE How old are you?

VANN For . . . ah, thirty-six.

They dance: Lee looks up at him, her expression serious.

INT. BEDROOM IN LEE'S HOUSE. DAY

Vann finishes making love to Lee: an explosive climax, after which they lie together for a moment, drenched in sweat. Eventually, Vann disengages gingerly, smiling across at Lee.

VANN That was something else.

She looks across at him, her expression candid, something fierce in her eyes. Vann leans across her, opens a drawer, reaches in and brings out a small wrapped parcel, which he hands to her.

Happy birthday.

LEE Thank you.

She puts it to one side, reaches up and draws Vann's head down, so she can kiss him. Eventually, he breaks free.

VANN Can I take a photograph of you opening your present?

She looks at him again, the same strange faraway expression in her eyes.

LEE You can do just whatever the hell you like.

EXT. SO DO. DAY

The canary-yellow pick-up makes its way through the hamlet: the children from the hospital are sitting in the back, each clutching a balloon and a sponge bag of the kind distributed by airlines, bouncing as the truck jolts over uneven ground.

Close on the little girl Vann first noticed in the schoolroom. Her lip has been repaired. It's still rather pink and raw and not entirely unscarred, but it's hugely improved. As the truck slows, she takes a plain oblong mirror out of her sponge bag and studies her new lip.

EXT. SCHOOL AT SO DO. DAY

Mme Tu waits outside the school with a number of parents and children. The eager anticipation of the adults is almost palpable. The pick-up pulls up and the Vietnamese surge forward as Vann and Ramsey jump out and begin helping the children down.

Vann finishes by lifting the little girl out of the back of the truck and carrying her over to the group of Vietnamese. She stretches her arms out towards a young, heavily pregnant woman, her mother. The mother takes her, holding her awkwardly because of her condition, but radiantly delighted when she sees the child's upper lip. She inclines her head to Vann in dignified gratitude and Vann smiles at her. Then he turns away as Mme Tu arrives at his elbow.

TU This is very good, Mr Vann, what you have done.

VANN We're supposed to be here to help you, aren't we?

TU That's right; but some of you have trouble remembering this.

Vann signals to Ramsey and they extricate themselves from the crowd and climb back into the pick-up.

INT. PICK-UP CAB. DAY

Vann reverses the truck and begins turning it round.

VANN I like that woman, the teacher.

RAMSEY She's the VC medical officer for this village.

A moment's silence, as Vann absorbs this information. Then he glances across at Ramsey.

VANN Well, hell, if I was a Vietnamese, I guess I'd join the VC, wouldn't you?

RAMSEY No doubt about it.

EXT. RANGER HQ. DAY

A sleepy-looking ARVN Ranger, armed with an M-14, wanders out of the house, attracted by the sounds of the children and the truck.

INT. PICK-UP CAB. DAY

Vann looks at the Ranger and snorts sardonically.

VANN Jesus, a guard, things are looking up.

He looks back at the school for a moment, frowning.

Listen, I meant to ask you, how come the school doesn't have any goddamn walls?

He accelerates away, waving to the crowd, as Ramsey looks at him for a moment, uncertain.

I mean, you said this was one of ours.

RAMSEY Have you any idea how much cement fetches on the black market in Saigon?

VANN We supply them with cement and they sell it?

RAMSEY The ARVN sell our arms to the VC: you think the civilians don't want a piece of the action?

Vann glances across at Ramsey; then he stares ahead of him at the road, his expression settling into one of determination.

VANN OK, who do we see?

Ramsey looks at him for a moment, as if he needs to make sure Vann is serious: there's no doubt that he is.

RAMSEY Most of the construction work in the province is handled by one contractor. His name is Ngo Duc.

INT. DINING ROOM OF NGO DUC'S HOUSE IN CU CHI. DAY

Lunch is being cleared away by servants in Ngo Duc's comfortable house in Cu Chi. Duc, a plump, shifty-looking middle-aged man, sits at the head of the table, flanked by Vann and Ramsey and facing his wife, a delicately pretty woman, considerably younger than her husband. Ramsey has some papers spread in front of him and is conducting a kind of interrogation. Dialogue in Vietnamese.

RAMSEY Aluminium sheets for roofing: the school in Phuoc Hiep used seventy fewer sheets than you claimed, and the maternity clinic twenty-five fewer sheets.

DUC Who gave you these figures?

RAMSEY We counted them ourselves.

There's a silence as Duc contemplates his fingernails. Then he shoots a glance at his wife.

DUC Come into my office: we'll look through the invoices.

He rises to his feet as Ramsey reverts to English, speaking to Vann.

RAMSEY He's going to show me some invoices.

Duc also makes an attempt at English.

DUC One moment, please.

Vann nods and Duc leads Ramsey out of the room, closing the door behind him. A moment's hiatus. Then Vann catches Mrs Duc's eye and smiles politely; whereupon Mrs Duc puts her napkin on the table, rises and, smiling angelically, moves around until she's close to Vann, at which point she falls to her knees. Vann half-turns towards her, startled. She smiles up at him and reaches for his belt, which she deftly begins to unbuckle. For a moment, Vann is too surprised to react; then he scrambles to his feet, does up his buckle, and hurries out of the room.

INT. NGO DUC'S OFFICE. DAY

Ngo Duc and Ramsey are still on their feet when Vann bursts into the room and bears down on Duc.

VANN I'm a married man, you two-bit chiseller, I got five kids.

Ramsey is gaping at him, completely bewildered.

Tell this shithead if he hasn't put walls around that school in ten days, I'm personally going to pour three kilos of cement up his ass.

Ramsey struggles manfully with the Vietnamese for this. He just manages to get it out in time to hurry out of the room after Vann, leaving Duc staring stonily after them.

INT. FRENCH RESTAURANT ON THE SAIGON RIVER. NIGHT

Vann is having dinner with Annie; she's seventeen now, slightly overawed by the circumstances, hanging on to Vann's every word and not only because of the inadequacies of her English.

VANN The truth of it is, I'm looking for someone to love.

Annie doesn't answer: she lowers her eyes in embarrassment.

How would you say that in Vietnamese, I'm looking for someone to love?

Annie tells him. Vann begins to repeat it, but gets off to a bad start and gives up. Annie says the sentence again. Vann tries it again, gets to the end, but his version is so garbled, it gives Annie the giggles. See how bad I am, I have a tin ear, I didn't even make it to the end of the course. We're just going to have to speak English.

ANNIE My English very bad, number ten.

VANN No, number ten is what the bar-girls say, you shouldn't say that. I can see I'm going to have to teach you.

ANNIE OK, and I teach you Vietnamese.

VANN That's going to be a little more difficult. But I'm a patient man.

INT. USOM BUNGALOW. NIGHT

Vann jerks awake as the first of a series of nearby mortar explosions shakes the bungalow. He gropes for a match and lights the gasoline lantern, begins throwing on clothes as Ramsey appears in the doorway. The flickering lantern light reveals a room now tidy to the point of austerity.

RAMSEY The VC are attacking So Do. We got half a message, then the radio went dead.

VANN OK, let's go.

EXT. USOM BUNGALOW. NIGHT

A blazing building lights the scene as Vann and Ramsey emerge from the bungalow. More shells land, further down the street, as the two of them make their way towards the pick-up truck, crawling and running.

EXT. SO DO. DAWN

A pall of smoke hangs over the silent hamlet as the pick-up screeches to a halt. The Ranger HQ in the south-east corner of the square is a blackened ruin, surrounded by bodies. Opposite, the school is now enclosed within new breeze-block walls, one of which has been damaged in an explosion. Vann and Ramsey jump down and hurry towards the Ranger HQ.

INT. RANGER HQ. DAWN

In the entrance hall is a uniformed Ranger corpse, slumped grotesquely on a chair. His throat has been cut and his weapon stolen. The floor is slippery with blood. Vann shakes his head and passes into –

INT. DORMITORY. DAWN

– the large room off the hall, which has been used as a dormitory. It contains a dozen or more corpses; one or two are on the floor, but the majority are lying on their beds in their undershorts, almost as if they were asleep: except that each of them has been shot in the face. Vann moves from bed to bed, checking them, grim-faced. Silence, except for the buzz of flies.

EXT. RANGER HQ. DAWN

As Vann and Ramsey emerge from the building, three F-5 Phantom fighter-bombers scream past overhead, flying low. In the area in front of the house, two or three badly wounded survivors lie in the mud. Vann stops beside them, looking down.

VANN No security. I told them. They were all asleep.

He looks up, as, in the middle distance, comes the crump of exploding bombs, shouting in exasperation.

What the hell use is that? Charlie's long gone.

He looks at Ramsey, shaking his head.

We can't win, you know that?

He makes an effort to pull himself together.

You stay here, do what you can, I'll drive into Saigon, get a mobile surgical team.

He moves back towards the pick-up, amid the roar and flash of more exploding bombs.

EXT. ROUTE I. DAY

The canary-yellow pick-up, driven by Vann, travels fast, leading a red-cross truck along the scarred and cratered road.

INT. SCHOOL AT SO DO. DAY

The schoolroom has been transformed into an emergency hospital and Vann watches as the surgical team performs some vital operation in an atmosphere of purposeful haste. He turns away just as the teacher,

Mme Tu, steps into the room and bears down on him, her face set in an expression of cold fury.

TU Come.

Her tone brooks no contradiction and Vann obediently follows her out of the schoolroom.

EXT. SCHOOL AT SO DO. DAY

Mme Tu emerges from the school and Vann, following her, stops dead: his mouth drops open and for a second he seems, unprecedentedly, totally at a loss.

Facing him is the mother of the little girl with the harelip: or what's left of her. She's been napalmed and the upper half of her body, her arms and face are scorched black. She seems quite calm, no doubt owing to shock, and her lidless eyes stare penetratingly at Vann.

TU Last month you took her daughter into Saigon to fix her lip, remember? Today you kill that daughter and a son and all her family when they are cutting cane; and you do this to her. Even your kindness is poisoned.

VANN Let's get her treated.

His voice comes out as a croak. Mme Tu says something to the woman in Vietnamese and leads her gently into the schoolroom. Vann stands for a moment, poleaxed, before turning to follow them.

INT. BEDROOM IN LEE'S HOUSE IN SAIGON. DAY

Vann stands looking in the mirror, doing up his tie. In the background Lee moves around the room, dressing.

LEE I like it when you get dressed up.

VANN That's what my daughter used to say.

He freezes, immediately aware of his mistake.

LEE Your daughter?

He turns away from the mirror, moves over to her and puts a hand on her shoulder.

VANN I lied to you, I'm sorry, yes. I do have a daughter.

LEE How old is she?

VANN Nineteen. And I also have four sons.

Lee's jaw drops.

And I'm five years older than I said I was. I'm sorry. I wanted you so bad, I didn't want to risk losing you.

He leans in and kisses her forehead. She's looking up at him, frowning, but she doesn't pull away.

Forgive me.

Lee draws back and looks at him for a moment.

LEE You're pretty good for such an old man.

VANN And you're pretty good for such a young woman.

She smiles, defusing the tension. He turns back to the mirror to check his tie.

LEE Anyway, why you dressing up? You got another girl?

VANN No, I have a very important meeting.

Lee is looking at him, her expression sceptical.

Would I lie to you?

They both burst out laughing.

INT. OUTER OFFICE IN MACV HQ, SAIGON. DAY

Vann, uncharacteristically dapper in suit, tie and highly polished shoes, sits waiting, nursing his briefcase. Presently, an aide comes into the room.

AIDE General Westmoreland will see you now, Mr Vann.

Vann springs to his feet and follows the aide.

INT. GENERAL WESTMORELAND'S OFFICE. DAY

General Westmoreland, fifty-one now and brimming with energetic bonhomie, springs to his feet and swoops around his desk to pump Vann by the hand. His deputy, Lt. General Throckmorton, sits on one side in an armchair.

VANN Thank you for agreeing to this, General.

WESTMORELAND Not at all, John, I'm looking forward to your briefing, believe me. You know John Throckmorton, don't you?

As he speaks, he's piloting Vann into a hard-backed chair and returning to behind his desk.

I've been talking to your people here in USOM and they agree with me you're wasted out there. I understand they're going to offer you a promotion momentarily and bring you back to Saigon.

Vann's too surprised to be able to conceal his dismay.

VANN I want to be able to finish what I've started, sir. I hope I don't have to leave right now.

WESTMORELAND Well, that's a conversation you need to have with your people.

THROCKMORTON In the meantime, we'd really like you to share some of your concerns and perceptions with us.

They sit back, waiting, as Vann swiftly organises his thoughts.

VANN I wanted to talk to you about unobserved H and I.

WESTMORELAND Go ahead.

VANN Well, sir, I believe this random bombing and shelling is totally counter-productive. The VC are very little affected by it, by far the majority of the victims are friendly, many of them women and children. It's not efficient and it's not right. I have five kids of my own: I know how I would feel if they were killed by someone who said he was defending my liberty.

WESTMORELAND You have to remember, John, the Oriental doesn't put the same high price on life as we do. And I guess however careful you are, accidents will happen. Doesn't mean we're not aware of the problem.

VANN Seems to me if you're admitting things are so insecure you have to make free-fire zones twenty-five miles outside Saigon, that's a real propaganda boost to the enemy.

Silence. Westmoreland nods, considering. Then he turns to Throckmorton.

WESTMORELAND Why don't we suspend H and I in Hau Nghia province on an experimental basis, see what happens?

THROCKMORTON Fine, I'll see to it.

VANN Thank you, sir.

WESTMORELAND What next?

VANN Corruption.

WESTMORELAND Ah. More your department than ours, isn't it, now you're a civilian?

VANN I would say that you're paying more than twice as many salaries to regional forces as there are men. Just check the names on the payroll. Half of them don't exist.

Silence.

And half the equipment we provide is being sold direct to the enemy. We make deals with crooks which make us look bad in the eyes of the population – and at the same time we're arming the VC at our own expense.

WESTMORELAND I know what you're saying, John, but it's hard for us to interfere in the affairs of a friendly government. We're not colonialists, after all; and we don't want to be perceived that way.

THROCKMORTON Anything else?

VANN We're losing the war is all.

Silence. Westmoreland looks away for a moment, then decides to rise above this remark.

WESTMORELAND I'm going to tell you something in confidence, John. President Johnson is very aware of our problem. And I believe I've convinced him we need more manpower. When you were serving over here, how many men did we have?

VANN Seventeen thousand.

WESTMORELAND I'm asking for two to three hundred thousand.

VANN Will you integrate the forces?

Westmoreland frowns: he hasn't anticipated this response.

VANN Put a Vietnamese platoon in each company and have a Vietnamese deputy commander?

WESTMORELAND You've just been telling us how corrupt and incompetent they are.

VANN But it's their country, it's their war. What, are we going to win all by ourselves and just go home? Then what's going to happen? We have to train them and motivate them and help them. And join them.

WESTMORELAND You understand the Vietnamese better than anyone, John. I respect that. But my job is to deal with the enemy. And I intend to. I'm going to stomp them to death.

INT. HOSPITAL WARD IN SAIGON. DAY

Vann puts a bunch of flowers on the bed of the napalmed woman. Her torso and face are wreathed in bandages and her arms have been amputated at the elbow. Her baby is in a crib next to the bed. Her eyes stare out at Vann through the bandages. A young Vietnamese doctor stands next to Vann.

VANN Just tell her if she needs anything she should let me know.

The doctor speaks to the woman in Vietnamese and she answers, speaking with some difficulty.

DOCTOR She thanks you for your kindness.

Vann looks away from her intense stare.

VANN Her eyes are . . .

DOCTOR She has no eyelids now.

Vann looks down at the tiny, week-old baby.

VANN The baby's OK, is she?

DOCTOR Yes, the baby is fine. Only she cannot feed her. You burned away her breasts.

INT. HOTEL ROOM IN SAIGON. EVENING

Vann rolls off Annie and looks over at her: her face is streaked with tears.

VANN That was your first time, wasn't it?

Annie nods, not trusting herself to speak.

VANN I had no idea, why didn't you tell me?

He reaches out to wipe away a tear.

VANN So I'm your first man?

ANNIE First and last.

VANN Wasn't that bad, was it?

ANNIE No, I mean . . .

She tries to work out how to say it, as the tears come faster.

I don't want . . . other man, never: I love you.

Vann doesn't answer. He strokes her hair, his expression pensive.

EXT. SCHOOL AT SO DO. EVENING

It's evening and the yellow pick-up stops near the school just as Mme Tu is leaving. Vann jumps down to intercept her. Ramsey joins them, moving more slowly.

VANN I wanted you to know I had them stop the H and I.

TU H and I, what is that?

VANN Harrassing and Interdiction. The bombing, the shelling, the napalm.

TU Good. Too late for some.

VANN I know that.

She looks at him shrewdly for a moment.

TU I make you some dinner.

EXT. MME TU'S HOUSE. EVENING

It's still not quite dark. Vann and Ramsey sit on a kind of porch at the back of Mme Tu's modest house on the outskirts of the hamlet, looking out across cane fields. They're eating, skilfully manipulating their chopsticks. Mme Tu watches them for a moment, her expression benign.

TU Why are you Americans in Vietnam?

Vann and Ramsey hestitate, looking at each other.

VANN You tell her.

Ramsey frowns in earnest consideration.

RAMSEY I would say the principal reason is, you know, to curb the expansionism of China.

TU China?

RAMSEY That's right.

TU China is your enemy?

RAMSEY I guess so.

TU Then why don't you go fight in China?

RAMSEY Well, because, this is the . . . er, cockpit.

Mme Tu shakes her head in the gathering dusk.

TU You know that China is our traditional enemy?

RAMSEY Well, yes . . .

TU We have been resisting Chinese expansionism for hundreds of years. With many wars.

RAMSEY The thing is . . .

TU If you want to fight the Chinese, we will be your ally.

RAMSEY I don't think that's exactly . . .

TU In fact, the only good thing about your goddamn war is when we beat you, the Chinese will be frightened to attack us ever again.

Ramsey falls silent, flummoxed. Vann gives an abrupt bark of laughter.

VANN I think she won the debate.

He raises his bowl to her.

INT. HOTEL ROOM IN SAIGON. DAY

Vann raises a camera to his eye and takes a photograph of Lee, who's posing for him on a rumpled bed. Strong light pushes through the closed blinds. A knock at the door. Vann moves over to it, putting down the camera, pulling on his dressing gown and laying a finger on his lips to indicate silence to Lee.

VANN Who is it?

RAMSEY (*voice over*) Doug.

INT. HOTEL CORRIDOR. DAY

Vann opens the door a crack.

RAMSEY Did I wake you?

VANN I was just taking a shower.

RAMSEY I think I found a way we can nail Ngo Duc.

VANN You got the pick-up downstairs?

Ramsey nods.

I'll be there in five minutes.

And, slightly to Ramsey's surprise, the door is closed in his face.

INT. NGO DUC'S OFFICE. DAY

Ngo Duc looks up, startled as Vann and Ramsey burst into the room. Ramsey speaks in Vietnamese.

RAMSEY The police chief has told us about your attempt to bribe him.

DUC Wait a minute . . .

RAMSEY You offered him ten per cent of your profits and said you'd paid Americans in USOM in Saigon to have us replaced.

DUC He must have been dreaming.

RAMSEY Pending an enquiry into this, we have asked the province chief to annul all your outstanding contracts.

Silence. Duc is flabbergasted. A look of steely rage comes into his eyes.

DUC This is the way the French colonialists treated us.

Ramsey reverts to English.

RAMSEY He says we're behaving like French colonialists.

VANN So what, he's behaving like the Cosa Nostra. Let's go.

As they leave, Duc is staring at Vann with undisguised hatred.

EXT. MME TU'S HOUSE. DAY

Mme Tu emerges from the house as Vann pulls up in the canary-yellow pick-up. He jumps down, holding a bunch of flowers, which he hands to Mme Tu, who, however, looks strained and upset.

VANN Thanks for last week.

TU Where are you going?

VANN Trang Bang.

TU You must not. Go back.

VANN What do you mean? Are you . . .?

He breaks off as two young men, wearing green uniforms and Ho Chi Minh sandals (made from used tyres) appear in the doorway of Mme Tu's house. Mme Tu hesitates, then hisses at Vann.

TU Go back!

EXT. ROUTE I. DAY

The pick-up truck speeds along the two-lane straight stretch of road.

INT. CAB. DAY

Vann is very attentive. He leans forward to peer through the windscreen.

EXT. ROUTE I. DAY

Vann's point of view through the windscreen: on his side of the road three soldiers in black pyjamas, armed with rifles, are shepherding a number of prisoners, stripped to the waist, moving towards him. One of the soldiers beckons to him to stop.

INT. PICK-UP CAB. DAY

Vann transfers his foot to the brake and starts to slow down.

Vann's point of view through the windscreen: the second soldier raises his rifle and aims it at Vann.

INT. PICK-UP CAB. DAY

Vann's foot moves as he changes gear and hits the accelerator. He waves to the soldiers as he passes, his expression friendly.

EXT. ROUTE I. DAY

The leading soldier waves back and pushes down his companion's rifle, as the truck passes, accelerating.

INT. PICK-UP CAB. DAY

Vann frowns, trying to make sense of what's happened.

His point of view: the needle on the speedometer touches seventy m.p.h. and passes it. Vann is still extremely puzzled. He moves his head.

His point of view: the road behind, spinning away in the rear-view mirror. None of the group of soldiers and prisoners has moved. They're all watching him.
Close on Vann: suddenly, out of sheer instinct, he ducks his head. A split second later, the windscreen blows in, as there's a burst of gunfire from up ahead. Fragments of glass spray into Vann's face, arms and chest, but he's saved himself from far worse damage, as a line of bullet-holes stitched across the back of the cab makes clear.

EXT. ROUTE I. DAY
Vann's point of view through the shattered windscreen: on the other side of the road, strung out at intervals, a dozen men in black pyjamas, alternately armed with rifles and sub-machine guns.
A cemetery runs along both sides of the road, a few feet lower in level than the road.

INT. PICK-UP CAB. DAY
Vann takes an immediate decision: he accelerates and swings the wheel to the left.

EXT. ROUTE I. DAY
Vann's point of view through the windscreen, as bullets from the ambushers smack into the truck: he's driving straight towards the nearest soldiers, who are forced to scatter at the last minute. The truck takes off into the air as it leaves the road, crashing down on to the earth of the local cemetery.

INT. PICK-UP CAB. DAY
Vann, bleeding from his glass-inflicted wounds, grapples with the wheel, picking his way between the gravestones, still travelling fast.
His point of view: above, the ambushers, silhouetted on the side of the road, have wheeled and are continuing to fire.

EXT. ROUTE I. DAY
Below, the truck is swathed in dust. One of the soldiers, armed with a Thompson, waits, watching as the truck swings back towards the road, biding his time.

INT. PICK-UP CAB. DAY

Vann's point of view through the windscreen: he's heading towards the road, guiding the truck up the verge towards the last of the ambushers.

EXT. ROUTE I. DAY

The young soldier raises his Thompson as the truck comes roaring back on to the road and fires carefully.

INT. PICK-UP CAB. DAY

Bullets zing through the cab as it jolts up on to the road, smashing the offside window and demolishing the remains of the windscreen. Vann is hanging grimly on to the wheel.

EXT. ROUTE I. DAY

The soldier fires after the retreating truck and hits one of the rear tyres. The truck lurches and plunges off the road on the far side. The soldier and his companions start running towards it.

INT. PICK-UP CAB. DAY

Back down in the cemetery on the other side of the road, Vann fights desperately to retain control of the vehicle. He just avoids a large funerary monument and fights the truck back up on to the road.

EXT. ROUTE I. DAY

The truck clatters away, driving on the rim of its punctured wheel.

INT. USOM OFFICE IN BAU TRAI. DAY

Ramsey looks on, concerned, as an ARVN medic removes a long sliver of glass from Vann's forearm. He has about a hundred small cuts on his forearms, face and chest. He shakes his head angrily, as the medic begins to paint his wounds with disinfectant.

VANN Stupid of me, I never thought he'd be able to hire the VC as hitmen.

RAMSEY The VC collect taxes from everyone. No more contracts, no more taxes.

Vann winces as the disinfectant stings, covering it by snapping at the medic.

VANN Would you hurry, I got a lunch date.

RAMSEY Is there anything I can do?

VANN Yeah. Have the truck repainted.

EXT. BACK ROADS. EVENING

The pick-up has been repaired and resprayed a bright blue: it's still identifiable by some bullet-holes in the door. It's bumping along an unmade-up road between rice fields in the red glow of evening.

VANN AND RAMSEY

This land is your land
This land is my land
From the DMZ
To the Gulf of Thailand . . .

INT. PICK-UP CAB. EVENING

Vann and Ramsey sing lustily, their Armalites resting across their knees. Enough time has passed for Vann's wounds to heal.

VANN AND RAMSEY

From the Mekong Delta
To the Central Highlands
This land was made for you and me.

EXT. PADDY FIELDS. EVENING

The pick-up is parked on a kind of promontory, looking down across the paddy fields. The sun is very low now, about to disappear behind a range of green hills to the west. A few small figures move about the fields below; buffaloes stand up to their knees in water, tails swishing away flies. It's a timeless vista, startlingly beautiful in the coppery light, serene and tranquil. Vann leans against the pick-up sipping Pepsi from a can, looking at the view; Ramsey sits on the ground, not far off.

VANN They offered me Chief Adviser to III Corps.

There's an instant's disappointment before Ramsey's face clears and he smiles generously.

RAMSEY Great.

VANN I said I wouldn't take it unless they made you province representative.

RAMSEY And?

VANN They bought it.

Ramsey looks up at him, delighted.

I'll come out from Saigon, often as I can.

He takes a drink, then turns to look down on Ramsey.

Don't travel alone or unarmed.

RAMSEY No, I learned that from you.

Vann looks out across the fields, pensive.

VANN Last six months, you know, the happiest time of my life.

Ramsey glances up at him, surprised by the depth of feeling in his voice. Vann continues to look out across the exquisite landscape.

Fade.

EXT. DOWNTOWN SAIGON. EVENING

1966. The atmosphere of Saigon has changed rapidly since the massive influx of US troops. The streets are full of GIs now, and street commerce is widespread and frenzied. There are piles of garbage on every street corner and a large number of roaming children, many of them beggars, with wounds or amputations. A green Toyota sedan noses its way through the heavy traffic.

INT. TOYOTA. EVENING

Vann is driving, Annie is the passenger. She's snuggled up to him, her head resting on his shoulder. He turns into a leafy suburban side street and pulls up.

EXT. SIDE STREET NEAR ANNIE'S HOUSE. EVENING

Vann walks round the Toyota, parked in the shadow of a large house with a walled-in garden. He opens the passenger door and Annie emerges. He's just closing the door when Annie's Father bursts from the shadows and slaps him hard in the face. Annie starts shouting at him in Vietnamese; meanwhile he is shouting at Vann in rather better English than his daughter can muster.

FATHER I know you, Vann, I have detectives. I can sue you. My daughter is still a teenager. We have laws in Vietnam! Where is your responsibility? My daughter drop out of school because of you!

Annie shouts at him again, her voice this time clashing with Vann's.

VANN I'd like to talk to you, sir, would you let me say something here?

FATHER No talk.

VANN I'd just like a chance to explain.

FATHER Not explain. Nothing to explain.

Annie shouts at him again and he delivers a stinging blow to her cheek and hurls an order at her. She begins to move away, nursing her cheek and bursting into tears. Before Vann can intervene, her Father turns back and shouts at him again.

You go buy girl in town if you want one. Stay away from here. From now on, the gate is locked. And you stay away!

As he speaks, he's pushed Annie down the street and shoved her in through the iron gate. He clangs it shut behind them. Vann is left alone on the sidewalk, for once entirely at a loss.

EXT. ROAD NEAR BAU TRAI. DAY

Ramsey is driving the blue pick-up; Vann is the passenger. Late afternoon.

VANN (*voice over*) What do you mean, everything is going wrong? We put that bastard Duc out of business, didn't we?

INT. PICK-UP CAB. DAY

Ramsey turns to Vann, his expression miserable.

RAMSEY The province chief told me he had to get hold of three quarters of a million pis or else they would replace him. The graft goes all the way up to Ky and Thieu.

VANN So what did you do?

RAMSEY I let him embezzle it from our budget. I figured if he went, we'd get someone worse.

VANN Right.

RAMSEY And they started H and I again.

VANN Jesus.

RAMSEY Whole village burned out up by Duc Hue.

VANN I've come to the conclusion, the only way to change anything is to get some real power. We have to move up the ladder.

RAMSEY No, I leave that to you.

INT. BEDROOM IN VANN'S HOUSE IN SAIGON. DAY

Vann and Lee are lying next to one another, quiet, when the phone rings. Vann reaches across her to lift the receiver.

VANN Hello . . . Frank . . . no, it's a good line . . . OK, when was this? . . . No, I'm coming, I'll be back, fast as I can, tomorrow . . . Well, you get the best, best there is, you hear, I'll pay for everything, all right? . . . Yes, I got that, I'll find you . . . OK, well, this is on your nickel, so we shouldn't talk all day . . . Yes, right, I'll see you, Frank, 'bye.

He puts the receiver down, turns to Lee and speaks in a small, bleak voice.

VANN My momma's dead.

INT. HOLLOMAN-BROWN FUNERAL HOME IN NORFOLK, VA. DAY

Myrtle Lee Vann lies in her plush grey coffin, a small, square-jawed woman in her sixties, with tinted reddish hair and a glass eye. The morticians have done their best to offset the effects of dissipation, without being able to conceal entirely the blackened teeth and broken veins of a confirmed alcoholic.

Vann stands looking down at her, his expression enigmatic. After a while, he turns abruptly, nods to the mortician, and heads quickly for the door.

EXT. PARKING LOT OF THE FUNERAL HOME. DAY

Vann leaves the building and strides over to his nondescript rented Ford. It's a sunny fall day.

INT. FORD. DAY

In the passenger seat is Vann's half-sister, Dorothy Lee Cadorette. Vann climbs in next to her and hands her a piece of paper.

Inset: the paper is a rough sketch of a tombstone, on which the following words have been written:

MYRTLE LEE VANN
JULY 20, 1905–SEPTEMBER 10, 1966
BELOVED MOTHER OF JOHN, DOROTHY, FRANK AND GENE

VANN (*voice over*) That's what I told them to put on the headstone, grey marble, I picked us out a good one.

He starts the car as Dorothy Lee frowns dubiously at the piece of paper.

DOROTHY LEE That's not her right name, John.

VANN What do you want, you want me to put the name of that goddamn drunk? Jesus Christ, Dorothy Lee, he took her eye out with a beer can. You rather have his name on here than your daddy's?

DOROTHY LEE She never loved Daddy.

VANN She never loved anybody except herself. And your daddy loved her. And us, he was mother and father to all us kids. Why do you think I took your daddy's name?

He breaks off, powerfully affected. The car is passing the dour industrial wasteland of Norfolk's Atlantic beach-front. Dorothy Lee stares straight ahead, her expression stubborn.

VANN The police think some guy killed her?

DOROTHY LEE Somebody beat up on her, anyways. She had a broken ankle and a fractured skull. They didn't think to check up on her, happened all the time, they'd find her passed out, so they'd just throw her in the tank.

VANN Do they have any idea who did it?

DOROTHY LEE Coulda been anybody. They thought maybe whoever it was took her underwear. I had to tell them she didn't have any underwear.

Vann drives on, his expression sombre.

EXT. CEMETERY IN NORFOLK. DAY

Vann stands by the graveside, expressionless, surrounded by his family: Dorothy Lee and her five children; her two brothers and their families; Myrtle's three sisters, a couple of whom are far from sober; and a frail, dejected-looking old man of sixty-eight: Frank Vann, Vann's adopted father. As the minister drones on in the background, the camera closes in on Vann's hard blue eyes.

EXT. LUMBERYARD IN NORFOLK. DAY

1937. The same hard blue eyes belong to a thirteen-year-old boy who runs up a huge pile of sawdust in the deserted lumberyard and does a backflip. Watching him is his friend Gene C. Rutchfield. Vann stands at the top of the pile, looking around him. Then something catches his eye and he gestures to Gene.

VANN Hey, come up here, take a look at this.

Gene makes his way to the top of the pile. He looks where Vann is pointing.

Their point of view: a black Model-T, discreetly parked by one of the empty worksheds. After a while, it becomes clear that the car is bouncing up and down in a regular movement. Presently, a man's foot, still shod, appears incongruously in the rear-seat side window. Vann and Gene both burst out laughing.

GENE Come on, John.

He runs off down the sawdust pile; Vann does another backflip and then a third, before hurrying after him.

EXT. WORKSHED. DAY

Gene creeps up to the Model-T and peeps in. The car has MD on the licence plate, indicating a doctor. Gene turns back to Vann, eyes brimming with hilarity, gestures him to hurry up and then returns to his ogling. Suddenly, however, he straightens up and moves, white-faced, to intercept Vann.

GENE Don't look.

VANN Why not?

They struggle for a moment, before Vann breaks free and approaches the car.

INT./EXT. MODEL-T. DAY

Vann cautiously peers in the window.

His point of view: the doctor, still more or less fully clothed, lies on the back seat, his eyes shut tight. On top of him, her buttocks bouncing energetically up and down, is a young woman with reddish hair: Myrtle Lee Vann.

Vann recoils and turns away from the car. A moment later, he begins striding away from it. Gene hurries after him, trying to think what to say. Eventually, he hits on something.

GENE Who's the guy?

VANN Am I supposed to know all her goddamn customers?

EXT. CEMETERY. DAY

1966. Vann throws a handful of earth into his mother's grave. Then he turns to follow the other mourners, strung out in a line between the grave and the line of parked cars, headed by the funeral home's baby-

blue hearse. Beside him, his face wet with tears, is the crumpled, shabby figure of Frank Vann.

FRANK This is real good of you, to pay for all this, Johnny.

VANN That's OK.

FRANK And the money you sent her every month, well, I know she drank most of it away, but she couldn'ta got by without it. She loved you.

VANN No, Frank, she never did want me, you know that.

FRANK That's not true, she was proud of you, she was so proud of you. She used to carry all your letters round in a shoebox, show them to everybody. You know how she kept on losing stuff, all the time, but she always kept a hold of that shoebox.

He's starting to cry again. Vann pats him on the shoulder.

VANN Take it easy, Frank.

FRANK I'm glad you had time to see her, Johnny, didn't she look pretty? Pretty as a picture, pretty as the first day I met her. Didn't she?

VANN Sure.

FRANK She never did go anywhere without that shoebox.

Vann nods, gritting his teeth.

INT. SITTING ROOM OF THE VANN HOUSE IN LITTLETON. DAY

Vann sits almost formally, at an angle to Mary Jane, an untouched plate of cookies on the coffee table in front of him. The atmosphere is strained.

MARY JANE Are you sure you can't stay over?

VANN I have to get to LA tonight. My flight's at six a.m.

MARY JANE Oh.

Vann opens his mouth to say something else, then thinks better of it. Silence.

INT. TOYOTA. EVENING

Vann is driving Lee to her school. She sits beside him, formally dressed, alert as ever. He seems a little stiff and uneasy.

VANN I talked to Mary Jane.

LEE Oh, yes.

VANN She doesn't want to give me a divorce.

Silence. Lee considers for a moment.

LEE I never wanted a Vietnamese husband, you know. They treat women like shit. My father has a mistress, he's never home, always at the house he bought for her. I don't want to be like my mother.

She breaks off and turns to Vann.

Maybe she change her mind, your wife. I can wait.

She reaches over to put a hand on Vann's hand. He raises it to his lips.

EXT. DIRT ROAD NEAR TRUNG LAP. DAY

The blue pick-up, driven by Ramsey and loaded with sacks of rice, bumps along the narrow road through a rubber plantation. It's late afternoon.

At the same time, the sound of a telephone ringing.

Four Viet Cong, armed with rifles, flit out of the plantation and block the road, levelling their arms at the pick-up.

INT. PICK-UP CAB. DAY

Ramsey reaches for his AR-15 rifle, next to him on the seat, lifts it and fires wildly through the side window. Two of the Viet Cong fire back. A bullet hits a five-gallon oil drum stowed in the cab and a jet of oil splashes in Ramsey's face. Blinded, he stalls the pick-up, which skids to a halt.

Meanwhile, the sound of the telephone cuts out as someone lifts the receiver.

VANN (*voice over*) Yes, John Vann, what is it?

INT. VANN'S OFFICE IN SAIGON. DAY

Vann sits bolt upright, the blood draining from his face.

VANN Jesus.

EXT. DIRT ROAD. DAY

Ramsey climbs out of the pick-up, his face stained with oil, his hands raised.

VANN (*voice over*) I'll be right over.

As the Viet Cong surround their prisoner, who towers above them, one of them strikes a match and throws it into the oil-saturated cab. The pick-up erupts into flame.

EXT. ROUTE I, NEAR TRUNG LAP. DAWN
Alone, driving fast in his Toyota, Vann turns off the main road on to the dirt track.

EXT. DIRT ROAD. DAWN
Vann stands by the burnt-out pick-up. He looks devastated, helpless for once, uncertain of what to do next.

INT. OFFICE AT 25TH INFANTRY DIVISION HQ, CU CHI. DAY
Vann is hectoring a number of junior officers, all considerably younger than he is.

VANN They'll be moving him out of the area, fast as they can, you have to send out search parties right away . . .
He breaks off as a very tall, distinguished-looking figure, Major General Fred C. Weyand, enters the room. The officers all snap to attention; but Weyand shows more interest in the visitor.

WEYAND Mr Vann?

VANN Yes, sir.

WEYAND My name's Fred Weyand, I was intending to contact you. We just moved in from Hawaii and I'm told you know this province better than anyone. I need a briefing.
Vann looks at him for a moment.

VANN I'll make a deal, General. My colleague Doug Ramsey's just been snatched by the VC. You give me three search parties and I'll brief you the whole goddamn weekend.
Weyand's surprised by his bluntness: but not unfavourably. He smiles.

WEYAND Fair enough.

INT. SCHOOLROOM AT SO DO. DAY
Mme Tu breaks off her lesson and looks up to see Vann standing in the doorway. He beckons to her, his expression peremptory. She says something to the children, begins moving over to him.

EXT. SCHOOL. DAY
Vann begins speaking almost before Mme Tu emerges from the schoolroom door.

VANN You know why I'm here. I want you to tell them this: I'll give them ten thousand dollars if they bring him back.

My own money. It's all I can get right now, but if they want more, they should say how much. Got that?

TU I will see what I can do.

VANN For Christ's sake, he was taking rice to refugees, what the hell do they think they're doing?

Mme Tu shakes her head, avoiding his eye.

EXT. ROUTE I. DUSK

It's raining hard on the deserted road. All along this stretch of it Viet Cong flags are flying and banners have been set up, one of which is in English: it says YANKEES GO HOME! *The Toyota roars down the road like a bat out of hell.*

INT. TOYOTA. DUSK

Vann has the windows open, grenades on the passenger seat and an Armalite across his knees.

INT. GEN. WEYAND'S OFFICE AT CU CHI. DUSK

Weyand looks up with a start as Vann crashes into the room with an armful of papers, which he dumps on Weyand's desk.

VANN Some reports for you to look at. I'll be back around midnight.

WEYAND You shouldn't move around after dark.

VANN This province used to be secure, when two of us were running it, instead of two thousand.

He turns abruptly and leaves the room. Weyand, impressed in spite of himself, watches him go.

EXT. PORCH OF MME TU'S HOUSE. EVENING

Vann waits, impatient. Eventually, he drops into a chair and, a moment later, Mme Tu emerges from the house. She hands him a slip of paper.

TU Here's the letter.

Inset: in the middle of the piece of paper, one line in Vietnamese handwriting.

VANN Great. What does it say?

TU It says: 'The American is alive. He will be released when it is quiet.'

She sighs, looking out across the cane fields.

It was young soldiers who took him, new in the area. They didn't know who he was. But of course, now they have him . . .

VANN And the money?

TU He said: dollars cannot redeem crimes.

VANN Crimes? What crimes?

The question dies on the air. Mme Tu turns to him and he looks away.

TU You should not come again. Not safe for you. Not safe for me.

VANN I want you to help me find Doug.

TU This letter says: when it is quiet.

VANN Yes?

He looks up at her in appeal: she meets his eye, speaks calmly and quietly.

TU For us this means: when the war is over.

EXT. BIEN HOA AIRBASE. DAY

Vann and Weyand stand on the sidelines watching troops filing aboard the big C-141 Starlifter transports.

VANN Can you tell me why General Westmoreland's moving all these men up to Khe Sanh?

WEYAND The theory is, the base will act as a lure and tie down vital sections of the NVA.

VANN So what if it does, it's crazy, it's taking pressure off the VC down here in the South, just to run some goddamn airbase up on the Laotian border. It's like those operations up in the DMZ last summer, it just takes one column of NVA to waggle its ass and he sends in the cavalry. He falls for it every time.

WEYAND I agree with you: but Westy is *Time Magazine* Man of the Year, what am I going to tell him?

VANN He's reading it all wrong.

He stares morosely at the emplaning troops; Weyand, meanwhile, is looking at him appraisingly.

WEYAND I don't have anyone else like you, you know? I need someone who drives through the country and spends nights at hamlets and doesn't bullshit me. I want us to meet every two weeks, OK?

VANN Whatever you say.

EXT. SIDE STREET NEAR ANNIE'S HOUSE. EVENING

Vann emerges from the Toyota and crosses to the wall. There's a rustle of leaves and Annie appears, about ten feet up, on top of the wall. She sits down on the wall and lets herself drop down into Vann's arms. She's extremely excited.

ANNIE Good news!

VANN What is it?

ANNIE I'm going to have your baby!

She flings her arms round his neck.

INT. HOTEL ROOM IN SAIGON. NIGHT

Annie sits on the end of the bed as Vann paces around the room. Her jaw is set, her expression stubborn, her face is streaked with tears. She shakes her head determinedly.

ANNIE No.

VANN It's not a good time for me right now.

ANNIE Of course: now you can get a divorce, we can be married.

VANN Well . . .

ANNIE People in love, it's right to have a baby.

VANN Have you told your father?

ANNIE I don't care what he says. I don't care what anybody says. I will have this baby.

INT. VANN'S OFFICE IN BIEN HOA. DAY

Vann looks up from his desk at the sound of a commotion outside. Voices raised in Vietnamese. Suddenly, the door bursts open and Annie's Father appears, shaking off the young woman secretary, who has been trying to hold him back. Vann makes a quick decision, nods to the secretary.

VANN It's OK, I'll see to him. Thank you.

The secretary, looking indignant, reluctantly releases Annie's Father and leaves the room. Vann considers him warily for a moment, then indicates a chair.

Sit down.

Annie's Father does so; it's clear from his expression he intends to spend no time on pleasantries.

FATHER I call you: you do not answer.

VANN It's been a busy time.

Annie's Father springs to his feet, quivering with passion.

FATHER Her mother and I, you think we want that she has your dirty baby?

VANN Listen –

FATHER No Vietnamese will ever touch her now. We are like you, we try to make her get rid of this baby, but she is dreaming, she cannot hear, she is in love with her disgrace. You must marry her.

VANN I'm already married.

FATHER Vietnamese marriage. And you must give her a house. With a maid. Everything she needs.

He rests his case. Vann looks up at him, bemused by these demands.

VANN Suppose I don't.

FATHER I have a letter right here. To the Ambassador. OK?

He produces the letter from an inside pocket and flourishes it in front of Vann.

VANN I need some time to think.

FATHER Tomorrow. Tomorrow I send the letter.

EXT. VERANDAH OF GENERAL WEYAND'S HOUSE. NIGHT

Vann and Weyand are having a pre-dinner drink, in Vann's case, Pepsi.

WEYAND I have some news, John, I hope you'll think it's good. Bruce Palmer's going back to MACV and I've been given command of III Corps.

VANN Well, that's great, congratulations.

WEYAND I need a civilian deputy who'll relate directly to me the way Ambassador Komer relates to Westy. What do you think?

Vann is delighted. He's temporarily speechless.

Westy warned me you'd be nothing but trouble; but I said, I can take it.

INT. DINING ROOM. NIGHT

Vann and Weyand are at the table: Vann has a heap of files at his elbow.

VANN All these B-52 strikes and this defoliation shit, Christ, it's like treating a toothache by cutting the guy's head off.

WEYAND I know.

VANN And what is this obsession he has with Khe Sanh? He thinks he's luring them and they've wound up luring him. Jesus, General Giap wrote these articles saying his intention is to entice the US forces to the borders, did anybody show them to Westy?

WEYAND He doesn't believe them.

VANN I'm telling you, Fred, I've never been so discouraged as I am now. You'd better look at these intel reports. There are three divisions active in this area now, if our estimates of NVA infiltrations are accurate. Plus around forty battalions of local guerrillas. They could walk into Saigon tomorrow. How can you get it through to him?

WEYAND I'll keep trying.

VANN You better succeed or he's going to wake up one night and find them getting in bed with him.

EXT. PORCH. NIGHT

Weyand sees Vann out on to the porch of his villa.

VANN This is wonderful, Fred, I feel like I'm back in the Army.

WEYAND Is there anything you're going to need?

Vann thinks for a moment.

VANN Could I have a military aide?

WEYAND You have anyone in mind?

VANN Anyone will do. Long as he brings his own helicopter.

Weyand considers. Then he nods in acquiescence.

WEYAND OK. You can have a new car too.

He waves a dismissive hand at Vann's Toyota, parked in front of the house.

And you're entitled to a house in Saigon as well as your house here, if that's any good to you.

Vann reacts, as a thought immediately strikes him.

EXT. HOUSE IN GIA DINH. DAY

Vann leads Annie up the front path through a small garden towards a comfortable two-storey house, surrounded by a brick wall topped with barbed wire. As they approach, the front door is opened by a maid, who bows to them, beaming. Annie's pregnancy is by now beginning to be visible. She looks up at the house, overcome with delight.

EXT. USO CLUB CAR PARK. EVENING
Vann and Lee stroll up to the parked Toyota, Vann takes the keys out of his pocket and holds them out to her. She hesitates, puzzled; but then beams as Vann makes an extravagant gesture conveying that the car is hers.

INT. DRAWING ROOM IN ANNIE'S FATHER'S HOUSE. EVENING
Vann, wearing a dark suit and tie and Annie, by now heavily pregnant, wearing traditional Vietnamese ao dai *stand in front of the house altar, which is decorated with a gleaming brass urn, candles, burning joss sticks and a brightly coloured box, containing betel leaves and areca nuts. Vann slips a gold wedding band on Annie's finger. Annie's Father and a small gathering of relations watch as Vann takes a joss stick and kneels in front of the altar. Annie kneels down next to him. Both of them bow low. The smoke curls up from the joss stick. Seen through it, Vann and Annie straighten up and he plants a decorous kiss on her cheek. She looks up at him, her eyes shining.*

EXT. HELIPAD NEAR BIEN HOA AIRBASE. DAY
A two-seater H-23 Raven helicopter lands on the pad and Vann jumps out before the engine stops, crouching and running towards the administration block.

INT. WEYAND'S OFFICE AT BIEN HOA. DAY
Weyand looks up, as Vann is shown into the room.

WEYAND I showed your intel report to Westy.

VANN And?

WEYAND He's agreed not to transfer any more troops out of the Saigon area.

VANN Well, that's great. Because it's sure as hell going to happen here, sometime in the New Year.

WEYAND We don't get any reinforcements, you understand, we just get to keep what we have.

VANN That's enough to hold Saigon.

WEYAND So you can go back to your family for the holiday and sleep nights.

VANN I had a call, they asked me to brief the Special Assistant to the President.

WEYAND Think you can paint him the picture without driving him crazy?

VANN I can try: but you know Westy's going to be in town too.

INT. NATIONAL PRESS CLUB, WASHINGTON. DAY

General Westmoreland, authoritative and confidence-inspiring, moves smoothly towards his peroration, in front of a large audience of diplomats, pressmen and TV crews.

WESTMORELAND We know you want an honourable and early transition to the fourth and final phase, the mopping up of the Vietnamese Communists; and with your support we will give you a success that will impact on every emerging nation in the world.

At the back of the hall is Vann, leaning against the wall, his expression mutinously sceptical.

EXT. THE WHITE HOUSE. DAY

A crisp day, snow in the air. Vann's profile in the back of a limousine, as it passes through the White House gates.

INT. THE SPECIAL ASSISTANT'S OFFICE, WHITE HOUSE BASEMENT. DAY

Vann sits at the opposite end of a sofa to Walt Rostow, the President's Special Assistant. A couple of other officials are present. Coffee on the table. Rostow is beaming at Vann.

VANN It's a great plan he has, no doubt about it.

ROSTOW Yes, it is, isn't it?

VANN Only problem is it can't work.

Rostow is taken aback by this.

ROSTOW What do you mean, why not?

VANN Because whatever's coming isn't going to be up on the Loatian border, it's going to be right in our backyard.

ROSTOW I understand that possibility's been covered.

VANN Just about; but only because I proved it was so strong.

ROSTOW Surely the important thing is that last month we finally reached the crossover point.

VANN The what?

ROSTOW You heard General Westmoreland: the moment we started to inflict casualties on the enemy faster than he can replace his losses.

VANN Oh, that, yes, well, that's just public relations bullshit.

Rostow gets up and moves over to stand at his enormous desk, his expression hardening.

ROSTOW On the contrary, we've been a great deal more cautious with the press than General Westmoreland's private estimates might have allowed us to be, isn't that right, George?

He surges on, before the Press Secretary can do more than murmur assent.

And as a matter of fact, every statistic we're looking at indicates that this thing will be more or less over in six months, what do you say to that, Mr Vann?

There's a pause; then Vann looks straight into Rostow's eyes.

VANN Well, hell, Mr Rostow, I don't know. I'm a born optimist. I think we can hold out longer than that.

Shocked silence; then Rostow organises some papers on his desk. His voice is icy.

ROSTOW I have another appointment, Mr Vann.

Vann rises to his feet. Rostow glances up at him.

I'm not sure a person with your attitude should be working for the US government.

VANN Yes, sir; may I say the feeling is entirely mutual.

He turns and heads briefly for the door.

INT. DINING ROOM OF THE VANN HOUSE IN LITTLETON. DAY

It's Christmas. The Vanns' children, now aged between twenty-one and twelve, sit around the table with various friends, and Mary Jane's mother and aunt make the numbers up to about a dozen. Mary Jane sits at one end of the table. Vann, at the other end, pauses, carving knife and fork in his hands, poised above the turkey.

VANN It's great to be back.

He leans forward to carve the bird.

INT. SITTING ROOM OF THE VANN HOUSE. DAY

It's the day after Christmas; Vann sits with his two younger sons, Tommy and Peter, working on a model of a helicopter in the shadow of the Christmas tree. Presently Mary Jane steps into the room, her expression grim.

MARY JANE Boys, will you leave us for a moment? I have to talk to your father.

Immediate protest by the boys, which Mary Jane quells with quiet insistence.

Do as I say.

The boys leave the room. Vann watches them go, frowning.

VANN What's the matter?

MARY JANE There's a cable for you. The mailman doesn't go out today so they called and read it out to me. Your daughter was born yesterday.

Silence.

VANN Jesus, that's three weeks premature.

MARY JANE Your . . . the girl fell downstairs and went into labour. Mother and child are doing well.

She looks at him, her eyes bright with anger.

How could you do this to us, John?

VANN Just happened.

MARY JANE I think maybe it's time we talked about a divorce.

VANN I don't want a divorce.

MARY JANE No, it just suits you, doesn't it, a marriage! Good excuse to give to all your whores over there. Is this one under age as well?

Vann gets up and leaves the room.

INT. BEDROOM. NIGHT

Vann opens the door and a rectangle of light falls into the room. Mary Jane sits up in one of the twin beds and puts on the bedside light. Vann advances with some reluctance into the room, closing the door behind him.

MARY JANE I have a suggestion.

VANN Yes.

MARY JANE Leave Vietnam, bring the child with you, we'll adopt it, start again.

Vann sighs heavily and sits down on the second of the two beds.

VANN I have more than two thousand men under me now, I have responsibilities; plus I understand Vietnam better than any other American. I knew if I stayed in the Army I could never be a general; but if things go on the way they're going, I stand a good chance of being one in everything but name.

MARY JANE And is that what's most important to you in the world?

Vann doesn't answer; and after a moment Mary Jane looks away, upset. She knows the answer to her question.

INT./EXT. VANN'S HOUSE IN GIA DINH. NIGHT

1968. Vann stands outside the front door, his arms full of presents, fumbling for his keys, when the door is opened by a distinguished-looking elderly Vietnamese woman: Annie's Grandmother. She lets him in and he steps into –

INT. FRONT HALL. NIGHT

– the front hall. A vigorous pantomime ensues, as Vann tries to indicate to the old lady which of the presents is hers, while Annie's Grandmother keeps pointing upstairs to indicate the whereabouts of the baby.

INT. BEDROOM. NIGHT

The night light is burning and Annie is already awake when Vann comes bounding through the door. The baby, Thuy Van, lies in her crib; she's only two weeks old, with the wizened, almost senile look of a premature child. Vann sweeps Annie up in his arms: she looks even more frail and child-like than usual.

VANN Couldn't wait for me to get back, huh?

ANNIE Oh, John.

The baby is looking up at him with enormous eyes. He kneels down beside the crib and lays his little finger in the child's palm. The tiny fist closes around his finger.

VANN My God, you forget, you forget all this.

He looks up at Annie, his eyes shining.

I left all the gifts with your grandmother. I don't think you should open them today, do you?

ANNIE Why not? Yes, I want to open them.

VANN No, I think you should wait until Tet.

INT. OFFICES AT BIEN HOA. EVENING

Vann comes out of his office and hands a sheet of paper to a male secretary.

VANN Looks like Charlie's on his way. I want this sent out to every province capital. Now.

SECRETARY OK.

VANN Add a final sentence, will you? 'I expect you to maintain maximum alert posture, especially during hours of darkness, throughout the Tet period.'

SECRETARY This is going to take a hell of a time to encode.

Vann thinks for a moment, then speaks decisively.

VANN All right: send it out in the clear.

EXT. VANN'S HOUSE IN BIEN HOA. NIGHT

Vann pulls up in his new car, a blue Ford Mustang, outside his modest two-storey house, close to the airbase. Lee opens the door to him as he springs up the stairs.

INT. BEDROOM IN VANN'S HOUSE IN BIEN HOA. NIGHT

Darkness. A couple of heavy explosions, the second of which briefly illuminates the image of Vann leaping out of bed, as Lee sits up in alarm. It's three a.m. Lee turns on a bedside light. Vann is throwing on his clothes.

VANN This is it. The offensive.

He's dressed in a matter of seconds and slides back the panel of a walk-in wardrobe to grab an M-16, talking to Lee as he does so.

You hear anything, anything at all, anyone in the house, you get in here and close the door, OK?

He rushes out of the room as the sound of another explosion rends the silence.

EXT. VANN'S HOUSE IN BIEN HOA. NIGHT

Vann bursts out of the front door as the night is abolished by a series of explosions, distant and close.

INT. TACTICAL OPERATIONS CENTRE. NIGHT

Vann hurries into the long Quonset hut where General Weyand is already directing operations. He looks up, smiling, as Vann arrives by his side.

WEYAND Right on time. Just when you said. And look at it this way, if it hadn't happened, we'd be in big trouble with Westy.

VANN Is this just Saigon or is it everywhere?

WEYAND Everywhere. The whole switchboard's lit up. And in Saigon Charlie's in the grounds of the Embassy.

VANN Where's my pilot? I'm going to get out and visit all my teams.

At this moment, there's a vast explosion. All the fluorescent light strips are blown out of their fixtures and shatter. Pieces of furniture collapse. Weyand and Vann seem relatively unmoved. In the darkness, Weyand calmly reaches for his helmet and puts it on his head.

Must be the ammo dump.

As Weyand's staff moves purposefully about the hut picking up furniture, testing telephones and lighting emergency gasoline lanterns, and as a series of secondary explosions follows, Vann finds his pilot and starts moving towards him.

Meanwhile, a dazed-looking Colonel hurries over to Weyand.

COLONEL Sir, the VC are right across the street.

Vann signals to his pilot and starts to hurry away, calling back to Weyand as he goes.

VANN Remember the Alamo, Fred.

EXT. BIEN HOA AIRBASE. NIGHT

Vann and his pilot run, silhouetted against spectacular explosions. As they approach the helicopter, the two-seater H-23, an M-113 trundles across the tarmac, firing its .50 calibre machine un at a fleeing row of Viet Cong in black, inflicting heavy damage, piling up corpses. Vann and the pilot scramble into their machine.

INT./EXT. H-23 RAVEN. NIGHT

The camera rises alongside the little helicopter above a scene of apocalyptic violence. The blazing ruin of the ammunition dump sends flames hundreds of feet up into the air which illuminate the beleaguered airbase, the wreck of a blazing F-4 Phantom, the helicopter gunships rising to attack the scattering column of VC, the M-113, its guns blazing, the isolated firefights in all directions.

Another angle on the helicopter as it pulls away, lit by the flames on the ground, until it is swallowed up into the darkness.

EXT. 25TH INFANTRY DIVISION HQ, CU CHI. DAY

Vann hurries across the landing strip towards the warming-up H-23 and scrambles aboard.

INT./EXT. H-23 RAVEN. DAY

Vann shouts to the Pilot, to be heard above the roar of the rotor.

VANN OK, we're secure here now, let's get back to Saigon.

PILOT Lot of street fighting, I hear.

VANN I've got a girl and a one-month-old baby in Gia Dinh.

The pilot lifts off without further ado.

EXT. STREETS OF GIA DINH. DAY

Seen from Vann's point of view, the helicopter passes first over a raging street battle, gunfire and mortars pounding to and fro between blazing buildings with empty window frames; then there's a roadblock, manned by Regional Forces, besieged by gesticulating civilians; finally the streets are eerily deserted, except for the occasional smouldering ruin of a car. Thick black columns of smoke rise in the distance and above the sound of the helicopter comes the irregular rattle of small-arms fire, erupting all over the city.

INT./EXT. H-23 RAVEN. DAY

Vann points down at his house, surrounded by its high wall topped by barbed wire.

VANN There it is.

The pilot loses height, circling the house. Nothing is stirring below.

Strange.

PILOT What?

VANN The gate is open.

And so it is. What's also clear, although Vann does not comment on this, is that most of the windows on the upper floor have been blown out.

VANN (*voice over*) Set me down by the province HQ.

The pilot begins to pull away from the house, skimming the pagoda on the other side of the street.

EXT. HELICOPTER PAD AT PROVINCE HQ. DAY
Vann jumps out of the helicopter, clutching his M-16. He shouts to the pilot, as he moves swiftly away.
VANN Be right back!

EXT. STREETS OF GIA DINH. DAY
Vann hurries through the empty streets, crouching low, keeping to the shadows, alert, showing no signs of fatigue, though his clothes are grimy and sweat-stained.

EXT. HOUSE. DAY
Vann pauses outside the gate, then darts through it, his M-16 raised. There's no one in the garden. He runs up the front path.

INT. BEDROOM. DAY
The door is open and the bedroom is silent. The windows have been blown in and the empty crib glitters with fragments of broken glass.
VANN (*voice over*) Annie!

INT. STAIRS AND LANDING. DAY
Vann moves cautiously up the stairs, ready to fire if necessary.
VANN Annie!

As he reaches the landing, a burst of fire rips into the house at the upstairs level, shattering more windows. Vann crouches and springs into –

INT. BEDROOM. DAY
– the bedroom, where he makes his way over to the window, keeping low. He peers through the window, crouching to one side of it.

EXT. STREET AND PAGODA. DAY
Vann's point of view: the garden, the wall, the street, the pagoda opposite. Suddenly, there's another burst of automatic fire. The shooting is coming from the upper levels of the pagoda.

INT. BEDROOM. DAY
Vann sits on the floor for a moment, his back against the wall, looking over his shoulder through the window, working out what to do next.

EXT. HOUSE. DAY

Vann moves away from the house, cautiously approaching the gate and slipping through it.

EXT. STREET. DAY

Overhead shot: one corner of the wall surrounding Vann's house. As he backs towards it, looking around him, he's unaware that a Viet Cong guerrilla is approaching at right angles armed with an AK-47, moving confidently, ignorant of Vann's presence, but on course to collide with him.

Another angle shows Vann, alone, as he moves ever nearer to the corner. At the last minute, by instinct or having heard a footfall, he spins; and his reflexes are quicker than the guerrilla's. He squeezes off a burst of fire which lifts the guerrilla off his feet and smashes him back against the wall, blood pumping from gaping wounds, beneath an expression of amazement. Almost immediately, there's a hail of fire from the pagoda and Vann makes a run for it, bullets buzzing round him like a swarm of bees.

EXT. SIDE STREET NEAR ANNIE'S HOUSE. DAY

Vann manages to scale the wall surrounding Annie's Father's house, the M-16 strung across his body.

EXT. GARDEN OF ANNIE'S HOUSE. DAY

Vann jumps down into the garden and runs to the front door, which is opened by Annie's Father, who looks at him, bemused.

VANN Is she with you? Is she OK?

FATHER I fetch her when it started. Took most of the day to get back.

Annie, holding the baby, appears in the doorway behind her father.

VANN I went to rescue you from the house.

ANNIE We were told there will be VC in the pagoda.

VANN Too right. I nearly got killed.

He sounds piqued. Annie smiles at him, trying to defuse the situation.

ANNIE What could I do, John?

INT. TACTICAL OPERATIONS CENTRE. EVENING

Vann arrives to join Weyand, who's sitting watching television. Close on the TV: General Westmoreland is giving a press conference amid the rubble and Viet Cong corpses in front of the American Embassy.

WESTMORELAND It's quite clear to me that this attack is merely a diversionary feint to try to draw us away from Khe Sanh and the DMZ, where I remain convinced the enemy's main thrust will soon be concentrated.

Weyand turns to look quizzically up at Vann. Neither of them has been to bed for twenty-four hours.

VANN How do you like that?

WEYAND So don't expect any thanks from him.

VANN How're we doing?

WEYAND We're in good shape. Saigon is going to hold.

VANN I meant to be here sooner, but I had to go into Gia Dinh, get my girl and the baby.

WEYAND They OK?

VANN Yeah, I killed a few VC, choppered them out.

Weyand gestures at the TV, where Westmoreland is still holding forth.

WEYAND You saved his ass. You were right every step of the way. It's going to take us a week or two to clear all the VC out of the city, but we'll do it. You personally saved Saigon.

Vann looks away, reddening with pleasure.

INT. SITTING ROOM OF VANN'S HOUSE IN GIA DINH. EVENING

Vann is watching television with Annie, who's paying more attention to the baby, Thuy Van. It's the end of February and Walter Cronkite is speaking to camera in New York.

CRONKITE Who won and who lost in the great Tet offensive?

Vann sits up, his brow furrowing in concentration, as Cronkite pauses impressively.

I'm not sure.

VANN What are you talking about?

CRONKITE It seems now more certain than ever that the bloody experience of Vietnam is to end in stalemate.

VANN Did you hear that?

ANNIE Not really, what's he saying?

VANN I think he's saying we're licked.

Annie doesn't really understand this: she returns her attention to the baby. Vann continues to watch, transfixed.

INT. SITTING ROOM OF VANN'S HOUSE IN BIEN HOA. DAY

Vann and Lee (in her dressing gown) are watching President Johnson's speech on TV of March 31, 1968 ('Accordingly, I shall not seek and I will not accept the nomination of my party for another term as your President.'). Vann's expression registers mounting irritation.

VANN I campaigned for this bastard.

He turns to Lee, exasperated.

What is this chickenshit? The VC just sustained their heaviest losses of the entire war. We killed twenty thousand in III Corps alone. Tet was a victory!

He shakes his head, angry and indignant.

It was my victory.

He turns back to watch Johnson. Meanwhile, however, Lee is looking at him, genuinely concerned.

INT. VANN'S OFFICE IN BIEN HOA. EVENING

A secretary puts his head round the door and Vann looks up from his paperwork.

SECRETARY Peter Arnett is here.

VANN Show him in.

A younger version of the figure familiar from his Gulf reporting is ushered in; Vann springs to his feet and shakes hands with him.

VANN Hi, Peter, long time.

ARNETT And a lot happening since we last met, the Tet Offensive, the President standing down, General Westmoreland replaced by General Abrams, what's happening, John? Is it like they say, are we losing?

He uses this to get himself organised, the pen, the shorthand pad and so on.

VANN Of course not, we've never been in better shape.

Arnett looks up at him, surprised into a grin.

ARNETT This is why we love interviewing you, John. For years while everybody else said we're going to wrap this up in six months, you kept saying we were in deep shit. Now everybody else is running scared and you're suddenly the optimist.

VANN That's because, as I keep saying, Tet was a victory: but it was also a clear message it's time for a new strategy.

ARNETT Care to give me an idea of what that might be?

VANN OK, first thing you do is you send home a hundred thousand Americans. All the clerks, latrine diggers, short-order cooks, every class of goddamn amateur, and you start to concentrate on training and equipping our ally to fight his own war. We could run this place far better with less than half the personnel.

ARNETT Westmoreland kept asking for more troops.

VANN No comment, except he's a total asshole. It's time we stopped wasting American lives for Nowherevilles like Khe Sanh. We have this massive air superiority, what we need to do is use it to break the enemy's back and then just send in our ground troops to clean up.

ARNETT You always used to be opposed to indiscriminate bombing.

VANN What I'm really opposed to is losing wars. And you don't lose them till they're over. So maybe it's time we took off the gloves.

INT. KITCHEN IN VANN'S HOUSE IN BIEN HOA. DAY

It's seven o'clock in the morning. Vann, in his dressing gown, breakfasting, looks up in surprise, as Weyand strides into the room and slams down an opened newspaper.

WEYAND For Christ's sake, John, how many times have I told you to keep your yap shut?

VANN It is attributed to me?

WEYAND Of course it is, it's a goddamn interview. You're in big trouble. How could you be such a stupid son of a bitch? Abe's going to hit the roof.

For once, Vann seems temporarily at a loss. His face is ashen.

VANN Can you do something for me, Fred?

WEYAND I don't know. I really don't know.

VANN It isn't part of my game plan to be fired at this point.

Silence. Weyand shakes his head.

WEYAND I'll see what I can salvage.

INT. KITCHEN IN VANN'S HOUSE IN GIA DINH. EVENING

The maid is serving dinner to Vann and Annie.

VANN You remember when I got into trouble talking to that journalist?

ANNIE Yes, I do.

VANN I had a letter today, told me my interview made so much sense it was like a breath of fresh air.

ANNIE From who?

VANN President-Elect Richard M. Nixon.

Annie looks impressed.

ANNIE You think he will be a good president?

VANN Long as he keeps listening to me.

INT. DRAWING ROOM IN LEE'S GRANDFATHER'S HOUSE. DAY

1970. Lee's graceful hands take a pair of earrings from Vann's palm.

EXT. AIRFIELD. DAY

The enormous bulk of a B-52 bomber heaves up off the runway.

INT. DRAWING ROOM IN LEE'S GRANDFATHER'S HOUSE. DAY

Vann and Lee are standing in front of the ancestral altar in a room of palatial splendour, watched by a number of family members, most conspicuously Lee's Grandfather, a former cabinet minister, whose house reflects his rank. This is an engagement ceremony, less formal than the marriage with Annie, but still an undeniably solemn occasion. Lee glances shyly at Vann and puts on the earrings.

EXT. SKY. DAY

The B-52 bomber flies way above the cloud cover at thirty thousand feet. It begins to release its bomb load.

INT. DRAWING ROOM IN LEE'S GRANDFATHER'S HOUSE. DAY

Vann and Lee approach the altar, sparer and more elegant than the one in Annie's Father's house, dominated by a resplendent portrait of Lee's Grandmother. Lee kneels in front of the altar and Vann puts his hands together and bows.

EXT. JUNGLE. DAY

Below, a series of vast explosions rips through the forest, causing appalling destruction.

INT. DRAWING ROOM IN LEE'S GRANDFATHER'S HOUSE. DAY

Lee rises from her knees and Vann leans over to plant a chaste kiss on her cheek.

INT. LA CAVE RESTAURANT. NIGHT

Vann is having dinner at Saigon's most fashionable restaurant with a plump Vietnamese civilian, who turns out on closer inspection to be Cao. The atmosphere between them is surprisingly easy. At the moment Cao is laughing delightedly at some sally of Vann's.

CAO You know, John, time has treat us kindly. You, chief of pacification in IV Corps; me, chief of psychological warfare.

VANN I'd rather be a general.

Cao looks at him for a moment.

CAO You know what you should do?

VANN What?

CAO When you were my counterpart, we had some problems. Of course; I had my own ideas. Now you should look for a general with no ideas. There are plenty like this. Then make yourself his counterpart.

VANN How could I do that? I'm not in the Army any more.

CAO We are not in uniform, John, but you and I will always be soldiers.

Vann reflects on this for a moment.

So many ways you have changed. You remember you used to fight me all the time, stop me from sending air strikes: now they call you Mr B-52.

VANN Is that right?

EXT. CAMBODIAN JUNGLE. DAY

The drone of approaching aircraft. Chained to a tree is a shockingly emaciated figure in ragged clothing: Doug Ramsey. His Viet Cong captors are hurriedly disappearing into a makeshift underground shelter. Presently, only Ramsey and six other scarecrow American prisoners are left in the clearing, each chained to his separate tree.

CAO (*voice over*) You see: takes a long, long time to understand our people.

VANN (*voice over*) Mr B-52, huh?

Close on Ramsey's pale, sore-scarred face: which tenses in terror as the appalling roar of the B-52's bomb load approaches like a giant's footsteps. Tears squeeze out of his red-rimmed eyes.

INT. BEDROOM IN LEE'S HOUSE IN SAIGON. NIGHT

Darkness. Vann cries out in a nightmare. Lee switches on a light as he sits up with a jolt. She smiles, trying to jolly him out of it.

LEE What's the matter? Bad conscience?

VANN What do you mean?

Lee is startled by his angry reaction. She reaches out a hand to smooth his sweat-matted hair off his forehead.

LEE Nothing. I'm sorry.

He continues to look haunted.

INT. GENERAL WEYAND'S OFFICE AT MACV HQ. DAY

1971. General Weyand looks up as Vann is shown into the room.

WEYAND Hi, John. Take a seat.

Vann moves somewhat gingerly across the room towards a chair.

Is something the matter?

VANN I guess I'm a little nervous.

Vann sits down; by now, Weyand is surprised and intrigued.

WEYAND You going to tell me why?

VANN I want to ask you a favour.

WEYAND Go ahead.

A pause. Then Vann takes a deep breath and plunges ahead.

VANN OK. I had a meeting with General Dzu in Dalat. I did a lot of work with him in the Delta when you were with the delegation in Paris and I got to know him really well, he was real co-operative.

WEYAND You mean he always did what you told him?

VANN Anyway, he said, at this meeting, that General Kramer was rotating back to the States in May, so he's going to need a new counterpart.

WEYAND Yes?

VANN I'm volunteering for the job.

Silence. Weyand is genuinely astonished.

WEYAND You're not in the Army, John, remember?

VANN I don't know where it says a senior adviser has to be in the Army.

Weyand thinks about this for a moment.

I know Dzu better than any other American knows him. He's a good man, but he needs help. He's going to request that I'm made his adviser. I'd just like you to support that request, if you feel you can.

WEYAND All right, John, I'll talk to Abe. See if he's forgiven you.

VANN What for?

WEYAND You need a list?

Vann relaxes; he sits back in his chair.

INT. SITTING ROOM IN LEE'S HOUSE. DAY

Lee walks into the room and is surprised to find Vann there. On the coffee table in front of him are a bottle of champagne and two glasses.

LEE What's this about?

VANN I have just been made the first civilian general in the history of the United States Army.

LEE Then open the champagne.

VANN Maybe we should go upstairs first.

He jumps up and sweeps her off her feet, heading for the staircase.

INT. LEE'S BEDROOM. DAY

Vann moves around the room, dressing. Lee watches him from the bed.

LEE I don't like so much you going up to the Central Highlands.

VANN It's where the next big offensive is coming, it's the place to be. And I'll come to Saigon as often as I do now. More probably.

Lee looks at him for a moment, before she decides to speak.

LEE When I met you, you were the only American here who saw what was wrong and told the truth. You wanted to help our people, I thought you loved us. And you were angry all the time. About the corruption, the bombings . . .

VANN It's different now, we're starting to use our resources correctly, we have a chance of winning this thing.

LEE Before you looked at the power, your eye was clear, you saw everything. Now you are the power, you have gone blind.

Vann doesn't answer. He looks at her, his expression bleak, evidently hurt.

I know you lie to me all the time, John, I don't like it, but I can live with it. But this is the first time I see you lying to yourself.

Vann sits on the end of the bed. Close on his face, as he contemplates what she has said, and the shock of the truth grapples with the strength and confidence of his self-image.

Fade.

INT. BASEMENT OF THE VANN HOUSE IN LITTLETON. NIGHT

The basement is a bedroom shared by Tommy and Peter Vann, now seventeen and sixteen respectively. A third bed has been moved into the room temporarily for Jesse Vann; he lies on it in his flower shirt and purple flares, smoking a cigarette. He's twenty-one now, and his curly blond hair flows down over his shoulders. 'Gimme Shelter' by the Rolling Stones is on the turntable, roaring out at maximum volume and Jesse's foot in its brown canvas shoe taps in time with the music. Vann appears at the top of the basement stairs, raising his voice to be heard above the music.

VANN I'm just leaving, kids: came to say goodnight.

Murmurs of 'goodnight' from the boys. Vann stays on the stairs, trying to think of something else to say.

VANN Hope you won't mind, your age it's so damn difficult to think what to buy; I'm just giving you some money for Christmas.

Tommy turns the record-player down a little.

That's better. Jesse, I hope that's a cigarette you're smoking.

JESSE Afraid so.

VANN You got that blue polyester suit I mailed you from Hong Kong? Why don't you think about wearing that tomorrow, your grandmother would like that.

JESSE Left it in Texas.

VANN Oh. Well . . .

He starts to turn away.

JESSE Dad.

VANN Yes?

JESSE You want to give us something for Christmas? How about checking out of this dirty war?

VANN Don't start in again, Jesse, shall we just try to hold it in these few days?

JESSE OK.

VANN See you tomorrow.

He moves away up the stairs. The boys call out 'goodnight' again, but he doesn't answer.

EXT. VANN HOUSE IN LITTLETON. NIGHT

Snow on the ground. Mary Jane is walking Vann to his car, a rented Ford. Their breath rises on the air.

VANN Where does he get off, lecturing me about the war? He may have to go fight there himself one day.

MARY JANE He's been classified 4-F.

VANN How come?

MARY JANE John Allen went to talk to the draftboard.

VANN Why?

MARY JANE He's the eldest, he's head of the family now.

Vann doesn't know quite how to react to this. He brings out his car keys.

Anyway, what Jesse said, it's just he's the most outspoken, we all feel that way.

VANN All of you?

MARY JANE It's an immoral war, John.

Silence. Vann fumbles with his keys. Then, abruptly, he looks up.

VANN Maybe I should stay tonight.

MARY JANE No, I don't think that would be right.

VANN OK.

He leans forward and pecks her on the cheek.

I don't get why you had to divorce me.

Mary Jane looks up at him, a world of pain in her eyes. They look at each other for some time, before Mary Jane dismisses all the possible answers to this remark and speaks quietly.

MARY JANE Drive carefully.

Vann gets into the car. Mary Jane turns away, her eyes full of tears.

INT./EXT. FORD. NIGHT

Vann's point of view: Mary Jane moves slowly up the path, through the snow. She opens the door, hesitates in the doorway and then moves into the house, blotting out the rectangle of light.

Vann's face in the car window.

INT. DINING ROOM OF THE VANN HOUSE. DAY

Once again, Vann stands ready to carve the turkey; in front of an older and larger family than at Christmas four years before. His daughter Patricia, twenty-five now, is married, for instance, with a baby son. Ostensibly, it's a happy Christmas tableau; but Vann has the air of being the thirteenth at table.

Over this, Vann's voice, urgently emphatic.

VANN (*voice over*) You got to promise me, Fred, two days after Christmas, you're going to call, you're going to say there's an emergency, you need me back.

INT. GENERAL WEYAND'S OFFICE AT MACV HQ. DAY

Weyand looks across at Vann and shakes his head.

WEYAND I don't want to do that, John.

VANN We don't know when the offensive is coming, but we know it's coming soon and I agree with Abe it's coming somewhere in my area; and when it comes it's going to be decisive.

INT. DINING ROOM OF THE VANN HOUSE. DAY

As the conversation with Weyand continues in sound and Vann leans forward to carve the turkey, the festive buzz at the table gives way to a different series of sounds, gradually increasing in volume as the scene proceeds. These are the sounds of war: the rattle of machine-gun fire, the dull thud of the bomb clusters, the rumble of tanks, the whistle and crash of artillery shells and, above all, the thunder of the helicopter gunships.

VANN (*voice over*) I need all the time I can get to prepare, Fred. So promise me you'll call.

WEYAND (*voice over*) You can afford to spend a little time in your home.

VANN (*voice over*) I have no home over there any more.

Vann has stopped carving. He glances blindly up at his family.

He looks as if he hardly knows where he is. The sounds rise to a crescendo.

EXT. FIRE BASE DELTA IN THE CENTRAL HIGHLANDS. DAWN
1972. Vann's four-seater OH-58 Kiowa (Ranger) helicopter leads a flight of three HU-1 Iroquois (Huey) slick-ships and two AH-1G (Cobra) gunships. They are flying through a spectacular mountain and forest landscape, past the massif known as 'Big Mama', towards a battle raging on the Fire Base below.
VANN (*voice over*) This is my home.

INT. RANGER. DAWN
Vann sits in the co-pilot's seat with his ARVN aide, Lt. Huynh Can Cai, behind him. His eyes are bright and throughout this last period he is to be suffused with rage and exaltation. He shouts into his head-set.
VANN OK, in you go now, fire at will, Cobras first.

EXT. FIRE BASE DELTA. DAWN
Below, NVA troops are surging through the breached wire on the perimeter of the Fire Base. The two Cobras zero in on either end of the line of infantry. The helicopters are armed with rapid-firing 7.62 mm miniguns, automatic grenade-launchers and rocket-pods. All hell breaks loose.

INT. RANGER. DAWN
Vann stares down at the carnage below. Faintly audible above the chatter of the rotors and the frequent explosions comes a curious sound: he's whistling the 'Colonel Bogey March'.

EXT. FIRE BASE DELTA. DAWN
The Ranger's point of view: the line of NVA infantry is decimated by the attack force of helicopters.

INT. TACTICAL OPERATIONS CENTRE IN PLEIKU. DAY
A secure bunker, the operational HQ of II Corps. Vann strides in, fresh from his helicopter, followed by Cai.
He's greeted by an enormous Hawaiian, Major Peter Kama. Also present are: Brig. General John Hill Jr., Vann's second-in-command;

his counterpart General Ngo Dzu, an affable-looking, round-faced man; Colonel Le Duc Dat, a slim, tense figure who chain-smokes Craven A cigarettes; and a number of other officers, American and Vietnamese. Kama accompanies Vann as he moves towards the others.

KAMA Glad you made it, sir.

VANN Let me tell you something. When I first came to Vietnam ten years ago, I'd forgotten to renew my passport and they wouldn't let me on the plane, even though I kicked up fifteen kinds of shit. The plane went down. Everybody killed. Ever since then I've known one thing. In the air, I'm invulnerable. OK, how are we doing?

KAMA The attack has been repelled, the two hundred assault troops who got in have been wasted and the Stingers are hitting the NVA north of the base. But they figure they're going to have to evacuate tonight.

VANN Oh? Why?

There's a slight hesitation; then Hill steps over to the map, using it to illustrate what he's saying.

HILL If the NVA manages to break through anywhere along here and cut Route 14, it'll be easy for them to surround our division in Tan Canh and cut them off. In which case, Kontum will be virtually undefended and, I would think, undefendable.

VANN So your advice, do I have this right, is to abandon all our forward positions and pull back to Kontum?

HILL Seems to me the only sure way to avoid disaster.

VANN Well, in General Dzu's judgement, we don't have to give up any territory at all, isn't that right, General?

DZU Exactly.

VANN So we take note of your opinion, John, we thank you for it and we overrule it. Peter, will you get me General Weyand on the radio?

As Kama moves off to deal with this, Vann turns back to the others.

Any other comments?

A dark American officer, Colonel Philip Kaplan, raises a hand and speaks.

KAPLAN We have a number of intel reports that the NVA are moving across the Laotian border in tanks.

VANN We get reports like that all the time, Phil. There's never once been positive ID of a tank in II Corps. Whenever we check, we find it's just a truck or a PT-76. You have M-72s, don't you?

KAPLAN Yes, sir.

VANN I'll see if I can get you more rounds for your 106-mm recoilless.

He makes a note and looks up, smiling.

You OK, Colonel Dat? No worries about tanks?

Dat snaps his fingers. An aide hurriedly breaks open a new pack of Craven A, hands him a cigarette and lights it. Dat inhales luxuriously and permits himself a thin smile.

DAT No worry about a thing.

Kama summons Vann over to the radio phone.

KAMA General Weyand's on the line, sir.

Vann takes the receiver from him.

VANN Hello, Fred? Yes, you heard right, we held Fire Base Delta. And we're going to hold Dak To and Tan Canh: all of our major positions. This time I promise you, every single one of our sons of bitches is going to fight or die.

EXT. 22ND DIVISION HQ AT TAN CANH. DAY

The post is under heavy bombardment from mortar fire and 122 mm rockets. There are a number of burnt-out vehicles (including M-113s) by the main gate. Over this, Kaplan's voice, calm but full of urgency.

KAPLAN (*voice over*) They're using some kind of wire-guided missile I've never seen before.

INT. COMMAND BUNKER. DAY

In the radio room, Colonel Dat snaps his fingers again. The aide hands him a Craven A and lights it, but this time, Dat's hand is shaking so much that the aide has difficulty managing. In the background, Kaplan is speaking into a radio phone.

KAPLAN I guess maybe it's a Sagger.

INT. TACTICAL OPERATIONS CENTRE IN PLEIKU. DAY

Vann is listening impatiently, standing not far from General Dzu and Brig. General Hill.

VANN Sagger, my ass, the NVA doesn't have anything like that.

INT. COMMAND BUNKER AT TAN CANH. DAY

Kaplan shakes his head doggedly.

KAPLAN I saw one land just now, it sort of curved around and –

He's interrupted by a tremendous explosion, which knocks him sideways. Sandbags pour into the bunker and the black supporting timbers catch fire. Kaplan scrambles to his feet, bleeding from a gash in his temple. Dat is also standing, but rooted to the spot, paralysed with fear. Several others in the room are quite seriously wounded. Kaplan pulls himself together.

All right, everybody out of here!

INT. TACTICAL OPERATIONAL CENTRE IN PLEIKU. DAY

Vann shouts into the radio phone.

VANN Phil? Tan Canh, hello, Tan Canh . . .

He turns to the others.

I'm going up there.

INT. LZ AT TAN CANH. DAY

Vann's Ranger comes in to land, leading a fleet of half a dozen Hueys. The Landing Zone is being peppered with mortar fire. Vann emerges from the helicopter and strides towards the command post, ignoring the exploding shells. Kaplan emerges from the reserve bunker near the officers' quarters, some of which are on fire, and hurries to meet Vann.

VANN You got fifty-two wounded?

KAPLAN Fifty-seven now.

VANN OK, load them up. Where's Dat?

INT. RESERVE BUNKER. DAY

Dat sits on a wooden chair, lighting one Craven A from another. He looks up listlessly as Vann appears.

DAT You must evacuate us tonight.

VANN What are you talking about?

DAT The North Vietnamese soldier is better than South Vietnamese soldier.

VANN What is the state of your artillery?

DAT We will be overrun.

Vann controls himself, turns and leaves the bunker. Dat remains where he is, catatonic.

EXT. LZ. DAY

The evacuation of the wounded continues, despite the intensity of the bombardment. Vann is taking leave of Kaplan.

VANN I want you to hang on as long as you can, Phil.

KAPLAN Those missiles, whatever they were, took out all but one of our tanks. So, if they do have tanks –

VANN Will you give up with these fucking tanks!

EXT. DIVISION HQ AT TAN CANH. DAWN

The silence is broken by a strange, squealing sound, like a barnyard full of pigs. The camera slowly rises, as the sound increases in volume, until it identifies the source of the noise: fifteen T-54 Soviet-built tanks, trundling inexorably towards the main gate, beneath grey skies and drizzle. From the camera's final position, at right angles to the advancing tanks, hundreds of ARVN troops appear, scrambling out of the slit trenches, running for their lives. As the tanks crash through the heavy barbed-wire defences, as easily as if they were cobwebs, something terrible begins to happen. The fleeing troops, in their panic, have chosen to escape across a minefield; and a regular series of explosions begins.

INT. RANGER. DAWN

Vann in the co-pilot's seat, takes a small three-by-five-inch spiral note pad out of his shirt pocket. He flips back the cover and begins to write. Inset: what he writes is as follows: '0700. Last will and testament.'

EXT. TAN CANH. DAWN

Vann's Ranger and another back-up Ranger dip down out of the low cloud cover.

INT. RANGER. DAWN

The Pilot reacts, appalled, to something he's seen.

PILOT Shee-it!

EXT. LZ. DAWN

The Pilot's point of view: the Landing Zone is occupied by a tank; its turret is swivelling and its 100 mm gun is winching up to point at the Rangers.

INT. RANGER. DAWN

As the Ranger swerves, Vann is shouting into his transmitter.

VANN Hello, Red Six, do you read? Over.

An answer comes through: Vann listens for a moment, then speaks into his headset.

VANN You're going to love this, boys. They want us to set down in a goddamn minefield.

At this moment, a shell from the tank explodes nearby.

EXT. MINEFIELD. DAWN

Nine or ten American advisers, including Kaplan, are crouched in a narrow fold in the ground. They're watching with bated breath as the two Rangers come in to land.

INT. RANGER. DAWN

The pilot, almost on the ground, closes his eyes at the last minute.

EXT. MINEFIELD. DAWN

The Rangers land, coming in 'hot', so that the rotor guard in the tail boom hits the ground; but there's no explosion. Vann is out of the helicopter in an instant, rushing over to Kaplan. As he speaks, the designated six advisers rise and run for their appointed helicopter.

VANN Thanks a lot, in a minefield, great.

KAPLAN The sergeant led us out here, we stood in the footprints of the ARVNs who got through.

VANN Where's Dat?

KAPLAN I don't know.

INT. RESERVE BUNKER. DAWN

Tracking shot through the smoke-filled bunker.

KAPLAN (*voice over*) He followed us out of the bunker. Then, when he saw what was going down, he went back.

The camera comes to rest on Dat, still sitting in his chair, his packet of Craven A in one hand and his service pistol in the other: he's blown most of his head off.

EXT. MINEFIELD. DAWN

Vann nods, then turns to get back on the helicopter.

VANN Be right back. Don't go away.

He runs to get aboard and both helicopters start to lift off. As they do so, a number of ARVN soldiers suddenly appear out of nowhere and rush forward to cling to the skids and radio antennae of the Ranger. By the time they pull away, Vann's Ranger is carrying four soldiers and the back-up helicopter five, all hanging on underneath.

INT. RANGER. DAWN

The pilot turns to Vann, speaking into his headset.

PILOT Can't get any height.

VANN That's OK, we'll just go to Dak To, we have to go back.

EXT. MINEFIELD. DAWN

Kaplan and the two remaining advisers are pinned down now, keeping back the advancing NVA with a hail of automatic fire.

Vann's Ranger comes over the horizon and lands, coming in 'hot' again. Vann opens the door and gestures and the three Americans run for the helicopter and start to pile aboard; at the same time, however, at least a dozen ARVN soldiers begin to converge on the Ranger.

INT./EXT. RANGER. DAWN

Vann stands in the doorway, brandishing his M-16. He begins to beat off the ARVN soldiers with the butt as they try to scramble on to the skid. Meanwhile, Kaplan and his two companions are doing their best to fight their way through the desperate melee. Eventually, they manage to scramble their way past Vann into the Ranger.

EXT. MINEFIELD. DAWN

Another angle shows, however, that on the pilot's side another dozen or so ARVN soldiers are getting themselves organised to hang on to the Ranger, invisible and inaccessible to Vann. Meanwhile, the NVA troops are seizing the opportunity to close in.

INT. RANGER. DAWN

Vann beats off a last invader and turns back to the pilot.

VANN OK, go!

EXT. MINEFIELD. DAWN

The Ranger starts to rise, painfully struggling: but the number of soldiers clinging to the pilot's side causes it suddenly to tip alarmingly.

One of the rotors hits the ground and fractures, shearing off and more or less decapitating one of the soldiers. The Ranger goes out of control, rolls over twice. The engine screams and dies.

In the eerie silence, Vann scrambles out of the top and jumps down, holding a portable radio. As, behind him, the others fight their way out of the wreckage, helping one of the advisers, who's been hurt in the crash, he starts to make adjustments to the radio. Nobody notices the four NVA soldiers who appear over the crest, bearing down on the beached Ranger. One of them steps on a mine. Vann sees the others, drops the radio, and fires at them with his M-16. Kaplan joins him, also firing, and a firefight is soon in progress. At a certain point, Vann judges it safe to turn back to his radio.

VANN Hello, Rattlesnake, this is Rogue's Gallery, come in please.

The speaker crackles in reply.

OK, Rattlesnake, our position is two hundred yards west of the Tan Canh compound. We are under attack from ground forces and our Ranger is down, repeat, down. We need a slick-ship to evacuate five of us, say a Huey and as many gunships as you can spare to cover. Got all that? Oh, one other thing, we're in a minefield, didn't want to make it too easy.

He puts down the portable radio and joins the others, firing at the advancing troops, standing full on to them, aiming carefully and coolly.

INT./EXT. HUEY. DAWN

On the minefield below, the battle is a fierce localised struggle around the shell of the crashed Ranger, seen from the point of view of the Pilot.

EXT. MINEFIELD. DAWN

As the Huey comes in 'hot', its two accompanying Cobras begin to strafe the NVA troops with rockets and grenades. Somehow, in the ensuing mayhem, Vann and Kaplan manage to get the hurt adviser from the Ranger and another, quite badly wounded, adviser into the Huey, which is itself taking a great many hits from NVA gunfire. After what seems an agonising scramble, the Huey finally lifts off.

INT. HUEY. DAWN

The interior of the Huey is still in some chaos as it pulls away. One or two of the ARVN soldiers have managed to slip aboard during the fighting. But Vann, squatting behind the Pilot, seems perfectly calm.

VANN Well, thank you kindly.

HUEY PILOT Ain't out of the woods yet.

He taps the fuel gauge, which is dropping alarmingly.

EXT. LZ AT PLEIKU. DAWN

The Huey lands at the pad beside II Corps HQ. First out is Vann, followed immediately by his Pilot. They pause beside the helicopter.

PILOT Jesus.

He points at the fuselage. The fuel cells have been punctured and fuel is running down the side of the aircraft.

One tracer bullet would have lit us up real good.

VANN Find another Ranger, I need to take something down to Brigade Command Post.

EXT. BRIGADE COMMAND POST AT VO DINH. DAY

Vann climbs out of another Ranger. He's carrying his brown footlocker. Major Kama hurries out of the command post to meet him. Vann hands him the footlocker.

VANN I want you to send this to rear command post at Nhatrang, OK?

KAMA Sure.

He takes the footlocker and, as he does so, Vann stuffs a piece of paper into Kama's shirt pocket.

VANN And take care of this. It's my will. I want you to sign it yourself, prove you've witnessed it; and keep it with you.

KAMA You told me you were invulnerable.

VANN I have a girl and a kid over here, want to make sure they'd be OK.

KAMA You got it. What's in the box?

Vann looks at him for a moment, then speaks, his expression neutral.

VANN I'm in the box.

He starts moving back towards the Ranger, calling back over his shoulder.

And I am invulnerable: it's the guys I travel with.

He scrambles back into the helicopter.

INT. VANN'S OFFICE IN TOC, PLEIKU. NIGHT

Vann sits alone in his office, in a pool of light cast by the standard lamp by his desk, sifting through papers. He looks up as John Hill lets himself into the room.

VANN I owe you an apology, John. You were right and I was wrong. The only part of your analysis that was inaccurate is that our people ran so fast the NVA didn't get time to surround them. I was wrong about Tan Canh and I was wrong about the goddamn tanks. Now I'm trying to figure out how we hold Kontum.

HILL General Dzu doesn't think we can.

VANN If we can't hold Kontum, we're going to lose the whole of the Central Highlands and that'll be the end of the war and the end of my career, which, I can tell you, is not on my agenda. So look. Our only hope is that the NVA is so fucking cautious. If they'd followed through, they could have been in Kontum tonight. But they always stop and think. So I reckcn we have ten days, two weeks if we're lucky. Which should give us time to plan and co-ordinate what I see as our only possible strategy at this stage.

HILL What's that?

VANN B-52s. We're going to drop more bombs on these mothers than anybody's ever had dropped on them before. Another thing, aren't we working on some experimental helicopter-mounted anti-tank missiles?

HILL Yes. TOW, stands for tube-launched, optically tracked, wire-guided. They're testing them in Yuma now.

VANN OK, I want you to ask General Weyand to call Arizona, tell them we'll test them out right here.

HILL What about Dzu? Suppose he insists on withdrawing?

VANN That's OK, I'll just tie him up and throw him in a closet.

He closes his eyes and pinches the bridge of his nose.

HILL When did you last go to bed, John?

VANN Last week sometime.

HILL Maybe you should get some sleep.

Vann looks at Hill: his eyes are red-rimmed but blazing.

VANN First we have to prepare for the battle; then we have to win it; after that, there'll be plenty of time for sleep.

INT. RANGER. DAY

Vann is in the co-pilot's seat staring down at the terrain west of Route 14.

EXT. ROUTE 14. DAY

Vann's point of view: there's some movement below, enough to alert Vann to the presence of troops.

INT. RANGER. DAY

Vann speaks into his radio.

VANN Hello, Moonwalker, this is Rogue's Gallery: I want you to give me an Arc Light, co-ordinates Delta Peter seven-one-niner-three-eight-six. That's the centre of your box and I want you to come in in echelon, not in line. Please confirm. Out.

He listens to the response, then turns to speak to the pilot.

OK, peel away.

EXT. SKY. DAY

The Ranger turns sharply, moving away from the immediate target area. Then, very soon, from above, the brassy drone of the approaching bombers. Eventually, the giant shapes of the three B-52s appear, flying in formation up at about thirty thousand feet. Each of them releases 108 five-hundred-pound bombs, which begin floating down like vertical formations of geese or baby sticklebacks expelled from their bloated mother.

INT. RANGER. DAY

Vann is looking up at the B-52s with some affection.

VANN Big ugly fat fuckers.

The blast as the first bombs hit the ground shakes the helicopter and the next minute is full of an almost unimaginable sound and fury.

EXT. ROUTE 14. DAY

Seen from above, the pattern of explosions spreads, one obscene flower after another. It's over with unexpected speed.

INT./EXT. ROUTE 14. DAY

Below, the flames and smoke slowly begin to clear. Inside the Ranger, Vann reaches across to open the side door.

VANN Let's go take a look.

The Pilot turns the Ranger and starts to lose altitude, moving down through the smoke. Suddenly, Vann grips his arm and points.

His point of view: below, a group of about forty uniformed NVA.

PILOT Are you sure?

VANN They'll be in shock for thirty minutes.

He picks up his M-16 and moves to the open door. Below, the NVA troops are indeed staggering around, entirely disoriented.

Vann takes aim and begins to fire. They're sitting targets, too confused to run away. Vann is able to inflict considerable damage.

EXT. AIRFIELD AT PLEIKU. NIGHT

Vann and Hill hurry across the tarmac towards an almost stationary C-141 jet transport. By the time they arrive, the back of the plane has been lowered to reveal one of a pair of brand-new Hueys. A mechanic drops to the tarmac, to be greeted by Vann.

VANN How's the weather in Arizona?

MECHANIC Hotter than hell.

VANN I want these operational by first light.

EXT. SLIT TRENCHES NEAR KONTUM. NIGHT

An NVA assault is in progress. Fantastic confusion of noise and flashing light. Vann runs up the trench, exhorting the defenders, shouting and pointing and cajoling. Eventually, he takes up a dangerously exposed position and begins blazing away at the enemy with his M-16.

INT. HUEY. DAWN

Vann is riding in one of the two new Hueys. The other flies alongside.

EXT. ROUTE 14. DAWN

Three T-52 tanks are moving south, trundling along at some speed.

INT./EXT. HUEY. DAWN

The two Hueys fire their TOW missiles simultaneously. Below, seen from Vann's point of view, two of the tanks disappear in vast explosions.

VANN Hallelujah!

Below, as he watches, the third tank tries to take evasive action: it reverses itself into a house, crashing through the wall, until it becomes invisible. The Gunner smiles back at Vann.

GUNNER No problem.

He fires another missile. Below, the entire structure, house and tank, vanishes in an orange fireball.

INT. BUNKER IN THE SPECIAL FORCES COMPOUND, KONTUM. DAY

Close on Vann: he's filthy, unshaven, demented-looking. He looks up abruptly.

VANN What's going on?

Hill stands at his elbow.

HILL Nothing. Nothing's going on.

VANN What do you mean?

HILL No assault this morning.

VANN Are you trying to say . . .?

HILL I think maybe I am.

EXT. SPECIAL FORCES COMPOUND, KONTUM. DAY

Vann emerges into the daylight, screwing up his eyes in the fierce light. He stands for a moment: then he sniffs the air.

VANN Wind's from the north, huh?

HILL I guess.

VANN Can you smell it?

He sniffs again.

I'm going to take a look.

INT./EXT. RANGER. DAY

Vann peers down at the ground. Below, the land around Route 14 and the road itself have been bombed into a landscape resembling the surface of the moon. Vann sees something. He draws the Pilot's attention to it.

VANN Set down.

PILOT You sure? I –

VANN Set down!

EXT. ROUTE 14. DAY

The Ranger lands in swirling dust on the rim of a deep crater. Vann, clutching his M-16, jumps down from the helicopter. He moves, like a man in a dream, towards the edge of the crater.

EXT. BOMB CRATER. DAY

Below is a scene out of Hieronymus Bosch. There's a pool at the bottom of the crater, though of what, it's not immediately clear. The whole area is strewn with bodies, whole and dismembered; a corpse, holding in its entrails, is surrounded by severed limbs.

Vann stands, looking down at all this, a strange, almost seraphic expression on his face.

There's some movement below, possibly a body stirring, more likely a rag of cloth flapping in the breeze. Vann raises his weapon and begins to fire into the crater.

He stands for a long time, firing down into the crater, his eyes wide and unblinking.

INT. OFFICERS' MESS AT PLEIKU. NIGHT

Vann, the only man in the room not in uniform, fills his glass and rises to his feet. He's been sitting between Weyand and Hill, for whom this has been a celebratory farewell dinner.

VANN When I first came to Vietnam, ten years ago, we were just out here doing a little advising. Trouble was, we were giving the wrong advice to the wrong people in the wrong government. Even when we happened to give the right advice, the goddamn government ignored it. So we brought over hundreds of thousands of our boys and Westy said he would fight a war of attrition; only thing he didn't realise was it was our side was getting attrited. Well, now we're back to advising. The wheel has come full circle; but this time it's rolling over General Giap's foot. We're getting it right at last – and that means we're going to win. So, John, I can't imagine why the hell you're leaving.

Hill joins the general laughter.

No, John, I'm real glad you're next and I drink to you: if we had some more like you, we could all go home.

He raises his glass and toasts Hill, as do the rest of the officers; and then sits down amid enthusiastic applause.

Weyand leans in to speak to him confidentially, under cover of the general hubbub.

WEYAND You know John's not the only one on his way home.

VANN Who else?

WEYAND Abe's been recalled.

VANN So who's going to be C-in-C?

Weyand doesn't answer. Instead, he grins broadly.

Jesus, Fred.

WEYAND I'm going to need your help. I don't know who else could have held Kontum.

VANN Maybe between us we could turn this war around.

Hill leans across, interrupting them.

HILL Why don't you stay tonight, John? Give yourself a break.

VANN No, I've been up in Kontum every night since this thing started. I'm going to take some food up for the guys.

EXT. LZ AT PLEIKU. NIGHT

Vann gets out of a jeep close to where his Ranger is warming up. He's carrying a cardboard box full of fruit, bread rolls, other food wrapped in foil and bottles of wine. He hands this to a young Captain, who sets off with it in the direction of the helicopter; and embraces Hill, who's ridden out with him to say goodbye.

INT. RANGER. NIGHT

Vann jumps aboard and straps himself in as the young pilot, Lt. Ronald Doughtie, leans over to him. The Captain is in the back.

DOUGHTIE You want me to sweep around to the west of Chu Pao?

VANN Hell, no. There'll be no triple-A tonight. Let's take the fast track.

DOUGHTIE Roger.

EXT. LZ AT PLEIKU. NIGHT

The helicopter rises into the limpid, starlit Vietnamese night.

INT. RANGER. NIGHT

Vann, the pilot, Lt. Doughtie, and the young Captain in the back are all singing at the tops of their voices.

ALL

This land is your land,
This land is my land,
From the DMZ
To the Gulf of Thailand . . .

EXT. CENTRAL HIGHLANDS. NIGHT

The Ranger passes, tiny against the moonlit mountains.

ALL

From the Mekong Delta
To the Central Highlands,
This land was made for you and me.

INT. RANGER. NIGHT

The three of them begin the song again: then, quite suddenly, the helicopter lurches to the right.

EXT. MOUNTAIN RIDGE. NIGHT

The Ranger hurtles downwards in a spiral, totally out of control; it crashes into an isolated clump of trees and explodes.

EXT. MONTAGNARD GRAVEYARD. DAWN

The helicopter has crashed in a graveyard, shaded by trees and adorned with strange, carved wooden statues of melancholy, squatting creatures. The camera begins close on Vann, who has been thrown clear and lies on the ground face down in his wellington boots and white golfer's jacket, his body more or less undamaged.

Slowly the camera pulls back, revealing the still smouldering pieces of wreckage, the damaged trees. Back and back it goes until it's above the swirling mist which runs along the summit of the massif.

As the sun starts to rise behind the mountain ridge, a caption:

JOHN VANN DID NOT MISS HIS EXIT
HE DIED BELIEVING HE HAD WON HIS WAR

Fade.

The Custom of the Country

INT. BEDROOM IN THE STENTORIAN HOTEL, NEW YORK. EVENING

It's just over a hundred years ago; and the occupant of the pretty white-and-gold room, with sea-green panels and a rose-coloured carpet, stands, in her elaborate and decorous underwear, looking at a long rack of expensive dresses, with an expression of ferocious concentration. She's a very beautiful, fair woman in her early twenties; there's something a little remote and disconnected about her pale eyes, but once encountered, she's someone who would not be easily forgotten: not least because her name happens to be Undine Spragg. She makes her selection, chooses a dress from the rack and turns. Beside her is her French maid, Céleste, at present holding an armful of dresses and consequently more or less invisible. Undine adds the dress she's just picked, causing Céleste to stagger slightly.

UNDINE On the bed, Céleste.

The maid decants the dresses on to the bed and begins to straighten them out as Undine hovers behind her, still giving her full attention to the matter in hand.

The main titles begin: and continue as Undine chooses one of the dresses and has Céleste help her into it. It's still early evening, but it's January and the light is beginning to go. As Undine inspects herself in the mirror, Céleste draws down the blinds and switches on one of the electric lights, lighting the wall brackets.

You can go now, I'll take off the dress myself.

Céleste bows slightly in acknowledgement and leaves the room.

Alone now, Undine springs into energetic activity. She drags the heavy pier-glass forward, changing its angle; she puts on elbow-length white gloves and finds a fan; she turns on all the lights, including the irritatingly intricate chandelier above; and she crosses to the door, turns, and, as if making an entrance, sweeps across the room and sinks gracefully into an armchair so that she's directly facing the mirror.

As the titles end, Undine sits, leaning a little forward now, her lips slightly parted, turning her head abruptly so that her golden hair in its complicated coiffure undulates and recomposes itself, finally looking directly at herself; so justifiably pleased by what she sees, one might think, that she can't help smiling: but no, the smile is just the first of a series of expressions she now begins, quite systematically, appraising with a professional's eye, to try out.

INT. DRAWING ROOM OF THE SPRAGG SUITE. EVENING

Undine's mother, Mrs Leota B. Spragg, is slightly dwarfed by the huge gilt armchair in which she reclines, in the vast room furnished in Louis XV style, its walls hung with salmon-pink damask and oval portraits of Marie Antoinette and others. Her manicurist, Mrs Heeny, a stout, red-faced party in black, has pulled up a smaller chair, so that she can attend to Mrs Spragg's nails, which she is presently buffing with practised skill. A selection of heavy rings lies on the nearby onyx table top. Mrs Heeny's awesomely capacious alligator bag stands on the floor at her side.

There's just a moment for this companionable tableau to establish itself; and then the double doors to the room are flung open with such force that the ladies are both considerably startled. Undine stands on the threshold, a tragic expression on her face: she's wearing a silk dressing gown.

MRS SPRAGG Why, Undine, whatever is the matter?

UNDINE I don't know what to do: I haven't a single thing to wear.

She strides over to the window, pulls back the layers of lace curtain and stares out for a moment at the twilight.

And I don't see why in the world I should go out to dinner with these people.

Mrs Spragg leans forward to murmur confidentially to Mrs Heeny.

MRS SPRAGG Undine met a Mr Popple yesterday here at the hotel.

MRS HEENY The society portrait painter?

MRS SPRAGG That's right: and she sorta took a liking to him.

UNDINE I don't care if I never see him again.

MRS SPRAGG So then an invitation arrives this afternoon; and she's naturally disappointed because it wasn't from Mr Popple, it was from some little fellow who was with him.

UNDINE Not even from him: it was from his sister.

MRS HEENY Well, when a young man in society wants to meet a girl another time, he'll always get his sister to ask her.

UNDINE What happens to the ones who don't have sisters? It must be fearfully poky for them.

MRS HEENY Why, they ask their mothers; or some married friend.

MRS SPRAGG Anyway, Mr Marvell's sister has some house way over on Thirty-Eighth Street.

Mrs Heeny stops what she's doing, her little eyes gleaming.

MRS HEENY Marvell? Is that Mr Ralph Marvell?

Something in Mrs Heeny's excited tone causes Undine to turn away from the window.

UNDINE Is he as swell as Mr Popple?

MRS HEENY As swell? Why, Claud Walsingham Popple ain't in the same league. And as for Mrs Henley Fairford . . .

MRS SPRAGG Who's she?

MRS HEENY Why, the sister, of course, the sister!

Undine is looking out of the window again.

EXT. WEST 72ND STREET. EVENING

Undine's point of view, through the slight distortion of the window glass: at the end of a row of brownstones on 72nd Street is the Park; and across, on the far side, the lights are beginning to twinkle through the bare branches.

UNDINE (*voice over*) And does he live on Fifth Avenue?

MRS HEENY (*voice over*) No, no, he lives in his grandfather's house on Washington Square.

MRS SPRAGG (*voice over*) Way down there?

INT. SPRAGG SUITE. EVENING

Undine turns back into the room, her eyes shining.

UNDINE Do you mean to say the Marvells are as swell as the Driscolls or the Van Degens?

MRS HEENY Wait a minute, I got something right here in my clippings.

She lays her nail-polisher down on the table amidst her bottles and files and plunges down into her vast handbag, coming up with a handful of newspaper and magazine cuttings. She rummages efficiently for a moment, licking her forefinger to facilitate the process; then reads out in a monotonous, unpunctuated drone:

MRS HEENY 'Mrs Henley Fairford gave another one of her natty little dinners last Wednesday. As usual it was smart small and exclusive and there was much gnashing of teeth among the left-outs . . .' That means the Driscolls and the Van Degens. See, Undine, the Driscolls and the Van Degens are just money: the Marvells and the Fairfords are real class. And if they ain't swell enough for you, Undine Spragg, you'd better go right over to the court of England!

MRS SPRAGG Well!

At which point the outer door to the suite opens and Undine's father, Abner E. Spragg, appears. He's tallish, grey-bearded and somewhat round-shouldered, with longish grey hair spilling down over his collar: but his piercing eyes and regular features give a clue to the origins of his daughter's beauty. He drops his overcoat and high hat across a side table and speaks in a cautious, dry tone.

SPRAGG Well, Mother? Undine. Mrs Heeny.

MRS SPRAGG Undine's been asked out to a dinner party with one of the first families in New York. What do you say to that? We were right to come here, weren't we, Abner?

SPRAGG I guess you two always manage to be right.

UNDINE I don't see how I can go, Father.

All three of them look at her in astonishment.

I don't have a single thing to wear.

MRS SPRAGG You shouldn't ask Father to buy more clothes right on top of those last bills.

SPRAGG I ain't on top of them, I'm way down under them.

UNDINE Well, I can't go looking like a scarecrow . . .

Mr Spragg holds the pause mischievously: finally, he breaks into a smile.

SPRAGG No, I guess you can't at that.

Undine runs over and throws her arms around him. But something is still troubling Mrs Spragg and she looks down at Mrs Heeny, who has circumspectly resumed buffing her nails.

MRS SPRAGG Why was the invitation addressed to me, Mrs Heeny?

MRS HEENY In the best society, everyone pretends girls can't do a thing without their mother's permission. You remember that, Undine. Always say you have to ask your mother first.

UNDINE Mercy! How'll she know what to say?

MRS HEENY She'll say just whatever you tell her to, of course.

MRS SPRAGG Does that mean I got to answer the letter?

There's panic in her eyes, but Mrs Heeny has an answer for this as well.

MRS HEENY Mrs Fairford don't know your writing. So why don't Undine do it for you?

INT. UNDINE'S ROOM. EVENING

Close on a sheet of blood-red notepaper with initials embossed in silver in the top corner: US. Undine's graceful hand comes into shot; and she writes in a startling white ink: 'Dear Mrs Fairford . . .'

Another angle reveals Undine, hesitating, sucking on her pen. Then, she makes a decision.

Inset: on the sheet of paper, she alters the first word to 'Dearest'.

Undine hesitates again, sighing in frustration. Then she tears up the page, pushes it aside and reaches for another sheet.

Inset: this time she writes: 'My Dear Mrs Fairford . . .'

Dissolve.

INT. DINING ROOM OF THE FAIRFORD HOUSE ON 38TH AND PARK. NIGHT

Mrs Laura Fairford, a small woman with a large nose and a no-nonsense air, sits at the head of a surprisingly modest table in a dingy, gas-lit, wood-fire-heated, book-lined room. She and her husband Henley, a nondescript bald fellow with a grey moustache, only have six guests this evening; and Undine, who is by some margin the most elaborately dressed and coiffed, sits between a distinguished elderly man, Charles Bowen, and Ralph Marvell, a slight, handsome young man with a blond moustache and a kind face. At the moment, we hear the general conversation, which is animated, as a mere background blur, and focus on Undine, who is staring at her plate, which contains a piece of grey meat and some overcooked vegetables, in ill-concealed dismay.

UNDINE (*voice over*) Of course, the food was simply sumptuous.

MRS SPRAGG (*voice over*) And was Mr Popple there?

UNDINE (*voice over*) Heavens, no, there were only six guests, it was very anteem.

The camera has now come to rest on another of the guests, an attractive, dark young woman, with an indefinably melancholy air: Clare Van Degen; and the sound comes into focus as she speaks.

CLARE Well, yes, he seems to be doing everyone's portrait this year; so we agreed to let him do me.

RALPH Is that a good reason?

He's spoken very lightly, but Clare colours and looks up at him, her expression defensive. Undine watches her closely, as Mrs Fairford takes up the conversation.

MRS FAIRFORD I sometimes think Claud Popple is the only gentleman I know; at least he's the only one who sees fit to tell me he's a gentleman every single time I meet him.

CLARE I thought you liked his things; otherwise I'd never have had him paint me.

RALPH I'm sure he'll do you capitally.

Clare looks away, clearly a little upset; and the sound fades, as Undine's voice returns.

UNDINE (*voice over*) But guess what, one of the guests was Mrs Peter Van Degen.

MRS SPRAGG (*voice over*) No!

UNDINE (*voice over*) I recognised her right away from her photograph in *Boudoir Chat*. She turns out to be Mr Marvell's cousin and I think she's a little bit sweet on him.

MRS SPRAGG (*voice over*) And what was he like, Mr Marvell?

UNDINE (*voice over*) Oh, he was a perfect gentleman: couldn't have been more attentive.

Ralph Marvell now has the water jug in his hand and turns somewhat nervously to Undine.

RALPH A little more water?

UNDINE I don't care if I do.

She's aimed for a casual tone, but it comes out rather aggressively, and Ralph, a little intimidated, pours the water and can't think what else to say; so Undine turns to address herself to Mr Bowen.

I went to see Sarah Burnhard last week. In *Fade*?

BOWEN Ah, I have tickets for next week, what did you make of it?

UNDINE I didn't know it was going to be in French.

BOWEN I imagine she was remarkable.

UNDINE Yes. Not as young as she has been.

Now it's Bowen's turn to be slightly flummoxed: but Ralph can't suppress an indulgent smile.

INT. FRONT HALL OF THE FAIRFORD HOUSE. NIGHT

Ralph is helping Undine on with her cloak, when Clare, who's already wrapped up and on her way to the front door, turns back, as if on impulse.

CLARE Ralphie.

Ralph turns to her immediately, abandoning Undine in mid-sleeve.

Come to the opera with me on Friday.

RALPH I'd love to.

CLARE We'll have a little dinner somewhere first: Peter's dining at his club.

By now, the butler has the door open; and Undine follows the others out.

EXT. EAST 38TH STREET. NIGHT

It's very cold; the street is coated with ice. Waiting at the bottom of the steps are a gleaming motor car and a hansom cab. At the top of the steps, Clare kisses Ralph lightly and smiles at Undine, her voice a little dry.

CLARE Goodbye, Miss Spragg.

She progresses down the steps, where her uniformed chauffeur waits with a fur rug to open the door and help her into the car.

Meanwhile, Ralph takes Undine's arm and pilots her down the steps. He helps her into the cab, where she clearly expects him to join her: instead, however, he closes the door and extends a hand through the lowered window.

RALPH Well, goodbye.

UNDINE Oh. Oh, goodbye.

She shakes his hand, blushing in confusion.

EXT. CENTRAL PARK. NIGHT

The cab clatters across the snowy expanse of the Park.

MRS SPRAGG (*voice over*) And did Mr Marvell escort you back here?

INT. CAB. NIGHT

Close on Undine: she's mortified, furious.

UNDINE (*voice over*) You don't understand, Mother, that's not how it works. This is the inner circle, not a clambake in Apex.

INT. BREAKFAST ROOM IN THE STENTORIAN HOTEL. DAY

The conversation is taking place in the stuffy and cavernous dining room on the ground floor of the hotel. Mrs Spragg looks up with a slightly affronted expression from her bananas and cream. Mr Spragg, meanwhile, is running an abstracted eye over the Times, *in front of the ruins of what has clearly been an heroic breakfast.*

MRS SPRAGG Well, I stand corrected.

Undine, who's been toying with a piece of toast, turns her attention to her father.

UNDINE Father, will you take a box for me at the opera on Friday?

Spragg looks up, startled. He puts down the paper, takes off his gold eye-glasses and hooks them into the pocket of his battered old black waistcoat. He raises his eyebrows.

UNDINE A parterre box.

SPRAGG Won't a couple of good orchestra seats do?

UNDINE No.

Spragg reaches out for a toothpick, fiddles with it nervously for a moment.

I owe a lot of hospitality to Indiana Binch.

MRS SPRAGG It's true, Abner, she does.

Spragg transfers his cold gaze to his wife for a moment.

UNDINE I only want it once.

SPRAGG You only want most things once, Undine.

UNDINE What's that supposed to mean?

SPRAGG Fact is, Undie, I'm a little mite strapped just this month; and I happen to know a parterre box costs a hundred and twenty-five dollars.

UNDINE It's taken me two whole years in this city to make the least little bit of progress; and if you're not going to help me build on that, we may as well go straight back to Apex.

She's said this between clenched teeth with great intensity; and Spragg, clearly rattled, exchanges an uneasy glance with his wife.

INT. METROPOLITAN OPERA HOUSE. NIGHT

The opera is Donnizetti's Lucia di Lammermoor, *and as the first act draws to a close, Undine, in her box, glances with annoyance at her neighbour, Millard Binch, who lolls, quite frankly asleep, with his mouth open, uttering occasional unattractive little grunts. His wife, Indiana Binch, a large, creamy person, seems oblivious to this, complacently absorbed in the opera. Undine leans forward and turns away from them and from the stage.*

Her point of view: one of the boxes in her eyeline is still completely empty.

While looking at it, she suddenly becomes aware that a stout, exophthalmic, imperiously ugly young man in the next-door box is staring at her quite truculently. He doesn't look away when she becomes aware of him; and, as she looks away herself, obscurely unsettled, she hears him murmur to his companion, a striking woman in black, who turns and studies Undine through a handsome tortoiseshell lorgnette studded with diamonds. Eventually, she speaks in a penetrating stage whisper, perfectly audible to Undine.

WOMAN No idea!

Undine's aware, as the first act ends, the lights come up, and the applause swells, that the frog-faced young man continues to stare at her, eavesdropping on the conversation which Indiana now initiates, as her husband wakes with a start.

INDIANA Why, look, Undie, there's Mr Popple over there!

She points to a tall, dark, imposing figure in a nearby box, leaning over in animated conversation with a beautiful woman; then she waves her playbill above her head, all but spilling out of her dress.

Yoo-hoo! Mr Popple!

Popple looks up and grants her the most vestigial possible nod, before returning to his conversation.

UNDINE I don't think you should beckon like that, Indiana.

INDIANA Why not? How else are you to let people know you're here?

UNDINE Nobody else is beckoning.

But Indiana is already irrepressibly surging forward, waving to someone down in the stalls. Undine edges away from her, glancing across again at the empty box.

Dissolve to – later, as during one of the quieter, romantic passages of the opera, Millard Binch wakes with a strangled gargle. He takes a moment to make sense of his surroundings, then leans forward between the women, speaking in what he fondly imagines to be a discreet murmur.

BINCH Guess I'll cut out, girls, I ain't really on to grand opera.

He scrapes noisily to his feet.

I'll be waiting outside when the show busts up.

UNDINE Yes, yes.

And as he cannons unsteadily out of the box, she sees another square of lighter darkness appear across the way; and Clare Van Degen appears in the empty box, escorted by Ralph Marvell.

Dissolve to – the second interval, and now the box is empty again and Undine is looking wistfully across at it. Indiana looms at her elbow.

INDIANA Why don't we take a stroll and see if we can't run into your friends?

UNDINE No!

At which point, the door to the box opens, Undine whirls around and her expression suddenly changes when the visitors prove to be Claud Popple, closely followed by the frog-faced young man.

POPPLE Mrs Binch, Miss Spragg, I don't believe you've met Mr Peter Van Degen.

Van Degen surges forward, dismissing Indiana with a brisk nod and seizing Undine's hand, leaning over her chair in so monopolistic a fashion, that Popple has no choice but to busy himself with Indiana.

VAN DEGEN I told Popple he had to introduce us before I was a minute older. I was sure I'd seen you before somewhere. Were you at the Motor Show the other day?

UNDINE No, I wasn't.

VAN DEGEN How long are you in New York?

UNDINE I live here.

VAN DEGEN Well, that's first-rate! Why don't I organise a jolly little dinner one night at the Café Martin?

UNDINE I'd like that.

VAN DEGEN Then we can go and see a show afterwards. Something a little more cheerful than this, huh?

UNDINE I went to dinner at the Henley Fairfords earlier this week and met your wife.

VAN DEGEN My wife?

His whole demeanour stiffens and changes and a blaze of anger flashes in his eyes. It takes a moment for his equanimity to be restored.

She never goes to restaurants. So we'll just have to arrange a foursome with old Popp and Mrs . . . you know, your fat friend here.

The house lights go down, the conductor emerges, the curtain rises.

Well, better skip, I suppose, delighted to have met you, can't wait to see how this turns out, huh, Popp?

He hustles Popple out of the box as abruptly as they appeared. Indiana, glowing, turns, anxious to discuss the encounter with Undine; but Undine's head is turned away. She's flushed and upset by Van Degen's blatant attempt to pick her up; and across the way she sees Clare being ushered back into her box by Ralph.

Dissolve to – the end of the third act: the curtain falls, the audience applauds, the lights go up. Undine turns decisively to Indiana.

UNDINE I'm sorry, Indiana, I'm going to go home, I'm not feeling so good.

INDIANA Oh, Undine . . .

UNDINE You stay where you are, I'll be all right, I'll find a cab.

Undine moves into the back area of the box where there's a mirror, silk curtains, a red damask sofa and a coat-rack. Undine is just reaching up for her cloak when the door opens and Ralph Marvell appears. He looks dismayed.

RALPH You're not leaving, are you?

UNDINE I thought you weren't coming.

Ralph is surprised and clearly delighted by the frankness of this admission.

RALPH I've been waiting so as not to clash with all your other visitors.

UNDINE There haven't been so very many.

Indiana turns and sees what's going on: she's about to lumber to her feet, but Undine quells her with an unambiguous glare and she subsides and turns back to studying the house.

UNDINE Won't you sit down?

She sits next to him on the sofa. He seems rather overwhelmed and there's a moment's silence. Undine's aware that he's greedily studying her in the mirror and she allows herself a graceful little sigh.

I don't know if I shall ever learn New York ways.

RALPH I hope you don't.

A fleeting puzzled frown travels across Undine's face, but instinct tells her not to query this unexpected assertion and she turns to look at Ralph, who's now gazing directly at her and manages, with a supreme effort, not to avoid her eye.

Dissolve to – sometime in the final act: as Lucia goes elaborately mad, Undine and Ralph sit in the back of the box, conversing in intimate murmurs.

UNDINE They're awfully lonesome at the hotel; and they moved here from Apex City entirely on my account.

RALPH Why?

UNDINE I always thought: this is where you came when you wanted to live. But New York's not very friendly to strange girls, is it? I suppose you have so many fascinating ones of your own.

RALPH I couldn't wait to get away: after Harvard, I made them send me to Oxford. Then I spent a year travelling all over Europe. In the end, I couldn't put it off any longer: I had to come back to my desk in the family law firm.

UNDINE You're a lawyer?

RALPH I wouldn't say that. I sit behind my desk. But what I really want to do is write.

Undine turns her head, interested; but the next moment she's wincing, her hair caught in the spangles of Indiana's dangling wrap. Ralph leans forward eagerly; and in the half-darkness, tenderly, scarcely daring to breathe, he painstakingly frees her hair. When the process is complete, they're very close, the music is swelling to a crescendo; and Ralph finally speaks in an ardent whisper.

May I call on you tomorrow afternoon?

UNDINE Yes. Yes, you may.

INT. DRAWING ROOM OF THE SPRAGG SUITE. DAY

Two months later; and this time, it's Undine sitting in the huge armchair, while Mrs Heeny finishes off her manicure under Mrs Spragg's indulgent eye. She drops her nailpolisher into her lap, reaches for an intricate old sapphire ring and slips it on to the fourth finger of Undine's left hand.

MRS HEENY Don't know as I've ever seen such a quaint old engagement ring, Mrs Spragg. Wouldn't be a bit surprised if it was his grandma's.

MRS SPRAGG Came in a Tiff'ny box, Mrs Heeny.

MRS HEENY Well, he woulda had Tiff'ny rub it up for her. But it'll be a family heirloom, you mark my words, that's the aristocratic way to do it.

MRS SPRAGG Long as they're not trying to scrimp on the ring . . .

Mrs Heeny ignores this unworthy suggestion, rises to her feet, disposes of her polishers and rolls back her sleeves in businesslike fashion.

MRS HEENY So you're off to visit the old gentleman, Mr Marvell's grandfather, this afternoon?

UNDINE How on earth did you know about that?

MRS HEENY That's what it says in my clipping I cut out of the *Radiator* this morning.

UNDINE I don't know why they insist on my dragging Mother along.

Mrs Heeny has been wrapping layers of lace and muslin around Undine's shoulders, now she begins taking the tortoiseshell pins out of her magnificent hair. Mrs Spragg looks on, her expression miserable.

MRS SPRAGG I'm sure you don't need to worry about me, Undine, I shan't open my mouth.

INT. DRAWING ROOM OF THE DAGONET HOUSE IN WASHINGTON SQUARE. DAY

Tea has been served and Undine and Mrs Spragg sit at either end of a large sofa facing the massed ranks of the Dagonet family: Ralph himself, his widowed mother Mrs Marvell, Mrs Fairford and the spry, sardonic, white-haired head of the family, old Mr Urban Dagonet. The sober, heavy, brownish-panelled room resounds to the inexhaustible garrulity of Mrs Spragg, which is already on the way to driving Undine to distraction.

MRS SPRAGG No, you see, it was after our two eldest were taken from us in the typhoid epidemic that Mr Spragg decided to start Apex Pure Water, he made a vow that no Apex child should ever again take a mouthful of infected water, that was the only idea he had in his head at the time, no thought of profit, I mean, but strangely enough, that was when we first began to be better off, wasn't it, Undine?

UNDINE Yes, Mother.

She's spoken between gritted teeth: but a slow pan has revealed that Mrs Spragg's audience is by no means bored; and as Mrs Spragg takes a restorative pull at her tea, Mr Dagonet seizes the opportunity to pay a graceful compliment in his reedy voice, making a flowing gesture with his free hand.

DAGONET I must say you could hardly have found a more appropriate name for your daughter, how prophetic.

Mrs Spragg doesn't altogether follow, but is scarcely discouraged.

MRS SPRAGG Well, Undie was named after a hair-waver my father put on the market the very week she was born, it's from *un*doolay, of course, the French for crimping, he was a phrase-maker, my father, he had a real knack for finding names, Goliath Glue, for example, that was one of them, and of course he was a minister for a while, right after he left the undertaker's and before he opened the drugstore and it was a great success, his hair-waver, one of his all-time most popular lines, ouf . . .

This last gasp is a result of Undine having discovered a way to kick her mother quite savagely under cover of the table; and Mrs Spragg now lapses into an abrupt and wounded silence.

UNDINE I keep telling Ralph he's going to have to hurry up and introduce me to some of his friends, we don't know a soul in New York.

MRS MARVELL What about the friends who were with you at the opera?

UNDINE The Binches? Well, Indiana Binch was a schoolmate of mine in Apex.

DAGONET What is Mr Binch's occupation?

UNDINE He's a broker.

DAGONET Ah, a broker.

He pronounces the word as if it describes some particularly contemptible species of insect; and Undine hastens to try to repair her unfortunate error.

UNDINE I guess Indiana will be looking to get a divorce pretty soon.

DAGONET A divorce? Why would that be? Has Mr Binch been misbehaving himself?

UNDINE Lord, no, but Millard's been a big disappointment to Indiana. She knows she'll never get anywhere until she gets rid of him.

There's a bewildered silence: Mrs Marvell, in particular, looks perfectly appalled.

DAGONET But if she 'gets rid of him', as you put it, for such a trivial reason, how do you suppose she herself would be situated?

UNDINE I guess her lawyer would fix it so she looked good. Isn't that what you people do?

Another silence is broken by a sudden bark of laughter from Ralph.

MRS MARVELL Ralph!

RALPH Yes, mother.

MRS MARVELL I'm pleased to say, Miss Spragg, that in spite of our growing indifference, a divorced woman in New York is still at a decided disadvantage.

UNDINE You mean Indiana would be even worse off?

MRS MARVELL That would entirely depend on what she wanted.

UNDINE Well, nothing but the best, of course. Just like everybody else.

In the ensuing silence, Mr Dagonet suddenly decides to defuse the situation. He leans forward and pats Undine's hand affectionately.

DAGONET If she looked like you, my child, there isn't a reason in the world she shouldn't get it.

INT. MR SPRAGG'S OFFICE IN THE ARARAT TRUST BUILDING, WALL STREET. DAY

Mr Spragg sits in his revolving chair behind his desk, his hands folded across his waistcoat, his feet crossed and balanced adroitly on a tilted waste-paper basket. It's clear from the view through the window that his office is towards the top of one of the taller New York buildings in the financial district. Facing Mr Spragg, dapper and compact, sits Mr Urban Dagonet.

DAGONET He has three thousand dollars a year from me; and I'm afraid that's all he can count on.

SPRAGG You mean he don't make a living from his law business?

DAGONET The law is not a business, Mr Spragg, it's a profession.

SPRAGG Oh, it's a profession? Well, maybe he ought to make his move now, go right into cooking stoves and be done with it.

DAGONET I am absolutely confident it would take him no time at all to make cooking stoves as unremunerative as the law.

Despite the gravity of the situation, the two men are finding their discussion not unenjoyable. Now Spragg permits himself a wintry smile and shifts his position slightly.

SPRAGG So, what can he do?

DAGONET He can write poetry.

SPRAGG Oh.

DAGONET Now and again he gets ten dollars for it from a magazine.

SPRAGG Well, looks as if they're going to have to live on two hundred and fifty dollars a month.

DAGONET I should have thought your daughter's dress allowance was higher than that.

Spragg glances at him, acknowledging the justice of this remark. He ruminates for a moment.

SPRAGG Perhaps I could put him in the way of something . . .

DAGONET Believe me, Mr Spragg, it will pay us both to keep him out of business.

INT. DRAWING ROOM OF THE SPRAGG SUITE. EVENING

Undine, alone in the room with her father, is looking at him with her mouth open and her expression shocked and incredulous.

SPRAGG All I'm saying, Undie, maybe you better wait awhile and look around some more.

UNDINE Look around? You talk as if I was marrying for money! If I wanted to do that I could marry some dentist and live on the West Side! Come to that, I could have married Millard Binch when he asked me. Don't you understand, if I broke off an engagement with a man like Ralph, nobody worth knowing would ever speak to me again! We might as well go right back to Apex; it wasn't my idea to leave in the first place! I don't know, I wish I was dead!

She bursts into stormy tears. Mr Spragg watches her for a moment, plucking at his beard in impotent distress.

SPRAGG Ain't you in love with the fellow, Undie?

UNDINE Well, of course I am, what do you think?

SPRAGG Then I don't see why you and he should mind beginning in a small way.

UNDINE I see, you want me to drag him down? Well, I'm not going to.

She wrenches off her engagement ring and flourishes it.

I'm sending this back this very minute!

By this time, Spragg has crossed over to her. He puts a hand on her quivering shoulder. his expression cowed and distressed.

SPRAGG All right, Undine, let me see what I can do.

INT. THEATRE FOYER. EVENING

As the fashionable crowd jostles in the interval, Ralph leans over Undine's hand and kisses it. She smiles at him abstractedly, her eyes darting around the foyer; then a thought strikes her.

UNDINE This ring, Ralph, was it your grandmother's?

RALPH My great-grandmother's, why?

UNDINE Oh look, there's your cousin.

She points out Clare Van Degen, at the other end of the foyer.

UNDINE Have you told her we're engaged?

RALPH Of course. She said she was going to call on you.

UNDINE Well, she hasn't. Shouldn't you go and talk to her?

Ralph looks at her uncertainly for a moment.

RALPH Won't you come with me?

UNDINE I'll be fine on my own.

Ralph hesitates another few seconds, then sets off through the press.

Undine watches him for a while, then decides to consult her playbill.

At which point, a hearty voice suddenly intrudes.

VOICE Well, well: Undine.

Undine looks up sharply to discover a slightly overweight, red-faced, prematurely balding man, with shrewd eyes and a large imitation pearl on his bulging shirt-front, looking coolly at her. This is Elmer Moffatt; and his appearance causes Undine to go white and drop her playbill. Moffatt picks it up for her, an ironic light in his dark eyes.

MOFFATT So: you do remember me, then.

Undine seems unable, for the moment, to speak.

Don't you want me to speak to you?

UNDINE No.

Moffatt seems surprised: he forms his lips into a noiseless whistle.

MOFFATT Well, that's a bit stiff.

UNDINE Look, I'll see you, I promise to see you, but please don't talk to me now.

MOFFATT Anything to oblige, as you know. But when will you see me?

UNDINE There's a tea room on the west side of Central Park. By the riding school. Tomorrow afternoon at four.

Ralph is making his way back towards them.

Now go!

MOFFATT Whatever you say. Oh, and congratulations on your engagement.

And he slips away before the arrival of Ralph, who's slightly surprised and pleasantly gratified when Undine grips his hand in both of hers and buries her face in his neck.

EXT. CENTRAL PARK. DAY

Undine, wrapped up against the cold wind in an unusually plain outfit, waits in a trellised passageway close to the tea room, the outside tables of which are more or less deserted. She's veiled, but her reaction is obvious as Elmer Moffatt appears, moving, despite his bulk, with a swaggering step. He draws up to her, smiling pleasantly, taking her limp hand in his gloved fist.

MOFFATT Well, this is very white of you, Undine.

UNDINE I said I'd come.

MOFFATT What you say and what you do . . .

UNDINE I don't see the use of starting like this.

MOFFATT Suppose we take a walk, seeing as it's so chilly? And suppose you let me see you?

After a moment's hesitation, Undine draws back her veil. Moffatt looks at her with frank appreciation.

I'm obliged to you: there's mighty few women as well worth looking at.

UNDINE And I'm glad to see you too, Elmer.

She turns and he joins her as she sets off down the path known as the Ramble.

MOFFATT You managed to conceal it quite well last night, Miss Spragg.

UNDINE I was taken aback. I thought you were out in Alaska.

MOFFATT I'm one of Harmon B. Driscoll's private secretaries.

UNDINE You *are*?

MOFFATT Maybe if you'd known that last night, you wouldn't have cut me.

UNDINE I didn't mean to, Elmer; but I'm engaged now.

MOFFATT I know that; but then you were engaged the first time I met you: to that stiff Millard Binch.

UNDINE I was a child.

MOFFATT That's a fact. So you were.

They fall silent for a moment, moving through the trees.

MOFFATT So just what is it you want from me, Undine?

UNDINE All I want is that nothing should be found out.

MOFFATT Why? You afraid I want to break into your gilt-edged crowd? 'Allow me to escort you to the bewfay.'

Undine stops and looks at him entreatingly, pressing close to him.

UNDINE It's my first chance, Elmer. Please don't let me lose it!

He looks down at her, frowning, surprised as tears begin to spill out of her eyes.

MOFFATT I never saw you cry before. All right, Puss, don't you worry, I ain't going to interrupt the wedding march. Cheer up!

He hums a few bars of the Lohengrin *wedding march and she smiles at him through her tears.*

UNDINE Thank you! I won't forget this.

MOFFATT Maybe you can make me one little promise in return.

Undine immediately looks anxious again, but Moffatt smiles reassuringly.

Don't mistake me, it's an easy one this time. Someday it might be handy for me to know one of your set in a business way. If so, would you fix it up for me? After you're married, I mean.

She smiles at him again, relieved; and holds out her hand.

UNDINE I promise.

But Moffatt bypasses her hand and moves in to kiss her on the lips.

MOFFATT Don't see why I shouldn't kiss the bride.

Undine pulls away; but not perhaps as violently as one might have expected.

EXT. STENTORIAN HOTEL. DAY

It's twilight already and the hotel facade is lit up as Undine turns in off the street, still veiled, her head down, moving fast.

INT. FOYER OF THE STENTORIAN. DAY

Undine taps across the marble vestibule of the hotel and steps into the elevator.

INT. ELEVATOR. DAY

Undine speeds upwards in the elegant, mirror-lined elevator, staring at the back of the elevator-operator's red uniform.

INT. CORRIDOR IN THE STENTORIAN HOTEL. DAY

Undine moves down the plush, brightly lit corridor and lets herself in through a double door.

INT. DRAWING ROOM OF THE SPRAGG SUITE. DAY

Undine pauses on the threshold, unpleasantly surprised: the sole occupant of the suite is Ralph Marvell, who drops the magazine he's reading and springs to his feet.

RALPH I know you asked me not to come, dearest, but I couldn't keep away.

Undine closes the door behind her and advances reluctantly into the room, drawing off her long gloves.

I'll only stay a moment. Just take off your veil and let me look at you.

UNDINE I look so terrible, if I showed myself to you, you might not come back.

RALPH Let me.

He undoes her veil and puts it back, then leans in for a tender kiss. He straightens up again, almost immediately.

You've been crying!

UNDINE I . . . got very hot and nervous at the dressmakers.

RALPH I hate to see you so done up. Why can't we get married tomorrow?

UNDINE Oh, I wish we could.

Ralph takes her in his arms, his expression ardent.

RALPH You mustn't say that unless you mean it.

UNDINE But I do, I do.

RALPH Then let's not wait another three months: let's get married just as soon as we can!

He hugs her to him, covering her face with kisses.

INT. THE SPRAGGS' BEDROOM. NIGHT

Mr and Mrs Spragg are in their adjacent twin beds; and Spragg is looking out at his wife from under his nightcap with an expression of the purest consternation.

SPRAGG Two weeks, Leota? I can't possibly do it!

MRS SPRAGG We don't have a choice, Abner.

SPRAGG Maybe I could have managed it by June, even though I wasn't expecting to have to give my son-in-law a pension like he was some Grand Army veteran: but right now I'm on the wrong side of the market, I just can't put my hand on the cash.

MRS SPRAGG She's seen Elmer Moffatt.

Spragg goes white: the implications of this seem immediately clear to him. He thinks for a moment, then his jaw sets and he turns back to her.

SPRAGG All right, Loot, let me see what I can do.

INT. ARARAT TRUST BUILDING. DAY

Mr Spragg, his expression preoccupied, leaves the elevator and moves with his loping stride down the corridor and into an outer office, where his extremely respectable-looking secretary sits at her desk behind a kind of counter.

SECRETARY Gentleman to see you, Mr Spragg.

The gentleman is Elmer Moffatt, who is already on his feet, a hand extended, which Spragg accepts without enthusiasm.

SPRAGG Step this way: but I warn you, I'm pretty busy.

MOFFATT I don't doubt it, Mr Spragg.

INT. SPRAGG'S OFFICE. DAY

Spragg leads Moffatt into the office, instals himself in his revolving chair and arranges his feet in his waste-paper basket, as Moffatt flops down opposite him, calm, playing idly with a large cameo ring.

SPRAGG Well?

MOFFATT Well, Mr Spragg, I guess I carry a legitimate grudge against you; but I'm here to put you on to a good thing.

Mr Spragg gives him the briefest and frostiest of smiles, consults his pocket watch and turns to stare out of the window.

You may not know this, but I'm working for Mr Harmon B. Driscoll.

SPRAGG Congratulations.

MOFFATT Thank you. Now as you do know, Mr Driscoll has all the railroads and streetcars out in Apex; and what he needs next is the water supply.

SPRAGG I'm out of that a long time ago.

MOFFATT Sure. But the man Mr Driscoll is up against is your ex-partner, Representative James J. Rolliver.

Mr Spragg's eyelids have narrowed like a lizard's; now he peers through them for a moment at his interlocutor.

SPRAGG Driscoll tell you to come here?

MOFFATT No, sir.

SPRAGG Well, glad to have seen you, Mr Moffatt.

MOFFATT I understand Undine's getting married next week.

SPRAGG You go straight to hell.

Mr Spragg's feet are out of the waste-paper basket and his face is black with rage. Moffatt, on the other hand, still displays a calm and amiable front.

MOFFATT Don't you worry yourself. I ain't angling for an invitation. But I do want to get out of Driscoll's office and start up on my own. And all I need for that is to put my hand on let's say fifty thousand dollars; and if you was to come round with me to old Driscoll's office, I happen to know I could put my hand on double, yes sir, double that sum.

SPRAGG You want me to tell Driscoll what I know about James J. Rolliver?

MOFFATT I want you to tell him the truth.

SPRAGG Rolliver and I always stood together.

MOFFATT I don't see as you've done so well out of it.

Spragg brings his hand down with a crash on the dusty desk.

SPRAGG I can't do it: I'm not going to do it!

MOFFATT Well, so long.

He springs to his feet, his expression serene, seems about to leave the office, but pauses in the doorway.

I saw Undine the other day, she tell you? She don't beat about the bush the way you do. She wants the Marvells to think she's right out of kindergarten. And I'd really like to be able to oblige her, even though you didn't hesitate to kick me when I was down and there's a kinda poetic justice in your being the man to help me up. But I need that fifty thousand dollars and you're the only man who can get it for me. Oh, and by the way, the other fifty's yours. Now do you see where we're coming out?

Spragg stares at him, motionless, his hands in his waistcoat pockets, through a long silence.

SPRAGG I'll think about it.

MOFFATT No, sir. Your news ain't worth a dollar to Driscoll if he don't get it today. So it's you speak to him; or I speak to the Marvell family.

At which point, the secretary puts her head around the door.

SECRETARY Mr Marvell is here.

And Ralph appears immediately, beaming, apologetic.

RALPH I hope I'm not in the way, sir, turn me out if I am.

SPRAGG Mr Moffatt, Mr Ralph Marvell.

Ralph and Moffatt shake hands.

MOFFATT What a pleasure, Mr Marvell. I was just on my way out.

He turns a charming smile on Mr Spragg.

And I hope to see you again later in the day, Mr Spragg.

SPRAGG Let me see what I can do.

Moffatt slips out of the office; and with a considerable effort, Spragg brings himself to focus on young Ralph.

And now what can I do for you?

EXT. HILLSIDE NEAR SIENA. DAY

Close on Ralph: a curious angle, seen from above, his head resting in his palms, as he lies in the grass.

RALPH Happy?

UNDINE (*voice over*) Hot.

Another angle reveals that Ralph is lying in the shade of an ilex grove; while Undine sits, a little way off, her back resting against a tree, her posture conveying a certain discomfort. Around them, the vivid colours of the Tuscan hills, the cypresses, the vines, the long yellow walls of an old villa, the fierce blue of the brilliant July sky.

I thought you said there'd be a breeze up here.

RALPH Wasn't it as hot as this in Apex?

UNDINE I didn't marry you to go back to Apex.

RALPH Sometimes I wonder why you did marry me.

He's spoken very lightly and laughs happily, but Undine says nothing; and presently Ralph scrambles up, moves over to her and drops on one knee beside her. He takes her hand, studies the back of it, then turns it over and contemplates the palm; then he glances shyly up at her.

I don't think I've ever seen you look so beautiful.

He kisses her palm and her wrist with all the tenderness he can muster.

And I've never been so happy in my life.

She looks down at him, serene and enigmatic.

EXT. OPEN CARRIAGE. DAY

Ralph and Undine, side by side, rattle towards the walls of the city. The sun blazes low on the horizon.

UNDINE Don't people generally come here earlier in the year?

RALPH That's why I chose to come now: so we could have the place to ourselves.

He's aware that this doesn't seem to Undine a particularly satisfactory idea.

Shall we go and sit in the cathedral? It's always cool at sunset.

UNDINE We've sat in the cathedral at sunset every day for a week.

The carriage moves on, through the exquisite Tuscan landscape.

EXT. MAIN SQUARE IN SIENA. NIGHT

Ralph sits at a café table, alone, nursing an espresso. Sloping away from him is the extraordinary expanse of the central piazza in Siena. The soft light of gas lamps, the silver wash of a full moon, isolated knots of strollers and loafers, occasional low flights of birds, odd echoes of footsteps or fragments of conversation: all contribute to a unique atmosphere which Ralph drinks in, enchanted.

EXT. STREET IN SIENA. NIGHT

Ralph strolls back along the narrow, deserted, cobbled street, lost in a reverie; and turns in at the entrance of a modest hotel.

INT. HOTEL CORRIDOR. NIGHT

Ralph knocks at a door, waits a second, then opens it.

INT. UNDINE'S ROOM. NIGHT

Undine, in her nightdress, is sitting on a window seat in the open window, with her legs drawn up. Céleste, her maid, is turning down one of the single beds in the room. Undine glances across at Ralph, as he enters the room.

UNDINE Enjoy your walk?

RALPH Beautiful place.

UNDINE That'll do, Céleste. And put out the lamp as you go.

CÉLESTE Madame.

She turns out the lamp and leaves the room, scarcely acknowledging Ralph: but he doesn't notice and as soon as the door closes behind her, he hurries over to Undine's side, leaning over her to kiss her.

RALPH How's your headache?

UNDINE Not much better, I'm afraid.

RALPH Oh, I'm sorry.

Undine lets out a small, melancholy sigh; Ralph looks down at her, concerned.

RALPH What's the matter?

UNDINE I don't know . . . maybe I'm homesick.

RALPH Homesick?

UNDINE I don't think I like Europe. It's dirty and smelly and there are beggars and the rooms are stuffy and the food's disgusting. New York's so much nicer.

RALPH New York in July?

UNDINE At least there are people round. This place is like a cemetery.

Ralph is very disturbed by this outburst: he thinks for a moment, his expression miserable.

RALPH Well, should we go back, then?

Undine looks up, assessing him for a moment before answering.

UNDINE Céleste tells me Paris is wonderful.

RALPH Céleste?

UNDINE And it'll be full of people we know.

Ralph considers briefly; then capitulates with a rueful smile.

RALPH When would you like to go?

Undine whoops with delight: she's on her feet in an instant.

UNDINE First thing in the morning.

She throws her arms round Ralph and kisses him.

I do love you, Ralph.

She kisses him again, more penetratingly this time.

RALPH What about your headache?

UNDINE Never mind my headache.

EXT. HOTEL ST JAMES ET ALBANY, PARIS. DAY

A carriage draws up in front of the little hotel on the Rue de Rivoli. As the coachman helps Undine down, followed by Céleste and Ralph, swarms of uniformed hotel staff begin to unload huge quantities of luggage.

INT. DRAWING ROOM OF THE SPRAGG SUITE AT THE STENTORIAN HOTEL. DAY

A bellboy carries a trunk out on his back, while another gathers up numerous irregular brown-paper parcels and miscellaneous ornaments. Mrs Spragg has been closely supervising the whole procedure; now, momentarily overcome, she dabs a handkerchief at the corner of her eye as Mr Spragg, his expression sombre, takes her arm.

INT. FOYER OF THE ST JAMES ET ALBANY. DAY

Bellboys push two large chariots stacked with luggage into the service elevator, while a clerk from reception escorts Ralph and Undine over to the passenger elevator.

INT. FOYER OF THE STENTORIAN. DAY

Spragg signs various documents at the reception desk, as Mrs Spragg, still looking distraught, waits nearby; and a stream of bellboys file by with all kinds of odd objects: cushions, lampshades, hatboxes, a sewing machine.

INT. SUITE AT THE ST JAMES ET ALBANY. DAY

Undine and Céleste direct the bellboys where to put the various pieces of luggage in a small, but comfortable sitting room, while Ralph, his expression somewhat constrained, distributes what seem to be generous tips.

EXT. STENTORIAN HOTEL. DAY

Spragg watches Mrs Spragg being helped into a cab in front of an ungainly open carriage on which a lifetime's accumulation of possessions has been piled. Ignoring the army of bellboys, he hands the doorman a dismayingly small coin, takes a farewell glance up at the hotel's impeccable facade and clambers in after his wife.

EXT. PRÉ CATALAN. NIGHT

Ralph and Undine are dining al fresco in the conservatory restaurant in the Bois de Boulogne with three other American couples, including the Binches. Undine is laughing uproariously at something; whereas Ralph, though not apparently unhappy, seems a little apart, not speaking to either of his neighbours. Presently, he looks up, his attention caught by a slight commotion at the door to the Orangerie, where the maître d'hôtel is dealing with a raucous party of arrivals. Leading them, Ralph notices, is Peter Van Degen: and his party consists of a couple of substantial American men and a number of what appear to be chorus girls. As soon as Van Degen sees Ralph, he abandons negotiations and makes his way over to him.

VAN DEGEN How's the honeymooners?

RALPH As you see.

VAN DEGEN I'm glad I've found you: you must pay a visit on Clare, if you can catch her away from the sale rooms. We're at the Nouveau Luxe.

RALPH Thank you, I will. How is she?

But his question goes unanswered: Van Degen has caught Undine's eye, exchanged a smile and is now setting off up the table to greet her, abandoning Ralph in mid-sentence.

INT. HOTEL SUITE IN NEW YORK. DAY

Mrs Spragg sits at a plain round table, at present doing duty for a writing desk, her pen poised, her expression, as ever when confronted by the horrors of composition, anguished. It's a fairly tight shot, but there's enough evidence to reveal that the Spraggs' new quarters, though sober and respectable, are nothing like as lavish as those at the Stentorian. Mrs Spragg braces herself and begins writing in a round, childish hand: 'Dearest Undie'.

INT. CORRIDOR IN THE ST JAMES ET ALBANY. DAY

As Ralph approaches the door to his suite, it opens to disgorge an impeccable blond-bearded Frenchman with the red ribbon of the Légion d'Honneur in his lapel, followed by a neat lady assistant, who carries a number of black velvet-covered boxes. The Frenchman bows and sweeps past; and Ralph steps into the suite.

INT. SUITE AT THE ST JAMES ET ALBANY. DAY

Undine looks up: she's slipping on her wedding and engagement rings and looks far from happy.

RALPH Who was that? He looked like an ambassador.

UNDINE Just that jeweller I was telling you about.

RALPH Jeweller?

UNDINE I thought I might have one or two old things reset.

RALPH Not your engagement ring?

UNDINE I would have cancelled his visit altogether, if I'd had time: you see, I've just had a letter from Mother.

RALPH Is anything wrong?

UNDINE I should say so. Father's been speculating. He's lost a lot of money.

RALPH I'm sorry, that's hard on him.

UNDINE Hard on us as well. He can't send us any more money for at least three months.

RALPH I see.

He looks away for a moment: this is obviously a bitter blow. Undine watches him, her eyes cool.

UNDINE Couldn't your people do something? Just this once.

Ralph flushes, turns back to her: he looks mortified.

RALPH My grandfather does everything he can for me and my mother has nothing but what he gives her.

Undine nods, taking this on board; then she adds, quite calmly, as if it were the most natural suggestion in the world:

UNDINE What about your sister?

EXT. THOMAS COOK'S. DAY

Ralph emerges from the offices of Thomas Cook's, near the Opéra. He pauses by a steamship poster to collect himself, closing his eyes briefly, his face white and strained.

INT. VOISIN'S. DAY

Undine pushes the silver instrument into the relevant cavity and produces a succulent white piece of lobster which she pops into her mouth. She shakes her head at Ralph, sweetly reasonable.

UNDINE I can't possibly get myself ready by Saturday.

RALPH But, you see, next week the rush season begins and the fares are practically double.

UNDINE We were going to Chantilly on Sunday.

RALPH There is a slow boat in two weeks' time. Sailing from Plymouth.

UNDINE No, if we don't have a deck suite, I'll be terribly sea-sick.

RALPH Then we'd better go on Saturday.

UNDINE I need more time, I must have some clothes to go home in.

Ralph looks at her across the dazzling tablecloth and the sparkling glassware, at a loss for words.

You don't understand what a saving it is shopping here. Have you any idea what a dinner-dress costs in New York?

RALPH But, Undine . . .

UNDINE I'm sure your sister wouldn't want me to go back to New York without a rag.

RALPH You can't have everything, Undine.

She looks across at him, not in the least annoyed, but faintly exasperated, as if he's just said something entirely ridiculous.

EXT. COMÉDIE FRANÇAISE. DAY

Ralph stands outside the columns on the Rue Richelieu, looking up and down the street, as the matinée audience flows into the theatre. Presently, a carriage pulls up and Clare Van Degen descends from it. Ralph hurries forward to meet her, kisses her slim brown hand and shepherds her into the foyer. The play showing is Phèdre.

INT. SUITE AT THE ST JAMES ET ALBANY. DAY

Sitting with his feet up on the chaise longue, finishing a cup of tea, is Peter Van Degen. Undine sits opposite in an armchair, her expression animated.

VAN DEGEN Well, of course, I shall be bowling home as usual on the 'Sorceress'.

UNDINE The 'Sorceress'?

VAN DEGEN My steam yacht. She's being refitted at the moment at Greenock.

He looks at her for a moment, his eyes narrowing shrewdly.

You and Ralph should come along. We generally have a pretty good spin.

UNDINE Would there be room?

VAN DEGEN Acres. Clare never comes, she's off to Italy with some long-haired friends of hers. But we always manage to have a jolly time.

He slips a gold cigarette case out of his pocket and lights a cigarette.

UNDINE Well thank you, I'm sure we'd love to.

VAN DEGEN Well, good, that's settled.

He looks at her greedily for a moment.

I must say, marriage suits you, you look absolutely stunning.

Undine smiles, pleased, but before she can reply, the door opens and Ralph appears. He hesitates for a second on the threshold, successfully suppressing his displeasure at seeing Van Degen.

Hello, old man, how was the show?

UNDINE Oh, Ralph only likes plays where they walk around in bath towels and talk poetry.

VAN DEGEN I can't take those five-barrelled affairs at the Fransay any more: we must get a party together, go off and see something with a chorus-line. Have a cup of tea.

RALPH Thank you.

His voice comes out a little stilted and sarcastic: they watch him with amiable indifference, as he reaches for the teapot.

INT. PAILLARD'S. NIGHT

A waiter fills Undine's champagne glass and she beams at Ralph across a plate of oysters. She reaches for the glass.

UNDINE You don't know it, but this is a celebration.

RALPH It is?

UNDINE I've just saved you thousands.

RALPH What have you done, decided not to buy a tiara?

UNDINE No, I've got Peter Van Degen to invite us to go home on his private yacht.

Ralph's jaw drops. He looks across at her, appalled.

Did you ever know such luck?

RALPH Out of the question.

UNDINE What?

RALPH Everybody knows about that boat. Half the chorus-world of New York have kept the beds warm. No decent woman would be caught dead aboard that floating cathouse.

He breaks off, a little surprised by his own vehemence. Undine is watching him, her expression cold.

UNDINE Just because your cousin won't go near it. Why do you believe all those stories she tells you? Everybody in New York knows she's crazy about you. That's why Peter has to take up with other women.

Ralph is astonished by this outburst. Finally, he manages to blurt out:

RALPH Well, you're not going on his yacht, the subject is closed.

Silence. Undine pushes aside her oysters, untouched.

UNDINE In that case, as long as you're on your high horse, you can get us a proper deck suite on a proper liner, in three weeks' time, when everyone else is going back; because I've done all I can.

INT. CORRIDOR IN THE ST JAMES ET ALBANY. DAY

Ralph hurries up to the door of his suite and unlocks it.

INT. SUITE AT THE ST JAMES ET ALBANY. DAY

The room looks as if a bomb has hit it. Every chair is hidden under piles of dresses, the floor space is largely taken up with yawning trunks overflowing with tissue paper, every surface is piled with hatboxes and shoeboxes and glossy pasteboard cartons. In the midst of all this, Undine is stretched out on the chaise longue, a hand over her eyes, crying. Ralph hurries to her side.

RALPH What's wrong? Why haven't they finished?

UNDINE I sent them away.

RALPH Why, my dear girl, what is it?

By now, he's on his knees beside her, holding her hand.

Tell me what's the matter?

She goes on sobbing for a while: then, abruptly, she wrenches her hand away from his and sits up.

UNDINE Stop staring at me like that: what do you think's the matter?

The answer to the question dawns on him: and he reclaims her hand.

RALPH But, darling, are you sure, that's wonderful!

UNDINE Wonderful? Wonderful?

RALPH Well, isn't it?

UNDINE I feel horribly ill, what's wonderful about that?

RALPH Oh my poor girl, I'm so sorry.

She wrenches her hand away again and jumps to her feet.

UNDINE Sorry? *You're* sorry? What earthly difference does it make to you?

And, still sobbing, she runs out of the room, slamming her bedroom door behind her. For a moment, Ralph stays where he is, shocked and uncertain. Then his eye falls on a small velvet box in the middle of the nearest table. He looks at it for some time; then, unable to contain his suspicion, he reaches for it and opens it. Undine has had the stones from her engagement ring reset in a fanciful art nouveau gold setting. Ralph stands for a long moment, the ring in the palm of his hand, racked with bitter thoughts.

Fade.

INT. DRAWING ROOM OF THE DAGONET HOUSE. DAY

There's silence in the big, gloomy room, except for the Empire clock on the white marble chimney-piece, which is striking five. A slow pan around the room first discovers young Paul Marvell, a none-too-happy-looking child, sitting on the starched knee of his nurse, a severe figure in uniform; then, bolt upright, with an aggrieved expression, Mrs Marvell; Mr Urban Dagonet, dozing in his armchair; a large mahogany sideboard, on which stands a birthday cake with two candles, a pile of plates and heaps of sliced, buttered bread, dishes of jam and rock cakes; Mr and Mrs Henley Fairford, rigid with disapproval; and finally, standing at the window, peering out into the darkening square below, Clare Van Degen. Eventually, the silence is broken by Henley Fairford.

FAIRFORD Well, I'm afraid I'm off to my bridge.

Mrs Marvell leans forward and taps Mr Dagonet's knee.

MRS MARVELL Wake up, Father, it's time for your nap.

DAGONET Where's Undine, isn't she here yet?

CLARE It's too bad, I'm afraid she's simply forgotten.

Paul starts to wriggle and whimper on his nurse's knee.

INT. CLAUD POPPLE'S STUDIO. DAY

A monumental portrait, almost complete, of Undine in a dazzling low-cut dress is being admired by Peter Van Degen. Popple, to one side, in his impeccable mouse-coloured velveteen suit, is just packing up his paints for the day. Van Degen turns to him.

VAN DEGEN It's damn good, Popp, you've hit her off remarkably. It's just the pearls ain't big enough.

There is a low laugh from behind the portrait; and another angle reveals that Undine is rising from a monumental pseudo-Venetian armchair on a dais on which she's been posing.

UNDINE It's not his fault, poor man; he didn't give them to me.

INT. OFFICES OF THE PLYMOUTH ROCK REALTY COMPANY. DAY

Ralph sits behind his desk in a kind of open-plan large office. He finishes writing something, then sets down his pen, gets up and moves over to where a glass partition marks off a separate office for one of the senior partners, Mr Danforth. He raps on the glass and puts his head round the door as Mr Danforth looks up, frowning.

RALPH I was wondering if I might leave a few minutes early today?

DANFORTH You're not working for your family firm any more, Mr Marvell.

RALPH I know that; but it's my boy's birthday.

INT. CLAUD POPPLE'S STUDIO. DAY

Undine sits in the main body of the studio, sipping at a cup of tea.

UNDINE Who'd have thought it was such hard work, sitting still all day? And is it me or is it frightfully hot in here?

Van Degen looks up from a sideboard, where he's pouring himself a cocktail from a jug.

VAN DEGEN Popp always likes to keep the place at low neck temperature in case the portraits catch cold.

UNDINE You know that nagging feeling, when you keep thinking you've forgotten something?

INT. DRAWING ROOM OF THE DAGONET HOUSE. EVENING

Paul is waiting in his nurse's arms as the remains of the company, Clare Van Degen, Laura Fairford and Mrs Marvell, sing 'Happy Birthday'. Then, as Mrs Fairford cuts the cake, Ralph hurries into the room.

RALPH Sorry I'm late, I couldn't get away.

He takes Paul from the nurse and holds him up in the air.

What's all this then? Crying on your birthday?

He looks around, as a thought strikes him.

Where's Undine?

MRS FAIRFORD She hasn't come.

RALPH Hasn't come?

He swings Paul gently in his arms until the crying stops.

There we are. You poor little chap.

INT. ENTRANCE HALL IN POPPLE'S APARTMENT BUILDING. EVENING

Peter Van Degen follows Undine across the marble floor of the entrance hall. Both of them are wearing fur coats.

VAN DEGEN You'd better let me give you a lift, you'll never get a cab on a night like this.

EXT. POPPLE'S APARTMENT BUILDING. EVENING

The lamps are already lit; snow is piled high on the street. Van Degen turns and with a familiar gesture turns up the collar on her fur coat.

VAN DEGEN Not afraid of being seen with me, are you? Ralph will still be swinging on a strap in the elevated.

He opens the door of his big open car and she climbs in.

INT. CLARE VAN DEGEN'S CAR. EVENING

Clare's car is closed and Ralph sits next to her, tucked under a rug, partitioned off from the uniformed driver and Paul, asleep in his nurse's arms.

CLARE Is it awful, working at that real estate office?

RALPH No, sometimes it's really quite interesting.

He looks across at Clare, who's gazing at him with great sympathy.

Not that I'm any good at it, of course.

EXT. CENTRAL PARK. EVENING

Peter Van Degen leans over towards Undine, raising his voice to make himself heard above the roar of the engine as the car thunders across the snow-coated park.

VAN DEGEN Why don't we run up to the Heights, cool you off a bit before dinner?

EXT. WEST END AVENUE. EVENING

Clare Van Degen's car draws up in front of the Marvells' little house.

INT. CLARE VAN DEGEN'S CAR. EVENING

Ralph turns to Clare with a wan smile.

RALPH Thank you.

CLARE See you later on. I suppose, at the Chauncey Ellings'.

RALPH I suppose.

Clare reaches out a gloved hand.

CLARE Why don't you ever come to see me? I miss you more than ever.

Ralph smiles ruefully, squeezes her hand and climbs out of the car without answering.

EXT. MORNINGSIDE HEIGHTS. EVENING

Undine shakes her head, declining Van Degen's hip flask, as they sit in the car looking out over the misty snowscape. She lets out a heartfelt sigh; Van Degen is instantly alert.

VAN DEGEN What's the matter?

UNDINE Oh, nothing.

VAN DEGEN No, go on.

UNDINE Just the usual. Too many bills this time of the year; and Ralph has trouble covering them.

VAN DEGEN Would a couple of thou be any help?

Undine looks sharply at him, torn between protest and eager acceptance.

I'll send round a cheque in the morning.

Suddenly, Undine's hand flies to her mouth.

UNDINE Oh my God!

VAN DEGEN What is it?

UNDINE It's the boy's birthday today. I knew there was something I'd forgotten.

INT. RALPH'S BEDROOM. EVENING

Ralph sits in an old armchair in his small bedroom, lit only by the glow of the firelight, staring into space. After a while, he gets up and crosses to the window.

EXT. WEST END AVENUE. EVENING

Ralph's point of view: Peter Van Degen's car, travelling as fast as it can, turns into the deserted street and screeches to a halt outside the house. Undine jumps out of the car and runs up the front steps.

INT. LANDING AND FRONT HALL. EVENING

Ralph emerges on to the landing as the front door opens. He waits in the half-darkness as Undine starts up the stairs. When she's halfway up, he steps forward. If she's startled, she doesn't show it; she flashes him a dazzling smile.

UNDINE Well?

RALPH They waited for you all afternoon at Washington Square. Have you forgotten the boy's birthday?

UNDINE Popple was finishing off the portrait. He took hours over some bit of the dress. I telephoned, but nobody answered. Then I couldn't get a cab. They never want to come out here, you know how it is.

RALPH The boy cried his eyes out.

UNDINE Oh dear.

She pushes by him on the landing.

I'd better go and dress or we'll be late.

INT. DINING ROOM AT THE CHAUNCEY ELLINGS'. NIGHT

Close on Ralph: he sits silent as around him swirls the colossal racket of a fashionable dinner party. The noise is enormous, unnaturally amplified.

His point of view: far down the table, half-obscured by flower arrangements and dazzling crystal decanters, Peter Van Degen leans in to murmur something to Undine, who erupts in joyous laughter.

As Ralph watches, the sound gradually diminishes, until finally, even though the party is as animated as ever, there's absolute silence.

INT. LANDING AND FRONT HALL IN THE MARVELLS' HOUSE. NIGHT

Ralph bolts the front door, puts out the lights and sets off up the stairs. He's heading for his room when, to his amazement, he's suddenly intercepted by Undine, still in her exquisite evening gown and cloak. She puts a hand on his arm.

UNDINE Ralphie . . .

She leans towards him, lips apart, a dreamy expression on her face, beautiful, infinitely available. But Ralph leans forward, avoiding her lips and gives her a formal peck on the cheek.

RALPH Goodnight.

He moves off crisply and vanishes into his room, leaving Undine marooned and astonished.

INT. UNDINE'S BEDROOM. DAY

Céleste comes into the room with Undine's breakfast tray, which she settles across Undine's knees. The day's mail is neatly piled on a corner of the tray.

UNDINE Where's Mr Marvell?

CÉLESTE He's already left for his office, madame.

She opens the curtains and leaves the room; meanwhile Undine's attention has been attracted by a bulky envelope, which she's in the process of opening. There's a smaller envelope inside with her name on; and a long box covered with blue velvet. She eagerly snaps open the box, which turns out to contain a magnificent rope of pearls; and a card, which she picks up.

Inset: the card is Peter Van Degen's. Undine turns it over. On the reverse is written: 'Have him repaint the pearls.'

EXT. HOUSE IN CONNECTICUT. DAY

There's still snow on the ground around the modest frame house in the wooded Connecticut countryside; and Van Degen's easily recognisable open car is parked in the driveway.

Over this image, the sounds, the grunts and gasps of a physical struggle.

INT. DRAWING ROOM OF THE CONNECTICUT HOUSE. DAY

In the corner of a sofa in the low-ceilinged, cosy room, Undine is grappling with Peter Van Degen; she's mostly hidden by him as he tries to kiss her. Eventually, she succeeds in pushing him away; and he recoils, out of breath, eyes popping, unpleasantly flushed. Undine is wearing her pearls.

UNDINE I don't think you're yourself today, Peter.

VAN DEGEN Look, I don't mind the instalment plan; but ain't you a little behind on your payments?

She flashes an indignant look at him: he gets up and moves around the room a little, huge and looming, roughly straightening his waistcoat.

Anyway, I'm going to let the interest accumulate: you won't have to see me again till I get back from Europe.

UNDINE Europe. When are you leaving?

VAN DEGEN First of April. Good day for a fool to acknowledge his folly.

There's a silence, as Undine calculates how best to react to his news. She settles on a melancholy sigh.

UNDINE Well, then, I guess this is goodbye.

VAN DEGEN Won't you be turning up in Paris? To get your things for Newport?

UNDINE You don't understand. You should have heard the wailing and gnashing of teeth when he had to rent this little place. And you know I only come out here because my doctor says I have to have country air. So we're going to spend Ralph's summer break in the Adirondacks; and it doesn't matter what I wear there because nobody I care about will see me.

VAN DEGEN Isn't that a little hard on Ralph?

She joins in his laugh for a moment, then looks sombre again.

UNDINE You know what I mean. But perhaps it's best you're leaving.

VAN DEGEN Why?

UNDINE Because I feel I've let a . . . misunderstanding arise between us.

Van Degen is trying to work out how best to advance; he returns to sit on the sofa.

VAN DEGEN Why don't you let me pay for your trip to Europe? It could all be so easy . . .

He begins edging gradually towards her; and she sees it's time to quell him again.

UNDINE You seem to forget I'm married.

This has some of the desired effect in that it stops his approach; but it's angered him and he now looks her directly in the eye.

VAN DEGEN Well, goddamn it, so am I.

INT. SPRAGG'S OFFICE. DAY

Spragg's feet are crossed in his waste-paper basket. He looks across his desk at Undine, watchful but expressionless.

UNDINE I need a change, Father, I've never really felt well since the baby was born; and there are other reasons.

SPRAGG Never knew you short on reasons, Undine.

UNDINE There's one more serious than all the others.

SPRAGG More bills?

UNDINE No.

She hesitates, flashes a quick glance at him.

I'm unhappy at home.

SPRAGG Unhappy!

Spragg is so startled he overturns the waste-paper basket. He stoops to gather up the scraps of paper that have spilled on to the carpet, using the activity to collect himself.

SPRAGG Why, he worships the ground you walk on!

UNDINE That's not always enough for a woman.

Spragg frowns: the discussion is straying into areas he doesn't wish to enter.

It's been a mistake from the very beginning. His people have always hated me and now Ralph's had to go into business, they'll never forgive me. And look at the way they treat you and Mother.

SPRAGG What do you mean? We never so much as set eyes on them.

UNDINE Exactly. All they want from you is your money.

Silence. Spragg turns this over for a moment in his mind.

SPRAGG I don't see how Europe's going to help you out. You go away, you just got to turn round and come back again.

UNDINE Maybe not.

SPRAGG What are you talking about?

UNDINE There's someone over there in Paris, who might do anything if I was free . . .

Spragg strikes his palm on the arm of his chair.

SPRAGG You stop right there, Undine Marvell. Are you sitting there in your sane senses talking about what you could do if you were free?

UNDINE I know exactly what I could do, I could –

SPRAGG You stop right there!

She looks across at him, her jaw mutinously set: but this time he's looking back at her with exactly the same expression.

INT. VESTIBULE OF THE ARARAT TRUST BUILDING. DAY

As Undine emerges from the elevator into the crowded lobby, a figure leaning against a column smoking a cheroot steps forward to intercept her: she's startled to see Elmer Moffatt.

UNDINE What are you doing here?

MOFFATT Waiting to speak to you. I have an office in this building now. I don't see much of your father since our bit of business together which got off to a very good start and then backfired on us. But you probably know about that.

UNDINE No, I don't; and if you don't mind, I'm in rather a hurry.

MOFFATT I won't hold you up: I just wanted to call in that promise you made me before you were married, remember?

UNDINE Yes, I do.

MOFFATT There's someone I'd like to meet in the way of business and you could make the introduction for me.

UNDINE Who?

MOFFATT Your husband.

Undine laughs in amazement.

UNDINE My husband?

MOFFATT I'm interested in a piece of real estate controlled by your husband's company. For various reasons, I'd rather not go to his office, I'd prefer a private approach.

UNDINE Well, I'm not sure . . .

MOFFATT Let me put it this way: there'd be a fat commission in it for your husband's company; and ten thousand dollars for him personally.

Undine has slowed down to listen to him; now she comes to a standstill. Moffatt hands her a business card.

Here's my number. Perhaps you could let me know quite soon.

He nods pleasantly to her and slips away.

INT. DRAWING ROOM AND FRONT HALL OF THE MARVELLS' HOUSE. DAY

Undine stands at the door peeking out into the front hall, as Ralph shows Moffatt out of the study opposite, shakes hands with him and shows him out.

MOFFATT I'll hear from you tomorrow, then?

RALPH You will.

Undine moves away from the door so that by the time Ralph arrives, she's over by the fire.

RALPH Amazing fellow. You say you met him in Apex?

UNDINE Once or twice.

RALPH I met him once in your father's office.

UNDINE They fell out. Some business thing.

RALPH I couldn't make out whether what he was proposing was absolutely straight. I thought I might consult your father about it this evening.

He lights a cigarette as Undine, her expression thoughtful, settles in an armchair near the fire.

UNDINE I wouldn't mention him by name if you want an objective opinion.

RALPH No, all right, I won't.

He reflects for a moment, drawing on his cigarette.

There could be quite a good commission in it, you'd like that, wouldn't you?

To his surprise, Undine turns her head away, suddenly close to tears.

RALPH What's the matter?

UNDINE You must think I'm so selfish and odious.

RALPH No.

He crosses to her, starts to stroke her hair.

No.

INT. STUDY IN THE MARVELLS' HOUSE. NIGHT

Mr Spragg chews on his cigar, puzzled, looking up at Ralph. He narrows his eyes.

SPRAGG Can't make out what your trouble is.

RALPH That's what I was hoping you'd explain to me.

SPRAGG Is this party of yours under any personal obligation to the fellow he's trying to buy the property from?

RALPH As far as I know, they've never met.

SPRAGG Then where's your trouble? I don't see the conundrum. It's up to people to take care of their own skins.

RALPH I see. Thank you.

EXT. WASHINGTON SQUARE. DAY

It's a fresh spring day and Undine emerges from the Dagonet house with Paul in her arms. She hasn't gone more than a few yards when she runs into Elmer Moffatt, who looks very dapper, with a bunch of violets in his buttonhole. They shake hands.

MOFFATT Well, well, this must be the heir apparent.

UNDINE He's been visiting with his grandfather, Mr Urban Dagonet.

MOFFATT He looks a bit of an armful.

UNDINE We'll pick up a cab on the corner.

MOFFATT Why don't you let me carry him that far?

Undine only hesitates for a second; then she hands Paul over to Moffatt.

Let's go for a ride.

He swings the delighted little boy up on his shoulders.

I don't suppose he knows what a friend I've been to him lately.

UNDINE When he's old enough to understand I'll tell him. Meanwhile, let me thank you for coming to Ralph.

MOFFATT I gave him a leg up and he did the same for me. I've been able to make a fresh start.

UNDINE Good.

MOFFATT Your husband was telling me you're off to the Adirondacks this summer.

UNDINE He is, with the boy. I'm going over to Paris.

MOFFATT Oh I see. Now your husband's able to blow you off to the trip.

UNDINE Yes, it's all thanks to you.

MOFFATT Well, didn't I always say I meant to act white by you?

They walk on for a moment in silence, Undine pensive.

MOFFATT Oh, some Apex gossip for you. You remember Indiana Binch, who went back to Apex when her husband Millard keeled over?

UNDINE Yes, of course.

MOFFATT Well, guess who she's snagged? Representative James J. Rolliver!

UNDINE Oh.

She's dreadfully taken aback by this and Moffatt's observant enough to notice.

MOFFATT She always was a bright girl. Not in your class, of course.

He flags down a cab for her, lifts down the little boy and gives him a resounding kiss on the lips before handing him back to Undine.

Now you take care over there in Europe.

UNDINE I will.

INT. RESTAURANT OF THE HOTEL NOUVEAU LUXE IN PARIS. NIGHT

Undine, a little more simply dressed than usual and looking especially dazzling, sits with Peter Van Degen at a big table near the orchestra, crowded with Americans, among them Indiana Rolliver, as she now is, and her beefy, genial, shifty-looking husband Representative James J. Rolliver. Everyone seems to be in riotous good spirits.

Another angle shows Undine's point of view: she's noticed that her sister-in-law's friend, Ralph Bowen, is making his way across the restaurant, accompanied by a tall, slim, distinguished-looking man in his late thirties. Bowen inclines his head, with a tactful smile, to Undine. It's a perfectly cordial greeting, but he doesn't seem inclined to stop and speak to her.

Bowen's point of view: Undine murmurs a word to Van Degen: who immediately springs to his feet and intercepts Bowen and his companion.

VAN DEGEN How long have you been over? Mrs Marvell wants to pump you for all the latest New York news.

Bowen smiles urbanely, indicating his friend.

BOWEN Mrs Marvell, this is the Comte Raymond de Chelles.

Chelles bows over Undine's hand and kisses it.

CHELLES *Enchanté.*

BOWEN And this is Peter Van Degen.

As Chelles shakes hands with Van Degen, Bowen murmurs to Undine.

We net on a trip up the Nile, we always dine when I'm in France.

VAN DEGEN Come and join us for coffee on the terrace.

UNDINE Yes, how is everyone in New York? Have you seen my little boy?

INT. PUBLIC PARLOUR AT THE MALIBRAN HOTEL, NEW YORK. DAY

The hotel where the Spraggs have now landed is dingy and dispiriting and its ground-floor public rooms are full of exhausted businessmen and elderly ladies. Little Paul Marvell has his arm plunged up to the shoulder in Mrs Heeny's enormous bag, spilling jars of face-cream and bundles of clippings on to the floor under the indulgent eyes of Mr and Mrs Spragg. Ralph, on his feet, watches his son anxiously, his expression constrained. Finally, Paul emerges from the bag with a sticky, fluff-encrusted piece of toffee, which he flourishes in brief triumph before tucking into it.

MRS HEENY That's right! And look, here's the clipping I was telling you about.

She picks up a battered cutting, holds it at arm's length and begins to read in her usual loud, unpunctuated monotone.

'It's no wonder the New York set in Paris has struck a livelier gait than ever with a sprinter like Pete Van Degen to set the pace and no one lags behind less than the fascinating Mrs Ralph Marvell who is to be seen nightly in all the smartest restaurants and naughtiest theatres with so many devoted swains in attendance that the rival beauties of both countries are making catty comments . . .'

RALPH I'd better be getting along. I'll collect him around six. Not too many candies, Paul.

MRS SPRAGG Now why do you suppose your old popper is so strict with you, eh?

Ralph's aware that Mr Spragg is looking up at him with considerable sympathy.

EXT. TERRACE OF THE NOUVEAU LUXE. NIGHT

The company has redeployed for coffee and takes up two tables in the softly lit formal gardens of the hotel. Undine has contrived to sit herself next to the Comte de Chelles, while Peter Van Degen, to his fairly obvious displeasure, finds himself at the other table talking to Bowen.

CHELLES I'm sorry, I didn't understand which of these gentlemen is your husband.

UNDINE My husband's not here, he's in New York.

CHELLES Diligently increasing the family fortune?

UNDINE I'd like to think so.

CHELLES If I had such an exquisite wife, I don't know if I would allow her to go to Paris without me.

UNDINE We're not so feudal in America.

CHELLES No, it always seems to me the great American ideal is to find a way to be respectable without being bored.

Undine finds this subject a little too theoretical to pursue. There's a pause, during which she becomes aware that Van Degen is glaring at her.

UNDINE So you're not married then?

CHELLES One knows it is something that has to come. Like death.

UNDINE Oh, mercy, it needn't be that bad.

CHELLES And, of course, one hears of nothing else at home.

He looks at her for a moment.

We have an old family place in Burgundy: I would like you to see it.

EXT. MALIBRAN HOTEL. DAY

Ralph walks up to the depressing facade of the hotel. It looks like a grain elevator. He vanishes into it.

INT. MALIBRAN HOTEL. DAY

Ralph advances into the hotel, across the scuffed linoleum of the foyer. All of a sudden he stops in his tracks, his expression dismayed.

His point of view: Paul, hanging on to Mrs Spragg's hand, is wearing a new outfit in kaleidoscopic tartan and a green velvet cap with a silver thistle.

MRS SPRAGG Go on, you show Poppa: we done a bitta shopping, didn't we?

RALPH Very nice.

The words have come out in a vicious undertone. He stoops to take Paul's hand.

MRS SPRAGG Wait a minute! You mustn't go without your piecer cake.

EXT. MALIBRAN HOTEL. DAY

As they emerge from the hotel, Ralph stoops again and gently removes from Paul's hand a glutinous chunk of cream cake, which he drops in a convenient trash can.

EXT. OPEN CARRIAGE. DAY

Undine sits with Indiana Rolliver, clattering through the Burgundian countryside in a heavy brougham. The carriage swings round a long bend and Undine's eyes widen as she reaches for Indiana's arm.

UNDINE Oh, my God, Indiana, that can't be it, can it?

EXT. THE CHATEAU DE SAINT DÉSERT. DAY

A huge rectangular château with towers at the corners and crenellated walls, surrounded by a moat. The carriage, tiny against the high walls, travels down an avenue of poplars, clatters across the drawbridge and under the portcullis and draws up in the spacious courtyard beyond. Undine and Indiana look at one another, entranced. An old male steward helps the ladies down from the carriage, by which time the tall, imposing figure of the Comte de Chelles is bearing down on them across the courtyard.

INT. THE LONG GALLERY AT THE CHATEAU DE SAINT DÉSERT. DAY

Undine gasps as she's shown into the long upstairs gallery, which overlooks the moat and the avenue of poplars, not least because of the extraordinary series of tapestries of mythological scenes after Boucher which stretch away down the length of the inside wall. Chelles watches, quietly enjoying the reactions of Undine and Indiana. Indiana gestures vaguely at the tapestries, not quite sure how to describe them.

INDIANA Why, these . . . ah, are amazing.

CHELLES The tapestries? They were given to my family by Louis XV himself.

UNDINE What a beautiful room!

CHELLES I love to show friends around the château. And since my parents, the Marquis and Marquise, are not here this week, you will have to accept me as your guide.

UNDINE I think we can accommodate to that, don't you, Indiana?

They follow him as he progresses down the gallery, suppressing with some difficulty the desire to giggle.

INT. RALPH'S BEDROOM IN THE WASHINGTON SQUARE HOUSE. DAY

Popple's finished portrait of Undine, the pearls suitably enlarged. Another angle reveals Ralph, sitting quite still, staring at the portrait with a perplexed expression. Eventually, his lips tighten, he tears his eyes away from the picture, rises and picks up the telephone.

INT. CHINESE DRAWING ROOM IN THE VAN DEGEN MANSION. EVENING

The smaller drawing room in Peter Van Degen's Fifth Avenue palazzo is full of Chinoiserie: vases, camphorwood chests, lacquer screens, everything black and red and gold. Clare sits in a low armchair with the light behind her; and Ralph sits nearby in the corner of a sofa.

CLARE Why haven't you been to see me before?

RALPH I wasn't sure you were still in town.

CLARE I suppose it's difficult for you to get away.

RALPH My partners work me very hard. They know I can't afford to lose the job.

He looks away for a moment, reflecting.

I'd never realised before how murderous uncongenial work could be.

CLARE How do you like being back at your grandfather's house?

RALPH It's strange. And of course unnecessary, since this man Undine found to rent our house came unstuck on Wall Street and has vanished without paying the rent.

CLARE I'm afraid he was Peter's recommendation.

RALPH So I gathered.

There's a slight pause, before Clare asks her unavoidable question.

CLARE How is Undine?

RALPH I don't know, I haven't heard from her in a while. Only thing that's certain is she won't be very pleased with me.

CLARE Why do you say that?

RALPH I've had to ask her to come back: the money's run out.

CLARE Oh, Ralph.

She stretches out her hand to him and he takes it. Their eyes meet for a moment; but then Ralph sighs and looks away.

INT. UNDINE'S SUITE AT THE RITZ. EVENING

Undine stands looking out of the window at the Place Vendôme below, when the door suddenly bursts open and Van Degen, flushed and agitated, is in the room.

UNDINE Didn't anyone ever teach you to knock?

VAN DEGEN Where have you been?

UNDINE I asked Céleste to telephone you.

VAN DEGEN Couldn't you have done that yourself?

UNDINE Chelles invited me down to his château in Burgundy. I went off in rather a rush.

VAN DEGEN You went to stay with Chelles?

UNDINE I had Indiana with me.

VAN DEGEN Indiana! Don't you know what that means over here, going to stay with a man?

UNDINE I've always been unconventional, you know that.

She looks at him shrewdly, seizing the opportunity he's given her.

And at least he isn't married.

Van Degen flushes an even deeper colour and begins to bluster.

VAN DEGEN What difference does that make?

Undine looks at him coolly and he looks away, momentarily at a loss. Undine decides to press her advantage.

UNDINE I don't see what difference any of it makes, since Ralph has ordered me home next week.

VAN DEGEN Ordered you home? But you can't go!

UNDINE It's no use saying things like that. I sail on Wednesday.

She looks up at him, her expression candid.

I'm a poor man's wife.

INT. SUBWAY CAR. DAY

Ralph hangs from a strap in the crowded carriage. It's obviously a hot day outside, but Ralph's face is streaming with sweat in a quite conspicuous way. He looks greenish, exhausted; his eyes are closed.

INT. FRONT HALL AND STAIRCASE IN THE WASHINGTON SQUARE HOUSE. DAY

Ralph moves unsteadily across the black and white flagstones of the front hall and begins climbing the stairs. He's halfway up when Paul

emerges from one of the first-floor rooms and runs towards him with cries of delight. Ralph kneels to take the child in his arms and submits to his kisses; but as he starts to rise, something happens in his head and he overbalances and collapses. The little boy looks down at him for a moment, and then begins to wail; whereupon his nurse, Mrs Marvell and Laura Fairford appear from various quarters, converging on Ralph's prone form. Mrs Marvell scoops up Paul and turns to the nurse.

MRS MARVELL Tell Jones to fetch the doctor right away.

The nurse hurries away, as Ralph comes to with a groan.

RALPH What happened?

MRS MARVELL You're to go straight to bed.

MRS FAIRFORD Can you get up?

She helps him up; he's extremely shaky and still streaming with sweat.

MRS MARVELL The doctor will be here soon.

RALPH Will you send a telegram to Undine?

MRS MARVELL She's sailing in a day or two, isn't she?

RALPH Please, I want her to know.

MRS FAIRFORD I'll do it.

She starts to help Ralph up the remainder of the stairs.

INT. UNDINE'S SUITE AT THE RITZ. DAY

As before, the suite is full to overflowing with clothes and boxes and half-packed trunks. Peter Van Degen stands among them, at a loss to know which way to turn. Undine watches him from her position over by the window.

VAN DEGEN Won't you at least have dinner with me if this is your last evening?

UNDINE I can't.

VAN DEGEN Are you dining with Chelles, is that it?

UNDINE I don't like to be cross-examined.

VAN DEGEN It's not too late to change your mind, you know. I could easily make it all right for you to stay.

UNDINE By paying my bills, you mean? I'm not going to make that mistake again.

VAN DEGEN But you can't go back to that deadly life!

UNDINE You're right, something's going to have to change.

Van Degen considers this remark for a moment, frowning.

VAN DEGEN You're not thinking of marrying Chelles, are you?

UNDINE I'll never forgive you if you tell anyone.

VAN DEGEN You mean you are? My God!

There's a knock at the door and a concierge enters with a telegram, which he hands to Undine. She tears open the blue slip, pulls out the cable and reads.

Inset: the cable says RALPH DANGEROUSLY ILL DOUBLE PNEUMONIA. DOCTORS ADVISE YOUR IMMEDIATE RETURN. GOOD WISHES. LAURA FAIRFORD.

Undine looks up from the telegram, a spark of anger in her eyes.

VAN DEGEN What is it?

UNDINE Nothing.

VAN DEGEN You're white as a sheet.

UNDINE It's from Laura Fairford. She says Ralph wants me home.

VAN DEGEN What business is it of hers?

UNDINE Exactly. As if I wasn't going back anyhow!

VAN DEGEN Is that all she says?

UNDINE Yes.

She crumples up the telegram and throws it into the waste-paper basket. Van Degen stares at her for a moment, his face working.

VAN DEGEN Come down with me to Trouville. I'll take a villa.

UNDINE Kiss me goodbye, Peter.

He crosses to her and takes her in his arms, leaning to give her a long kiss on the lips. Finally, she breaks away, evading him as he tries to repeat the kiss.

And now you must go.

VAN DEGEN Is that all you have to say?

UNDINE There can't be anything else as things stand.

He turns abruptly and stamps over to the door, passing out into a kind of ante-chamber, where he picks up his hat and stick. Undine watches him, tense and motionless in the centre of the room. For a long moment, Van Degen stands in the outer room, head down, with his back to her. Then, suddenly, he throws down his hat and stick, turns and strides back into the room.

VAN DEGEN I'll do anything you want, Undine. Anything in God's world.

He flings his arms round her; and this time she lets him kiss her again and plant feverish kisses all over her face and throat. She doesn't even resist as he begins to tear clumsily at her clothes.

INT. RALPH'S BEDROOM IN THE WASHINGTON SQUARE HOUSE. DAY

Undine's portrait slowly swims into focus. It's seen from Ralph's point of view: he's lying in bed, drawn and emaciated, but obviously on the road to recovery. A nurse is moving purposefully around the room; and Laura Fairford sits nearby, reading a book.

RALPH Laura.

Mrs Fairford looks up, surprised. She puts her book down hurriedly and moves over to sit next to Ralph, taking his hand.

MRS FAIRFORD Ralph. How are you feeling?

RALPH How long have I been here?

MRS FAIRFORD Nearly two months, Ralph. We've been very worried about you.

RALPH Call Undine.

Mrs Fairford doesn't answer for the moment: she looks very constrained.

I'd like to see her.

MRS FAIRFORD She's not here right now.

RALPH Out shopping, is she?

He manages a tired smile: but Mrs Fairford looks grimmer than ever.

MRS FAIRFORD No. I mean she never came back.

Ralph impels himself up on to one elbow.

RALPH But where is she?

INT. SPRAGG'S OFFICE. DAY

Spragg, looking fagged and sallow, stares across his desk at Ralph.

SPRAGG Well, right around now, I imagine she's somewhere between Chicago and Omaha.

RALPH I don't understand.

SPRAGG Enn rowt to Dakota.

RALPH Are you trying to tell me Undine's in the United States?

SPRAGG Well, let's see now, I think they made Dakota a state, didn't they?

Ralph springs violently to his feet, causing Spragg to react by removing his own feet from the waste-paper basket.

RALPH She's with another man.

SPRAGG My daughter is not that style, sir. She's travelling on her own and she's on her way to file her decree. I believe in such cases the usual plea is desertion.

RALPH You mean Undine's divorcing me? For *desertion*?

He bursts out laughing. Spragg looks at him, extremely uncomfortable. Ralph stops laughing, suddenly, and flushes with sudden passion.

Does she imagine I'm going to give in without a fight?

Spragg looks thoughtful: he rises carefully to his feet.

SPRAGG I assume you know as well as I do that once Undine's set on a thing, it ain't so easy to change her.

Ralph's mind is racing: he stands there, lost in thought, ignoring Spragg, who stands, jingling the loose change in his trouser pocket. Suddenly, Ralph comes to himself with a start and seizes his hat. Slightly to his surprise, Spragg intercepts him, putting a hand on his sleeve.

SPRAGG I'd'a given anything, short of my girl herself, not to have this happen to you, Ralph Marvell.

RALPH Thank you, sir.

He shakes hands with Spragg.

SPRAGG But it *has* happened. And you'd do well to bear that in mind.

INT. RALPH'S BEDROOM IN THE WASHINGTON SQUARE HOUSE. EVENING

Ralph sits, as before, staring at Undine's portrait. Then, abruptly, he jumps up and begins to move around the room collecting up the various framed photographs of Undine, all different shapes and sizes, which stand on the mantelpiece and bookshelves or hang on the wall. When he has them all, he manages to open a more or less empty drawer in a large chest; then he bundles them all in and, not without some difficulty, closes the drawer. After this, he turns his attention back to the portrait itself; getting it down from the wall is an easy enough matter, but where else is it to go? Ralph turns, holding the painting in his outstretched arms to consider one potential site after another.

Finally, all he can think to do is to jam the picture behind the monumental wardrobe in which his suits and topcoats hang.

INT. THE SPRAGGS' ROOM AT THE MALIBRAN HOTEL. EVENING

A kind of partition between sitting room and bedroom constitutes an attempt to confer on the Spraggs' quarters the status of a suite: it's abundantly clear, however, why they now choose to receive downstairs. Mr Spragg sits in one of the cavernous armchairs, his feet up on a low table, idly scanning the newspaper; while Mrs Spragg, more industrious, sits at a round table playing solitaire. Both are considerably startled by a soft knock at the door.

Eventually, Mr Spragg folds his newspaper and crosses to open the door. Undine is standing outside, obviously in a state of real agitation, sheathed in uncharacteristically dull travelling clothes, carrying a holdall. She surges into the room as Mrs Spragg, very alarmed, rises to her feet.

UNDINE He wasn't there!

MRS SPRAGG Who wasn't there?

UNDINE He promised faithfully he'd meet me in Chicago. We were going out to Reno to get married, after our divorces had come through.

SPRAGG Hold up a minute . . .

UNDINE Now what am I going to do?

She drops her holdall and Spragg enfolds her in his arms; her body is shaking with silent sobs.

INT. ATTORNEY'S OFFICE. DAY

The attorney, a grey, reedy figure, looks across his desk at Ralph and Laura Fairford; he holds a document in his hand.

ATTORNEY So you have no wish to contest these charges?

RALPH I simply want to turn my back on the whole business.

MRS FAIRFORD My brother is anxious not to make a scandal. For the child's sake.

ATTORNEY Quite. Well, in that case, you have only to abstain from any further action, which means, among other things, that you will have no need of my services. And the law will take its course.

RALPH Fine.

INT. DINING ROOM AT THE MALIBRAN HOTEL. DAY

The insalubriousness of the basement dining room at the Malibran seems to have had no effect on Mr Spragg's appetite and he's resolutely tackling an enormous plateful under Mrs Spragg's fond gaze, when Undine arrives at the table in one of her more eye-catching outfits. Mr Spragg looks up at her in surprise.

SPRAGG You're up early today, Undine.

UNDINE I want to go to the opera this evening.

She takes a seat at the table, as her parents look at her in surprise.

SPRAGG I suppose nothing less than a box will do?

UNDINE No. Two stalls will be quite sufficient. And you're to come with me, it's *Cavaleeria* this evening, you'll enjoy that.

INT. FOYER AT THE METROPOLITAN OPERA HOUSE. NIGHT

The opera is over and the stockholders' entrance is congested with chattering groups in cloaks, furs and jewels. Undine, wearing her pearls and a sensational evening dress moves slowly with her father in his battered old dress-suit, through the crowds, attracting a great deal of attention.

UNDINE I told you you'd enjoy it, it does you good to get out once in a while.

Spragg doesn't answer; he's uncomfortably aware that Undine is the focus of much discreet pointing and whispering; while, at the same time, people who know her and sense she's about to greet them are turning their backs on her and pretending not to see her. Finally, she finds herself almost nose to nose with Claud Popple, who has some fearsome dowager on his arm.

Mr Popple.

POPPLE Is that your footman over there? I can never remember what the fellow looks like.

And so saying, blushing, but ignoring Undine completely, he steers his substantial escort towards the exit. Spragg takes Undine's arm and, mustering all the dignity he can, moves her resolutely away from the crowd.

EXT. CENTRAL PARK. NIGHT

It's snowy again; the cab trundles through the park.

INT. CAB. NIGHT

Undine is lost in her own thoughts; presently, Spragg turns to her.

SPRAGG Did your husband give you those pearls?

Undine gives a snort of derision.

UNDINE Ralph?

SPRAGG Then I guess you better send them back to the party they belong to.

UNDINE They belong to me!

SPRAGG You send them back to Peter Van Degen first thing in the morning! You hear me?

Undine's too taken aback to protest or even answer.

INT. UNDINE'S ROOM AT THE MALIBRAN. DAY

Undine's still in bed, the curtains are drawn and the breakfast tray is untouched: the room is a mere bedroom. The string of pearls lies forlornly on the small bedside table. There's a knock at the door.

UNDINE It's open.

Mrs Heeny, clutching her giant handbag, lets herself into the room.

MRS HEENY Land sakes, Undine! Do you know what time it is? And you look's if you been sitting up all night with a remains.

Undine picks up the pearls and flourishes them at Mrs Heeny.

UNDINE I want you to take these and . . .

MRS HEENY Take 'em? Why, good land alive, that's a fortune you got there in your hand.

Undine frowns in thought as Mrs Heeny reverently handles the pearls.

UNDINE What do you suppose I could get for them?

MRS HEENY Well, let's see now . . .

UNDINE I want you to sell them for me. Get the very best price you possibly can.

Mrs Heeny weighs them for a moment in her palm. Then, with a wolfish smile, she drops them into the depths of her bag.

MRS HEENY Don't you worry; there'll be others.

INT. SUITE AT THE HOTEL NOUVEAU LUXE IN PARIS. DAY

The vast gilded drawing room is reminiscent of the vulgar splendours of the Stentorian, with two high baskets of orchids as centrepieces.

Undine lifts her teacup under the benevolent and patronising eye of Mrs Indiana Rolliver.

INDIANA I do admire your enterprise; I'd never have the gumption to set off for Europe without Mr Rolliver by.

UNDINE I came into a little money and I thought it might be amusing to rent a small apartment. I do love Paris so; and I wanted to exorcise all the bad memories of last year.

Indiana shakes her head sympathetically.

INDIANA If only you'd come straight to me, I could have given you one tip right off: and that's to get your divorce first thing. You should have attended to that before you *began* with Peter Van Degen.

UNDINE I've never been calculating like that.

INDIANA All the same, it's a golden rule: never *never* give way to your feelings before you get your divorce.

She considers Undine shrewdly for a moment.

There isn't anybody else, is there?

UNDINE Anybody else?

INDIANA You know, now you've got your divorce, anybody else it could come in handy for?

UNDINE It's Mr Van Degen's responsibility . . .

INDIANA Yes, sure, I know that, but that's just talk. So if there is anybody else . . .

UNDINE I just know if I could see him one more time, I could make it all right . . .

Silence, as Indiana turns this over in her mind.

INDIANA Well, then, why don't Mr Rolliver and I just ask him to dinner, you know, without telling him beforehand: and there you'll be!

UNDINE Oh, Indiana, would you do that for me?

INDIANA We Apex girls should stick together.

UNDINE If there's ever anything I can do in return; anything at all!

INDIANA Just one thing. You know poor Millard Binch was crazy about you till the day he died: so I'd be much obliged if you'd keep your hands off Mr Rolliver.

INT. TEA ROOM IN THE RUE DE RIVOLI. DAY

Undine and Indiana are at a table near the door: so they can't fail to notice the commotion caused by a couple steering an ancient lady through the narrow entrance to the fashionable tea room. The man is the Comte de Chelles; and the moment he sees Undine he's bowing over her hand and, with markedly less enthusiasm, Indiana's.

CHELLES Ladies! Allow me to present my great-aunt, the Duchesse de Dordogne, and my cousin, the Princesse Estradina. *Ma tante, ce sont les dames américaines que j'ai invitées au château pendant l'été, Mme Marvell et Mme . . .*

INDIANA Rolliver.

CHELLES Rolliver, *c'est ça.*

DUCHESSE *Il faut les inviter,* Raymond.

CHELLES *Oui, bien sûr.* My aunt is at home on Thursday afternoons; she would be, we would all be, very happy to see you. I will leave a card at your *hôtel.*

INDIANA I'm at the Nouveau Luxe.

CHELLES *Parfait.* How nice to meet you again.

The group moves off, the aged Duchesse complaining volubly about something or other; Indiana leans forward, her eyes shining.

INDIANA Well, was he pleased to see you!

Undine has not failed to notice this; but at the moment, she has more important matters on her mind.

UNDINE Indiana, I hate to be persistent about this, but have you spoken to Mr Van Degen?

Indiana sits back in her chair, suddenly embarrassed.

INDIANA I'm sorry, I've been meaning to tell you; the dinner's off, I'm afraid.

UNDINE You told him I was going to be there?

INDIANA He asked point-blank, you know, knowing we were friends; and I couldn't very well deny it.

UNDINE And he doesn't want to see me?

Indiana shakes her head, visibly troubled.

Did he give you a reason?

INDIANA You'll hate me if I tell you.

UNDINE If you don't, I'm going to go straight off to his hotel . . .

INDIANA You mustn't do that!

UNDINE Then tell me now!

Indiana sighs. She looks away. Finally she speaks in a mumble.

INDIANA It was something he found out about you . . .

UNDINE About me?

INDIANA Something to do with the way you treated your husband.

UNDINE The way I treated Ralph?

INDIANA It was one particular thing. He says the day you went off with him, you'd had a cable saying Mr Marvell was desperately ill.

UNDINE How did he know?

Now it's Indiana's turn to be shocked.

INDIANA You mean it's true? Oh, Undine . . .

Undine's mind is furiously racing; she ignores Indiana's protestations.

I'd never have believed it was true.

UNDINE Who told him?

INDIANA Your husband's sister sent him a cable saying you'd never answered the one she sent you, and would he ask you to go back?

UNDINE He never did.

INDIANA He said he knew you didn't want to go.

UNDINE How?

INDIANA He said he asked you when the first cable came what was in it and you said not a thing.

UNDINE So he knew about it all along.

INDIANA And he said in the end, when you were away, he got to thinking: how would she be to me, if I was dying?

Silence: eventually, Indiana nervously feels the need to extract a moral.

Men have their feelings too, Undine . . .

She breaks off as Undine raises her head and glares fiercely at her.

INT. RECEPTION ROOMS AT THE HOTEL DE DORDOGNE. DAY

A footman leads a palpably impressed Undine and Indiana through an extraordinary series of gilded rooms opening on to one another. At the end of the long perspective sits the Duchesse de Dordogne in a wheelchair surrounded by her guests; and as Undine and Indiana approach, pausing to glance at cabinets full of Sèvres china or painted ceilings, the Conte de Chelles detaches himself from his great-aunt's side and comes hurrying to greet them. Once again, he's unable to disguise his partiality for Undine; it's her hand he grasps first.

CHELLES It's so wonderful you were able to come.

EXT. TERRACE OF THE NOUVEAU LUXE. NIGHT

As before, Undine and Chelles sit next to each other on the fringes of a large and raucous throng. He is gazing at her with an almost comic intensity.

UNDINE This is where we first met, do you remember?

CHELLES How could I ever forget it?

He leans a little closer to her.

I know you don't live here at the *hôtel*. Won't you allow me to escort you back to your apartment?

UNDINE It's very gallant of you, but I don't think I can accept.

CHELLES Why not?

UNDINE It's so easy for a woman in my position to be talked about. I have my little boy to consider.

Chelles inclines his head, disappointed but respectful.

INT. THE ROLLIVER SUITE AT THE HOTEL NOUVEAU LUXE. NIGHT

Representative James J. Rolliver lolls back asleep in his armchair, his mouth open, emitting occasional gulping snores. Indiana and Undine, meanwhile, are on the sofa, engrossed in confidential discussion.

INDIANA Everything but marriage, my dear.

UNDINE I don't understand why you say that.

INDIANA For one thing, the family will want a religious marriage.

UNDINE Of course: it's such a beautiful religion.

INDIANA Maybe, but it doesn't recognise divorce. And a man of position in France could never go through a civil marriage with a divorced woman: he'd ruin himself and her. That's why they have so many . . . arrangements over here.

UNDINE Arrangements?

INDIANA You know, provided appearances are kept up, people in France are very indulgent . . .

UNDINE Really, Indiana, how can you even suggest such a thing? I've made that mistake once already.

INDIANA I know, I'm just explaining the way the French look at things.

UNDINE I don't care how they look at things, Indiana, I'm an American.

INT. UNDINE'S APARTMENT NEAR LES INVALIDES. DAY

Undine looks up, surprised, as Chelles is shown into the room by Céleste. It's a pleasant, airy room with a balcony, up at tree-top level, looking out on to a row of horse chestnuts.

CHELLES I am sorry to make this intrusion on you, but it's something very important.

UNDINE I was expecting to see you at the Duchesse's this afternoon.

CHELLES Yes, this is why I am here. To ask you not to come this afternoon.

UNDINE Why not?

CHELLES Because my mother will be there.

Undine's expression hardens.

UNDINE I don't understand.

CHELLES You see, my mother would be very upset if she were to meet you there.

UNDINE Why?

CHELLES Because she knows I love you.

Silence. They look at each other for a moment.

UNDINE I take it she didn't mind when I visited the château last year?

CHELLES That was different. Then you were married: now you are divorced.

UNDINE I see.

She's upset, which she tries to conceal with as cold an expression as she can muster.

CHELLES I know you are not like other women and I respect you for it.

UNDINE It's a shame your mother can't feel the same respect.

CHELLES If it were possible, you know I would ask you to be my wife.

UNDINE Would you?

CHELLES Of course. Of course.

He's taken her hand: now, as she looks at him, obviously troubled, he leans towards her; but she pulls away from him.

UNDINE No. I can't.

Chelles lowers his head, baffled.

Isn't there any way we could be married?

CHELLES Only if your marriage was annulled. This has to be done by the Pope himself. And it's an expensive, I mean, a very expensive procedure.

UNDINE But it could be done?

CHELLES Yes; in theory.

He looks up at her, his eyes full of longing.

UNDINE I'd hate to be the cause of any disagreement in your family.

CHELLES I knew you would understand.

UNDINE And I'm sure you'll understand, but in the circumstances it will be impossible for me to continue to receive your visits.

Chelles looks up at her, shocked.

INT. THE ROLLIVER SUITE AT THE HOTEL NOUVEAU LUXE. DAY

Indiana looks at Undine in astonishment.

INDIANA Annulled? But that's an absolutely insane idea.

UNDINE Why?

INDIANA You don't imagine it would make the slightest bit of difference to his family?

UNDINE I don't see how they could prevent it.

INDIANA Yes, but . . . who's put this notion into your head?

UNDINE Raymond himself.

INT. FOYER OF THE HOTEL NOUVEAU LUXE. DAY

Undine's preoccupied as she sweeps across the foyer; so she doesn't notice the stocky, well-scrubbed figure of Elmer Moffatt, until he cheerily intercepts her.

MOFFATT Well, don't this beat the band?

UNDINE Elmer!

MOFFATT I'm on my way to talk a little business with our friend Representative Rolliver.

UNDINE I thought you'd fallen out with him.

MOFFATT No, no. He and your father don't have much love lost; but I kept myself well in the background that time.

UNDINE Well, he's out at the moment, so unless you want to talk to Indiana . . .

MOFFATT No, I was always able to take Indiana or leave her alone.

They smile at each other; and she's taken by a sudden impulse.

UNDINE Why don't you come back and have tea with me?

EXT. OPEN TAXI. DAY

The taxi whirls through the crowded streets of Paris.

MOFFATT Don't Paris just about beat everything?

UNDINE How well do you know it?

MOFFATT Oh, this is my very first look round.

He looks across at her.

Are you settled here now? I saw in the papers . . .

UNDINE Yes, it was a mistake from the beginning.

MOFFATT I never thought he was your form.

INT. UNDINE'S APARTMENT. DAY

Moffatt sits astride a lyre-back chair, concentrating the considerable energy of his attention on the problem Undine has put to him.

MOFFATT And you think if you could get a-hold of enough cash, you could fix the whole thing up with the Pope?

UNDINE So it seems.

MOFFATT Well, if I wasn't stone broke, I'd send the old gentleman my cheque in the morning.

UNDINE You couldn't manage to borrow some for me?

MOFFATT Right now I can't even seem to borrow any for myself.

She watches him, disappointed, as he rises and moves around the room, his quick eyes curiously darting. He picks up a photograph of Paul from an ornate little writing desk.

Long pants already! I declare!

UNDINE I can't tell you how much I miss him.

A thought strikes Moffatt: he works on it for a moment, eyes narrowed.

MOFFATT Who does he belong to?

UNDINE Belong to?

MOFFATT When you were divorced, who got him?

UNDINE Well, I did, but I couldn't afford to have him here.

MOFFATT If he was mine and you tried to get him away from me, I'd fight down to my last dollar.

UNDINE I haven't a dollar to fight with.

MOFFATT You're not following my thought. You ain't got to fight. He's yours. So why don't you send right over for him?

UNDINE I told you, I –

She breaks off: she's beginning to see what he's getting at. He resumes his position on the lyre-back chair, staring at her intently.

His father would never give him up.

MOFFATT That's what I'm saying. So all you got to do is sit tight and wait for the cheque.

They look at each other for a moment: Moffatt frank and Undine uneasy.

INT. FRONT HALL IN THE WASHINGTON SQUARE HOUSE. EVENING

Ralph lets himself in at the front door. He crosses the hall and gathers up his day's mail from its usual spot on the hall table. At which point, Mrs Marvell appears. He turns to greet her cheerfully, but the words die on his lips as he sees that she's obviously very agitated about something.

RALPH Is something the matter?

MRS MARVELL I've had a very strange telephone call from some woman with a name like Heeny. About Paul.

RALPH What did she say?

MRS MARVELL She said would I pack a trunk for him, because she's been asked to collect him on Saturday and take him over to Paris.

Some instinct causes Ralph to look down at the letters in his hand; one of them has a somewhat official appearance and he breaks it open and runs an eye hurriedly over the contents, which cause him to utter an involuntary murmur.

RALPH Sole custody . . .

MRS MARVELL What did you say?

He looks up at his mother, shocked but resolute.

RALPH What day of the week is it?
MRS MARVELL Wednesday.

INT. CAB. EVENING
As the cab rattles up Fifth Avenue, Ralph leans forward to rap impatiently on the partition with his stick.
RALPH Fast as you can, please!

EXT. EAST 62ND STREET. EVENING
Ralph stands outside a neat brownstone; presently, the front door is opened by the attorney consulted by Ralph about the divorce; he seems startled to see Ralph.
ATTORNEY Mr Marvell.
RALPH I'm sorry to trouble you at home, it's rather urgent.
ATTORNEY You'd better come in.

INT. STUDY IN THE ATTORNEY'S HOUSE. EVENING
The attorney looks up from the letter Ralph has given him.
ATTORNEY You see, the case is closed, I really don't know what grounds there might be to re-open it.
RALPH It says she's planning to remarry.
ATTORNEY Well, that would generally be regarded as something advantageous to the child.
Silence. Ralph gnaws at his lip.
Once you chose not to contest the case . . . it's a poor outlook, I'm afraid. The best you could hope is to arrange to see your boy at stated intervals.
Ralph still doesn't speak; he looks across at the attorney, despair in his eyes.

EXT. FIFTH AVENUE. EVENING
Ralph turns into Fifth Avenue, moving blindly through the soft summer twilight, his eyes bright with tears.

EXT. THE VAN DEGEN MANSION. EVENING
Ralph stands for a moment outside the imposing bulk of the Van Degen house. Then he summons his resolve, approaches and rings the doorbell. After a while, the door is opened by a tail-coated butler.
RALPH I was hoping to find Mrs Van Degen in.

INT. CHINESE DRAWING ROOM IN THE VAN DEGEN MANSION. EVENING

Ralph, under the sympathetic eye of Clare Van Degen, is quivering with rage and indignation.

RALPH I'll fight it, I don't care what it costs, I'll fight every inch of the way!

Clare considers him for a moment.

CLARE But if there's no prospect of winning, wouldn't it be better to offer the money directly to Undine?

Ralph looks at her, extremely surprised.

Why do you suppose she's suddenly decided she wants Paul?

RALPH He'll be living proof that she was always in the right. He'll give her the appearance of respectability.

CLARE You're like me, Ralph, you're hopelessly old-fashioned. I don't believe Undine cares a straw for the appearance of respectability. I think what she's after is the money for her annulment.

Ralph thinks about this: his incredulity slowly begins to dissolve.

RALPH You mean to say she wants me to buy Paul back from her?

CLARE Yes: and if I know her, she won't want to demean herself by selling him cheap.

He looks at her, bewildered; and she meets his gaze candidly.

So you must let me help.

INT. VESTIBULE OF THE ARARAT TRUST BUILDING. DAY

Ralph is not, as might be assumed, on his way to see Mr Spragg. Instead, he consults the directory carved into a black marble tablet, until he finds the name of Moffatt.

INT. MOFFATT'S OFFICE. DAY

It's a surprisingly well-appointed office, not the shabby, old-fashioned utilitarianism of Spragg's quarters, but a cool arrangement of blue leather armchairs and well-stocked mahogany bookcases. One of the bookshelves contains a row of exquisite Gallé vases. Moffatt sits behind his 'Washington' desk radiating bonhomie, as Ralph shifts uneasily in the depths of one of the armchairs.

MOFFATT A hundred thousand dollars.

RALPH Yes: and by the end of the month.

MOFFATT Well, I guess there isn't a sane man between here and San Francisco who isn't after that kind of a killing. But you did me a good turn and it is a first-rate time to buy right now. Now can you put up fifty?

RALPH I think so.

MOFFATT I reckon I can double that for you in three weeks. I can try, anyhow. Only don't tell the other girls.

He gets up, moves over to the bookshelf and picks up one of the vases, which he holds up to the light.

You like this?

Ralph makes some sort of polite sound of assent.

I must admit I have a weakness for pretty things.

There's something slightly menacing in the way he says this. Ralph doesn't notice, however, having hit on a way to extend the conversation.

RALPH I was afraid you might not be back from Washington.

MOFFATT Well, they thought I was going to be principal canary in the Harmon B. Driscoll Investigation. But do you know, when I got there, I found I couldn't remember a thing. And it looks as if it might turn out to have been an exceptionally profitable lapse of memory.

RALPH I'll try to let you have the money within forty-eight hours.

MOFFATT You better think it over.

RALPH No, I'll take your word for it.

He's rising to his feet. Moffatt smiles pleasantly at him.

MOFFATT How's that boy of yours? Last time I saw him, he was a stunning little chap.

Ralph is taken aback and slightly puzzled by this: but he manages a civil enough reply.

RALPH He's fine, thank you.

MOFFATT Good, good.

INT. PRINCIPAL DRAWING ROOM IN THE VAN DEGEN MANSION. DAY

The Van Degens' main room is a vast tapestried and gilded wilderness and Clare is perched on a high-backed sofa, beneath Popple's monumental portrait of her, in front of a low table groaning with gold plate. Facing her, as another angle will later reveal, is an equally massive painting of Peter Van Degen. Ralph is on his feet moving around the room, suffering his usual constraint when it comes to discussing money.

RALPH My grandfather understands the situation; he's released some money to me, which is my share of his estate.

CLARE But I've taken out twenty thousand dollars. I'll be very unhappy if you won't take it.

RALPH I couldn't.

CLARE Why not, it's my money, it's not his.

RALPH Supposing things went wrong?

CLARE If I've given it to you, what can possibly go wrong?

In her vehemence, she's risen and gone over to him; and they're now standing beneath the giant portrait of Van Degen. Suddenly Ralph takes Clare in his arms: he kisses her passionately and her response is eager. But a moment later, he detaches himself, once again afflicted by his embarrassed reticence.

RALPH Thank you, thank you! I accept.

CLARE Whatever I can do, Ralph. You just have to ask.

INT. OFFICES OF THE PLYMOUTH ROCK REALTY COMPANY. DAY

Ralph looks edgy and preoccupied: he looks around, checks the coast is clear and reaches for the telephone.

INT. MOFFATT'S OFFICE. DAY

There are a number of dark-suited, faintly alarming men in Moffatt's office, including the ox-like Representative Rolliver. The atmosphere is sombre. Moffatt, however, speaks into his phone with his usual confident good humour.

MOFFATT No, everything's first-rate . . . little bit of a hiccup last week, may hold us up a week or so; but we ought to be able to open a bottle of wine by the tenth.

He makes a face, for the benefit of his colleagues, conveying the thought: 'What else am I supposed to say?'

EXT. LONG ISLAND SHORELINE. DAY

A yacht glides into the landing stage at the end of the rolling lawn which runs down to the Sound from the Van Degens' summer house, a glittering white extravaganza, shimmering in a sunset glow. Ralph ties up, lifts Paul tenderly, depositing him on the landing stage, then jumps out himself to help Clare out of the boat. Paul sets off towards the house at a run, leaving them to stroll arm-in-arm up the lawn behind him.

CLARE There's something on your mind, something you haven't told me about.

Ralph hesitates; then decides to come clean.

RALPH Henley told me he'd heard talk in his office that Moffatt's consortium isn't going to get its charter.

CLARE And that would mean . . .?

RALPH I wouldn't be able to pay off Undine.

They walk on a few paces in silence.

CLARE You know how unreliable these Wall Street rumours can be.

Ralph brightens.

RALPH You're right. Besides, I have a feeling about this. I just know it's going to be all right.

CLARE And perhaps it might be the beginning of a new life for both of us.

Ralph smiles at her tenderly. Up ahead, silhouetted against the white palace in the dying light, the little boy turns and waves to them; there's something valedictory in the gesture.

INT. MOFFATT'S OFFICE. DAY

Close on another Gallé vase, a new acquisition, delicately turned to catch the light in Moffatt's chunky hand. He sits, calm, opposite the obviously distraught Ralph.

MOFFATT Well, I'm sorry. I don't how it leaked out; but somehow those reformers got a smell of what was going on and whenever they get to swishing around . . .

RALPH Do you mean to say the scheme's not going through?

MOFFATT Nope. We're high and dry.

RALPH So has the stock dropped?

MOFFATT Well, let me put it this way: you got to lean over to see it. But we'll get our charter in the end.

RALPH When will that be?

MOFFATT Oh, next year, I guess.

RALPH Next year? What earthly good is that to me?

MOFFATT I don't say it's as pleasant as driving your best girl home by moonlight. But it's safe enough.

RALPH You knew I had to have the money now.

MOFFATT I knew you *wanted* the money now. So did I.

RALPH You never warned me it was going to be risky.

MOFFATT I don't call it so risky lying back in your chair and waiting a few months for fifty thousand dollars to drop in your lap.

RALPH Well, I think you've misled me.

For the first time, Moffatt's equanimity slips a little: he flushes a dangerous-looking red.

MOFFATT Well, I'm in it a good deal deeper than you are: and if you get stuck, so do I.

Ralph's face crumples a little, as he acknowledges the logic of this.

RALPH I can't wait, you see.

Moffatt looks across at him with a kind of weary sympathy; and waits.

You spoke about my boy the other day . . .

MOFFATT I should say: as smart a little chap as I ever saw.

RALPH Well, you see, my wife, when we separated . . .

MOFFATT She got sole custody?

Ralph looks up, nodding miserably, surprised at the speed of Moffatt's deduction, but not disposed to query it. Moffatt ponders, his expression grave.

So that's what you want the money for?

RALPH Yes.

Moffatt half-swings round in his revolving chair and contemplates the tips of his shiny boots.

MOFFATT And why you want it in such a hurry?

RALPH I don't think she'll wait . . . or take less . . .

Moffatt looks up at him for a moment, scrutinising him through half-closed lids.

MOFFATT No: I don't believe Undine Spragg'll take a single cent less.

Ralph whitens. Then he rises to his feet, his expression fiercely indignant.

RALPH Look here, Moffatt: the fact I've been divorced from Mrs Marvell doesn't authorise anyone speaking of her to me to take that tone.

Moffatt looks up at him, calm to the point of truculence.

MOFFATT Well, if that's so, I guess I ought to feel the same way: I've been divorced from her myself.

For a moment, Ralph is stunned into silence; finally he blurts out:

RALPH What are you talking about?

MOFFATT Facts. Now and then it's mighty wholesome for a man to have a round with a few facts. Undine Spragg and I were made one in Opake, Nebraska, where we'd run off without telling her ma and pa. Wasn't what you'd call a society wedding. My, but was she a beauty then! Anyway, when they caught up with us, they put a stop to it and I lit out to Alaska.

Ralph has been listening in growing horror and disbelief. He seems to have difficulty speaking. He's gripping the back of a chair to steady himself.

RALPH You knew they hadn't told me?

MOFFATT I figured as much . . .

RALPH You knew the day we met in Mr Spragg's office?

MOFFATT Why, sure.

Ralph looks away, towards the window, his mouth working silently.

Now, listen, about the money . . .

But Ralph suddenly turns away and blunders out of the office.

INT. SUBWAY CAR. DAY

Ralph stands, holding on to a strap, completely oblivious to his surroundings, an expression of staring intensity on his face, marked enough to cause his fellow-passengers to avoid him. He's sweating again, perhaps not entirely as a result of the summer heat.

EXT. WASHINGTON SQUARE. DAY

Ralph strides across the square, moving fast, not looking to left or right; and hurries up the steps to unlock the heavy front door of the Dagonet house.

INT. FRONT HALL IN THE WASHINGTON SQUARE HOUSE. DAY

Ralph throws down his hat and stick and sets off, taking the stairs two at a time, hoping to go to earth before anyone can intercept him.

INT. RALPH'S BEDROOM. DAY

All the shutters are closed except one, so that a stripe of light bisects the cool shadow and expires against one of the walls. Ralph goes to close it; then loses interest and lets it be. He slumps into his old armchair. Then he does a curious thing. He begins to feel with his left hand the area below and behind his right ear, at the limit of the jawline's curve.

After a while he stops doing this, rises and, grunting with effort, drags Undine's portrait out from behind the wardrobe and sets it against the wall, where the light hits. He looks down at it for a moment, then utters a sardonic snort of protest, turns away, crosses to the door and bolts it. Then he moves, unable to tear his eyes away from the portrait, over to his bookcase, beneath which there is a single slender drawer.

He opens it a little way, puts in his hand and brings out a revolver.

He returns to his armchair, sits in it, releases the safety catch, feels for the place he found behind his ear and raises the revolver until the muzzle is resting against his chosen spot.

Close on Undine's portrait: enigmatic, overpowering in the bright shaft of light. Explosion.

Blackout.

INT. LONG GALLERY AT THE CHATEAU DE SAINT DÉSERT. DAY

Fade in on Undine's portrait: reframed in a heavier, ornate gilt frame and hanging at one end of the gallery above a roaring wood fire.

Standing looking up at it is Paul Marvell, now a touchingly earnest, slightly nervous child of seven.

After a moment, he turns away from the painting to look at its original: Undine is in mourning, a band of crêpe around her upper arm; she stands quite still, looking out across the moat, watching the mist on the fields and the heavy, monotonous November rain. He moves over to her, a little hesitant about seeking her attention.

PAUL Mother.

UNDINE Yes, dear?

PAUL When is father coming back? My French father, I mean.

UNDINE Well, he's late: so, very soon, I hope.

PAUL Oh, good.

UNDINE You like him, don't you?

PAUL Oh, yes.

Silence. Paul puts his hand up to touch her crêpe armband.

How long do you have to be in mourning?

UNDINE A year.

PAUL But he wasn't your father.

UNDINE No, but he was my husband's father and he was the head of the family and I'm part of the family now. You have to follow the custom of the country.

PAUL Did you have to wear mourning when father died? I mean, my real father.

Undine hesitates for a moment, then looks away, out of the window.

UNDINE No. No, I didn't.

PAUL I did. Aunt Laura made me.

To Undine's relief, the heavy brougham appears at the end of the avenue of poplars with a jingle of carriage bells.

UNDINE Here's your stepfather.

PAUL I'm going down to meet him.

He races out of the room. Undine stays where she is; and the camera slowly closes on her face as the jingle of carriage bells grows louder and then begins to recede.

EXT. COUNTRYSIDE NEAR APEX. DAY

The same bells jingle on the harness of a colt pulling a spanking new buggy along a dirt road cutting across the dusty mid-western plain. It's ten years earlier; and while it's clear the driver of the buggy is Elmer Moffatt and his passenger is Undine, the camera circles the buggy in long shot.

UNDINE (*voice over*) What do you mean, you found it? You can't just find a buggy, just like that.

MOFFATT (*voice over*) I could see you didn't want to go back into town in that dusty, crowded old stage.

UNDINE (*voice over*) I never met anyone like you before.

MOFFATT (*voice over*) That's because there isn't anyone like me.

INT. LONG GALLERY. DAY

Undine snaps out of her reverie as Chelles appears in the doorway, elegant in black, holding Paul's hand. Undine moves over to greet him and they kiss.

CHELLES You know, I've just been up to my mother's room and she's sitting up there without a fire.

UNDINE Why on earth is she doing that?

Chelles glances up the room; there's a second fire blazing in the gigantic matching fireplace at the far end of the gallery.

CHELLES She says we are using too much wood.

UNDINE Surely you don't want us to be cold?

She hurries on, before he has a chance to answer the question.

Anyway, how was your trip?

CHELLES A great success. Everything's settled.

UNDINE Tell me . . .

CHELLES Paul and I have an appointment at the stables, *n'est-ce pas*, old chap? Afterwards, maybe you would like to receive me in your room, we can discuss the whole business, what do you say?

He looks at her meaningfully, a smile playing about his lips.

INT. UNDINE'S BEDROOM IN THE CHATEAU. DAY

A heavy curtain has been roughly drawn across the high windows, cutting out a good deal of the light; but there's a blazing fire in this room too. Undine and Chelles lie snuggled up in the immense four-poster bed, but the atmosphere of lazy post-coital glow is somewhat undermined by the eagerness of Undine's interrogation.

UNDINE I still don't understand why you have to pay all your brother's gambling debts.

CHELLES It's a matter of honour. And it's the last time I shall have to pull the poor boy out.

UNDINE But if this American he's marrying is so rich, why can't she pull him out?

CHELLES Her father was very clear about this. He insisted on a clean slate. And he was right. But I was able to do some business with him. He's agreed to rent the house for Hubert and his bride.

UNDINE What house?

CHELLES The Paris house.

UNDINE Our house?

Undine looks at him for a moment, speechless with horror.

How could you do such a thing without consulting me?

CHELLES But, my darling, you're not interested in business, you always say it bores you. Naturally, I discussed it with my mother . . .

UNDINE Just because I don't think about money all the time, the way you do . . .

CHELLES I think about money because I have to: apart from everything, I have to look out for the future of that son we are going to have.

He reaches for her, looking as if he might be interested in starting again; but Undine allows him only the most perfunctory kiss before pulling away from him.

After all, why do we need that great house, when we will only be spending two months a year in Paris?

UNDINE Two months?

CHELLES Otherwise my place is here. Now I am the Marquis, I have to look after the family land, there is much to do.

UNDINE I'm sure I would use the house much more than that.

CHELLES I have said to you before, I don't like you to go to Paris on your own.

He's spoken in a perfectly reasonable tone, but one which brooks no contradiction. Undine, appalled, is still grappling with the implications of what he's said.

UNDINE Well, what happens when we do go up in the spring? Do Hubert and his wife move into a hotel?

CHELLES Of course not, don't worry, it's all arranged.

UNDINE Well, tell me!

CHELLES You and I will stay in the basement.

UNDINE The basement!

EXT. THE HOTEL DE CHELLES IN PARIS. NIGHT

The great house is a blaze of lights: there are sounds of an orchestra, silhouetted couples dancing past the windows. Chelles helps Undine down from the cab, sheltering her with his umbrella and taking her arm to help her down the steep steps which lead to the small, plain basement entrance.

INT. BASEMENT SITTING ROOM. NIGHT

The room is dimly lit by tapers floating in cups of oil, which provide enough light to reveal that the furniture is good but shabby. Chelles helps Undine off with her cloak.

The noise from above filters down. Undine and Chelles are both still in mourning.

UNDINE I wish we didn't have to come home every night to Hubert and his wife splurging around on top of our heads.

CHELLES Yes, she really ought to take a little more care: in her condition.

Undine looks away quickly, upset by the reference. Meanwhile, Chelles has picked up a document from a side table.

CHELLES Oh, yes, I forgot to give this to you.

Undine takes it, somewhat suspicious.

UNDINE What is it?

CHELLES A bill. From your dressmaker. For some reason it was addressed to me.

UNDINE Oh, I thought . . .

CHELLES My dear, you have the income from that hundred thousand dollars that came to Paul from your husband's investment. You didn't have to spend to get an annulment because the poor fellow did away with himself. And you have your father's allowance.

UNDINE Which he can ill afford.

CHELLES Nevertheless you accept it.

UNDINE What do you mean by that?

CHELLES All I mean is: you have your money, you have your expenses. You have only to be careful that the one bears some resemblance to the other.

Undine is baffled by the bland impermeability of his argument.

UNDINE Well, I'm going to bed.

She sets off towards the door, then stops, struck by another thought.

I hate having to creep around every night in my room so as not to wake up Paul.

CHELLES I can't very well have him in my room.

UNDINE Shouldn't we think about sending him away to school?

CHELLES Who's going to pay for it?

Silence, Undine turns away again, grim-faced.

Anyway, even if we could afford it, I don't think I would want to send him away. I'm too fond of him.

UNDINE Goodnight.

INT. THE ROLLIVER SUITE AT THE HOTEL NOUVEAU LUXE. DAY

Indiana Rolliver, even creamier and more substantial than before, beams indulgently at Undine across the groaning tea table set up in her suite, where Undine's mourning seems completely out of place.

UNDINE And then I'm supposed to go round everywhere with his sisters, who all look like the Curé's umbrella and play bridge with his aunts and have dinner with his cousins.

INDIANA Well, didn't I tell you, if it was amusement you were after, you'd've been better off not marrying him.

UNDINE And he's so jealous. I have to account for every hour I'm not with him.

INDIANA Well, isn't that kind of romantic? Mr Rolliver wouldn't bat an eye if I went up the Eiffel Tower in my shimmy.

UNDINE Of course it is. And he is romantic. And very . . . well, it's true what they say about the French.

INDIANA Yes, they are incorrigible; and to think they all have their . . . arrangements as well.

UNDINE Not Raymond.

INDIANA Doesn't he come up to Paris on his own?

UNDINE Yes, but he's trying to make a start in politics, he has to meet a lot of people . . .

INDIANA No politics after midnight.

UNDINE Oh, Indiana! . . .

INDIANA I'm sorry, Undine, I shouldn't have said anything . . .

UNDINE You mean you know something?

INDIANA I'm sure it's just rumour . . .

EXT. OPEN CARRIAGE. DAY

As before, the big brougham, now carrying Undine and Chelles, swings round the long bend. Paul is sitting on Chelles's knee.

EXT. CHATEAU DE SAINT DÉSERT. DAY

The château, huge and squat, comes into view.

EXT. OPEN CARRIAGE. DAY

For Chelles this is always an exhilarating moment. He reaches for Undine's hand. She lets him take it, but doesn't turn her head towards him.

Another angle reveals that she's fighting back tears.

EXT. COURTYARD OF THE CHATEAU. DAY

The brougham comes clattering off the drawbridge, under the portcullis, and pulls up in the courtyard in front of the welcoming party of staff, tenants and relations. Standing in the doorway at the top of the steps, dressed in uncompromising black, her hands crossed on the silver head of an ebony cane is a figure of daunting severity: the Dowager Marquise de Chelles.

INT. LONG GALLERY. DAY

Undine stands at the window staring out at the summer landscape, alone in the vast room.

EXT. AVENUE OF POPLARS. DAY

Paul shouts with laughter as he rides his pony, trying to keep up with Chelles, on his black horse. He sees his mother, standing at the window of the long gallery above and waves to her. She doesn't wave back.

INT. DINING ROOM. EVENING

A large company, all in black, including Undine, Chelles, Paul, the Dowager Marquise, the Curé and large numbers of mostly female relations sit around an enormous baronial table eating what looks like an excellent meal. Subdued murmurs of conversation. Chelles sits at the head of the table, his mother on his right; Undine faces him at the far end, several yards away.

EXT. TERRACE. EVENING

The company is split rigidly into two groups, according to gender. The women, with the single exception of Undine, are all engaged in embroidery or knitting; the men, a little way off, circulate the cognac, smoke, read the papers and argue. The sun has gone down, but the twilight is still balmy. Undine inspects her nails minutely, one at a time.

INT. PRIVATE CHAPEL. DAWN

Undine sits among all the women of the family at Early Mass. The Curé intones portentously. They're in a kind of balcony decorated with coronets, while the household staff sit below on plain backless benches. Undine smothers a yawn, then drifts into a dream, remembering something.

INT. BAPTIST CHAPEL IN APEX. DAY

The plain wooden interior could not be a greater architectural contrast, but the congregation, at present shuffling out of the chapel, is no less soberly dressed than the worshippers of Saint Désert. Mr and Mrs Spragg are on the threshold of the chapel with Undine between them.

EXT. EUBAW AVENUE IN APEX. DAY

There seems to be some commotion outside, the cause of which is not instantly identifiable. Scandalised remarks are being passed: 'He's drunk,' 'That's one of them girls from North Fifth Street.' Undine begins bobbing to and fro, trying to see over the heads of the people in front of her. Suddenly she's still.

Her point of view: sauntering down the road, his shirt open, his boots filthy, his chin unshaven, is Elmer Moffatt, dispensing cheery greetings left and right; and on his arm is a woman with far too much make-up, a plunging neckline and a scarlet dress. She's also waving at a few people she recognises, almost without exception men.

Mrs Spragg claps her hand over Undine's eyes: but too late.

INT. PRIVATE CHAPEL IN THE CHATEAU DE SAINT DÉSERT. DAY

Undine comes to herself with a start: the Dowager Marquise is anxious to get to the altar rail in response to the Curé's little bell; but Undine is blocking her way. She scrambles to her feet to let the old lady pass, then follows her down the narrow winding staircase to the floor of the chapel.

INT. UPSTAIRS CORRIDOR. DAY

The Dowager Marquise stands in her doorway, looking thunderously disapproving. A stream of servants passes in single file, each carrying an armful of packages, clearly the arrival of some massive order from a Paris clothes store.

INT. DINING ROOM. EVENING

The entire company as before, minus Undine, still all in black, are on their feet as the Dowager Marquise mumbles through some interminable Latin grace. She's still going, when the door opens and Undine appears, dazzling in a new cream silk dress. The Dowager breaks off, stares at Undine goggle-eyed, waits pointedly as she demurely takes her place at the far end of the table and resumes and completes the grace. Everyone sits down in total silence.

INT. LIBRARY. EVENING

Undine and Chelles are alone in the comfortable book-lined room, Chelles nursing a glass of Calvados, Undine staring angrily at the empty fireplace. Eventually, she breaks the silence.

UNDINE Well, the mourning is over, isn't it?

CHELLES Tomorrow.

UNDINE Oh.

CHELLES It really doesn't matter.

He reaches for a newspaper on the nearby table.

There's an interesting piece in the *Journal des Débats*. Let me read it to you.

UNDINE I don't think so.

CHELLES Good for your French.

UNDINE What's it about?

CHELLES The importance of the Family in the life of the Nation.

Undine hesitates, then shakes her head.

UNDINE I don't think so, thank you.

EXT. BATTLEMENTS OF THE CHATEAU. DAY

Undine comes to a stop and looks out across the dramatic Burgundian landscape. There's a sharp wind blowing; the low clouds scud by and there's obviously an autumnal chill in the air. Undine shivers and moves on.

INT. UNDINE'S BEDROOM. DAY

Undine stands in front of an inadequate cheval mirror on which the silvering is patched and blackened. There's a fire burning in the grate, she's alone and she's trying on clothes. From the amount of clothes scattered around the room, she might have been doing so for hours. She turns and turns again, checking herself in profile, obscurely dissatisfied.

INT. THE DOWAGER MARQUISE'S BEDROOM. EVENING

Undine sits a little apart from the Dowager and the other female relations, who are all clustered around the bright white light of a single carcel lamp with ground-glass shade, source of both light and heat. The room is dominated by the dim outline of a massive tapestried four-poster. The ladies are all still at their embroidery or knitting. Undine draws her shawl about her.

INT. LONG GALLERY. DAY

It's the depths of winter again; and once again Undine stands listlessly at the window staring out at the pouring rain and fires blaze at either end of the huge room. Chelles is sitting at the piano playing some étude, surprisingly well. Presently, he breaks off and looks up at Undine for a moment.

CHELLES I'm afraid I have some not so good news for you.

Undine turns to look at him, frowning.

UNDINE What?

CHELLES The rain has weakened the dam around the other side of the mountain. We have to rebuild or the vineyards will be in danger.

UNDINE Oh.

She suppresses a yawn.

CHELLES It's a very bad moment for this to happen: means we will have to give up our stay in Paris this spring.

Undine is suddenly wide awake, appalled.

UNDINE No!

CHELLES I know it's a disappointment. But this will be very expensive to repair.

UNDINE Can't I go and stay at the Nouveau Luxe with my American friends?

CHELLES I don't think that would be suitable.

UNDINE Suitable? You keep me shut up here, interfere with everything I want to do, you think that's suitable?

CHELLES I have never interfered with the way you spend your money.

UNDINE I should think not, when you grudge me every penny of yours.

CHELLES Of course I would take you to Paris if I had the money.

UNDINE You can always find the money for this place. If it's too expensive for you, why don't you sell it?

CHELLES Sell Saint Désert?

He's speechless with horror. But Undine can no longer stop herself.

UNDINE In America, if we can't afford to keep something, we're not ashamed to sell it. Or sell something. Sell those old tapestries, you keep telling me they're worth a fortune!

CHELLES You just don't understand, do you?

UNDINE I understand you'd rather I was unhappy than sell one of your great-grandfather's armchairs.

This is addressed to Chelles's back, since he's by now striding towards the door. Exasperated by this, she shouts after him.

Or maybe we'd better separate, maybe that would be the best thing!

He turns in the doorway and speaks with deadly finality.

CHELLES We don't do things like that.

He leaves the room, closing the heavy door behind him. Undine's face puckers; and for once she looks completely defeated and at a loss.

INT. UPSTAIRS CORRIDOR. NIGHT

The lighting, as in the Paris basement, is provided by tapers floating in oil, at lengthy intervals, so that the corridor is murky and shadowy. Chelles escorts Undine down the long corridor in silence. It's late and this evening Undine seems to have made a particular effort when dressing for dinner, with dazzling results. They come to a halt outside her bedroom door and Chelles clears his throat.

CHELLES I have reconsidered. We shall go to Paris for six weeks; but not a day longer.

UNDINE Oh, thank you!

CHELLES And we can't afford to give any dinners whatsoever, I want that clearly understood.

She dissolves in his arms, looks up and kisses him. Then she opens her bedroom door.

UNDINE Won't you come in for a while?

Chelles looks at her for a moment, taking a step back to do so.

CHELLES You are very beautiful, my dear. More beautiful than ever. Goodnight.

He turns and sets off, back down the corridor, his footsteps echoing on the stone flags. Undine watches him go, miserable and frightened.

INT. UNDINE'S BEDROOM. NIGHT

The room is lit only by the dying fire. Undine lies in bed, her eyes wide open and glittering in the darkness.

EXT. MAIN STREET IN APEX. DAY

The dusty expanse of Main Street simply peters out into a half-formed little park with a bandstand. Undine moves dreamily along the far end of the street, protected by a bonnet from the blazing sun, when Moffatt suddenly emerges from the shadows, startling her considerably.

MOFFATT You want to go for a walk?

Undine hesitates, then answers with a fine show of indifference.

UNDINE I don't care if I do.

They stroll along in silence for a while and almost immediately reach the little park. Moffatt somewhat ungraciously indicates a white bench in the shadow of the bandstand and, once Undine has settled herself, flops down unceremoniously next to her.

MOFFATT Lost my job, I suppose you know that.

UNDINE If you'd wanted to keep it, I guess you wouldn't have behaved the way you did last Sunday.

MOFFATT What do I care, one-horse hole like this?

He looks at her with a direct candour.

Hadn't'a been for you, I'd'a moved on months ago.

UNDINE What do you mean?

MOFFATT I went with that girl on purpose and you know it. It just makes me sick seeing you go round with that stiff Millard Binch, and him grinning as if he'd patented you.

UNDINE Just a minute, you got no right . . .

But he cuts her off with a kiss; and for a moment she writhes and struggles in his arms. Then she decides, quite consciously, to give way to the kiss.

INT. UNDINE'S BEDROOM. NIGHT

Undine still lies sleepless; she turns on her side and tears spill out of her eyes. Her shoulders begin to shake.

EXT. COURTYARD OF THE CHATEAU. DAY

Chelles embraces Undine perfunctorily and mounts his handsome black horse.

CHELLES I expect to be back this evening.

UNDINE I'll see you then.

CHELLES But don't wait up for me. I may decide to stay the night in Beaune. Depends what happens.

He digs his heels in and gallops away, out under the portcullis. Undine watches him go, her expression thoughtful.

INT. LONG GALLERY. DAY

For once, Undine is looking inwards: she moves up and down running her eyes over the Louis XV tapestries. A door opens and a small, dark, intelligent-looking man is shown into the room.

UNDINE Mr Fleischhauer.

The man bows formally to Undine.

FLEISCHHAUER Mme la Marquise.

But almost at once his attention is caught by the tapestries. He fits a pair of pince-nez attached to his pocket by a piece of elastic and begins to examine them with a sigh of satisfaction.

UNDINE They were given to the family by Louis the Fifteenth . . .

FLEISCHHAUER I'm familiar with their history.

Undine is embarrassed and falls silent: she watches as he examines the glorious expanses of pink and blue. Finally, he straightens up, his pince-nez snapping automatically back into his pocket, and turns to Undine.

Yes. I have a gentleman with me.

UNDINE A gentleman?

FLEISCHHAUER Probably the greatest American collector of our times.

UNDINE I didn't say the tapestries were for sale.

FLEISCHHAUER Yes, but this gentleman buys only things which are not for sale.

UNDINE I just wanted a valuation.

FLEISCHHAUER Let me watch him when he looks at them: then I can put a price on them.

UNDINE Very well.

Fleischhauer goes over to the door and opens it: the next room is another long gallery, less lavishly furnished, but by no means negligible. At the far end, with his back to them, studying a bust, is a stocky figure in a fur coat.

FLEISCHHAUER Mr Moffatt!

Undine gasps; Moffatt turns; then it's his turn to appear astonished. He advances into the room and takes Undine by both hands.

MOFFATT Well, I'll be . . . What are you doing here?

UNDINE I live here.

MOFFATT Well, so, these are yours?

UNDINE I didn't know you were a great collector.

MOFFATT The greatest!

UNDINE Not that the tapestries are for sale, of course . . .

MOFFATT Well, of course.

He looks at her fondly for a moment, then turns to Fleischhauer, suddenly aware of him.

You go take the train, send the motor back, I'll get a later one.

FLEISCHHAUER Just as you say, Mr Moffatt. Mme la Marquise.

He bows and slips away, leaving Moffatt and Undine gazing at each other for a long moment.

MOFFATT Sorter funny to see you in a place like this; but you look it. You always do.

UNDINE And so do you. You must be awfully rich.

MOFFATT Out of sight. I own pretty near the whole of Apex.

He indicates the tapestries.

I was thinking of buying these for my private railroad car.

UNDINE Well, if you really want them, I don't suppose I could stop you.

MOFFATT When I want something, nobody can stop me.

He's said this quite amiably, but nevertheless there's an undercurrent of menace. Now he decides to break the mood.

Surprised you're not up in Paris, all your old crowd are there. I came over with the Rollivers.

UNDINE I didn't know you knew them.

MOFFATT Oh, yes, Jim Rolliver's a Congressman now, you got to have a Congressman in your pocket. We're all at the old Nouveau Luxe.

UNDINE We've had to delay our trip this year, troubles with the estate, of course it just eats money.

Again, Moffatt gestures jovially at the tapestries.

MOFFATT Well, you want to get him to chip off one of his heirlooms.

Undine looks away, not knowing how to respond. This is not lost on Moffatt, but he's now busy looking up and down the length of the room.

MOFFATT Great place you got here. And what is it you are now, a Marquise? So this is what I helped you to.

UNDINE What made you do it?

He looks her up and down, blatantly appraising her.

MOFFATT Felt like it.

Undine doesn't know how to take this; she changes the subject.

UNDINE I hope you'll stay to lunch.

MOFFATT Just try and stop me.

UNDINE What are you planning to do next?

MOFFATT Business never sleeps.

UNDINE Besides business.

MOFFATT Everything I can.

He flops down in one of the big armchairs and stretches out his legs.

I'm one of those people who knows the best when he sees it: and once I see it, I mean to have it.

He looks at her penetratingly; and she looks away, troubled.

INT. BASEMENT SITTING ROOM AT THE HOTEL DE CHELLES. DAY

Undine sits in her dressing gown, sipping at a cup of chocolate. She looks up in surprise as Chelles suddenly surges into the room. He looks furious; and before she can speak, he bangs a letter down on the table in front of her.

CHELLES I suppose this is your doing!

Undine picks up the letter and looks at it; Chelles waits for a moment, but can't restrain himself from continuing in the same coldly angry tone.

And it was this Fleischhauer who brought a man to see the tapestries when I was in Beaune?

UNDINE That's right: I sent for him.

CHELLES You sent for him?

UNDINE Well, why shouldn't I? Something has to be done. We can't go on like this, scrimping and saving and not even being able to ask our friends to dine. What's the point of it, when you can just open your hand and have two million francs drop into it?

Chelles stands looking at her for a moment: finally he speaks, icy and deadly.

CHELLES You Americans, you're all the same. You come here from a country we don't know and can't imagine and which you care so little about, you've forgotten it before you've been here a day. You learn our language, but you never understand what we mean; you want what we want, but you don't know why we want it; and we are stupid enough to believe we can teach you what makes life decent and honourable.

Undine is no longer scared and apprehensive: she's looking at him with as much incomprehension as if he's just landed from another planet.

UNDINE You mean to say you're going to refuse the offer?

He leans forward, picks up the letter and violently rips it up, throwing the pieces in Undine's face.

CHELLES This is how I refuse it!

UNDINE Is that what you call decent and honourable?

Chelles picks up one of the fragments of paper and flourishes it.

CHELLES If you're capable of this, you're capable of anything!

He turns and strides out of the room. A moment later, the outside door slams heavily behind him. Undine rises decisively to her feet.

INT. UNDINE'S BEDROOM. DAY

Undine is dressed in her prettiest day clothes. She stands in front of the inadequate mirror in the dingy room, making a final minute adjustment to her make-up.

EXT. HOTEL DE CHELLES. DAY

Undine comes up the basement steps. It's a perfect spring day. A cab is passing and she flags it down.

EXT. HOTEL NOUVEAU LUXE. DAY

The cab pulls up outside the lavish façade of the Nouveau Luxe. Undine jumps out and pays.

INT. FOYER OF THE NOUVEAU LUXE. DAY

Undine receives instructions from the concierge and sets off across the marble foyer.

INT. CORRIDOR IN THE NOUVEAU LUXE. DAY

Undine hesitates for a second outside the door of a second-floor suite; then she knocks. The door's opened almost immediately by Elmer Moffatt.

MOFFATT Hello.

Undine puts out a hand and takes one of Moffatt's.

UNDINE Please don't send me away!

Moffatt frowns and shakes his head, breaking into a smile.

INT. SITTING ROOM OF MOFFAT'S SUITE IN THE NOUVEAU LUXE. DAY

Some time has passed. Moffatt's room looks not unlike Undine's hotel rooms on the eve of departure; only in his case it's not clothes but objets d'art *which cover every available surface and spread all over the floor: more art nouveau glass, a Greek marble bust, a lapis lazuli bowl, snuff-boxes, china and paintings. Moffatt and Undine are sitting at either end of the long sofa which stretches along one wall. After a moment, Moffatt breaks the silence.*

MOFFATT Well, he sounds darned low to me.

UNDINE He just doesn't understand; and, anyway he despises Americans. It's all been an awful mistake.

She looks across at him, gauging his state.

I keep thinking about that day in Apex, when you asked me to go for a walk. That's when I felt how strong you were. Stronger than any of them.

He's looking back at her, pensively assessing her.

MOFFATT You're not the beauty you were then; but you're real fetching.

Undine laughs, a little shocked by his frankness.

UNDINE I'm not sure how I should take that.

He seems at a loss for once; and, somewhat unexpectedly, he takes his watch out of his pocket and consults it.

UNDINE Do you have an appointment?

MOFFATT It don't matter.

UNDINE Another woman?

MOFFATT It don't matter.

Undine stands up; hope is ebbing away from her.

UNDINE Did you ever miss me?

MOFFATT You bet I did.

He's spoken with genuine bitterness; and what she says seems equally genuine.

UNDINE It's the only time I ever really cared: all through.

Moffatt stands up as well; they gaze at each other for a moment.

Is there someone else? You can tell me, you're going back tomorrow.

Moffatt shakes his head, gives a snort of laughter.

MOFFATT Too busy.

She moves towards him and puts a hand on his shoulder.

UNDINE Then couldn't we . . . ? They think differently about marriage over here. I can do what I like. My husband does.

MOFFATT You mean he goes with other women?

UNDINE So they tell me.

MOFFATT And nobody makes trouble if you know the ropes?

UNDINE That's right.

To her surprise, Moffatt recoils from her, causing her hand to drop from his shoulder. His face has grown harsh and dark. He crosses to the window and stands for a moment, looking out, his hands in his pockets. Eventually, he turns back to her.

MOFFATT I don't want you that way, Undine. You were my wife once and you were my wife first and if you want to come back, that's the way it has to be: not slinking in the back way when no one's looking.

She looks at him, not quite daring to believe he means what he's said.

Well? Is it yes?

UNDINE Yes?

MOFFATT Will you marry me?

UNDINE How can I? I'm a Catholic now, we can't do things like that. Couldn't we just . . . see each other sometimes?

MOFFATT When I want that kind of thing, I go down to North Fifth Street.

Undine is taken aback by his bluntness: she begins to prevaricate.

UNDINE Couldn't we just be friends?

MOFFATT Don't talk magazine stuff to me, Undine. I'm not saying we don't want each other the same way. I'm saying we've a different way of looking at things. You've settled for all these old European airs and graces. But there's a new century just around the corner and you know what: it's going to be an American century; and before you know where you are, people are going to start doing things our way.

Undine is confused: this has all gone much further than she'd anticipated.

UNDINE I suppose I'd better say goodbye.

MOFFATT So: you haven't got the nerve.

UNDINE What do you mean?

MOFFATT To come with me where you belong.

UNDINE I've told you, I can't get a divorce, my religion . . .

MOFFATT You were born a Baptist, weren't you? You come with me, I'll see you get your divorce. Who cares what they think over here? You're an American, ain't you?

UNDINE You don't understand –

She breaks off, aware that he's impervious to any reasoning. Moffatt moves over, until he's facing her, only a couple of feet away.

MOFFATT All right, Undine: I guess it'd better be yes or no here and now. Ain't going to do either of us any good dragging it out. So we shake hands now and say goodbye; or I'll book you a deck suite on the boat tomorrow. Now which is it to be?

Undine looks up at him. There are tears in her eyes and terror and exhilaration; and indecision.

Fade.

EXT. THE MOFFATT HOUSE IN PARIS. DAY

An imposing mansion in one of the quiet streets off the Champs Élysées. The black wrought-iron gates are topped with gilt ornaments; there's a semi-circular drive enclosing formal flower beds packed tight with spring blooms; and the house, which stands in its own grounds, is five storeys of gleaming pale stone. It's 1900.

INT. PAUL'S BEDROOM. DAY

Paul Marvell's bedroom in the new house is a large, impersonal room furnished with white fur rugs and brocade chairs. A maid is unpacking his suitcase, while Paul himself, who's now nine, opens drawers and cupboards in search of something which is clearly of some importance to him. Finally, he turns to the maid who's almost completed her task; she's quite young, her expression is impersonal.

PAUL I can't find my toys, do you happen to know where they are?

MAID *Hein?*

PAUL *Où sont mes choses? On m'a dit qu'elles seraient ici.*

MAID *Sais pas, moi.*

She closes the suitcase none too gently, transfers it to a cupboard, which she bangs shut, and briskly leaves the room. Paul, on his own now, looks around the room, his expression oppressed and cornered.

INT. DINING ROOM. DAY

In the immense marble dining room, supervised by a liveried footman, Paul sits at the vast gleaming table, picking listlessly at a plate of food. He reaches for the water jug, but the footman springs forward, snatches up the jug and pours water into the cut-glass crystal tumbler.

INT. LIBRARY. DAY

Paul looks up at the rows of books, beautifully bound and closed in behind gilt trellising. He reaches up to open one of the trelliswork doors; but it's locked.

INT. LANDING. DAY

Paul pauses outside the great double doors to the ballroom, from which can be heard sounds of furniture movement and hammering. He reaches up for one of the door handles, but a servant, passing with a tray of glasses, speaks to him sharply.

SERVANT *C'est fermé; on travaille.*

PAUL Oh, *pardon.*

He moves away, dejected.

INT. MAIN STAIRCASE. DAY

Long shot: the small figure of Paul, as he slowly climbs the unusually broad staircase.

INT. UPSTAIRS CORRIDOR. DAY

Paul moves along the corridor, then lets himself in one of the tall, dark doors.

INT. UNDINE'S BEDROOM. DAY

A beautiful, large room, pale and airy and feminine, with heavy velvet curtains. He passes through into –

INT. UNDINE'S DRESSING ROOM. DAY

– Undine's dressing room, a riot of mirrored cupboards and every kind of available lighting and dressing tables and tapestry stools and make-up cabinets. He carries on into –

INT. MOFFATT'S DRESSING ROOM. DAY

– Moffatt's adjoining dressing room, all mahogany wardrobes and rows of dark suits and shoes and boots in serried ranks. Paul moves on into –

INT. MOFFATT'S BEDROOM. DAY

– Moffatt's bedroom. Here he pauses in front of the room's centrepiece, lustrous against the brown wall. It's a Van Dyck portrait of a boy in grey velvet, his hand resting on the head of a big dog, his expression infinitely melancholy. Paul looks at this for a while then turns away and leaves the room, moving back into –

INT. UPSTAIRS CORRIDOR. DAY

– the corridor, which he crosses and knocks on a door. There's an indistinct squawk from the other side and Paul opens the door and steps into –

INT. MRS HEENY'S BEDROOM. DAY

– a big, pink room, lined with mirrors, in which is reflected the substantial figure of Mrs Heeny, sunk in a deep pink armchair, her trusty bag at her feet.

MRS HEENY Well, whatta you think of your ma's new house?

Paul closes the door carefully behind him.

PAUL She said she would be here.

MRS HEENY I told you, she had to go down to the Shatter-country with Mr Moffatt to look out something for one of his collections. She'll be back 'fore you know it. I must say I'm glad to be off of that boat, aren't you?

PAUL I suppose.

She notices that he's staring at her bag.

MRS HEENY You're remembering those Saturdays at Grandma Spragg's when you used to hunt through all this for taffy. Ain't any taffy in it now, I'm afraid. Still, let's see what we can find.

She leans forward, opens the bag, roots around and comes up with a handful of fresh clippings.

Let's see now: here we are. 'The highest price ever paid for a Vandick was raised at Thursday's auction at Sotheby's in London the purchaser Mr Elmer Moffatt . . .'

PAUL Can't you find one about my mother?

MRS HEENY Why, sure I can.

She starts laying out the clippings on the table in front of her.

Here we are: here's one of my favourites.

It's somewhat battered. Mrs Heeny smooths it out tenderly and begins to read:

'No case has ever been through the divorce courts of this State at a higher rate of speed than the divorce and remarriage of the Markweesy de Chelles of Paris France and the billionaire Railroad King Mr Elmer Moffatt who was the Markweesy's first husband every record has been broke as Mr Moffatt said last night the hearing began at seven-ten p.m. and by eight the happy couple were steaming out of the station at the trial Mrs Spragg de Chelles wore copper velvet and sables and gave evidence as to the croolty of her French husband . . .'

PAUL That's not true.

MRS HEENY What?

PAUL It isn't true, he wasn't cruel, my French father.

MRS HEENY Well, it's in the paper, sonny, it must be true.

The slightly awkward silence is broken by the sound of voices, calling from downstairs.

UNDINE (*voice over*) Paul!

MOFFATT (*voice over*) Paul Marvell, ahoy there!

MRS HEENY There they are, what did I say? Now you run along.

Paul gets up, but there's an unmistakeable moment of reluctance, until Mrs Heeny begins to look really surprised and Paul is shamed into beginning to move towards the door.

INT. MAIN STAIRCASE AND LANDING. DAY

Paul hurries down the broad staircase, reaches the first-floor landing and hesitates, uncertain which way to go.

Paul's point of view: he sees the backs of Undine and Moffatt. They're standing just inside the double doors to the ballroom, which are now open. All the chandeliers in the room are blazing.

Paul runs to them; but neither of them hears his approach or turns to greet him.

INT. BALLROOM. DAY

Reverse angle: Paul runs up to Undine and tugs at her dress. She turns her head and looks down at him.

UNDINE Mercy! Who cut your hair that way?

Moffatt turns and grasps Paul by the hand, pumping away cordially.

MOFFATT Well, Senator, how's it going?

PAUL Mother, mother!

Undine leans over to kiss him.

UNDINE Don't squeeze like that!

Close on Paul: he suddenly relaxes his grip on Undine, his eyes widening in shock.

His point of view: for the first time, it becomes apparent that the walls of the gigantic ballroom are lined with the Boucher tapestries from the Château de Saint Désert.

Paul gapes at the tapestries, stunned. Undine's also inspecting them, somewhat more critically.

They look smaller here.

She looks down at Paul.

And how are you?

PAUL I took first prize in English composition –

UNDINE Well, that's good. You tell me about it tomorrow. I have to go and change.

MOFFATT Can't you just give him a minute, Undine?

UNDINE I haven't even set out the place-cards.

She hurries out of the room, leaving Moffatt beaming awkwardly at the child.

MOFFATT You're a smart boy to remember these. I don't suppose you thought you'd ever see them here.

PAUL I don't know.

MOFFATT You wouldn't have done if he'd had any idea who was buying them: he'd rather have starved. As it was, getting them out of him was like drawing teeth.

To his amazement, Paul suddenly bursts into tears. He drops to one knee and takes him in his arms.

What is it, old chap, what's up?

Paul sobs and sobs.

Is it because your mother don't have time for you? That's the way she is, we got to learn to lump it.

He picks him up in his arms; he's beginning to quieten down, but his body is still convulsed.

That's better. I like you first-rate, you know, always have. And, you know what: one of these days you're going to be the richest boy in America.

Paul starts to cry again, burying his face in Moffatt's neck, sobbing his heart out.

INT. UNDINE'S DRESSING ROOM. EVENING

Mrs Heeny has finished helping Undine with her hair and is now assisting her to arrange an astonishing ruby tiara.

MRS HEENY This the one used to belong to Marie Anternette?

UNDINE That's right.

She leans forward to open a box on her dressing table.

And could you help me with these?

The box contains a rope of huge pearls, about five hundred of them, a necklace beside which Van Degen's gift retrospectively pales into insignificance. Mrs Heeny's hand flies to her mouth.

MRS HEENY My oh my oh my. Will you look at them pearls?

UNDINE Mr Moffatt found them in Vienna.

Mrs Heeny secures the clasp at the back of Undine's neck.

INT. BALLROOM. EVENING

Undine waits by the fireplace in her completely extraordinary regalia. Presently Moffatt saunters into the room. He carries a newspaper in one hand and uses the other to scoop up a handful of candies from a bonbonnière, which he throws into his mouth. His evening clothes seem a little too tight. In his buttonhole is the red ribbon of the Légion d'Honneur. Undine watches him approach, obscurely displeased. When he takes a proper look at her, he lets out a little tuneless whistle.

MOFFATT Boy.

UNDINE Don't forget, you have to take down Mme de Follerive; and don't keep calling her Countess.

MOFFATT Why not, she is one, ain't she?

UNDINE And I've put Peter Van Degen's new wife on your left.

MOFFATT Oh yeah? I hear she's hardly out of school.

UNDINE I hope you're not going to leave that newspaper lying around.

MOFFATT Oh, I brought it in to show you. I'm going to have to buy myself another Congressman.

UNDINE Why?

MOFFATT 'Cause Jim Rolliver's been appointed Ambassador to England.

Undine looks at him, horrified.

UNDINE Rolliver? Does that mean . . .?

MOFFATT Yup. Indiana at the Court of St James.

UNDINE Well.

MOFFATT Yes.

UNDINE Why don't you ever try for something like that? You don't have a spark of ambition.

MOFFATT Wouldn't do me a bit of good if I did.

UNDINE What do you mean?

Moffatt sticks his thumbs in his waistcoat armholes and laughs.

MOFFATT Because of you. You're divorced. They won't have divorced Ambassadresses.

UNDINE Why not?

MOFFATT I guess they want to cut down on the number of pretty women in embassies.

UNDINE Well, that's just about the most insulting thing I ever heard!

She's genuinely upset. Moffatt makes an ill-judged attempt to jolly her out of it.

MOFFATT Cheer up!

She looks at him coldly.

UNDINE We'd better go down.

INT. LANDING AND MAIN STAIRCASE. EVENING

Undine and Moffatt emerge from the ballroom and move down the stairs between the ranks of liveried footmen.

EXT. THE MOFFATT HOUSE. NIGHT

The courtyard is jammed with motors. The house is a blaze of light and noise.

INT. DINING ROOM NIGHT,

The dinner party is in fully swing. Close on Undine, at the head of the table, as the sound swells and roars, once again unnaturally amplified. Undine's point of view: there are about forty guests at the long table, all dressed and bejewelled up to the hilt. Among the guests, we recognise Popple and Van Degen. But Undine's attention is focused, above the crystal and the épergnes and the gold plate, on the far end of the table, where Moffatt is enjoying a joke with the woman on his left, who must be the new Mrs Van Degen, who's not much older than twenty, and is quite exquisitely beautiful. Slowly, as before, the sound gradually diminishes to absolute silence.

INT. UPSTAIRS CORRIDOR. NIGHT

Moffatt escorts Undine down the well-lit corridor to her bedroom door. They pause outside the door.

MOFFATT Slap-up success, wouldn't you say?

UNDINE You were getting on very well with the new Mrs Van Degen.

MOFFATT He's a lucky fellow.

He looks up quickly.

Not as lucky as me, of course.

He can't help sounding rather forced and hollow. Undine opens her bedroom door.

UNDINE Would you like to come in for a while?

MOFFATT Better not. Early start tomorrow.

He leans in and pecks her on the cheek in a comradely fashion.

Goodnight.

He turns and sets off down the corridor; Undine watches him go, chewing at her lip, hurt in her eyes.

INT. UNDINE'S DRESSING ROOM. NIGHT

All the lights are on and Undine has taken off her tiara and necklace and just stepped out of her dress. Now she leans forward for a moment, studying her face in the mirror. She opens one of the cupboard doors slightly, so that in its mirror she can see her back as well as her face; and her profile, when she chooses.

She leans forward again and smiles; and her hand goes to the crow's feet which appear at the corner of her eye. She tries it again; and this time manages a smile in which her eyes take no part. Then she begins, as at the beginning, to run through her repertoire of facial expressions, checking them full-face and profile. It's like a litany of familiar exercises, but this time there seems to be some new element not seen before in Undine's face and it's not simple tiredness or strain: it's fear.

Slow fade to black.